THE TRUE LAW OF KINGSHIP

THE TRUE LAW
OF KINGSHIP

Concepts of Monarchy
in Early-Modern Scotland

J. H. BURNS

CLARENDON PRESS · OXFORD
1996

Oxford University Press, Walton Street, Oxford OX2 6DP

Oxford New York
Athens Auckland Bangkok Bombay
Calcutta Cape Town Dar es Salaam Delhi
Florence Hong Kong Istanbul Karachi
Kuala Lumpur Madras Madrid Melbourne
Mexico City Nairobi Paris Singapore
Taipei Tokyo Toronto
and associated companies in
Berlin Ibadan

Oxford is a trade mark of Oxford University Press

Published in the United States
by Oxford University Press Inc., New York

British Library Cataloguing in Publication Data
Data available

Library of Congress Cataloging in Publication Data
Burns, J. H. (James Henderson)
The true law of kingship : concepts of monarchy in early modern
Scotland / J. H. Burns.
p. cm.
Includes bibliographical references (p.   ) and index.
1. Political science—Scotland—History—16th century.
2. Monarchy—Scotland—History—16th century. 3. Scotland—History—
James VI, 1567–1625. 4. Scotland—Politics and government—16th
century.
JA84.S26B87 1996
320.441'09'031—dc20 95-17980
ISBN 0-19-820-384-5

1 3 5 7 9 10 8 6 4 2

Typeset by Best-set Typesetter Ltd., Hong Kong
Printed in Great Britain
on acid-free paper by
Biddles Ltd., Guildford & King's Lynn

In memory of
my father and mother
and of our forebears
from Tweeddale to the Merse,
in Lothian, and in Fife

Preface

THIS book is, in one sense, a sequel to my 1988 Carlyle Lectures, published in 1992 as *Lordship, Kingship, and Empire: The Idea of Monarchy, 1400–1525*. The respective subtitles indicate a measure of common ground and a degree of chronological overlap between the two enquiries. In another aspect, however, *The True Law* looks back much further, to the beginnings, almost half a century ago, of my interest in the ideas with which it is concerned. While writing it, I have had on my desk the dissertation on 'The Theory of Limited Monarchy in Sixteenth Century Scotland' for which I received the degree of Ph.D. from the University of Aberdeen in 1952. It would be neither credible nor, perhaps, creditable to suggest that the book is a revision, after all these years, of that thesis. None of the eight chapters in the present text corresponds at all closely to any chapter in the earlier work; and at least half of the material examined now played no part then. Yet I may owe it to my former self to say that some at least of the conclusions reached in the 1940s and 1950s have survived in the 1990s, relatively unscathed amid the demolition and reconstruction of much else.

It is proper, at all events, that this preface should express my gratitude to the University of Aberdeen and to my colleagues there between 1947 and 1960 for the richly rewarding first phase of my professional life, and that a special word of thanks should be said for the access I enjoyed to the rich resources of what was then the library of King's College, where I first read the works of John Mair and struggled to read the manuscript of John Ireland's commentary on the *Sentences*. Had it not been for the availability of those texts, what has been a lifelong interest might never have germinated.

In more personal terms, this preface enables me to acknowledge another debt which goes back to the very beginning of my work in this field. To John Durkan I owe more than I can adequately express for over forty years' friendship and for constant access to his unequalled knowledge and expertise in the intellectual history of Scotland (and not only of Scotland) in the

late-medieval and early-modern period. He has, I suspect, sometimes viewed with reserve the more ambitious conclusions I have
now and then been tempted to draw; but what is certain is that,
time and again, I should have gone sadly astray and missed
essential evidence had it not been for his unstinting generosity in
sharing his knowledge and his unflagging enthusiasm for the
quests in which we have engaged.

Cognate with my debt to John Durkan is that which I owe to the
successive editors of the *Innes Review*, who have afforded me, like
so many others, the possibility of publishing work in areas which,
thanks in large measure to the *Innes* and its sponsors, have been
rescued from the neglect in which they once languished. Parts of
the text, again, have been presented at seminars in Cambridge
and in St Andrews, and I am grateful to the organizers of these
groups and to those who took part in the discussions for the
opportunity to try out and to refine my ideas.

Having made particular reference to the library facilities I enjoyed in Aberdeen, I must not fail to mention also the recurrent
debt all scholars owe to such institutions as the National Library
of Scotland, the British Library, the Cambridge University Library, and the Bodleian Library. In this case I should also like to
thank the authorities of the Signet Library in Edinburgh and the
Folger Shakespeare Library, Washington, DC, while without the
splendid facilities of the London Library work on many parts
of the book would have been much harder to complete ex-
peditiously. Similarly I must thank Professor R. L. Greaves for
his generous gift of a copy of his *Theology and Revolution in the
Scottish Reformation*, which gave me ready access to his important
articles collected in that volume. My thanks are due also, for
assistance and advice on various points, to Drs Jane Dawson,
Craig McDonald, Norman Macdougall, Sally Mapstone, Roger
Mason, and Jenny Wormald.

In regard to publication I am once again deeply grateful
to Tony Morris of Oxford University Press for his unfailing
encouragement and assistance; and also to Anne Gelling and
Anna Illingworth of the Arts and Reference Division, Michael
Belson (Desk Editor), and, for invaluable copy-editing, Mary
Worthington.

To my wife, who has lived with the subject-matter of this book
for almost as long as she has lived with its author, what I owe is,

as always, far beyond my capacity to express it. I can only hope that she knows how deeply conscious I am of that indebtedness.

London   J. H. B.
February 1995

Contents

Abbreviations

APS
: *Acts of the Parliaments of Scotland*, 12 vols., ed. T. Thomson and C. Innes (Edinburgh, 1814–75)

Cal. Scot. Pap.
: *Calendar of State Papers Relating to Scotland*, ed. J. Bain *et al.* (Edinburgh, 1898–)

Chronicles, 1531
: John Bellenden, *The Chronicles of Scotland*, ed. R. W. Chambers, E. C. Batho, H. W. Husbands, 2 vols. (Edinburgh, 1938–41)

In Mattheum
: John Mair, *In Mattheum ad literam expositio* (Paris, 1518)

In quartum, 1516
: John Mair, *In quartum Sententiarum* (Paris, 1516)

In secundum, 1510
: John Mair, *In secundum Sententiarum* (Paris, 1510)

Meroure, i, ii, iii,
: John Ireland, *The Meroure of Wyssdome composed for the use of James IV., King of Scots A.D. 1490 by Johannes de Irlandia Professor of Theology in the University of Paris*, vol. i, ed. C. Macpherson, 1926; vol. ii, ed. F. Quinn, 1965; vol. iii, ed. C. McDonald, 1990 (Scottish Text Society; Edinburgh)

MPW
: *Minor Prose Works of King James VI and I*, ed. J. Craigie and A. Law (Scottish Text Society; Edinburgh, 1982)

Quartus, 1509
: John Mair, *Quartus Sententiarum* (Paris, 1509)

Quartus, 1512
: John Mair, *Quartus Sententiarum* (Paris, 1512)

RPC
: *Register of the Privy Council of Scotland*, ed. J. H. Burton and D. Masson, 14 vols. (Edinburgh, 1877–98)

Super tertium
: John Mair, *Super tertium Sententiarum* (Paris, 1517)

A Note on Quotations

IN quotations from primary sources, the spelling, etc. in the editions cited has in general been followed. However, in the case of texts written in Middle Scots, the symbols þ and ȝ have been replaced respectively by 'th' and 'y' (or 'z' as appropriate). It is hoped that this will have spared the printers, and may spare some readers, a certain amount of difficulty. Unfamiliar words and forms in such quotations have been elucidated by 'translations' in square brackets where this seemed likely to be helpful.

Introduction

Upon the King, let us our lives, our souls,
Our debts, our careful wives,
Our children, and our sins, lay on the King

(Henry V, IV. i)

'Political ideas' in late-medieval and early-modern Europe were preponderantly, and inevitably, ideas about kings and kingship. Whatever importance may be ascribed to the 'republicanism' of Renaissance humanists—and part of that importance lay in the interaction between republican ideas and the traditional relationship between king and subject—it was necessarily of secondary importance in the 'real world' of politics. The Europe of the Renaissance and the Reformation was a Europe dominated by royal power. In so far as a 'modern state' took shape and emerged in that period, it was a monarchical state. Even in the few societies where republican institutions had established and maintained themselves between the eleventh century and the fifteenth, monarchy was, in most cases, taking over both the substance and the form of government.[1] In view of this monarchical predominance it is possible to claim that the investigation proposed in this book, into the concepts of kingship that were current in Scotland from the latter part of the fifteenth century to the first quarter of the seventeenth, may exhibit, among other things, a microcosmic view of a wider world of ideas. There is no need to exaggerate the European importance of a small realm on the fringe of the continent. Scotland was, in fact, by no means negligible in its dynastic (and therefore diplomatic) significance in the sixteenth century; and the deposition of a queen in 1567 added an element of notoriety. It is not surprising, though it remains noteworthy, that the polemical debate precipitated by the vicissitudes of Mary Queen of Scots is a major factor in the development of the 'royalist' and 'monarchomach' ideologies which were to play so large a part in political controversy and conflict throughout the seventeenth

---

[1] Milan and Florence are obvious instances, Venice is the obvious exception.

century and beyond. Such dramatic developments, however, serve merely to throw into sharper relief the point that concepts of kingship in early-modern Scotland reflect the general and fundamental political preoccupations of the period.

One such preoccupation is suggested by the Shakespearian epigraph to this introduction. Kingship was, quintessentially and inescapably, a matter of personal rule. The personality of the king, therefore, the formation of his character, the virtues (and vices) he possessed and displayed, were matters of great political importance. This is reflected in the steady output of works in the 'mirror of princes' tradition. That tradition stretched back, of course, to a point very near the start of European thinking and writing about government; and it is a tradition widely shared by other cultures; but it can be claimed that the period with which this book is concerned was, in Europe, especially fertile in the production of this crop. Scotland, no doubt, fell below the average in this respect. Yet it is still the case that, at the outset of the more specific discussion here, we shall encounter John Ireland's *Meroure of Wyssdome*: not, indeed, a classic instance of the *Fürstenspiegel*, yet addressed to a young king lately come to the throne and, in the last of its seven Books, manifesting many of the characteristic concerns of the genre. And towards the end of the enquiry, alongside James VI's *True Lawe of Free Monarchies* (which gives the present book its title), we have his *Basilikon Doron*, which exemplifies precisely the nature and purposes of the many princely mirrors that had preceded it.

To be a king, however, was more than a matter of bringing personal character and power to bear upon the problems of government: more even than doing this with the adjustments necessitated by the particular circumstances of the realm to be ruled. It was also an institutional role. The stage on which the king played his part was set with structures which he had not designed and which he could rarely alter in any radical way. Limited scene-shifting, adjustments, modifications, might be within his power, but rarely changes on the scale achieved by Henry VIII when he brought about the abolition of papal jurisdiction within his realm. Nor could change, whether minor or major in scope, be a matter of mere royal *ipsedixitism* (to adopt one of Jeremy Bentham's coinages). Reflection indeed may suggest that the metaphors of stage scenery and even of 'structures' are not altogether appropriate for the setting in which royal power had to operate. It was rather as though the king found himself in a landscape, of which the features were subject to natural or organic change at rates ranging from the almost insensible to the more or less rapid. Such processes might afford greater or smaller opportunities for the intervention of artifice: royal power might be used to accelerate institutional development, to retard it, or to alter its direction. In no case, however, could a king—to change the metaphor again—inscribe his sovereign will on a blank sheet. However 'absolute' a king's power might be (or might be conceived to be), politics even for such a ruler could never be simply (in Michael Oakeshott's formulation) 'waking up each morning and considering, "What would I like to do?"'[2] Royal government had to work with and through instrumentalities which were to a substantial extent the given conditions of the problem and had to be accepted as such.

Nor were these considerations confined to the area of institutions in a formal sense. Such institutions were themselves rooted in soil constituted by the social and economic realities of a particular community. This may not always have been appreciated in historians' attempts to characterize and assess the achievements and failures of particular monarchies or individual kings. Indeed, it was by no means always recognized by those who wrote at the time about the nature and capacity of royal government. A lack of such awareness of the concrete circumstances of kingship is perhaps especially characteristic of the typical 'mirror of princes' treatment of the subject, where conventional and stylized morality may often appear to be deployed at a level somewhat remote from the dusty arena of real-life politics. One of the distinctive features of the *Basilikon Doron* is precisely its author's first-hand observation of just that kind of reality.[3] It follows that, while a particular realm and the concepts of kingship which prevailed there may indeed illustrate more general themes, the development of those themes in that realm can be properly understood only by reference to the conditions constituting a

[2] M. Oakeshott, 'Political Education', in id., *Rationalism in Politics and Other Essays* (1962; London, 1974), 114.
[3] James VI and I, *The Basilicon Doron of King James VI*, ed. J. Craigie, 2 vols. (Scottish Text Society; Edinburgh, 1944, 1950; hereafter Craigie edn.): see esp. Book II, 'Anent a King's Duetie in his Office'; and cf. Ch. 7.

specific environment. At this point, accordingly, it is necessary to turn to an examination of the character of Scottish kingship and the circumstances in which it had to function.

If it were permissible to have a second epigraph at this point, the following sentences might be appropriate: 'There are two basic and fundamental duties of government. The first is defence of the realm. The second is the enforcement of sensible and updated laws.'[4] No one in the fifteenth century, in Scotland or elsewhere, would have had any great difficulty in endorsing this view—expressed, as it happens, by a Scots law professor in 1992. It is true that the term 'updated' seems at first sight as inapposite in substance as it would have been unfamiliar in form five hundred years ago. Yet further consideration suggests that even this would not have seemed wholly out of place in the late-medieval context. One historian has seen 'the massive legislative programme of the March 1504 [Scottish] Parliament' as 'a serious attempt to reappraise the whole arena of civil and criminal law'.[5] More generally it can be argued—how convincingly may be debatable—that even the reign of James III, to say nothing of that of his son, saw genuine attempts to 'update' both law and government in Scotland.[6] The evaluation of such endeavours, while essential to our understanding of the nature of late-medieval Scottish kingship, is obstructed by the gaps in the surviving evidence, by the enigmatic characters of the two kings, and by the fact that each reign has, in various ways, been the subject of obfuscating myth, legend, and stereotyping. The myth-making process was particularly intense in regard to James III. Here the legend of a weak, unwarlike, sensual ruler, at the mercy of flatterers and acting on the advice of 'low-born favourites', degenerating into tyranny and justly deposed and slain as a result, was the work of sixteenth-century chroniclers increasingly driven by polemical motives. There will be a good deal to say about this in the context of the debates set off by another deposition, eighty years later.

In the case of James IV, though the term 'legend' has also been applied, the problems have arisen largely from stereotyping by

---

[4] Ross Harper, 'Modernizing Scotland's Laws Should be Priority', *Scotsman*, 6 May 1992.

[5] L. J. Macfarlane, *William Elphinstone and the Kingdom of Scotland 1431–1514: The Struggle for Order* (Aberdeen, 1985), 423.

[6] See on this esp. Macfarlane, *Elphinstone*, 407 ff.

modern historians.[7] To see him as a 'Renaissance prince' is an obvious temptation; scarcely less strong is the attraction of such terms as 'new monarchy' and 'the aureate age' to describe the political and cultural aspects of his reign.[8] Yet such phraseology may be only a little less unhelpful than the statement by an eminent historian, taking a broader canvas, that 'Scotland had to wait for Knox before drawing a line under its messy medieval politics'.[9] Nor is it easy to repress altogether a sense of frustration when one finds that the 'revisionist' scholarship which seemed to have established a 'new orthodoxy' in the interpretation of both reigns has itself fallen victim to fresh revisions, to heterodoxies which, if they do not quite restore the status quo ante, do seem to take us to a similar point on the next twist in the historiographical spiral.[10]

This is certainly not the place for any attempt to resolve issues so complex and so controversial. All that can be attempted for present purposes is to consider a selection of more specific problems in the period and suggest some provisional positions as part of the background to the more central issues in this investigation. And it is possible at least to begin with something fairly unequivocal, which arises, appositely, in the area where ideas meet, or at all events come close to, the world of practice. In 1469, at the outset of James III's personal reign—he had succeeded to the throne in 1460 at the age of 8—an act was passed regarding the competence of notaries in Scotland. The subject may not seem to be one of major importance; but the principle involved in the legislation was potentially crucial. The substantive effect was that the king could now appoint notaries public within the realm, where, moreover, notaries appointed by the emperor would no longer have authority to act. This assumption of what was in principle an imperial prerogative was backed, logically enough, by the claim that the king of Scots had 'ful jurisdictioune and fre

---

[7] N. Macdougall, *James IV* (Edinburgh, 1989), pp. v–x.

[8] These terms are used in the titles of chs. 17 and 18 of R. Nicholson, *Scotland: The Later Middle Ages* (Edinburgh, 1974).

[9] G. R. Elton, *New Cambridge Modern History*, vol. ii, *The Reformation 1520–1559* (Cambridge, 1958), 8.

[10] The point may be seen by comparing the general line taken by N. Macdougall, *James III: A Political Study* (Edinburgh, 1982), with, on the one hand, the older view represented by Nicholson, *Later Middle Ages*, esp. chs. 15 and 16, and, on the other hand, the interpretation offered by Macfarlane, *Elphinstone*, chs. 5 and 8.

impire within his realme'.[11] Sovereignty *ad extra*, we may say, was being asserted; and, as it happened, the assertion was made in respect of a realm which, with the virtual annexation of Orkney and Shetland, was about to achieve its full territorial extent.[12] The English claim to suzerainty which had led to the protracted War of Independence, even if (as the event was to prove) it refused to lie down, was effectively dead. Other vestiges of subjection to external authority were also about to disappear. Notably, the raising of the see of St Andrews to archiepiscopal rank in 1472, though achieved in controversial circumstances, and initially, given those circumstances, unwelcome to the king as well as to the other Scottish bishops, at least meant the final extinction of the claims in Scotland of the see of York.[13]

In such developments as these—ecclesiastical autonomy, territorial integrity, jurisdictional sovereignty—Scotland was joining in movements that had begun in the central Middle Ages and were proceeding at an accelerating pace in the fifteenth century. All this brought, in general, an enhancement of royal power. Even in regard to ecclesiastical jurisdiction, the papacy of the post-conciliar restoration had to come to terms with temporal rulers unwilling to surrender control of appointments that were essential to the effective governance of their realms. Scotland under James III—and indeed throughout the three reigns which preceded the onset of the Protestant Reformation—shared in these tendencies to a considerable extent.[14] Nevertheless a degree of caution is advisable in assessing the general development of political authority during the period. If there was a process that can

---

[11] *APS* ii (Edinburgh, 1844), 95; and cf. the comments by Nicholson, *Later Middle Ages*, 483–4; J. Wormald, *Court, Kirk, and Community: Scotland 1470–1625* (London, 1981), 3–6; Macdougall, *James III*, 97–8; Macfarlane, *Elphinstone*, 330.

[12] Nicholson, *Later Middle Ages*, 413–18; Macdougall, *James III*, 90–1. Berwick, recovered in 1461, was lost again in 1482 and might since then be regarded as *Scozia irredenta*.

[13] Macdougall, *James III*, 104–7; L. J. Macfarlane, 'The Primacy of the Scottish Church, 1472–1521', *Innes Review*, 20 (1979), 111–29.

[14] Macdougall, *James III*, 222–5; Nicholson, *Later Middle Ages*, esp. 469–71, 556–62; J. A. F. Thomson, 'Innocent VIII and the Scottish Church', *Innes Review*, 19 (1968), 23–31; Macfarlane, 'Primacy of the Scottish Church'; id., *Elphinstone*, esp. 426–30; C. Burns, 'Papal Gifts to Scottish Monarchs: The Golden Rose and Blessed Sword', *Innes Review*, 20 (1969), 150–94; G. Donaldson, *Scotland: James V to James VII* (Edinburgh, 1971), esp. 45–8; M. Mahoney, 'The Scottish Hierarchy, 1513–1565', in D. McRoberts (ed.), *Essays on the Scottish Reformation* (Glasgow, 1962), 39–84; W. J. Anderson, 'Rome and Scotland, 1513–1625', ibid. 463–83.

be called 'the shaping of absolutism' in fifteenth-century Europe[15]—a foreshadowing of what emerged as the characteristic 'absolute monarchies' of the early-modern period—care must be taken both to understand the term 'absolute' correctly and to recognize the continuing availability and currency of other ways of envisaging royal power. In the case of Scotland, it has been argued that 'For almost twenty years, at a time when Europe was racked by strife between monarchy and aristocracy, James III had promoted the royal authority . . . It was [his] concept of monarchy, not the medieval constitutionalism of the magnates, that James IV would pursue.'[16] This evidently implies that some kind of 'absolutism' was, in contrast and even conflict with 'constitutionalism', being promoted and pursued. It is an implication which calls for careful and critical scrutiny.

The claim to 'imperial' kingship, asserted in the act of 1469, has been seen as reflecting 'a high-flown view of royal authority';[17] as manifesting James III's 'alarming belief in the sanctity of his office' and thus 'a dangerously exalted view of Scottish kingship'.[18] And the theme of 'empire' continued—in James's coinage of the 1480s[19] and, in his son's reign, in the imperial crown which still tops the chapel tower of King's College in Aberdeen.[20] In regard to the actual exercise of power the evidence is somewhat less decisive. There are certainly clear indications that James III was regarded as acting in an arbitrary and high-handed manner. In particular, the liberality with which he granted remissions aroused adverse criticism. This was voiced as early as 1473, when the estates asked the king to 'closs his handis for al remissiounis and respettis [respites] for slauchter . . . for a certane tyme'.[21] A dozen years later the problem was still a matter of parliamentary concern: in 1484 and again in 1485 James undertook to refrain from granting such pardons for three years.[22] And almost at the

---

[15] As to this see J. H. Burns, *Lordship, Kingship, and Empire: The Idea of Monarchy 1400–1525* (Oxford, 1992), esp. ch. 4.

[16] Nicholson, *Later Middle Ages*, 539–40.

[17] Ibid. 483.

[18] Macdougall, *James III*, 98.

[19] I. H. Stewart, *The Scottish Coinage* (2nd edn., London, 1967), 67.

[20] Macfarlane, *Elphinstone*, 330: 'As for the crown on top of the tower, Boece tells us specifically that this was an imperial, not a royal one.'

[21] *APS* ii. 104; and cf. Macdougall, *James III*, 99; Nicholson, *Later Middle Ages*, 430–1.

[22] *APS* ii. 165, 170; and cf. Macdougall, *James III*, 201.

end of the reign, in October 1487, parliament secured a similar royal undertaking, this time for seven years.[23] Venality was doubtless the root problem in all this; but whether greed or need was the motive, the issue at stake was the fundamental royal responsibility for law-enforcement and the disregard of that responsibility involved in the arbitrary overriding of the established legal rules. 'Due process' was again denied in such episodes as James III's handling of the earldom of Lennox between 1471 and 1473. By a grant which has been called 'the most scandalous of the reign', he conferred the liferent of the earldom on the chancellor, Andrew Stewart, Lord Avandale, in total disregard of three hereditary claimants. And when the *title* was conferred on one of those claimants, John Stewart, Lord Darnley, this was ultimately made conditional on his acceptance of Avandale's liferent and of other royal grants from the lands of the earldom. The king was treating the earldom as being, effectively, in his gift, for which there was no legal basis.[24]

What cannot safely be claimed, however, in the absence of relevant evidence, is that James III's arbitrary acts were backed by any doctrine or ideology of 'absolutism'. If we compare the situation with, for example, the controversies over royal power in Castile earlier in the century, what we shall not find in the Scottish case is anything corresponding to the battery of absolutist formulae which was at the disposal of Juan II and Enrique IV and formed a focal point in constitutional debate as well as part of the armoury of factional strife. Those formulae, moreover, were part of an absolutist tradition which could be traced back for two centuries to the work of the Bologna-trained jurists who had advised Alfonso X on the drafting of his *Siete Partidas*.[25] Scotland, in the period with which we are concerned, was doubtless acquiring, from canonists as well as civilians, the seeds from which a mature and sophisticated legal culture would develop from the

[23] *APS* ii. 176; and cf. Macdougall, *James III*, 202–3, For a less hostile view of James's policy in this respect, see Macfarlane, *Elphinstone*, 111–12, referring to the 'problem of tempering justice with mercy'.

[24] Macdougall, *James III*, 101–2. A more lenient view of the case is taken by Macfarlane (*Elphinstone*, 174), who says simply that 'James had rashly and, as is now evident, wrongly given [Avandale] the liferent of the earldom of Lennox'.

[25] See Burns, *Lordship, Kingship, and Empire*, 72–8.

sixteenth century onwards.[26] In the fifteenth century, however, even a professional judiciary remained at best an aspiration: 'lions under the throne' were conspicuous only by their absence.

This is not to imply that we can simply revert to the traditional stereotype of an essentially weak Scottish monarchy, bedevilled by protracted royal minorities and perpetually embroiled in a losing battle with its 'over-mighty subjects'. Whatever revisions may overtake the 'new orthodoxy' which, in the past twenty years or so, has modified that traditional picture, some of its conclusions will surely stand. Thus James III, James IV, and James V, whatever their mistakes, misconceptions, and mishaps may have been, were plainly not weak kings. Nor does it seem fully adequate to say that they were merely continuing an established pattern, whether this is presented in a specifically Scottish or in a more general European form.[27] The character of kingship was changing—in Scotland as elsewhere—as social conditions and the demands of political situations changed. It may be true that an attempt (perhaps no more than half-hearted) by James III to introduce a greater degree of centralization in the administration of justice was premature, and that his two successors on the throne achieved greater success by reverting to the tradition of itinerant royal justice.[28] Yet in 1532 the College of Justice was established; and however mixed or even tainted James V's motives may have been in promoting that establishment, it was none the less a milestone along a road on which (we may perhaps claim) his

[26] See on this Macfarlane, *Elphinstone*, esp. chs. 2 and 3. For the legal culture of the 16th c. and its background, see J. W. Cairns, T. D. Fergus, and H. L. MacQueen, 'Legal Humanism and the History of Scots Law: John Skene and Thomas Craig', in J. MacQueen (ed.), *Humanism in Renaissance Scotland* (Edinburgh, 1990), 48–74.

[27] For a vigorous summary of the 'new orthodoxy' see Wormald, *Court, Kirk, and Community*, esp. ch. 1. Reservations as to this view are apparent in Macfarlane, *Elphinstone*: see esp. ch. 5, 'The Struggle for Order in the Reign of James III 1460–1488'.

[28] See Wormald, *Court, Kirk, and Community*, 14–15; Nicholson, *Later Middle Ages*, 429–30, and as index under 'Justice, Ayres'; Macdougall, *James III*, as index under 'Justice'; id., *James IV*, as index under 'Justice Ayres'; and perhaps esp. Macfarlane, *Elphinstone*, as index under 'ayres, justice'. Macfarlane (*Elphinstone*, 441) sums up by saying that 'royal justice in Scotland . . . was still thought of in terms of peripatetic justice *coram rege*'.

much-maligned grandfather had set out sixty years before.[29] James III and his advisers certainly seem to have tried to introduce some differentiation of functions in the administration of justice and to have shown some concern for the quality of legal knowledge deployed at different levels in the system.[30] In the wider field of governance—*gubernaculum* as distinct from *jurisdictio*, according to one (perhaps questionable) formulation— the crucial area is inevitably the royal council and the critical question relates to the actualities of 'conciliar' royal rule. This is an area where clear-cut conclusions may be hard to reach and to justify, especially since such records as survive relate largely to the judicial, rather than the 'governmental' functions of the 'Lords of Council'. It must also be borne in mind that, since pure autocracy is, in its literal sense, inconceivable in any ongoing system of government, the king's council in one form or another had always had an essential part to play in royal rule. It may, none the less, be possible to detect signs of significant development, if not of radical innovation, in the conciliar aspect of Scottish kingship in this period.

The conciliar body with which we are concerned is not, of course, the relatively large 'general council', which could and did act at times as a surrogate for the full assembly of the estates in parliament. The focus here is on what was later called the privy council and has been described, with reference to this period, as '[a] small group of familiars, both clerical and lay, who had access to the king . . . and formed his inner or "daily" Council'.[31] The term 'familiars' might, to be sure, hint at something which, from the standpoint of the magnates as the king's traditional 'natural counsellors', could wear a sinister appearance. The king's 'familiars' might, in this view of the matter, be courtiers or 'favourites' who had usurped positions of influence to which they had no proper claim. Such a view is reflected, for instance, in the 1482 addition to one of the manuscript copies of Andrew Wyntoun's

---

[29] See Donaldson, *James V to James VII*, 46–8, for a fairly sceptical view of the establishment of 1532: 'All that had happened was the inadequate endowment of the "session" of semi-professional and specialist judges which had already been taking shape.' A rather more positive view, perhaps, is taken by Wormald, *Court, Kirk, and Community*, 24–5.

[30] See Macfarlane, *Elphinstone*, 95–6, for a general account of this problem in 15th-c. Scotland, and pp. 109–12 for some aspects of James III's policy.

[31] Ibid. 407.

Orygynale Cronykyl of Scotland, complaining that James III 'wrocht mair the consaell of his housald at [that] war bot sympill na [than] he did of thame that was lordis'.[32] Much more recently it has been argued that the making of policy had become a matter for the king's 'court', with 'the king's official counsellors . . . relegated to such tedious tasks as assessing royal lands, auditing accounts, hearing literally hundreds of cases . . .'.[33] Now the suspicion that some kind of 'kitchen cabinet' has supplanted the legitimate wielders of power and influence is an endemic feature of political life; and it is always a suspicion that is hard to confirm or to allay. On balance, however, it would appear to be more probable that the members of the king's effective council 'were chiefly his officers of State—the Chancellor, Keeper of the Privy Seal, Secretary, Treasurer, Comptroller, Master of the King's Household and Chamberlain . . . backed by their professional information officers, the lord Clerk Register and the Director of Chancery, and supported by a team of royal and personal clerks and scribes . . . If anybody had political power,' the same historian adds, 'these were the men.'[34] If we take into account also the evident improvements in the keeping and care of administrative records, it will be sufficiently clear that the machinery of government in Scotland, however limited and intermittent its effective operation might be, was undergoing significant development as the fifteenth century drew to an end.[35] That development could only tend to enhance the power of the crown and the strength of the monarchy.

That point will seem to be further corroborated when we recall the fact that we are dealing with a period long before anything like an effectual 'separation of powers'—or even a clear distinction among the various powers of government—had begun to take shape. It is salutary to remember that, in Scotland as elsewhere, the king's council 'retained legislative and judicial powers, and was never reduced to an advisory capacity'.[36] That second clause must, it is true, be interpreted with some caution if we are not to attribute to the council greater independence of

---

[32] The text of that part of this chronicle which relates to James III's reign is printed by Macdougall, *James III*, Appendix A. The phrase quoted above is on p. 312.

[33] Nicholson, *Later Middle Ages*, 504.

[34] Macfarlane, *Elphinstone*, 407.

[35] Ibid. 407–8, on record-keeping; and for a general assessment, pp. 444–5.

[36] Wormald, *Court, Kirk, and Community*, 22.

action than it really had (at least when an adult king was ruling). It is useful to recall what was reported of James IV by Pedro de Ayala, the Spanish ambassador in 1496–7: that the king 'lends a willing ear to his counsellors, and decides nothing without asking them; but in great matters he acts according to his own judgment'.[37] Thus the really important consequence of the council's having 'retained legislative . . . powers' (we may leave aside the judicial aspect at this stage) was that it provided a means whereby *the king* could legislate. Yet the author who reminds us of these crucially retained powers also remarks, a page later, that 'King-in-parliament was the law-giver';[38] and it is necessary now to consider the parliamentary element in the structure of government.

It is interesting to recall in this connection the work of Sir John Fortescue—and the fact that he had spent some time as a Lancastrian exile in Scotland.[39] Fortescue makes a celebrated distinction between two forms of kingship—one he calls *dominium regale* and the other *dominium politicum et regale*. The latter is of major concern to him because, he believes, it is the form of kingship which operates in England; but he also notes other examples, and one of these is, indeed, Scotland.[40] Now one crucial differentia between the two forms of monarchy is the source of the laws by which each is governed. Under *dominium regale* the laws are made by the king: the maxim *Quod principi placuit legis habet vigorem* applies fully throughout the legal system. Under *dominium politicum et regale*, in contrast, laws, while they are indeed made by the king, are so made only with the assent of his subjects. Here— as also in respect of taxation—there is a critically important role for the parliamentary assembly. Fortescue's perception of Scotland as a case of *dominium politicum et regale* would thus indeed imply that 'King-in-parliament was the law-giver'. How are we to assess this in the light of what is known of the Scottish parliament in the period with which we are concerned?

It may be acknowledged at once that we are faced with a body very different from what the English parliament had by that time become. One crucial difference lay in the position, under the two

[37] Quoted by Nicholson, *Later Middle Ages*, 572–3.
[38] Wormald, *Court, Kirk, and Community*, 23.
[39] For the Lancastrians in Scotland, between the winter of 1460/1 and the summer of 1463, see Macdougall, *James III*, 57–61.
[40] *De laudibus legum Angliae*, ed. S. B. Chrimes (Cambridge, 1942), 32.

systems, of the 'third estate'. Scotland had developed nothing like the English House of Commons with the knights of the shire joining borough representatives in what was already a significant and was to become the predominant factor in the system. Burgesses did indeed attend the Scottish parliament, though with varying regularity, never in large numbers, and restricted throughout to representatives of *royal* burghs. Preponderantly, however, it was an assembly of prelates and magnates; the total membership was never large, sessions were brief, and much business was delegated to committees. On the other hand, strikingly at a time when tendencies in other realms—including England—were decidedly in the opposite direction, meetings of the estates in Scotland were, until the mid-1490s, frequent and fairly regular. Annual parliaments were the norm for most of James III's personal reign and in the early years of his son's. Thereafter, to be sure, there was a sharp, almost startling change, which will call for comment in a moment. First, however, we must consider what these frequent, if brief, parliaments were about.[41]

Parliament was, among other things, the supreme court in the realm, and judicial business was always an important part of its activity. For one thing—a point of some importance in what were often troubled times—it was in parliament that proceedings leading to forfeiture and the other penalties of treason took place. Yet, in the context of the more ordinary business of government, legislation was indeed a major item on the parliamentary agenda. Throughout the period from James I's return from his English captivity in 1424, the estates legislated on a vast range of topics, ranging from the essential to the seemingly trivial.[42] So much was this the case that James VI's fifteenth-century predecessors might well at times have anticipated his plaintive remark: 'in this country we haue alreadie mo good lawes then are well execute'.[43] It may well have been the case generally, as it surely was in a good

---

[41] See, for a concise analysis, Donaldson, *James V to James VII*, 8–9. Later, introducing his account of the 17th-c. constitution, Donaldson says: 'The organs of the Scottish constitution must be viewed not as the embodiment of theories of representation and consent, but as the machinery by which the government of the country was conducted, as the instruments by which effect was given to the will of the individual or the faction in control' (ibid. 276).

[42] A good indication, though by no means an exhaustive list, of the topics dealt with may be seen in the index entry 'Parliament, Scottish, Acts' in Macfarlane, *Elphinstone*, 509.

[43] *Basilikon Doron*, Craigie edn., i. 58–9.

many instances, that most of those who attended parliament had little interest in the legislative process as such. That process, for what it was worth, could be used by the king or by his immediate advisers to promote with some ease such measures as they thought desirable. A good illustration would be the so-called 'education act' of 1496, almost certainly the work, essentially, of William Elphinstone, and perhaps typical in being more notable for admirable intentions than for manifest effects.[44] As for taxation—that other touchstone for Fortescue's *dominium politicum et regale*—it is again the case that parliamentary consent was a prerequisite; but it 'was rare and was granted . . . only for extraordinary expenditure on royal marriages, diplomacy, or military preparations'. In this respect there is, predictably, more evidence for parliamentary concern and opposition. However, attempts to collect taxes, once granted, were so ineffectual that, it has been said, 'Taxation may . . . be ignored in any examination of the royal revenues'.[45] It follows that fiscal policy did not provide any real leverage for parliamentary control of the king's government.[46]

When all this is said, the fact remains that the Scottish estates cannot be dismissed as a mere tool to be manipulated by the king—or by any individual or group who might, for the time being, have the power of the crown at their disposal. The parliamentary assembly, for all its limitations, is more properly seen as a medium for the co-operation between king and magnates, which was ultimately essential for the proper functioning of the political system. That co-operation could not be taken for granted. There is clear evidence, not only of parliamentary criticism of royal policy, but of downright opposition—notably, but by no means only, in the early and doubtless over-confident years of James III's personal rule.[47] Despite this, annual—or virtually an-

---

[44] On the 1496 act see Macfarlane, *Elphinstone*, 312–13. More generally, Macfarlane refers (ibid. 112) to 'James III and his legislators' and the legislators are not, of course, the estates at large, but 'men like Andrew lord Avandale, Colin Campbell, John Drummond of Stobhall, John Ross of Montgrennan, Elphinstone, Alexander Inglis, and the king's secretary Archibald Whitelaw'.

[45] Nicholson, *Later Middle Ages*, 453. These comments refer specifically to the reign of James III; but the difficulty in collecting taxes was a persistent problem.

[46] It is, however, worth noting that taxation was very frequent in the early years of James IV's reign, but much less frequent later: see Macdougall, *James IV*, esp. 147–50. This should perhaps be borne in mind in relation to the 'demise of parliament' discussed below.

[47] Macdougall, *James III*, 94–7; but cf. 109–10: '[James] had discovered for himself that extraordinary taxation provoked opposition in parliament. Yet the strictures of the July parliament of 1473 may not have worried the king unduly.'

nual—meetings continued to be held, in which the king and his immediate advisers had to come to terms with the estates of the realm, and in particular with those magnates whose opinions and effective power could not safely be ignored.[48]

In the light of these points, a question, already adumbrated here, necessarily arises over what has been termed 'the demise of parliament' during the greater part of James IV's reign.[49] From the start of the reign in the summer of 1488 until June 1496 the estates met in full parliament on ten occasions. In the remaining seventeen years of the reign there were only three parliaments, the first of them meeting almost eight years after its predecessor.[50] Such a contrast cries out for explanation; but the cry is not easily answered. In part, the explanation may be that the king possessed, and availed himself of, other means of achieving the essential royal purposes usually served by parliament. In particular, a general council, attended by prelates and magnates, but not by burgesses, might provide the necessary forum. It may well have done so on several occasions, but the evidence is unfortunately far from adequate.[51] In any case, short of the formal convening of a general council, the ordinary council might be 'afforced' with additional members. And indeed, having regard to the trends that are generally apparent in European monarchies at this period, it is hard to resist the conclusion that in Scotland too a 'new monarch' was 'playing down the role of representative assemblies and placing heavy reliance on conciliar government'. Nor is it in any way inconsistent with this that 'there appears to have been no great enthusiasm for parliament on the part of the estates in general'.[52]

[48] During the twenty years of James III's personal reign, 1470, 1476, and 1486 are the only years in which there was no parliamentary session.

[49] Macdougall, *James IV*, ch. 7.

[50] See ibid. 171, for a convenient tabular summary.

[51] On the somewhat vexed question of the status and history of such general councils, see Nicholson, *Later Middle Ages*, esp. 21, 407. Macdougall, *James IV*, 191–2, shows how fragmentary and inferential the evidence for that reign is, as well as illustrating the difficulty of distinguishing between a formally summoned general council and an 'afforced' sederunt of the ordinary council. See also Macfarlane, *Elphinstone*, 430–4, for an account of the general council which met in 1513 to deal with the problems following the defeat at Flodden.

[52] Macdougall, *James IV*, 170, 192; and cf. Wormald, *Court, Kirk, and Community*, 10, suggesting 'a parallel with the policy of other European rulers: the attempt to play down the role of the "representative" assembly of estates, and build up more directly controllable conciliar government'. Also noteworthy, however, is the point that 'professional civil servants' seem still to have been eager to use parliament for lawmaking: they are said to have 'rushed to legislate given virtually their only chance in 1504' (Macdougall, *James IV*, 192).

Even at much later periods, after all, and in countries with far more mature parliamentary institutions, such enthusiasm was often wanting.

If, then, we were to look for a turning-point in the late-medieval development of Scottish kingship (and it would be rash indeed to see it as a point of transition to a distinctive 'early-modern' phase), we might be tempted to find it in the mid-1490s. The years 1495–7 have indeed been called 'the watershed', at least in the context of James IV's reign.[53] Certainly recent historical scholarship would warn us against adding the end of the previous reign to Seeley's 'Eighty-eights' as a critical moment in history, even if we restrict our view narrowly to Scotland.[54] Yet we surely cannot ignore the débâcle of 1488 or the crises that had preceded it. If we accept the view that James III was not a feeble *rex inutilis* and that the monarchy was, however hesitantly, gaining in strength and efficiency during his reign, then we also have to face the fact of his crashing failure. It can no doubt be argued that had it not been for the contingency of the king's death at Sauchieburn, 'the rebellions [of 1482 and 1488] would never have assumed the constitutional importance later given to them'.[55] Yet it has also been said of the first of those rebellions that '[t]he seizure of James III at Lauder in July 1482 was an event without parallel in fifteenth century Scottish political history'; and while the threat that James would be replaced on the throne by his brother Albany as 'Alexander IV' was no more than a brief phase in the struggle, the fact remains that the events at Lauder were 'immediately followed by a re-markable revolution in governmental personnel'.[56] As for 1488, we have no means of knowing what would have ensued had not the king 'happinit to be slane on the feild of Stervilin';[57] but we do know that the king had aroused the opposition of a substantial group of nobles who had, in one way or another, induced the heir to the throne to take up arms against his father. We may con-clude that James III was 'an aloof, overbearing and vindictive ruler whose dangerously exalted concept of Scottish kingship

---

[53] Macdougall, *James IV*, ch. 5.
[54] Sir J. Seeley, 'The Eighty-eights', *Good Words*, 29 (1888), 373–80.
[55] Macfarlane, *Elphinstone*, 182.
[56] Macdougall, *James III*, 158.
[57] *APS* ii. 210: this was the view presented in the parliament of October 1488. See further Macdougall, *James IV*, 58–60; Nicholson, *Later Middle Ages*, 532–3.

confounded his friends and eventually proved a godsend to his enemies'.[58] Or we may prefer to see him as 'an intelligent but frustrated ruler who understood his country's weaknesses much better than his people did, but without whose cooperation he risked political disaster'.[59] There can in any case be no doubt as to the disaster; and perhaps little doubt as to the existence of serious disequilibrium in the Scottish realm as James IV succeeded James III. The ensuing century was to produce situations even more likely to generate political conflict and controversy. This was the seedbed for the divergent views of kingship with which the chapters that follow are concerned.

[58] Macdougall, *James III*, 299.   [59] Macfarlane, *Elphinstone*, 171.

1

Theology and Politics
John Ireland and John Mair

BEFORE the battle of Sauchieburn on 11 June 1488, according to
one account, James III 'wes confessit . . . with maistir Johne
Yrland proffesor of theologie'.[1] The statement cannot be corroborated from any other source, but it is plausible enough: Ireland
(*c*.1440–95) had certainly been the king's confessor during the last
half-dozen years of his reign, besides serving him as counsellor,
judge, and ambassador.[2] If he did indeed perform the last service
of hearing the king's confession on the eve of the final disaster of
his reign, there is a certain appropriate irony in the fact. Ireland's
Meroure of Wyssdome was probably begun in the late 1480s and
intended originally for presentation to James III. In the event,
completed in 1490, it was presented to James IV, who had taken
the field at Sauchieburn against his father.[3] An exercise in 'popular theology', distilling in the vernacular the essence of what its
author had studied and taught in Paris between the 1460s and the
early 1480s, the *Meroure* has, especially in the last of its seven
Books, a good deal of the character of a typical *Fürstenspiegel*. It
would be naïve to argue that, had James III only followed the
conventional advice which (though the *Meroure* was not there for
him to read) must surely have reached his ears through Ireland's
preaching at court, the débâcle of 1488 might never have occurred. Yet it is hard to suppose that, as Ireland completed the

---

[1] Adam Abell of Jedburgh, 'The Roit and Quheill of Tyme' (National Library of
Scotland MS 1746). The relevant portion of the text is printed in Macdougall,
James III, Appendix B: the quoted phrase is on p. 315.

[2] On Ireland see J. H. Burns, 'John Ireland: Theology and Public Affairs in the
Late Fifteenth Century', *Innes Review*, 41 (1990), 151–81.

[3] The text of the *Meroure* has been published by the Scottish Text Society under
the title *The Meroure of Wyssdome composed for the use of James IV., King of Scots A.D.
1490 by Johannes de Irlandia Professor of Theology in the University of Paris*: vol. i, ed.
C. Macpherson, 1926; vol. ii, ed. F. Quinn, 1965; vol. iii, ed. C. McDonald, 1990
(hereafter *Meroure*, i, ii, and iii respectively).

writing of the *Meroure* and as James IV read it, or heard it read, they were not acutely conscious of a special kind and degree of relevance to the situation in the realm of Scotland as they knew it. Discount as we may, and no doubt must, the conventional (and, as we shall see, derivative) wisdom Ireland had to offer, we can still conclude that theology and politics did indeed meet in this text and context.

John Ireland was certainly the most distinguished theologian Scotland had produced since Duns Scotus (if we may accept the traditional view of Scotus's ethnic origin). That his distinction was vastly less is obvious enough; nor indeed can he be compared, whether in range or in originality, either with his older contemporary Gabriel Biel or with his compatriot John Mair in the next generation.[4] Any exact evaluation of Ireland's work is, to be fair, made difficult by the fact that so much of it is lost.[5] Nor has sufficient expert work yet been done on what survives.[6] It is clear, however, that he was not a negligible figure, and it is at least becoming possible to locate him with some confidence in the complex spectrum of fifteenth-century theology—and, up to a point, philosophy.[7] A starting-point may be found in the position Ireland seems to have adopted in the conflict of schools of thought in Paris in the early 1470s. When, in 1474, the opponents of the *via moderna* teaching which had so largely predominated there secured a royal ban on the crucial nominalist texts, Ireland (then within two years of becoming a fully qualified teacher of theology) was prominent in the resistance to the decree. He had himself 'followed' Ockham in works (no longer extant) deriving from his years of teaching in the arts faculty.[8] And the two or three

---

[4] Biel died in the same year as Ireland, but (though the date of his birth is uncertain) he was probably twenty-five or thirty years older. Because the strictly academic phase of his career came unusually late in life, there is little likelihood and no indication that Ireland was aware of his work. On him see esp. H. A. Oberman, *The Harvest of Medieval Theology: Gabriel Biel and Late Medieval Nominalism* (1963; 3rd edn., Durham, NC, 1983).

[5] See the list of Ireland's works appended to Burns, 'John Ireland', 172–3.

[6] There are two useful articles by Brother Bonaventure Miner: 'The Popular Theology of John Ireland', *Innes Review*, 13 (1962), 130–46; 'John Ireland and the Immaculate Conception', *Innes Review*, 17 (1966), 24–39.

[7] On the philosophical side see A. Broadie, *The Tradition of Scottish Philosophy* (Edinburgh, 1990), ch. 2, 'The Mirror of Wisdom: Philosophy in the Scots Tongue'.

[8] See items 8 and 9 in the list cited in n. 5 above. Ireland's career as an arts faculty teacher covered some fifteen years from his graduating MA in 1460.

years following the repeal of the ban in 1481 appear to have yielded his most substantial work—the commentary on the four books of Peter Lombard's *Sentences*, of which Books III and IV survive—together with several parerga said to have been written at the request or prompting of his royal patrons Louis XI and James III.[9] Thereafter, for the last dozen years of his life, Ireland turned away from the academic world, but not (despite the demands of the varied tasks he was called upon to perform in royal service) from theology. His theological learning was now directed towards the unlearned audiences who might hear his sermons or read his vernacular works.[10]

Two fundamental and related themes emerge with particular clarity and emphasis in even a cursory survey of Ireland's work. The first is the problem of predestination and of God's 'presciens' or foreknowledge, and of the relation between these factors or forces and human freedom. It hardly needs to be recalled that these problems, always crucially important in Christian theological thinking, had been the subject of particularly intense debate for at least a century and a half when Ireland wrote. The nominalist theology of the fourteenth century could be interpreted as implying a 'Pelagian' or perhaps a 'semi-Pelagian' view in which human beings, acting purely by means of their own natural powers and virtues, might achieve, or at least contribute to, their eternal salvation. Now Ireland is at pains, on every available occasion, to assert and to underline his rejection of any such view. He cites with significant approval the work of the greatest advocate of 'the cause of God against the Pelagians', Thomas Bradwardine, *doctor profundus*.[11] So fundamental was the importance Ireland attached to the subject that, even when he was consciously writing for lay readers rather than for 'clerkis' like himself, he felt that he must 'heir discend to the subtilite of this

[9] The surviving part of the *Sentences* commentary is Aberdeen University Library MS 264. The sole survivor among the 'parerga' is the 'Tractatus de Immaculata Conceptione Virginis Mariae' (Trinity College Dublin, MS 965).

[10] In addition to the *Meroure* and to sermons no longer extant, Ireland's vernacular work included the treatise *Of Penance and Confession* preserved in the Asloan manuscript and printed in W. A. Craigie's edition of that collection, vol. i (Scottish Text Society, 1923), 1–80. Ireland also mentions a vernacular treatise on Christ's passion, no longer extant (item 15 in the list cited in n. 5 above).

[11] Burns, 'John Ireland', 127 and n. 128. The suggestion (ibid., n. 159) that Ireland also invoked Richard FitzRalph, archbishop of Armagh, in this connection appears to be mistaken.

mater'.[12] The whole of Book V of the *Meroure* is devoted to these
intricate problems—admittedly one of the shorter sections of the
work, but still occupying nearly forty exacting pages in the
printed text. It is not surprising, then, to find that, in a strictly
academic context, with full scope for 'mony reulis conclusiouns
and correlaris', Ireland evidently dealt with the subject at length
and in depth, drawing on a wide range of sources from Augustine
to Pierre d'Ailly.[13]

The second of the two particularly prominent themes in
Ireland's theology mentioned above is closely linked with the
first. It responds indeed to a crux arising inevitably from Ireland's
position in regard to human freedom and God's power. On the
one hand he vigorously asserts man's 'liberte, that is fre will' as
the most essential element in the 'gret dignite' which God conferred by making human beings in his own image.[14] But the gift
was, of course, abused, so that 'our natur was filit and corrumpit
be the syn of Adam'; and the saving remedy for this cannot be
found in 'our awne wertu and power'. To claim that it can is,
precisely, the Pelagian heresy Ireland so strenuously rejects. Only
divine power manifested in the gift of grace can enable us to
perform any 'noble operacioun meritor of the lif eternale'. This,
however, left open the question of the form taken by 'the
assistaunce help and suple that god gevis to man'.[15] For Ireland,
an important part of the answer lay in what he called *auxilium
speciale*, the 'singulare and speciale help of god' which was
'necessare to all merit and gud werkis'.[16]

To invoke the notion of *auxilium speciale* was to enter one of the
debatable lands of late-medieval theology, and Ireland's use of
the term was not simply casual or occasional: he devoted an entire
treatise (or at least a substantial part of it) to the topic.[17] It
seems certain that we can detect here the significant influence of
one of the outstanding theologians and philosophers of the

[12] *Meroure*, ii. 145.
[13] Ibid., referring specifically to 'the first buk I wrait on the sentens in paris'.
[14] Ibid. 84.
[15] Ibid. 131. The last phrase is in the chapter-heading on p. 130.
[16] *Meroure*, i. 48.
[17] See the latter part of the passage cited below at n. 21. In another passage
Ireland refers to the book as having been 'a maist all of this mater, provand that the
help and suple of god that is callit *speciale auxilium* . . . is necessare to all merit and
gud werkis' (*Meroure*, i. 48).

mid-fourteenth century, Gregory of Rimini. Gregory's commentary on the *Sentences* is cited by Ireland at least five times in three
of his surviving works; and, apart from the reference in the treatise on the Immaculate Conception, the tone is always one of
approval.[18] The context, again, is consistently that of the debate on
grace and free will, usually with specific reference to the concept
of *auxilium speciale*.[19] No doubt the most significant of these cita-
tions occurs in Ireland's own *Sentences* commentary. In that work,
he tells us, this problematic area had been dealt with in three out
of the four books;[20] and in the surviving commentary on Book III
we have the following passage:

alia vero est opinio quod deus semper permouet [?] pulsando et exitando
[*sic*] ad graciam et ad opera bona per mociones bonas et speciale auxilium
et quod hoc subsequitur consensiendo [*sic*] operibus bonis . . . et pro hac
opinione est illud apochalipsis 3° ego sto ad hostium [*sic*] et pulso foris et
hec opinio est multum catholica de auxilio speciali et eam tractat
subtiliter magr. gregorius in fine 2ⁱ [Sent.] et doctor profundus brauardin
[*sic*].

This, moreover, is immediately followed by the fullest and most
informative reference we have to Ireland's own treatise on the
subject:

et etiam multa pro hac opinione tractaui in V libris quos scripsi ad
illustrem regem scotorum de gratia, uirtutibus, auxilio speciali et
partibus penitencie in sequendo prefatos doctores . . . [21]

In following Gregory of Rimini along this line of thought,
Ireland was evidently taking a position opposed to writers whom
in other connections he certainly respected. Gregory, in his

---

[18] See Miner, 'Ireland and the Immaculate Conception', 37, where it may be
indicated that Ireland detected some hesitation on the issue in Gregory. An earlier
Scottish theologian, however, described Gregory as *robustus adversarius in hac
materia* (quoted by H. McEwan, ' "A Theolog Solempne," Thomas de Rossy,
Bishop of Galloway', *Innes Review*, 8 (1957), 24. Certainly there seems to be nothing
equivocal in the view expressed by Gregory of Rimini in his *Lectura in Primum et
Secundum Sententiarum*: this can now be studied in the splendid edition under the
general editorship of A. Damasus Trapp and Venicio Marcolino, 6 vols. (Berlin,
1979–82: hereafter Trapp edn.).

[19] *Meroure*, i. 48; ii. 131, 145: the last reference is in the broader context of
predestination and divine foreknowledge. See also the passage cited below at
n. 21.

[20] *Meroure*, i. 48: 'j haue writtin of this mater apone the sentens j haue red in paris
apone the foure bukis, jn the secund thride and ferd.'

[21] Aberdeen University Library MS 264, fo. 64ᵛ.

lengthy discussion of *auxilium speciale*, identifies the following as 'modern Pelagians' who reject the concept: Duns Scotus, Ockham, Robert Holcot, Durand de St Pourçain, and (perhaps especially) Adam Wodeham.[22] Apart from Scotus, who will be considered further presently, these names all belong, in one sense or another, to the tradition of fourteenth-century nominalism with which Ireland plainly allied himself in important respects. At the same time he was quite ready to differ from these thinkers (all of whom he cites), mentioning (for instance) his explicit refutation of Holcot on a point of major significance.[23] There is therefore no difficulty in accepting, as we must, that Ireland endorsed Gregory of Rimini's censure of these 'modern Pelagians', though there may be room for doubt as to whether he would have endorsed the full rigour of Gregory's severely Augustinian position. Nor, in any case, did following Gregory's lead imply deserting the nominalist camp. There has, to be sure, been much debate as to Gregory's precise relationship to that school of thought; but he was regarded in his own time as 'the standard-bearer of the nominalists'; the first printed edition of his *Sentences* commentary followed closely upon the lifting of the royal ban on nominalist texts in Paris; and in our own day Heiko Oberman has argued that he is best regarded as 'a right-wing nominalist'—'a *doctor modernus* who combats the unorthodox excesses of nominalism'.[24]

If, however, there is a 'right-wing nominalism' to be found in the theology of Gregory of Rimini, its manifestations are not restricted to the doctrine of *auxilium speciale*—important though that evidently was both to Gregory and to those who, like John

[22] *Lectura*, I, dist. 26–8 (Trapp edn., vi. 17–114). There are references, either explicit or precisely identified by the editors, on e.g. pp. 18, 32, 62. On pp. 60–4 there is an extended refutation of the view taken by Wodeham, who, together with Scotus and Ockham, is again subjected to lengthy refutation on pp. 64–87.

[23] *Meroure*, i. 104: 'ilk man be werray law and obligacioun of natur suld trow the cristin faith, and refus the contrar. And this haly faith is nocht agane natur na ressoune natural, thocht sum part of doctouris as Robertus holcot of ingland say the contrar, bot his subtill and sophistic ressouns I haue assolyeit in the first buk of the sentens in the proheme in the first questioun, quhar I haue tretit of this mater at lenth, *doctrinaliter profunde et scolastice.*'

[24] See Burns, 'John Ireland', 166–7, and the references given there. In regard to the 1482 edn. of Gregory's commentary on Book I of the *Sentences*, it is worth noting that Domenico Mancini's dedicatory verses refer explicitly to Louis XI's lifting of the ban: 'Reddidit hunc nobis Ludouici gratia Regis | Reddidit et dogma a nomine nomen habens.' For Oberman's comments see *Harvest of Medieval Theology*, 199, 204.

Ireland, followed his lead in that direction. There were theologians of a generally Ockhamist outlook, such as Pierre d'Ailly and Gabriel Biel, who plainly 'held Gregory in high regard' but who none the less parted company with him on the still more fundamental issue of predestination. Gregory of Rimini's 'right-wing position', according to Oberman, 'is marked by his outspoken defence of predestination *ante praevisa merita*'. This was the position adopted by Duns Scotus; but Gregory 'goes beyond Scotus . . . in also holding to reprobation *ante praevisa demerita*'.[25] Where are we to locate John Ireland in this context?

There can, to start with, be no doubt as to the importance of Duns Scotus for Ireland's thinking. No other post-patristic theologian is cited so frequently in his writings and there are clear indications that Ireland 'followed' Scotus on a number of points.[26] So far as the critical issue of predestination is concerned, however, the relationship between the two is not altogether easy to determine. It seems clear that Ireland's most fully developed discussion of the subject was in his commentary, now lost, on Book I of the *Sentences*; and he provides a list of the authorities he referred to in that discussion which is too comprehensive to afford any adequate clue to the line he took.[27] We are left with the discussion in the *Meroure*, which can perhaps be seen as reflecting the difficulty Ireland found in expressing highly technical points in a language which, native to him though it was, he wrote—as he himself acknowledged—with less facility than the Latin in which his professional life had been carried on for

---

[25] Ibid. 204–5.

[26] The number of references to Scotus so far found in Ireland's works should be higher than the fifteen given in Burns, 'John Ireland', 165: Miner, 'Ireland and the Immaculate Conception', 37, says that there are 'very few references to Duns Scotus' in the 'Tractatus de Immaculata Conceptione', not (as in Burns) that he 'is cited only once' there. For instances where Ireland explicitly follows Scotus, see e.g. Aberdeen University Library MS 264, fos. 202ʳ, 213ᵛ; and, perhaps esp., *Meroure*, ii. 106 ff.

[27] *Meroure*, ii. 145: 'Of the mater of predestinacioun and presciens . . . I haue tretit at lenth in the first buk I wrait on the sentens in paris eftir the maist subtile doctouris, that has writtin of it, as augustin and the auld doctouris, and specialy the new doctouris Okam gregor de arimino de aliaco de hoeta . . .'. There is some interest in the overlap between this list and that given by Wendelin Steinbach in the introductory letter to his edition of Gabriel Biel's work on the *Sentences*, where he says that 'next to the *veteres theologi*, Biel esteems a second group as highly: Occam, Holcot, Gregory [of Rimini], Adam [Wodeham], Oyta, and d'Ailly' (Oberman, *Harvest of Medieval Theology*, 203).

decades.[28] Such as it is, however, this is the evidence we have to use.

We may begin, as Ireland does, with definitions:[29]

Predestinacio est diuinum propositum dandi vitam eternam. Predestinacioun is the will and purpos of god to gif to a creatur resonable or intellectual eternale lif in ioy and blis . . .

Reprobacio est diuinum propositum non dandi vitam eternam. The reprobacioun of the creatur is the wil and purpos of god that knawis the syn and iniquite of the man or of the creatur that will euir perseueir in syn and nouthir do pennaunce na ask mercy and tharfor he wil nocht gif him eternale lif na ioy final.[30]

It is perhaps significant that Ireland here makes a point of specifying the demerits of the reprobate but not the merits of those predestined to eternal salvation. However, it is soon made quite clear that both predestination and reprobation derive from absolutely free divine decisions reached 'befor the creacioun and making of the waurld'. What God 'ordanis . . . of his fre liberte' is not so ordained 'for ony caus'. The 'will and plesaunce of god' is God's 'self': as such it 'is eternale and na creatur may be caus of god na yit of a thing necessar and eternal'.[31] We are being offered a rigorous view of God's omnipotence, omniscience, and inscrutability, in which, to quote a telling phrase from Alexander Broadie, 'No creature, by being righteous, forces God's hand'.[32]

To say this, however, is not to deny that there is any kind of 'causal' relationship in the matter. Ireland makes a distinction: 'this terme caus amang gret clerkis philosophouris and theologis is tane twa wais'. In the fundamental sense of *causa essendi et reali* no creature, as we have seen, can be said to cause any act or aspect of God. But if the term be taken *large pro causa cognoscendi*, the result is rather different. Here we are dealing with the logical sense in which an antecedent may be said to be the cause of its consequent in a valid proposition of that kind. Thus, in asserting

[28] Ireland himself refers to Latin as 'the tovnge that j knaw bettir' than 'the commoune langage of this cuntre', *Meroure*, i. 164).
[29] These come, by way of Book I of Peter Lombard's *Sentences*, from Augustine.
[30] *Meroure*, ii. 145.
[31] Ibid. 146–7.
[32] Broadie, *Tradition of Scottish Philosophy*, 18. I am greatly indebted to Professor Broadie's brief but lucid discussion of these aspects of Ireland's thought (ibid. 13–19).

the proposition *quia homo est racionalis homo est risibilis*, we are claiming that man is capable of laughter *because* he is rational: his rationality is in some sense the cause of his capacity for laughter.[33] What Ireland sees as 'the hard and difficil questioun' is whether this sense of causality can be applied in the case with which he is concerned. Can the fact or proposition that God predestines or reprobates someone be seen as the consequent in any truly causal proposition? Ireland notes the sharp differences of opinion on this point among theologians, eventually stating his own view in the following terms:

this proposicioun, god predestinat sanct iohne baptist Sanct iohne the euangelist sanct petir sanct paule and richtsua of vthir almaist infinit, is conseqwent in a proposicioun causale Logicale, the antecedent of it beand trew and veritable; bot the antecedent is formyt of the termes in diuinite and nocht of the creaturis precise [i.e. absolutely].

It was God's 'presciens'—his foreknowledge from all eternity of the ways in which his rational creatures would use the freedom he had given them—that 'caused' his decree of predestination or reprobation.[34] This would seem to suggest that, in so far as the terms *ante* and *post* have any meaningful application in statements about the timeless being of God, Ireland's doctrine is one of predestination and reprobation *post praevisa merita/demerita*. Interestingly, he claims that 'this is the determinacioun of the maist subtil doctouris and gretest clerkis that euir has writtin in this mater, specialie in the nobile and excellent vniuersite of paris'.[35] In the end it is perhaps the concept of God's 'presciens' or foreknowledge that is central in Ireland's view of these problems.[36] And it is important to note and to emphasize that this is fully compatible with his equally strong insistence on the freedom

[33] *Meroure*, ii. 147. In regard to the stricter sense of *causa essendi*, Ireland makes the further point that even God himself is not the cause of his decrees in the matter of predestination and reprobation: 'for in the diuinite is nocht properlie causalite bot produccion *ex origine* without causalite properly accepit'.

[34] Ibid. 148–9.

[35] Ibid. 149. It may be worth recalling here an observation by Oberman (*Harvest of Medieval Theology*, 211): 'it is not surprising that the fourteenth-century syncretistic Parisian school, where the positions of the Scotists and nominalists were often fused to the point where their boundaries are difficult to discern, occupied itself primarily with a discussion of the relation of foreordination and foreknowledge.'

[36] This may, however, leave open the question whether Ireland would, as one scholar has expressed the point, 'collapse *praedestinatio* into *praescientia* . . . in the

and dignity of man. It was, to be sure, no longer possible, since the
Fall, for human beings to perform acts deserving of eternal happi-
ness without the 'special help' of God; but it was still for those
human beings to exercise their free choice in performing the acts
made possible by that help. God's foreknowledge of the way in
which that choice will, in each instance, be made does not pre-
empt the freedom of those who choose. If the intricacies of
predestinarian theology seem remote from the world of politics
and government, the dignity of man as a free agent is surely
fundamental to Ireland's (or any other) understanding of man
as a 'political animal'.

That, however, is not the only point at which Ireland's theology
may be seen impinging upon his 'political thought'. The tradition
of soteriology to which, in one of its variant forms, Ireland evidently adhered had among its central elements a distinction between the 'absolute' and the 'ordained' or 'ordinary' power of
God—between the infinity of things God could do by virtue of his
total freedom and the specific ways in which he had in fact chosen
to use his power and could be regarded as having bound himself
by covenant to act in his dealings with his creatures. As Ireland
himself says,

And thus thocht god be his infinit wertu and power absolute mycht
remyt our synnis and gif ws grace and glor without the operacioun of the
creaturis, yit his power ordinate and regulat be his devin wisdome has
ordand and disponit that thir operaciounis sal be maid and the gud
deidis of men acceipt befor his maieste be meyn and mediacioun of his
glorius passioun.[37]

That distinction, when applied to papal or royal power, was to be
a crucially important element in late-medieval and early-modern
political thinking. This was not a theme Ireland himself was

---

manner of both Ockhamists and so-called "left-wing" nominalists' (M. S. Burrows,
Jean Gerson and De Consolatione Theologiae *(1418): The Consolation of a Biblical and
Reforming Theology for a Disordered Age* (Tübingen, 1991), 170). Burrows refers on
this point to the work of Oberman, from whom the terminology of 'left-wing' and
'right-wing' nominalism derives. In that spectrum, it may be noted, Gregory of
Rimini, with his severely Augustinian views, stands on the far right.

[37] *Meroure*, ii. 70. Cf. ibid. 100: 'mar dignite and honour to ws and our natur is
to afferme that this man [Christ] lufit ws sa gretlie that be werray wertu iustice and
ardent cherite he wald obey to the fader of hevin and offer his precius lif for our
redempcioun na [than] to afferme that be his power absolut . . . he has deliuerit
ws'.

particularly concerned to develop; but it was surely part of what he had in mind when he considered royal power, whether in its own temporal terms or as an analogy to assist our understanding of the power of God.

The image of God as king or emperor is in fact a very important one for Ireland, most vividly invoked, perhaps, in the elaborate dialogue of 'the four daughters of God' in Book II of *The Meroure of Wyssdome*.[38] The 'daughters' are 'the foure hevinly wertuis'— Mercy, Truth, Equity (or Justice), and Peace. The context of their debate is the 'merwalus discord and dissencioune' brought about by mankind's lapse into sin. This 'gret syn and offens' is here identified as 'hurt maieste', the *crimen laesae majestatis* or *lèse majesté*.[39] One result of that crime was that the virtues with which man had been endowed in paradise are now in exile from their intended abode. Here they act as 'secretaris and wiss counsalouris' assisting 'the hie and sacret counsall of the trinite' in determining the remedy for man's fallen state.[40] The language Ireland uses here, and as the discussion develops, is the institutional language of royal government as he knew it; and there are, as Sally Mapstone has argued, some striking echoes of the Scottish system and situation in which Ireland had himself been involved. It does not seem fanciful to catch, now and then, the reverberation of some of the conflicts and crises briefly encountered in the introduction to this book; and what we can do hesitantly Ireland's contemporary audience would surely have done with far greater sharpness and immediacy.

More is involved here than the fairly obvious general point, made at the outset of the discussion and reiterated when the problem is about to be resolved by the counsels of Peace: the destructive effects of 'discord and dissencioune'. It is true that, when this theme is resumed, it is very directly linked to the point 'that all nobile citeis and realmes, all gret empyris be strif has bene

---

[38] *Meroure*, i. 106–25. This passage has been thoroughly analysed, with indications of parallels and possible sources (especially in *The Court of Sapience*), by Dr Sally Mapstone, 'A Mirror for a Divine Prince: John Ireland and the Four Daughters of God', in J. D. McClure and M. Spiller (eds.), *Bryght Lanternis: Essays on the Language and Literature of Medieval and Renaissance Scotland* (Aberdeen, 1989), 308–23.

[39] *Meroure*, i. 106. Ireland goes on (pp. 106–7) to refer to Adam and Eve's 'inobediens agane thar souerane lord and ouris, king of angellis and all creaturis'.

[40] Ibid. 107–8.

wndone'.[41] But more specific issues are considered in the course of the debate. One of these lies between mercy and justice—the issue, it has been argued, confronted by James III in the matter of 'remissions'.[42] Mercy pleads the case for pardoning sinful man. Truth, backed up by Justice, argues the overriding need for God as king to adhere to his 'behest & promyss': 'thi wourd mone stand, thi law mone be kepit . . . thi sentens and jugisment mone stand ferme jn execucioune'.[43] Precedent too is cited to the same effect: the rebel angels were punished, and so 'justice and ressoune wauld that auld Adam and his linage knew thi power and wertu, thi justice and equite'.[44] Equity, however, is seized upon by Mercy and used in accordance with the classic scholastic account of it to mitigate the rigour of strict law by looking rather to 'the entencioune of the legislatore'. One of the instances cited is Jonah's effective plea that Nineveh be spared: 'The sentens was nocht put in execucioune, for it was condicionale and comminiatore.' In such cases, Mercy tells her sisters, 'oure mychtie fader suspendis and reuokis his hevy and bitter sentens'.[45] These arguments prevail: with Mercy, Charity, and 'the souerane lady, dame sapience' ranged against them, Truth and Justice 'gretlie desirit . . . to haue hartlie pess and concord'.[46]

It is at the next stage, when peaceful resolution of the issue is formally and substantially achieved, that the 'institutional' character of Ireland's thinking emerges most clearly. So far we have had 'the sacret counsale of the hie and nobile king of paradice' assisted by the four daughters as 'secretaris'.[47] Now we are to see the king himself acting upon the counsel he has received. Before that final act, however, the advice of the 'sacret counsale' is to be consolidated and confirmed by the 'gret counsale'. The whole court of heaven assembles; 'the thre gerocheiss'—the hierarchical

---

[41] *Meroure*, i. 118.
[42] Macfarlane, *Elphinstone*, 111–12.
[43] *Meroure*, i. 109.   [44] Ibid. 110.
[45] Ibid. 111–13. Mapstone, 'A Mirror for a Divine Prince', 322 n. 28, draws attention to Macfarlane's references (*Elphinstone*, 33–4, 89–90) to 'the conceptual place of equity in the thought and practice of William Elphinstone'. It may also be apposite to recall that Gerson, who was profoundly influential on other aspects of Ireland's thought, contributed significantly to the discussion of equity: see Z. Rueger, 'Gerson's Concept of Equity and Christopher St German', *History of Political Thought*, 3 (1982), 1–30, and cf. J. H. Burns, 'St German, Gerson, Aquinas, and Ulpian', *History of Political Thought*, 4 (1983), 443–9; also Burrows, *Jean Gerson and De Consolatione Theologiae*, 223–4 and n. 30.
[46] *Meroure*, i. 117.
[47] Ibid. 107–8.

orders of angels—petition God as 'the thre nobile staitis of his hevinly realme'; and it is in this parliamentary setting that God gives 'his sentens diffinitive'.[48] The language is studiously legalistic. Christ's incarnation and passion are to cancel the 'cyrogrof and lettir of perdicioune of humane linage': in its place a

charter of grace and of mercy sal be subscriuit be the consent of the haly spreit, and selit with the sing of the haly croce, that all the trinite sall euir vse eftir this jn lettiris of grace and remissioun. And this lettir of grace be the consent of the hale trinite is geuin jn oure gret counsale of hevin the fyrst yere of grace, the day and houre of the blist incarnacioune of jhesu my sone, that js god omnipotent and of maieste.[49]

What must be carefully noted here is that the effective decision is God's, although (the godhead in question being a trinity of persons) that decision is in some sense a collective act. It may be fair enough to say that 'the heavenly king's decision is both his own and one taken constitutionally with his counsellors';[50] but the last phrase must be interpreted with some caution if we are to understand the kind of kingship Ireland envisages. Outside the circle of the Trinity (where the impenetrable life of God is lived), counsel may operate but consent is not required. It would seem that the notion of consent occurs only within the trinitarian context: explicitly with reference to the Holy Spirit, implicitly with reference to God the Son.[51] There is indeed a 'constitutional' procedure: the divine decision is promulgated 'in plain parliament'. Yet, we may perhaps suppose, this is a matter of *potestas ordinata*, which leaves intact the divine king's absolute power to act otherwise if that seems good to him. Not all of this need, and some of it plainly cannot, apply to terrestrial rulers, but we have none the less been given important clues, in Ireland's theological drama, to his understanding of kingship.

The central importance of justice and equity in that understanding will emerge even more fully when we come to consider the most explicitly 'political' part of Ireland's writings, the seventh and last Book of *The Meroure of Wyssdome*. First, however, there is another aspect of his theology to be examined: his ecclesiology. Ireland's adult life fell in a period when the great issues in

---

[48] Ibid. 119–23.   [49] Ibid. 123–4.

[50] Mapstone, 'A Mirror for a Divine Prince', 319.

[51] *Meroure*, i. 123: 'be the consent of the haly spreit, and selit with the sing of the haly croce'—where sealing with the sign of the cross clearly implies the consent of the Son.

ecclesiastical politics that had dominated the years of the councils of Constance and Basle were, if not entirely dormant, at least relatively quiescent. Accordingly we do not find in his work the elaborate ecclesiological arguments that are so prominent in the writings of John Mair. At the same time, he has enough to say on the subject to merit our attention here.

The magisterial authority of the church is taken for granted throughout Ireland's surviving works. In his treatise *Of Penance and Confession*, for instance, his approval of 'the translacoun of haly writ in ynglis toung' is subject to the proviso that the vernacular scriptures must be 'declarit . . . with the mind of the gast [i.e. the Holy Ghost] the kirk and profound doctouris'.[52] In the *Meroure* he goes out of his way more than once to submit the views he expresses to ecclesiastical correction. But what was meant by 'the kirk'? This could be a vexed and difficult question; and even in the 'popular theology' of *The Meroure of Wyssdome* it was a question calling for an answer. In Book III, the examination of the Apostles' Creed necessarily includes a chapter on the article affirming belief in *sanctam ecclesiam catholicam*. Ireland begins by glossing this article as

I trou that the vniuersale kyrk of ihesu that is constitut of all the haly persouns that has bene at is and that sal be in the faith of ihesu to the end of the waurld was is and sal be haly throu the speciall ordinaunce of god.[53]

The church is thus primarily the *universitas fidelium*, the whole body of the faithful; and the chapter in which Ireland expounds the implications of this fundamental postulate proves to be very largely a vehement statement of the conciliarist ecclesiology which was received wisdom in the university of Paris.[54] Both the Old and the New Testament, he argues, teach us that 'the determinacioun of the haly kirk' is the final and infallible authority in matters of faith and morals; 'And the generale counsal represents it.' Ireland insists repeatedly that 'all man and woman lifand in Erd' owe submission to this authority and that this specifically includes 'pape empriour king and all maner of persoune'.[55] The Bible itself has canonical authority only from the

---

[52] Craigie edn., 4. [53] *Meroure*, ii. 64. [54] Ibid. 64–9.
[55] Ibid. 64–5, and cf. 67: 'nouthir king empriour paip or pepil be battale be Errour or any vthir way may prevale na haue victorye agane the kyrk and haly spous of ihesu.'

ecclesiastical power vested in the general council.[56] That is the only power able to deal effectively with 'herretikis and scismatikis'.[57] It is an authority unimpaired by the 'euill lif' that may be led by 'the kyrkmen that cummys to the counsale', for it is guaranteed by 'the assistence of the haly spreit and the promys of ihesus'.[58]

Throughout this chapter the pope is effectively mentioned only as the ultimate subject, so to speak, of the supreme authority of the whole church as represented in the council. Christ's prayer for Peter, that his faith should not fail, is cited indeed; but it is interpreted in the classic conciliarist sense:

And thocht he spak to Sanct petir it is the faith of the halikyrk that he spak of and nocht the personale faith of sanct petir . . . ihesus said to sanct petir singulary to schaw the vnite of the kyrk and of the faith.[59]

Inevitably, however, there was more than this to be said about the papacy; and when Ireland comes to deal with holy orders as one of the sacraments which are his subject in Book VI of the *Meroure*, it may well seem that a somewhat different ecclesiology is being presented. Here, for one thing, the essentially hierarchical character of the church emerges decisively.[60] And while Ireland still insists that Christ built his church on the faith of *all* the apostles, the primacy of Peter and his successors is also made clear. The unity of the church now seems to require the monarchical rule of a single head: 'he that succedis to Sanct petir is vicar general of ihesu hiest in the cristianite *Cum plenitudine potestatis* heid of all cristin pepill and representis the persoune of ihesu.'[61]

---

[56] Ibid. 65. Ireland refers in this connection to a standard *locus* from Augustine: 'Euangelio non crederem si autoritas ecclesie non me moneret.' See on this Burrows, *Jean Gerson and De Consolatione Theologiae*, 231–2 and nn. 46, 47; Oberman, *Harvest of Medieval Theology*, 385. Gerson, whom Ireland does not follow in this instance, had replaced the verb *commoveret* in Augustine's text by *compulisset*. Ireland's *moneret* should prehaps read *moueret*.

[57] *Meroure*, ii. 68. Interestingly, Ireland's concern over heresy is linked here with his ideas about freedom and divine foreknowledge. He singles out for special condemnation 'thai that trowis that this waurld is gouernit be natur be necessite be fortoun or sic maner and that it proffitis nocht to do gud or euill becaus of the sciens and presciens of god . . . all this is herresie' (ibid. 69).

[58] Ibid. 65.   [59] Ibid. 68.

[60] See generally *Meroure*, iii. 78–90. A characteristic statement is this (ibid. 80): 'the haill congregacioun of the cristin pepil is diuidit in twa partis, and that is les of dignite that is callit *pars laicalis*, and the tother of mar dignite is callit *pars clericalis*, and thir kyrkmen are of mar dignite and nerrar to god'.

[61] Ibid. 90.

This theme is developed in a chapter which 'declaris the gret excellence of the louetenand and vicar generale of ihesu' and where papal prerogatives are emphatically asserted.[62]

To reconcile these seemingly divergent views of authority in the church may be said to have been the principal preoccupation of fifteenth-century ecclesiology; and it is not difficult to show that Ireland achieves that reconciliation in conciliarist rather than papalist terms. Thus, close examination of the passage to which reference has just been made reveals that the prerogatives reserved to the pope, extensive and important as they undoubtedly are, do not trench upon the fundamental area of the *magisterium* where the universal church represented in a council is sovereign. Moreover, crucially, while jurisdictional supremacy lies normally with the papacy, the council has, in the last resort, jurisdictional power over the pope. In his commentary on Book IV of the *Sentences*, Ireland—citing the standard canon-law text *Si papa*, which stated that 'no mortal' (*nullus mortalium*) had power to judge the pope—writes as follows:

judicial authority is thus denied to individual mortals but not to the universal church or the general council, which could correct [the pope] if he offended. This is clear by natural reason; for we see that, although the head in the human body is ordained for the direction and government of the members and though no member is entitled to withdraw its obedience from the head, none the less, if the head were to become weak or infirm and act so as to undermine the whole body, it would be legitimate for the members to restrain it lest the weakness affect the whole body. In the same way, if the pope were to run mad with a sword in his hand and leave his palace with a mind to kill whomever he met, then his subjects and inferiors might legitimately seize and bind him. Now if this is permissible for subjects for the sake of physical security, it must be still more so for a general council to intervene for the salvation of souls, lest by misgoverning the church and giving scandal [the pope] should lead the souls of his subjects down the path to damnation.[63]

---

[62] *Meroure*, iii. 91–4.

[63] Aberdeen University Library MS 264, sig. l 10ᵛ: 'Non obstat dictis capitulum *Si papa* ubi dicitur "si papa animas subditorum catervatim ad inferos deduceret, nullus mortalium posset eum iudicare ne deprehenderetur a fide devius," quia illud seipsum solvit cum dicitur "nullus mortalium"; quia denegatur iudicium singulis mortalibus, sed non denegatur universali ecclesie nec consilio generali, quae possunt eum corrigere si delinqueret. Quod patet per rationem naturalem, quia videmus quod licet caput in humano corpore sit ordinatum ad directionem et circa gubernationem membrorum eo quod non sit licitum membro a capite et eius obediencia recedere. Si tamen caput in humano corpore efficiatur languens seu infirmum, agens ad tocius corporis destruccionem, licitum esset membris ipsum

We may feel entitled to assume that Ireland should logically have applied this argument from 'natural reason' to temporal as well as to spiritual authority. Unsurprisingly, however, we find little if any trace of such arguments when, in Book VII of *The Meroure of Wyssdome*, he turns directly to kingship and its problems. Certainly the 'advice to princes' here has nothing to do with arbitrary or despotic power. We are after all dealing with an authority that is to be exercised over subjects to whom Ireland has explicitly ascribed the attributes of dignity and freedom; and he sees the relationship between king and people as one where there is 'double obligacioun of athir syd'. No doubt we need to be cautious in our interpretation of such a phrase; and yet it is interesting to note that it appears to be an instance in which Ireland made an insertion of his own in what is otherwise one of the most notably derivative portions of his work.[64] Certainly he is prepared, for most of Book VII, to follow a lead given him above all by Jean Gerson; and, just as certainly, there is nothing of striking novelty in either the original or the copy. Ireland's king, like Gerson's and like so many other conventional medieval stereotypes, is to serve his people above all by establishing and upholding justice. *Diligite justitiam*—'love justice'—is the text of the Gerson discourse from which Ireland borrows the exordium of Book VII, setting out 'the original foundament of all law police iurisdiccioun & dominacioun vsit amang men be the ordinaunce of god'.[65] Two points in this opening chapter—the 'foundament of all that folowis', as Ireland says in its closing line[66]—are worth special notice here. Each is a case in which Ireland makes an addition of his own to the material he is exploiting. The first of these has to do with the Aristotelian schema of forms of

ligare ne langor totum corpus invadat; ita etiam si papa incideret in furiam, habens [gladium] in manu, et exiret palacium volens occidere quos sibi obviam reperiret, tunc itaque liceret subditis et inferioribus eum capere et ligare, et in multis aliis casibus pro salute corporali licitum est ei resistere: modo si hoc liceret subditis pro salvatione corporis multo magis liceret generali consilio pro salute animarum sibi obviare, quin male regendo ecclesiam et scandalizando animas subditorum ad viam dampnacionis induceret.' Ireland goes on to say that the contrary view is directly against divine law and the purpose for which power has been entrusted to the pope: 'non est data potestas ad destruccionem ecclesie, sed ad edificacionem.'

[64] *Meroure*, iii. 127. Cf. Jean Gerson, *Œuvres complètes*, ed. P. Glorieux, 10 vols. (Paris, 1960–73; hereafter Glorieux edn.), vii. 1155: the substance and much of the detail in the two passages is the same, but the phrase about 'double obligacioun' is not in Gerson.

[65] *Meroure*, iii. 105.   [66] Ibid. 114.

government. Here Ireland gives an explicit reference to Aristotle which is not in the Gerson text and considerably expands what, in that text, is the briefest of summary statements.[67] He makes it clear, of course, that 'the best of all maner of police' is monarchy. He does not (as Gerson sometimes did) indicate any inclination to favour the triple *politia mixta*; yet it is clear that the 'aristocratic' and 'democratic' elements in the kingdom he has in mind have their own intrinsic value and their own parts to play in the system.[68]

The other passage to be particularly noted occurs when the subject under discussion is the role of 'the noble ciuil law' in securing justice. Gerson, in the corresponding passage of *Diligite justitiam*, seems concerned primarily to insist that the function of that law is to direct mankind to the ultimate spiritual goal. Ireland would not, of course, dissent from this view; but his concern is rather with the distinctive character of positive human law, and especially with its flexibility in comparison with the immutable rigidity of divine and natural law. Specifically, he makes the point that 'the law . . . may be interpret & dispensit be [by] the prince and Souerane be prudence and a wertu that is callit *Ephekea* that aristotil spekis of and that is quhen werray ressoune & equitie repungnis to the wourdis of the law'.[69] Bearing in mind the earlier reference to equity in this sense in the debate of the Four Daughters of God, we may conclude that the theme was one of special importance for Ireland. It should be borne in mind too that the ruler who exercises *epieikeia* is wielding this equitable power over laws he has himself made. These laws must not, to be sure, be repugnant to the law of nature; but 'for the complet and perfit gouernans of the pepill' they must extend to points which do not simply follow logically from fundamental moral principles. Human laws are genuinely positive laws 'maid . . . be wis men'.[70] Clearly this is an important area for the influence of counsel; and yet it is the 'Souerane' who 'is callit *legislator*'—who makes the law and gives it obligatory force.[71]

---

[67] *Meroure*, iii. 108. Cf. Gerson, *Œuvres complètes*, Glorieux edn., vii. 605.

[68] The impact of what Ireland says (*Meroure*, iii. 108) is somewhat muffled by his anodyne repetition of the insistence that each estate should be 'wertuis and haly'; but he does at least make it clear that the aristocratic element comprises 'the princis and lordis that has the steir [direction] and gouernaunce under' the king.

[69] *Meroure*, iii. 112.   [70] Ibid. 111.

[71] Ibid. 107–8. It may be noted that Ireland's discussion of both lawmaking and

Having laid his 'foundament', Ireland proceeds to develop the central theme of justice, drawing extensively and especially, though not only, on Gerson's sermon *Vivat rex*.[72] There is no need here to follow in detail this essentially derivative account of such matters as the virtues required by a king if he is to discharge effectively the heavy responsibilities he bears as 'louetennand of god'[73] and head of the *corpus mysticum* in which man's 'lif ciuil and polethik' is necessarily lived.[74] Questions of selection and emphasis naturally arise in our reading of such material. Thus it is perhaps significant that Ireland seems to depart from his source to lay special emphasis on the 'doctrine . . . that the king suld be of gret power that na vthir in the realme may contend or preuale agane him . . . And tharfor it is nocht conuenient that in a realme be a perygall or compeir to a king'.[75] The value of a 'wertuis and haly' nobility is, we may infer, one thing; the emergence of over-mighty subjects is quite another.

One passage in Ireland's *regimen principis* which seems to be wholly his own is concerned with the king's marriage. Addressing the young James IV directly, he urges him 'to iune thi hienes with a lady of hie and noble blud of farnes wertu and beute that thou may tak plesaunce in and haue noble generacioun of'.[76] In the concluding chapters, however, the text again becomes heavily dependent on Ireland's sources: Gerson once more, this time in the 1413 sermon directed against Jean Petit; and Chaucer's version of the *Tale of Melibee*. It is from the latter source that Ireland takes an injunction which, nevertheless, must have struck both him and the young king as peculiarly apposite to the situation in Scotland in 1490: 'the noble king or prince suld nocht tak his auld innemy that is recounsalit to him of his tendyr and sacret counsale.' And Ireland's explication of the point is very much his

---

'equity' is quite similar to the accounts given by Aquinas: see e.g. *Summa Theologiae*, Ia IIae, 95–7 (on human law); IIa IIae, 120 (on *epieikeia*).

[72] See McDonald in *Meroure*, iii, p. xxvii, for an analysis of Ireland's use of *Vivat rex*.

[73] *Meroure*, iii. 129.

[74] Ibid. 115.

[75] Ibid. 130. A similar point is made by Gerson in the sermon *Rex in sempiternum vive* (Glorieux edn., vii. 1018): 'authorité royale doit estre plus forte en armes et en conseil que aucun de ses subjets'. Ireland does draw on this sermon elsewhere in the *Meroure*, but neither the form of words he uses here nor the quotations from Virgil and Lucan he cites in support occur there.

[76] *Meroure*, iii. 135.

own: 'for thar remanis yit ane euill rute in his mynd and mony thingis that he dois to the prince he dois be dissimulacioun'.[77]

One chapter in Book VII of *The Meroure of Wyssdome* has been passed over in this discussion so far. This is in fact the point at which Ireland considers most directly what we would regard as a problem in 'political theory': the issue between elective and hereditary kingship. Once again the discussion has its basis in another text; but in this case Ireland's concern is explicitly to refute, not to follow. His target is the defence of elective monarchy by Marsilius of Padua in the *Defensor Pacis*; and in standard scholastic style the case for each side of the question is stated before Ireland indicates his own position and disposes of the contrary arguments.[78] He decides firmly enough, of course, in favour of hereditary succession. Yet, in one of the most interesting parts of the discussion, he shows an awareness that the matter is not altogether as simple as that. It is true, in Ireland's opinion, that inheritance is to be preferred to election because on this basis the king will have that concern for his realm and its well-being which men are apt to have for what is their own property. A hereditary kingdom which the ruler knows will pass to his heirs 'is mekle mar his and proper to him . . . na and he had it bot for his lif'.[79] Yet, although 'a persoune may cum to a realme be sempill & pur successioune as to ane vthir heretage, this maner', Ireland says, 'is nocht best'. The reason lies in a crucial difference between 'the rial dignite' and 'ane heretage particular or pryuate': the latter 'may be changit or sauld', not so the crown, which (we are implicitly told) is inalienable. Rejecting both simple inheritance and a purely elective basis, Ireland would seem to be feeling for what, eighty years or so earlier, Jean de Terrevermeille had defined as 'quasi-hereditary succession'.[80] Ireland's version of this is a system—found, he says, in 'fraunce and scotland & mony vthir realmes', in which 'the eleccioun of ane noble hie wertuis &

[77] *Meroure*, iii. 162. On Ireland and Chaucer see C. McDonald, 'John Ireland's *Meroure of Wyssdome* and Chaucer's *Tale of Melibee*', *Studies in Scottish Literature*, 21 (1987), 23–34.

[78] *Meroure*, iii. 144–54. Ireland refers to Marsilius explicitly at the end of the previous chapter, associating him with 'mony gret clerkis of paris and vthir placis' (p. 142). McDonald (*Meroure*, iii, pp. xl–xlii) gives a convenient 'tabular' summary of the arguments and counter-arguments.

[79] *Meroure*, iii. 146.

[80] Ibid. 147. On Terrevermeille's view (in his *Contra rebelles* of 1418), see Burns, *Lordship, Kingship and Empire*, 43–6.

excellent lynage that the hail pepil fyrst has chosin to gowerne the realme' is followed by 'successioun discendand of that noble linage'. For this system Ireland claims both Aristotelian warrant and biblical authority.[81] And indeed, while it is doubtless true to say that, in Ireland's view of kingship, 'There is no exaltation of the monarch's quasi-divine status nor declaration of his absolute right to the throne',[82] it is important to recognize that, without 'exaltation', there is still a firm insistence on the analogy between the earthly king and the 'divine prince'. Ireland argues that the crucial hereditary element in his preferred system 'is nerar and mar conuenient with the vniuersal regimen and gouernaunce of the waurld that god be his infinit power wisdome and beneuolens gouernis'. It is true that no authority vested in mortal men can be like that of God, who is 'euir ane without mutacioun or changeing'; but 'successioun fra the fader to the sone' gives royal authority the closest approximation to divine permanence that is to be had.[83] Ireland does not write in total abstraction from the realities of the world in which political authority has to be exercised. Indeed his rejection of the elective principle derives in part from the conviction that fallen human nature could not sustain the demands of such a system;[84] and he is fully aware that conquest and usurpation may, on the one hand, be the effective basis of power, and yet that such power may acquire legitimacy despite these origins.[85] Yet in the end, of course, Ireland writes as a theologian and *sub specie aeternitatis*. It is entirely appropriate that he should bring *The Meroure of Wyssdome* to an end by recalling his qualifications and status as theologian, preacher, and confessor, and by invoking 'the verite and haly doctrine of theologie in all thingis pertenand to the faith and saluacioun of thi hienes and pepil'.[86]

In turning from John Ireland to John Mair (1467/8–1550) we move, manifestly, on to a much higher level of intellectual

---

[81] *Meroure*, iii. 147–9.

[82] Sally Mapstone, 'The Advice to Princes Tradition in Scottish Literature, 1450–1500' (Oxford University D.Phil thesis, 1986), 439, quoted by McDonald, *Meroure*, iii, p. xliii.

[83] *Meroure*, iii. 148.

[84] See e.g. ibid. 147–8: 'Alsua be this sammyn way [hereditary succession] is put out of the hartis of mony men ambicioun, that is *libido dominandi*'.

[85] Ibid. 151–2.   [86] Ibid. 164–5.

achievement and significance. Even if all the writings Ireland is known or believed to have written survived, they would not constitute a body of work remotely comparable with that which Mair published between 1499 and 1550.[87] Again, while we know nothing of Ireland's pupils, we can refer meaningfully to a 'school' or 'circle' with Mair at its centre. He was a figure of substantial importance in the intellectual history of the early sixteenth century; and if the derisory comments made by Melanchthon and by George Buchanan reflect a decisive cultural shift away from the traditions Mair upheld, the influence of those traditions survived such ridicule and outlived even the octogen-arian Mair. The range as well as the scale of Mair's scholarly output must also be emphasized. Before embarking on his theo-logical career he had written half a score of treatises on various aspects of logic, as well as editing works by Johannes Dorp and Jeronimo Pardo. In the last five years before his final return, in 1531, from Paris to Scotland, he produced substantial commen-taries on Aristotle's *Physics* and *Ethics*. And if it was to theology that his greatest efforts were directed—resulting in extensive commentaries on the *Sentences* (several times revised) and two substantial scriptural commentaries—he also made a significant contribution to historical writing with his *Historia Majoris Britanniae* (1521).

Mair's historical work clearly has particular importance for the present enquiry—not only in its own right, so to speak, but be-cause it reflects a more general aspect of his thinking: his acute sense, for all his scholasticism, of what is concrete and experi-ential. And it will indeed be in the context of history rather than theology that we shall, in the next chapter, give our fullest consideration to his 'political ideas'. The fact remains that, as with Ireland, so to at least as great an extent with Mair: his ideas about society and government are deeply rooted in a theological under-standing of the world. It lies, plainly, far beyond the scope of the present enquiry to undertake more than a sketch of certain aspects of Mair's theology. The subject has, not surprisingly, at-tracted a good deal more scholarly attention than the peripheral work of John Ireland; and the philosophy which underpins or accompanies Mair's theological thinking has also attracted

[87] See J. Durkan, 'The School of John Major: Bibliography', *Innes Review*, 1 (1950), 140–6.

considerable attention.[88] Even so, there is no comprehensive study to which we can turn for a definitive location and assessment of Mair as a theologian; and some brief general comments may be useful before some specific issues of significance for the present subject are examined.

To describe Mair, summarily, as an 'Ockhamist' may be accurate so far as it goes; but it does not go very far.[89] That he adhered to a Parisian tradition in philosophy which looked back to Ockham as the *venerabilis inceptor* is certain; and his studies in Paris had begun a dozen years or so after the lifting of the 1474–81 ban on the texts that were crucial to that tradition. It is clear too that Mair had great respect for the English, and specifically the Oxonian, nominalists who can be regarded as especially prominent on what, in Oberman's terminology, we may call the 'left wing' of the *via moderna*.[90] Yet the logic to which Mair and his pupils were to contribute extensively had a complex history which cannot simply be interpreted in a unilinear 'Ockhamist' sense. Thomas Torrance, approaching Mair's theology by way of his philosophy, has strongly emphasized his concern 'to make a way through the confusions generated by the controversies between realism and nominalism'; even 'to use the tools fashioned by logical analysts in order to establish a form of realism'. This may be offset to some extent by an over-elaboration of logical distinctions; but the fundamental aim is to bring to light the objective reality of things. In this, Torrance argues, Mair was influenced by Augustine, Anselm, Grosseteste, Aquinas, and—

---

[88] See esp. T. F. Torrance, '1469–1969. La Philosophie et la théologie de Jean Mair ou Major de Haddington (1469–1550)', *Archives de philosophie*, 32 (1969), 531–47; 33 (1970), 261–93; A. Ganoczy, 'Jean Major, exégète gallicane', *Recherches de science religieuse*, 56 (1968), 457–95; A. Broadie, *The Circle of John Mair: Logic and Logicians in Pre-Reformation Scotland* (Oxford, 1985).

[89] He is so described both in N. Kretzmann *et al.* (eds.), *The Cambridge History of Later Medieval Philosophy*, 868 ('An Ockhamist in theology and politics'), and in C. B. Schmitt *et al.* (eds.), *The Cambridge History of Renaissance Philosophy*, 825 ('Scottish Ockhamist philosopher, theologian, political theorist'). It may be remarked that there are more, and more substantial, references to Mair's work in the second of these volumes than in the first.

[90] Mair edited the 1512 Paris edn. of Adam Wodeham's commentary on the *Sentences* and wrote a short life of Wodeham for that edn., reprinted by A. Constable in his edn. of Mair's *History of Greater Britain* (Scottish History Society; Edinburgh, 1892; hereafter Constable edn.), 431–2. See ibid. 22–3, for Mair's list of notable philosophers and theologians produced by Oxford, among whom Ockham and some of his boldest followers are prominent.

above all—by Duns Scotus, 'whom he seems always to have considered as his great hero'.[91] The result of all this may be seen as eclecticism harnessed to a theological programme of 'sane and genial conservatism'.[92] Yet it may be better to see it as an attempt to reconcile and synthesize divergent schools of thought—an attempt broadly characteristic of a substantial part of the theology of the late fifteenth and early sixteenth centuries. Gabriel Biel's name again comes to mind as another nominalist or Ockhamist whose ideas reflect a good deal more than such labels might suggest.[93]

Much could be said of Mair's handling of some of the basic theological themes considered above in an attempt to locate Ireland's doctrinal position. Enough has already been said, perhaps, to indicate that they shared a tradition and a doctrinal approach, though that approach was a good deal more fully developed by Mair than by Ireland.[94] The purposes of the present enquiry will, however, be better served at this stage by examining some topics with which, so far as we know, the older thinker did not deal. Mair, in this investigation, may well emerge as a more arid writer than Ireland: we shall not find in his work anything like the debate of the Four Daughters of God. We shall, on the other hand, find at least the elements of such a theory of society as we should seek in vain in John Ireland. That there is common ground even here is both true and unsurprising. Like all Christian theologians, Mair and Ireland found the starting-point for their exploration of the human condition in the Garden of Eden. In that original state a natural virtue and, specifically, a natural justice had prevailed, only to be forfeited by the sin that had,

---

[91] Torrance, '1469–1969', 532: 'il fut influencé profondément . . . par dessus tout par Duns Scot, élève le plus distingué qu'ait produit sa propre école à Haddington et qu'il semble avoir toujours considéré comme son grand héros.' Torrance draws attention in n. 4 to the important edition, supervised by Mair, of Scotus's _Reportata Parisiensia_ (Paris, 1517–18).

[92] J. Durkan, 'John Major: After 400 Years', _Innes Review_, 1 (1950), 134. The reference to Mair's 'eclectic views' is on p. 135.

[93] See on this e.g. J. L. Farthing, _Thomas Aquinas and Gabriel Biel: Interpretations of St Thomas Aquinas in German Nominalism on the Eve of the Reformation_ (Durham, NC, 1988).

[94] In view of the discussion above of _auxilium speciale_, it may be appropriate to mention Mair's handling of the theme in his _Sentences_ commentary (_In primum Sententiarum_ (Paris, 1510), dist, xxv, q. 1, fos. 47–9): he dissents from the view taken by 'eruditi viri Oxonienses conterraneus [Scotus] Okam & Adam [Wodeham]', while acknowledging that it is 'not improbable'.

fundamentally, created the circumstances within which society and government had to operate. From this point of departure Mair developed some important theoretical conclusions, which have a bearing—albeit not an unequivocal bearing—upon his 'political theory' and his concept of kingship.

The most important aspects of this inchoate theory emerge, predictably, in Mair's discussion (increasingly elaborate as editions of his commentary succeeded one another) of 'restitution' in the context of the fifteenth 'distinction' of Book IV of the *Sentences*.[95] This affords him the opportunity of analysing the notion of *dominium*; and he does so along lines laid down by Gerson, more particularly in his *De vita spirituali animae*.[96] A crucial question here for Mair concerns the origin or basis, and the character, of *dominium civile, sive politicum*. This includes, as we shall see, what we should think of as 'political authority'; but its connotation for Mair is much wider, extending to all aspects of the control exercised by rational creatures, and specifically by human beings, over the world in which they live. In particular, it includes private property, held by individuals. Now Mair is quite clear that *dominium* of this kind had not been established by either natural or divine law: it was the work of human law after the Fall, 'on account of sin'. Before that transformation of the human condition, what God had given mankind was enjoyed in common. Mair did not deny that it would have been *possible* for men in their original state to have brought in private appropriation; and indeed there must, for obvious reasons, have been individual *use* of parts of a whole which was, none the less, held in common. He acknowledged the reality of *dominium naturale*, but insisted that its basis was *need*. Such needs could still overrule the rights of private *dominium*, if there was no other way in which the

---

[95] Mair wrote, essentially, two versions of this commentary. The first, published for the first time in 1509, was reissued with some modifications in 1512, and is cited below as '*Quartus*, 1509' or '*Quartus*, 1512'. The second, considerably expanded version appeared for the first time in 1516: it was reprinted, seemingly with only minor variations, in 1519 and 1521 (cited as '*In quartum*, 1516' etc.). See for these editions Durkan, 'School of John Major', 142–5; and for fuller bibliographical descriptions, T. G. Law in Mair's *History* (Constable edn.), 407–8. Law, however, fails to note the not unimportant point that Mair's dedicatory epistle to bishops Gavin Douglas and Robert Cockburn appears in the 1516 as well as the 1519 and 1521 edns.

[96] Glorieux edn., iii. 144–57; and see the discussion in Burns, *Lordship, Kingship and Empire*, 37–9.

necessitous individuals could be preserved. In general, however, the sinful nature of man now demanded those rules of *meum* and *tuum* which were necessarily made by a human lawgiver.[97]

Before pursuing the strictly political implications of Mair's view, it will be as well to pause and consider where he stands in regard to an issue much debated in recent scholarship: the relationship between *dominium* and *ius* or right. He deals with the subject briefly towards the end of his commentary on distinction 15, where his concern is to differentiate various forms or modes of access to property. As distinct from, for instance, usufruct, or from *dominium utile*, true *dominium*, strictly construed, 'is a right of having, possessing, and using something at one's will and pleasure [*pro libito*]'—provided (Mair is interestingly careful to add) 'there has been no limitation by way of positive law issuing from some superior authority'. *Dominium* then is, in one way or another, a right: where there is *dominium* there is *ius*. The converse, however, is not true. There can be rights—such as those children may claim from parents, wives from husbands, subjects from their lords or rulers—which do not imply that the claimants have *dominium* over the other parties in the relationships in question. And indeed it is possible to interpret *dominium* in a looser sense, in which it can be equated with *ius*: the essential point, for Mair, is always the degree of 'legitimate power' (*potentia licita*) the claimant has—that is the measure of his right.[98]

It is noteworthy that in the passage just examined, as in the earlier, more general discussion, Mair sees a crucial role for the authority from which positive law emanates. And this leads him into what we might call a preliminary statement of his central political theory. He does not follow Gerson in developing a distinction between, on the one hand, different forms of *dominium* and, on the other, corresponding forms of *ius* and of *regimen*.[99] Arguing essentially in terms of *dominium* itself, and recognizing that rulers, by whom positive laws are made, enjoy a form of *dominium*, he poses crucial questions about the nature and basis of

[97] *Quartus*, 1509, dist. xv, q. vi, fos. 86[r–v]; and cf. *In quartum*, 1516, dist. xv, q. x, fos. 74–5.

[98] *In quartum*, 1516, dist. xv, q. x, fo. 77. Mair's discussion has some points in common with that by Antoninus of Florence in his influential *Summa Theologiae*: see on this Burns in id. and Goldie (eds.), *Cambridge History of Political Thought 1450–1700*, 141–2.

[99] Glorieux edn., iii. 141–4.

this kind of 'lordship'. It can, for one thing, take a variety of forms: Mair deploys the usual Aristotelian schematism and voices the standard medieval preference for monarchy. So far as monarchy itself is concerned, again, there are several ways in which it may be, or may be supposed to have been, established. Mair acknowledges that the Augustinian *libido dominandi* so characteristic of fallen human nature had been a common foundation of what became royal power. There can, however, be more 'honourable' ways of using one's strength and prowess to achieve 'the sweet fruition of an earthly crown'. Those, for instance, who lead others to occupy hitherto unclaimed lands may properly be regarded as having vindicated their claim to rule.[100]

Already, however, the focus of the discussion is shifting in some degree from the strong man who rules to those over whom his rule is to be exercised; and it is at this point that we begin to see something of what has been called the 'communitarian' element in Mair's thinking. Yet his position is complex and not unambiguous. Some of the ambiguity may, to be sure, reflect a degree of development in Mair's thought to which insufficient attention has been paid.[101] And—a more important point—it may be that to find ambiguity merely betrays an inadequate understanding of the totality of Mair's position. However that may be, the seeds of what appears, at least superficially, to be problematic are already present in the earliest evidence we have—the 1509 commentary on Peter Lombard's fourth Book. Here, on the one hand, we have the hypothetical case of a group of 'equals' recognizing their need of governance and choosing the best man for the task. We also have the earliest statement of a recurrent principle in Mair's theory: 'the king exists for the sake of the country, not the country for the sake of the king.' Yet between these two points there is an emphatic assertion of the importance of ensuring the king's supremacy in resources and power; while, immediately afterwards, Mair asserts just as emphatically the superiority of hereditary to elective monarchy. As for monarchy as such, its excellence is sharply contrasted with the deficiencies of *communitates*—the republican regimes which, Mair maintains,

---

[100] *Quartus*, 1509, fo. 86ᵛ.

[101] The term 'communitarian' is used by Richard Tuck, *Natural Rights Theories: Their Origin and Development* (Cambridge, 1979), 30. The question of development in Mair's ideas is taken up at the beginning of the next chapter.

were continuing to manifest their well-established weakness in
the Italian politics of 1508–9.[102] Other elements in this early phase
of Mair's thinking, which will be more usefully considered in the
next chapter, confirm the impression that we have here a vigorous
and positive account of kingship. There may be little if any indication that Mair was attracted by analogical arguments or images
drawn from the theology in which his thought was rooted: he
seems in general to have been sceptical about rhetorical devices of
that kind, nor did he have John Ireland's occasion to employ
them.[103] The 'divine prince' will not appear on this scene; but the
figure we see there is 'every inch a king'.

At the same time it must be borne in mind that this discussion
of kingship arose in the context of Mair's theory of *dominium*. A
question could be posed here which, though it seems to have
remained latent at first, eventually demanded and received
Mair's close attention. Given that those in political authority—
specifically, kings—enjoyed a form of lordship, how did their
dominium stand in relation to that which was enjoyed by ordinary
private property-owners? Did the king in respect of his realm (or,
for that matter, the pope in respect of ecclesiastical benefices)
have the same control as *dominium* implied in the private sphere?
Once the question was posed Mair had no doubt as to the answer.
Rulers do *not* have *dominium* of that kind. The nature of what they
do have will emerge more fully later; but the essential point is that
a king has no legitimate power to alienate or otherwise dispose of
the realm he rules.[104]

Yet it is also the case that the property-owner's rights themselves depend on, derive from, political authority. Mair develops
this point by reference to two moments in the scriptural history of
mankind—the situations following, respectively, the Fall and the
Flood. He argues that Adam certainly possessed authority over
his progeny; but this was the natural authority exercised by a

---

[102] *Quartus*, 1509, fos. 86ᵛ–87ʳ.

[103] Cf. *In quartum*, 1516, fo. 160ᵛ: 'ex mystica theologia debile capitur
argumentum . . . Item vulgo dicimus: argumentum a simili claudicat uno pede'.

[104] Ibid., fo. 76ᵛ: 'Rex non potest transferre ius regni sui & politiam regalem in
quemcunque velit . . . Ex isto patet . . . quod rex non habet ita liberum dominium
in regno ut ego in biblia mea'; and cf. *In Mattheum ad literam expositio*, 1518
(hereafter *In Mattheum*) fo. 73ᵛ: 'rex non habet ita pingue ius in regno suo sicut ego
in caputio meo'; also *Historia Majoris Britanniae*, 1521 (hereafter *Historia*), fo. 78ʳ:
'non ita pulcrum & liberum dominium in regno rex habet sicut in suo dominio
particularis dominus.'

father over his children: it was not political in character and could not, of itself, suffice for the tasks incumbent upon political authority. Specifically, Adam—and the same would apply to Noah in the world after the waters had receded—could not divide up the earth among his sons, allocating *dominium* in respect of different lands, otherwise than by an authority that was not paternal but political. That kind of authority, Mair maintains, has no natural basis or warrant. It could have been exercised by Adam and later by Noah only because their sons had requested a division of the earth among them.[105] Fundamentally, then, political authority exists by the *consent* of its subjects.

That consent may be given in various ways to rulers or ruling groups who have achieved power on different bases; but consent in some sense there must be if legitimate political authority is to exist; and we should bear in mind that legitimacy—*potentia licita*—is, in Mair's view, essential to all *dominium*, whether that term be strictly or broadly interpreted. It is noteworthy that, when discussing the question of prescriptive rights to property, Mair makes interesting use of a concept which in the more familiar context of John Locke's *Two Treatises of Government*, is called tacit consent. In Mair's terminology it is either *consensus virtualis* or *consensus interpretativus*; and in his later statement of the point he wants to make he says that every reasonable person must be supposed to consent to the laws enacted or allowed by the lawgiver, provided that those laws are themselves reasonable: irrational dissent does not affect the authority of the laws.[106]

That rulers, ruling thus by consent of their subjects, exercise at the same time an authority ordained by God is, of course, something Mair accepts and assumes, without supposing that it has any tendency to undermine the arguments just examined here. The word 'ordained' is especially apposite, for this is the manner in which God proceeds on the basis of his *potestas ordinata*. There

---

[105] *In quartum*, 1516, fo. 76ʳ. When the matter arises in the earlier version of Mair's commentary (*Quartus*, 1509, fo. 86ᵛ), the point about paternal and political power is not made.

[106] *In quartum*, 1516, fo. 77ᵛ; and cf. *Quartus*, 1509, fo. 88ʳ, where the point is made with reference to the consent of the *populus* rather than of the individual subject. The distinction between express and tacit consent is also used in Mair's *Historia*, fo. 44ʳ: 'Rex . . . non potest se bello exponere sine populi consensu vero vel interpretativo.'

remains in reserve, so to speak, his *potestas absoluta*; and Mair could not deny or doubt that God had sometimes intervened in a more direct way in the appointment of rulers. Plainly this was the case with the government of Israel as described in Old Testament history. Even more crucially for Mair, it was the case when God was providing for the government of the church. Inevitably Mair's ecclesiology has a claim to be regarded as the most important element in his theology for our understanding of his contribution to political thinking. The subject cannot be fully explored or evaluated here;[107] but some themes which interpenetrate with Mair's political ideas demand consideration. It would be an exaggeration, no doubt, but not an extravagant one, to say that the theology of the church and the theory of government are for Mair two sides of the same coin. It is at any rate the case that the essential notion of community is central in both aspects of his thought. Thus he follows the tendency in late-medieval juristic thinking to use the term 'mystical body' (*corpus mysticum*) to refer, not only to the church (the theological context in which the term had its origins), but to all organized societies, to any *universitas*. As a theologian Mair was, of course, well aware that the church was, in this respect *sui generis*. It was the mystical body *of Christ*, with all that this implied for its place in the economy of salvation. Yet at the same time the church was present here on earth, visible as a terrestrial organization: there were, therefore, characteristics it shared with the other *corpora mystica* of the social and political world.[108]

One of the most important of these was the need for governance. Mair had no inclination to deny that the church rightly exercised jurisdictional authority as well as preaching the gospel and administering sacramental grace. And, given its supreme

[107] The fullest analysis is in Ganoczy, 'Jean Major'. See also J. K. Cameron, 'The Conciliarism of John Mair: A Note on *A Disputation on the Authority of a Council*', in D. Wood (ed.), *The Church and Sovereignty c. 590–1918: Essays in Honour of Michael Wilks*, Studies in Church History, Subsidia 9 (Oxford, 1991), 429–35.

[108] The term *corpus mysticum* as such is used sparingly by Mair, but he consistently analyses the political community as a corporate entity, especially in regard to the authority of its head. Characteristically, however, he is sceptical about pushing analogy too far. Thus he rejects (*Historia*, fo. 69ʳ) the argument from the pre-eminence of the head in a natural body to a similar pre-eminence of the ruler over the rest of the 'mystical body', repeating the remark that argument from analogy 'pretty frequently limps'. For the church as *corpus Christi mysticum* the most important passage is perhaps *In Mattheum*, fo. 70, where, among other things, Mair insists that its *caput essentiale* is Christ himself.

importance, its government must be the best of all possible governments. This, following Aristotle (as Mair understood him), meant monarchy. That the church was indeed a monarchy was, in one sense, self-evident. It was God's church, and God himself—specifically, God in the second person of the Trinity—was its founder and ruler. To give laws to the people is, for Mair, the most essential duty of any ruler; and Christ was the *legislator optimus*.[109] Christ, however, while always, of course, in some sense present, was, in another perspective, like a king who had to provide for the government of his realm in his absence. Nor is Mair in any doubt as to the identity of Christ's vicegerent or vicar: it is indeed and of course the pope who in this sense wields monarchical authority in the church.[110] It was the precise nature of this authority that posed the questions which divided papalists from conciliarists; and Mair was writing at a time when such divisions had been re-opened in vehement controversy.[111]

Mair took no part in the immediate debate at the time of the council of Pisa–Milan in 1511–12. Nor had he found it necessary to include, in his writings before that date, any extended statement of the conciliarist view with which, nevertheless, he certainly agreed.[112] Even when, in 1516, he expanded considerably his commentary on Book IV of the *Sentences* and inserted a substantial discussion of the temporal power of the papacy, taking a predictably firm Gallican view of the matter, the conciliarist side of that medal is not displayed. Mair indeed goes out of his way to disclaim any intention of dealing with the

---

[109] *In quartum*, 1516, fo. 158ᵛ: 'Christus legislator optimus, optimam policiam in ecclesia instituit'; *In Mattheum*, fo. 69ᵛ: 'Christus legislator optimus reliquit optimam policiam in ecclesia.'

[110] Ibid., fo. 69ᵛ: 'Christus ascendit ad patrem: vicario vices suas commisit.'

[111] For the debate at the period of the council (or *conciliabulum*) of Pisa/Milan (1511–12) see esp. O. de La Brosse, *Le Pape et le Concile: La Comparaison de leurs pouvoirs à la veille de la Réforme* (Paris, 1965): this concentrates largely on the polemical interchanges between Mair's pupil Jacques Almain and Tommaso de Vio (Cajetan). For a briefer discussion which takes other contributions into account see J. H. Burns, 'Conciliarism, Papalism and Power, 1511–1518', in Wood (ed.), *The Church and Sovereignty*, 409–28.

[112] Brief indications of this appear in Mair's commentary on Book II of the *Sentences*, first published in 1510 (hereafter *In secundum*, 1510), fo. 100ʳ: 'concilium in aliquibus causis dat ei [*sc.* Papae] libellum repudii'; and *Quartus*, 1512, fo. 131ʳ, where Mair refers to a conciliar decree and says, 'romanus pontifex non potest ad nutum eius in illo statuto dispensare & ipsum reuocare . . . cum . . . concilium est supra papam'. This passage seems to be one of the additions made in the 1512 edn.; and Mair refers to a discussion of the matter in the Paris theology faculty some years previously, before he himself was a member.

subject.[113] With the changed relations between the French crown
and the papacy leading to the Concordat of 1516, Francis I had, in
January, forbidden further controversy on the matter. However,
within little more than a year of Mair's having completed his 1516
edition, circumstances altered once more. The Concordat itself
was the subject of vigorous controversy in the university of Paris,
and Mair felt free, in his commentary on St Matthew's gospel,
published towards the end of 1518, to deal at last and at length
with the question of conciliar authority.[114]

The peg on which this discussion hangs was provided by
Christ's words in Matthew 18: 15–18, on the theme of 'fraternal
correction', and in particular the injunction (in the Vulgate text),
dic ecclesiae—'tell the church'. It was from the church as a whole,
as a community, that the ultimate sanction would come. One
problematic point here, clearly, is the meaning to be attached to
the term *ecclesia*. This was a question Mair had discussed at an
earlier stage in his *In Mattheum*, dealing with chapter 16: 13–19. In
this passage Christ interrogates his disciples as to what men were
saying about his identity; and the climax is of course Peter's 'Thou
art the Christ, the Son of the living God', followed by Jesus's
response, 'Thou art Peter, and upon this rock I will build my
church'. Mair proceeds to list several ways in which the term
ecclesia can be interpreted. Primarily,[115] he argues, it means the
whole 'assembly of the faithful', those still on earth (in 'the church
militant') and those already in 'the church triumphant'. The term
may also be used, however, to denote only the first of these
groups; and again it may be used to mean no more than those
Christians who live in a particular province or even in a single
household. Yet again it may refer to the ruler (*ille qui praesidet*)
over one or other of these 'congregations'; and finally the term

[113] *In quartum*, 1516, fo. 158ᵛ: 'Impresentiatrum enim de preeminentia inter
maximum pontificem & universale concilium loqui non propono.'

[114] *In Mattheum*, fos. 68ʳ–72ʳ. This passage was reprinted as *Disputatio de
auctoritate concilii super pontificem maximum* in Gerson, *Opera Omnia*, ed. L. E. Du
Pin (Antwerp, 1706), ii. 1131–45; and an abridged translation by J. K. Cameron is
in M. Spinka (ed.), *Advocates of Reform* (London, 1953), 175–84. Mair's language
when indicating his intention of discussing the problem is of some interest: 'Ego
autem licet possem ab hac questione declinare, cum ita patenter incidat in caput
quod tracto, vix possum dissimulare' (*In Mattheum*, fo. 68ᵛ).

[115] The primacy is doctrinal rather than textual. Perhaps characteristically, Mair
lists first the sense in which 'church' refers to a building—'Primo modo capitur
pro domo materiali laudibus diuinis deputata'.

'church' may be applied only to clerics.[116] It will also be useful to consider what Mair says in this context about the interpretation of Peter's position. Following a well-established line, which we have already encountered in John Ireland, he insists that Peter had spoken in the name of all the disciples, and that the 'rock' on which the church was to be built was not Peter but Christ himself. He did not deny a certain priority to Peter, any more than he questioned the special authority enjoyed by the pope as Peter's successor. These things, however, were, in Mair's view, to be interpreted in such a way as to save the authority of the church as the *congregatio fidelium*.[117]

With these points in mind we may now go back to the problem of *dic ecclesiae*. Which of the possible meanings of 'church' are we to apply here? If we take it as referring immediately to the *praesidens* or *praelatus*—and Mair would for certain purposes be content to do so—we shall face the question of what is to be done when the sinful brother to be corrected is himself the *praelatus*; and that question will be most sharply posed if we are dealing with a 'prelate' who has no superior in the hierarchy. How, to put the point directly, is an offending pope to be dealt with? For papalists there could be no answer in juridical terms: no one on earth had authority to judge the pope.[118] For Mair, and for the whole conciliarist, Gallican, and, more specifically, Parisian tradition to which he adhered, this was unacceptable. Fraternal correction was applicable to every Christian. In the case of an erring pope, *dic ecclesiae*, since it could not refer to any other 'prelate', nor, for that matter, to any particular church, must imply an appeal to the authority of the church as a whole. In practice, since the whole *congregatio fidelium* could not act in a single assembly, this meant the church represented in a council; and Mair now has to define that body. There is perhaps a degree of studied imprecision in his definition: 'A council . . . is an assembly drawn from

[116] *In Mattheum*, fo. 60ʳ.

[117] Ibid., fo. 60ᵛ. See Ganoczy, 'Jean Major', 464–5, for an interesting discussion of the significance of Mair's having preferred to call Peter *apostolorum praecipuus* rather than *principalis* in this passage. It is perhaps unfortunate, even in a brief discussion, that Cameron seems not to take account of this earlier part of Mair's commentary, referring only to 'the exegesis of the word "church"' in Mair's commentary on Matthew 18: 15–18 ('Conciliarism of Mair', 431). It is clear, however, that the latter analysis presupposes the former.

[118] This is of course a somewhat over-simplified statement: for one thing, it was always recognized that a special case arose in regard to a *heretical* pope.

every rank in the hierarchy whose concern it is, summoned by those whose business it is to do so, with the common purpose of considering the public weal of Christendom'. Such a council, 'duly convened and representing the universal church, is superior to the pope'; and here, Mair argues, we must take the term 'church' as denoting the whole body of the faithful apart from the pope.[119] There is, of course, a sense in which the pope (whose status as, ordinarily, the monarchical ruler of the church Mair at no point denies or questions) is superior to the community he rules. He is superior in authority to every individual member of that community and to each of the particular 'churches' into which the church as a whole is divided. But it is essential to Mair's position that the universal church as such, as a *universitas*, rightly claims the final authority.[120] Only in extreme circumstances, to be sure, will that authority have to be asserted; but, when it is asserted (in the case of a pope whose behaviour threatens the well-being of the community whose servant, rather than 'lord', he is), it will extend to the ultimate sanction of deposition. [121]

It is neither necessary nor possible here to explore in detail Mair's conciliarist ecclesiology. There will be an opportunity in the following chapter to consider some of the striking comparisons he makes between the *politia regalis* in the church and the essentially similar (though not identical) 'polity' he finds in temporal kingdoms. Here the consideration of Mair's doctrine may conclude by emphasizing some aspects of his ecclesiology which are of special significance for his 'political ideas'. The first of these

[119] *In Mattheum*, fo. 168ᵛ: 'Concilium ... est congregatio ex omni statu hierarchico quorum interest convocata ab his quibus incumbit ad tractandum communi intentione de utilitate publica christians ... Conclusio sit ... concilium rite congregatum universalem ecclesiam representans est super maximum pontificem; et capio ecclesiam pro ecclesia ab eo separata.' Ganoczy ('Jean Major', 476) seems to overlook the crucial qualification in the words *quorum interest*, but is still correct in interpreting Mair's position as precluding an exclusively episcopal council.

[120] Mair subjects these points to close analysis: see esp. *In Mattheum*, fos. 70ᵛ–71ʳ. A point of particular importance, to be examined in the next chapter, is his use of the distinction between the ordinary power which is wielded *regulariter* by the ruler and the reserve power which *habitualiter et virtualiter* (or *casualiter*) remains with the community: 'Sic romanus pontifex regulariter [est] super totam ecclesiam ... sed habitualiter et virtualiter ecclesia est super ipsum' (ibid., fo. 70ᵛ).

[121] Mair brusquely dismisses the suggestion that prayer is the only recourse in such a situation: 'Ergo si papa est incorrigibilis est deponendus ... In hoc igitur dicere quod oportet pro eo solume rogare deum, & quod non est aliud remedium, est unum extraneum sine ratione' (ibid., fo. 69ʳ).

aspects is the quite fundamental importance for Mair of the Christian community as a whole. He is of course a conciliarist: only through the instrumentality of a general council can the corporate life of the church manifest itself to any purpose. But what finally matters is the community that is represented, not the representative body in itself. When Mair faces the question of the *plenitudo potestatis*, the fullness of power claimed by papalists for the pope, his main concern is to argue that it was upon the church as a whole that Christ conferred that power. He insists vehemently that the life of the church in which Christ has promised his presence 'even unto the end of the world' cannot be embodied in the perishable person of a pontiff. It inheres in the mystical body itself; and Mair strikingly invokes the authority, not simply of the Scriptures, but of Aristotle's *Politics* to the effect that the continuing vitality of a society lies with the *valentior pars* of its members.[122]

In terms of 'political theory', this may imply that the community has the last word—that it is, to use language Mair himself did not use, ultimately sovereign. Ecclesiologically, however, the same conclusion cannot hold; and the reason for this may itself have 'political' implications, even if these are such as Mair himself would have rejected. It was, he held, true that the authority of the church, acting through the council, was less limited (*illimitatior*) than that of the pope. Yet it was not, any more than the pope's power was, *un*limited. Such power—power that was both *regularis* and *casualis*, and also independent—did exist; but it was the divine power of Christ himself.[123] There had been, and there would be again, those who would see in this at least an analogy for the power of kings. John Mair, as we have seen implicitly already and as we shall see more directly in the next chapter, could not accept that analogy for either king or pope.

---

[122] *In Mattheum*, fos. 69ᵛ–70ʳ. The passage is further discussed in Ch. 2.

[123] Ibid., fos. 71ʳ⁻ᵛ. Ganoczy ('Jean Major', 486, where, *casualis* and *casualiter* are mistakenly printed as *causalis* and *causaliter*) also refers to Mair's concept of a power that is *fontalis* (as to which see Ch. 2). He seems to suggest that, in the church, only Christ is credited with such power by Mair. However, it is at least implied (fo. 70ʳ) that the community has this kind of power in both civil and ecclesiastical society: 'in regno et in toto populo libero est suprema fontalis potestas inabrogabilis . . . Sic est in ecclesia . . .'.

2

Politics and History
John Mair and Hector Boece

THE dedicatory epistle in John Mair's commentary on the gospel according to Matthew is dated from the university of Glasgow on 22 November 1518.[1] Sometime earlier in that year—precise dating is impossible—Mair had left Paris for Scotland. This was certainly not his first home visit; and it seems fairly clear that efforts to induce him to return to Scotland had been made unsuccessfully eight or nine years previously. The successful persuasion now was probably the work of Gavin Douglas, bishop of Dunkeld, and Robert Cockburn, bishop of Ross, during a diplomatic mission in France which occupied one or other or both of them for much of 1516 and 1517.[2] Paris had been the scene of Mair's highly successful career for a quarter of a century at least, and he was, by 1518, arguably at the height both of his powers and of his reputation and influence. He had been teaching in the faculty of theology for a dozen years, and his principal works in that field had now been published.[3] Three substantial works were still to come, two of them of considerable importance for the present subject: the *Historia Majoris Britanniae* (1521), and the commentary on Aristotle's *Ethics* (1530).[4] By the time the latter work was

[1] The letter is printed in *History* (Constable edn.), 435–6. Mair described it as having been 'hurriedly set down' (*raptim exaratam*). The date is mistakenly given as 22 Dec. in J. H. Burns, 'New Light on John Major', *Innes Review*, 5 (1954), 90.

[2] Douglas, then Provost of St Giles, Edinburgh, appears in a dialogue with Mair's pupil David Cranston printed in Mair's *In primum Sententiarum*, 1510, where he is represented as being anxious for the author to return to Scotland (repr., *History*, Constable edn., 425–8). It was he, presumably, who obtained for Mair crown presentation to the treasurership of the Chapel Royal on 31 Dec. 1509 (D. E. R. Watt, *Fasti Ecclesiae Scoticanae Medii Aevi ad annum 1638: Second Draft* (St Andrews, 1969), 339). Mair dedicated his *In quartum* to the two bishops on 24 Nov. 1516 (*History*, Constable edn., 437). See Burns, 'New Light', 89–90 and n. 54.

[3] His commentary on the *Sentences* had been completed with the *Super tertium* of 1517. After the *In Mattheum*, Mair's only substantial addition to his theological work was the commentary on the four Gospels (Paris, 1529).

[4] The third was *In quatuor Euangelia*, mentioned in the preceding note. Mention

published Mair's second, briefer Parisian period was almost over. For seven years or so, between the latter part of 1518 and sometime in 1525–6, Mair taught in Scotland, first in Glasgow as principal regent and then in St Andrews (which was also to be the scene of the last two decades of his long life).

Our concern in this chapter will be largely, so far as Mair is concerned, with his interpretation of the history of his native land. This, however, will—precisely because of Mair's conception of his task as a historian—entail close attention to the interaction of history and theology, of empirical fact (or what was believed to be so) and general principles. Before directly considering the *Historia Majoris Britanniae*, therefore, it will be useful to identify, so far as possible, the political position from which Mair approached its writing. In particular, as suggested in the last chapter, there are questions to be raised in regard to a possible development in Mair's thinking on such matters as political authority and forms of government.

There are, obviously, some constant factors. Mair's preference for monarchy is consistent throughout; nor is there any evidence to suggest that he changed his 1509 view as to the instability of republican regimes. Again, in regard to monarchy, the decisive view in favour of hereditary succession expressed in the 1509 *Quartus Sententiarum* is still present in what was virtually Mair's last published work, the *Ethica Aristotelis* of 1530.[5] And we have already seen, in Mair's early writing on these matters, an emphasis on consent as the essential basis of truly political power, which will certainly be found pervasively in his later works. Yet there are at least interesting shifts in emphasis or changes of perspective. In 1509 and 1510, it would seem, Mair was particularly concerned to lay stress on the 'absolute' character of royal power. This is *not*, it must be emphasized, to suggest that his view corresponded to what became known, much later, as 'absolutism'.[6] It does, however, mean that we cannot readily associate Mair with

should also be made of modifications in the later edns. of Mair's *Sentences* commentary, esp. perhaps the *In primum* of 1530, and of his logical works. Hubert Élie, *Le Traité 'De l'infini' de Jean Mair* (Paris, 1938), p. xviii, describes these edns. as 'emasculated'.

[5] *Quartus*, 1509, fo. 86ᵛ; *Ethica Aristotelis . . . Cum Jo. Majoris commentariis* (Paris, 1530), fo. 135ʳ.

[6] See on this J. H. Burns, 'The Idea of Absolutism', in J. Miller (ed.), *Absolutism in Seventeenth-Century Europe* (London, 1990), 21–42, esp. 24–5.

what we ordinarily think of as 'limited monarchy'—certainly not in the early phase of his thinking. Consider, for instance, the following passage from the 1509 commentary on Book IV of the *Sentences*:

It is better to have one supreme monarch in the realm, at whose will and pleasure everything is governed, provided that he takes counsel of wise men and then, with or without their consent, decides the issue as seems best to him.[7]

It is true that the account of counsel in Mair's 1510 commentary on Book II seems somewhat different. Here he appears to argue that a king must, on pain of mortal sin, accept counsel that is genuinely wise, and even envisages situations in which a king who is evidently and incorrigibly addicted to misgovernment might legitimately be deposed. Yet in that same passage he develops one of the most important elements in his positive account of royal authority: the legislative power.

Mair's concern here is to safeguard his position as essentially a monarchist one. Anticipating an argument with which his pupil Jacques Almain also had to deal in his 1512 controversy with Tommaso de Vio (Cajetan),[8] Mair denies that to admit the essential role of counsellors, or even the ultimate right of deposition, is to convert the realm in question from monarchy to aristocracy. The critical point is that the king 'lays down laws with authority, and has power to dispense from those laws'.[9] The theme of the king as the good or wise lawgiver was one that Mair was to develop further when he commented on the third book of the *Sentences*. That commentary was not published for the first time until 1517, though it is reasonable to suppose that Mair had lectured on the text some years before that. In any case, the position he adopts is both emphatic and interesting. What was at issue was an Aristotelian question: whether it was better for a community to be ruled by a good man or a good law. Mair's answer is decidedly in favour of the former. Part of his argument is based on the need for flexibility in dealing with human situations: the rigid provisions of the law must be tempered by means of equity or *epieikeia*, and this, for Mair as for Ireland and Gerson and so many

---

[7] *Quartus*, 1509, fo. 87^r.   [8] See above, Ch. 1 n. 111.
[9] *In secundum*, 1510, fo. 100^v: 'auctoritatiue condit leges positiuas in quibus dispensat'.

others, it is the business of the ruler to exercise. Again, the good man as ruler is himself a 'living law'. Most important for present purposes, however, is Mair's insistence that good laws—he is, of course, speaking of human law—are themselves dependent upon the authority that enacts and promulgates them: 'No law is good unless it is made [*lata*] by a wise man.'[10] Mair does not deny that human judgement is fallible, nor that the rules of law can have a clarity and certainty ordinary human decisions will frequently lack. He insists however that there is a specific kind of wisdom (*prudentia*) which enables those endowed with it to make, precisely, the kind of law in which clarity and certainty are, so to speak, crystallized. This is a form of *prudentia politica* (itself differentiated from, and superior in value to, both *prudentia monastica*, directed to individual goals, and *prudentia oeconomica*, directed to the management of the household). 'Political prudence' is, to be sure, needed by subjects as well as rulers; but the latter have—or should have—that particular form of it which Mair calls *prudentia legis positivae*—the skill that is manifested in the making and administering of positive law.[11]

These elements in Mair's thought are to some extent elaborated and taken further in his 1530 commentary on Aristotle's *Ethics*. For the moment, however, enough has been said, on the basis of Mair's earlier writings, to indicate that his monarchism was both decided and dynamic. The change, if change there was, in the position he had reached by 1518 consisted, not in any abandonment of that monarchism, but perhaps in the perspective in which it was viewed and presented. Already in 1512 Mair condensed and modified the passage in his *Sentences* commentary where, in 1509, he had laid most stress on the 'absolute' nature of royal power. And when, as we saw in the last chapter, he expanded considerably the discussion of *dominium* in which that passage had occurred, the emphasis seems to have moved quite markedly towards the 'communitarian' basis of political power and the consequential limits to which that power is subject. Nothing, perhaps, is said in Mair's 1516 commentary on Book IV which had not been either said or at least implied in the earlier version of that work or in the 1510 commentary on Book II. Yet the

---

[10] *Editio Ioannis Maioris . . . super tertium Sententiarum de nouo edita* (Paris, 1517; hereafter *Super tertium*), fo. 101ᵛ.

[11] *Super tertium*, fo. 81ʳ.

impression remains that the author's concerns are now somewhat different.[12]

It was undoubtedly, however, the elaboration of his conciliarist ecclesiology in the *In Matthaeum* of 1518 that prompted the further development of Mair's 'political theory' in what has been seen as a constitutionalist or even radical direction.[13] As a final preliminary to the discussion of the *Historia*, it will be useful to look more closely at some passages in the commentary which was the last work he completed before leaving Paris for Glasgow. Essentially these are passages in which Mair turns directly to the temporal realm in order to elucidate the nature of the *politia regalis et optima* that is supremely exemplified in the divinely ordained constitution of the church. Thus, in explaining the relationship between the pope and the church, Mair writes:

Francis is commonly said to be king of the whole realm of France; and as such he is superior not only to any single province of France but to the whole of it categorically. Nevertheless, the remainder [of the realm, apart from the king himself] is superior to him, because it is the source of his authority. The realm cannot, however, be taken away from the king without a reasonable and extremely grave cause.[14]

And Mair later develops the point by means of the argument, already noted briefly at the end of the last chapter, that the king is not superior to the whole community of his realm *regulariter et casualiter*, nor is such comprehensive sovereignty essential to a *politia regalis*. What *is* essential is that, together with the king's supremacy *regulariter* over the whole realm and over every individual subject, there should be recognized the 'reserve power' vested in the community of the realm and effective, when necessary, *casualiter et in aliquo eventu*.[15]

[12] For the further discussion of *prudentia politica* see *Ethica Aristotelis*, fo. 98ᵛ. The relationship between the 1509 and 1512 versions of the commentary on Book IV of the *Sentences* calls for more detailed scrutiny than is possible here; but cf. *Quartus*, 1512, fo. 85ᵛ; 1509, fo. 87ʳ. For the account of *dominium* in the 1516 and later edns. of the *In quartum*, see above, Ch. 1.

[13] See e.g. Q. Skinner, *The Foundations of Modern Political Thought*, 2 vols. (Cambridge, 1978), vol. ii. *The Age of Reformation*, 118–23.

[14] *In Mattheum*, fo. 70ᵛ.

[15] Ibid., fo. 71ʳ: 'ad policiam regalem non requiritur quod rex sit super omnes sui regni tam regulariter quam casualiter ... sed sat est quod rex sit super unumquemlibet, et super totum regnum regulariter; et regnum sit super eum casualiter et in aliquo euentu.'

Similarly, the theme of royal *dominium*, developed in the *Sentences* commentary, is taken up in the *In Matthaeum*: 'The king of France is not permitted to give his realm to someone else, for he does not have as full a right over his realm as I have over my cloak.'[16] The question of *dominium* in the sense of property recurs in a part of the *In Matthaeum* not so far considered: the discussion of taxation prompted by Christ's response to the question of paying tribute to Caesar. Mair's view is clear but carefully balanced. Taxation duly levied must be paid; but it is paid to the king as 'the common servant of the people'. If he upholds justice, maintains peace, and provides for the common security, then he deserves to be supported as *rex et pater patriae*. Otherwise—if, for example, the king is waging, or seeking to wage, an unjust war—his subjects are under no obligation to pay the taxes needed to meet his expenses.[17]

Such topics, together with other aspects of regal *dominium*, will call for further consideration in the more concrete setting of Mair's historical work. For the moment it may be more useful to turn from *dominium* to *potestas*. Already, in the discussion of Mair's ecclesiology, something has been seen of his views in this respect. Not surprisingly, however, these views are stated with special clarity in their civil or temporal bearing:

Thus, in the kingdom of France or of Scotland, there is a supreme power vested both in the realms as such and in their kings. It would indeed be better to say that there are two powers, one of which is superior to, and less limited than, the other, which is in fact subordinated to it.

Mair goes on to characterize this superordinate power—lodged as it is 'in the realm and the free people as a whole'—as *suprema fontalis potestas inabrogabilis*.[18] The most interesting term in that formulation is also the least translatable: no English word seems to capture the full force of *fontalis*. What it means is clear enough, and politically crucial. This supreme power is the *source* of all other powers in the state. It is indeed—though such terms were not available to Mair—what we would call a constituent or constitutive power. Mair takes care to insist (despite the problems this creates for the parallel he wishes to draw between the civil and ecclesiastical polities) that a 'free people' has the right, if there are

---

[16] Ibid., fo. 63^v.   [17] Ibid., fo. 82^r.   [18] Ibid., fo. 71^{r-v}.

reasonable grounds, 'to change the form of government' (*policiam mutare*).[19]

In comparison with this supreme power (even though the supremacy is functionally limited in the scope of its operation), the king's power is essentially 'ministerial': the king is indeed, as Mair was to call him in a passage already cited, 'the common servant of the people'.[20] And with this in mind, we may summarize the view of kingship, of *politia regalis*, which Mair had formed by 1518; which he regarded as being exemplified in the two realms he knew best at first hand, France and Scotland; and which he applied in his historical analysis. It is a view in which the king, succeeding by hereditary right, none the less rules essentially by consent of the community, whose servant he is. Yet his 'ministry' is a powerful one. Within the limits of a *dominium* which certainly precludes the possibility of any arbitrary disposal of the kingdom, the king enjoys a power which he shares with nobody else in the realm. It includes, in particular, the power to legislate, to lay down laws which, while they must, of course, to be valid, conform to the principles of natural and divine law, are indeed positive human laws, deriving their binding authority from the will of the ruler.[21]

That it is entirely appropriate to approach Mair's *Historia Majoris Britanniae* with such considerations as these firmly in mind, is demonstrated by what the author himself tells us about his conception of the historian's task—or at least of his own task in writing history. It is, he says, the theologian's business to define issues of faith, religion, and morals; and thus a theologian who writes history will legitimately deal, not only with what has happened in the past and why, but also with the rightness or wrongness of what was done. And the purpose here is didactic: addressing the young James V in his dedicatory preface, Mair suggests that reading such a history will, when the time comes, enrich with the experience of centuries the king's

[19] *In Mattheum*, fo. 70ᵛ.

[20] Ibid., fo. 71ᵛ: 'in rege . . . potestas ministerialis honesto ministerio'; fo. 82ʳ: 'Rex est communis servus populi'.

[21] To insist that positive law is a *preceptum pure humanum* is a recurrent theme in Mair's discussion of the subject, together with the postulate that law as such is always indicative of the will of a lawgiver: see perhaps esp. *Super tertium*, fos. 109ᵛ. 117ᵛ. There are problems in regard to the authority of customary law, but even there the mandate of the ruler as *legislator* is decisive.

judgement in determining what use he should make of the royal power he will then possess.[22] The clear implication is that what we might call a 'value-free' historical account would fail in this essential purpose.

Yet the fact remains that, in writing the *Historia*, Mair was turning in an unusual direction for a professional theologian, and it seems necessary to ask questions about his reasons for doing so. Such questions are often, to be sure, more easily asked than answered; and it may be as well to begin with what is perhaps an easier problem—the dating of Mair's new enterprise. That the book was in hand by the spring or early summer of 1518 is clear from a passage in which Mair mentions both that year and the fact that the young king of Scots (born on 12 April 1512) was then 'entering upon his seventh year'.[23] Indeed, since that reference occurs at the very end of the fifth of the six Books into which the work is divided, we might deduce that Mair had by then been at work on the *Historia* for some considerable time. We cannot, however, safely assume what is in fact rather unlikely—namely, that the whole book was written consecutively. The only other indication we have as to date comes from a passage in Book VI which would seem to have been written sometime in 1520.[24] And we know that the whole work had been completed and printed by April 1521 and that Mair was in Paris in the early part of that year to see this, and perhaps editions of other works, through the press.[25] The safest conclusion is perhaps that Mair embarked on the writing of his history at a time when he knew that he was about to return to Scotland, if indeed he had not already done so;

[22] *Historia*, sig. A ii[v]; Freebairn edn., p. xxx; Constable edn., pp. cxxxiv–cxxxv. The Latin text is somewhat more accessible in the edition by Robert Freebairn (Edinburgh, 1740), page-references to which and to the Scottish History Society translation (Constable edn.) are given below, as here. The translations in text and notes, however, are in general my own.

[23] *Historia*, fo. 113[r]; Freebairn edn., 259; Constable edn., 309. Mair had earlier referred, in rather less precise terms, to James V as 'a boy of six' at the time of writing (*Historia*, fo. 76[v]; Freebairn edn., 175; Constable edn., 212). R. A. Mason, 'Kingship, Nobility and Anglo-Scottish Union: John Mair's *History of Greater Britain* (1521)', *Innes Review*, 41 (1990), 182–222, seems to have overlooked this reference (cf. 217 n. 17).

[24] *Historia*, fo. 142[r]; Freebairn edn., 324; Constable edn., 384. Mair refers there to the forfeiture and execution of Alexander, third Lord Home (not 'first', as in Constable edn., 384 n. 2), which took place in Oct. 1516, as an event 'Quarto proximo anno cum hoc scriberem elapso'.

[25] Burns, 'New Light', 91.

and that the work was completed and revised during the first three years or so of his sojourn there.

The question as to why Mair wrote the *Historia* at all is less easily answered. The 6-year-old James V might be the obvious recipient of the formal dedication, but the need for a 'mirror of princes' in historiographical form was scarcely urgent enough to prompt the effort of writing it. The book may indeed be seen as having a political 'message' which, in the conditions governing diplomacy in the early sixteenth century, might have had, if not immediate then reasonably short-term relevance. Mair wrote, we must not forget, a history, not of Scotland alone, but of 'Greater Britain, of England as well as Scotland'. Resolute though he is in upholding Scottish independence against what he regards as manifestly false English claims to suzerainty, he is nevertheless convinced, and concerned to argue, that the only peaceful and prosperous future for both realms lies through a matrimonial union of the crowns.[26] There is an obvious temptation to see this in the context of Scottish 'party politics' during James V's minority; but the matter is by no means straightforward. The political situation to which Mair returned in 1518 was complex to the point of being chaotic. The 'natural' regent, the king's cousin and heir presumptive, John, duke of Albany, had withdrawn to France in 1517 as part of the *détente* between Henry VIII and Francis I, the latter then standing on the threshold of the protracted Habsburg–Valois conflict. It is true that the Franco-Scottish alliance had been renewed in August 1517 and that a future French marriage for the young king of Scots was then envisaged. None the less there might have seemed to be an opening at this juncture for a pro-English policy; and an 'English party' might have developed at just the moment of Mair's return to Scotland, as it certainly did later. That, it seems clear, did not happen.[27] The ineptitude of the probable leader in such a development, Archibald Douglas, earl of Angus, and the breakdown of his marriage to James IV's widow, Margaret Tudor, may largely account for this. At all events, however seriously or otherwise we should take the factor of Mair's presumed Douglas loyalties as an East Lothian man

[26] See on this Mason, 'Kingship, Nobility and Anglo-Scottish Union'.
[27] See Donaldson, *James V to James VII*, 36–7; and cf. Mason, 'Kingship, Nobility and Anglo-Scottish Union', 194–205, for other aspects of Mair's possible attitude to the contemporary Scottish political situation.

(and Gavin Douglas had indeed been one of his patrons), we cannot with any plausibility interpret his *Historia* as mere party propaganda. After all, Mair had evidently returned to Glasgow with the still more powerful patronage of its archbishop, James Beaton, chancellor of the realm since 1513; and Beaton was clearly supporting the pro-French policy of James Hamilton, earl of Arran, then 'undoubtedly at the head of affairs'.[28] We must perhaps conclude, therefore, that in writing as he did Mair was simply writing as he thought and urging a policy in which he believed, rather than seeking to further the interests of a faction.[29]

The case for a peaceful union between Scotland and England was not, in any case, the only lesson Mair sought to teach in his avowedly didactic *Historia*. Of most immediate concern here is the view of kingship he wished to advocate—to represent, indeed, as operative in the actual institutions of the Scottish realm, but also to uphold as the embodiment of the true character of the *politia regalis et optima*. To this theme we must now turn.

The discussion can scarcely begin at any point other than with Mair's extensive discussion (in the seventeenth and eighteenth chapters of Book IV) of the problem of the disputed succession following the deaths of Alexander III in 1286 and of his granddaughter Margaret in 1290. It is, however, worth pausing for a glance at Mair's first discussion of the subject, which occurs a little earlier in the text. His concern here is primarily to dispose of what he calls 'the silly fabrications' of 'Caxton the English chronicler'. The reference is to accounts of English history published by Caxton in 1480 and 1482 in which (following a tradition going back to Geoffrey of Monmouth) Scotland was treated as a dependent appanage of the English crown.[30] This was extended by 'Caxton' to cover the homage done by John Balliol to Edward I, following the latter's judgement in his favour in the Great Cause. In this connection Mair gives a cautious account of the end of Balliol's reign, in which King John, after various vicissitudes, found that he was 'despised in his own country' and 'went to France, that he might there lead a quiet and private life'.[31] This

---

[28] Donaldson, *James V to James VII*, 35.

[29] See on this Mason, 'Kingship, Nobility and Anglo-Scottish Union', 184–5; and cf. J. H. Burns, 'The Political Background of the Reformation', in D. McRoberts (ed.), *Essays on the Scottish Reformation* (Glasgow, 1962), 3 and n. 8.

[30] *Historia*, fos. 68ʳ–69ᵛ; Freebairn edn., 158–61; Constable edn., 191–5.

[31] *Historia*, fo. 69ᵛ; Freebairn edn., 160; Constable edn., 194.

might be regarded as amounting to 'constructive abdication'; but no explicit 'constitutional' point is made. Mair has not yet disclosed the full force of the view he intends to develop. Even when, a couple of chapters later, he offers his own narrative of events and not just a critique of 'Caxton', he leaves some crucial points less than wholly clear. Now we are indeed told of Balliol's secret undertaking to hold the crown of Edward as his overlord; now his three years' reign is presented as essentially an attempt 'to subjugate Scotland as far as in him lay to the English king'; and now the end comes, not with Balliol's 'abdication by flight', but with his 'expulsion' by the Scots.[32] This is followed by an account of relations between Robert Bruce and the Red Comyn and of Bruce's assumption of the crown and taking up the government of the realm.[33] What still awaits discussion is the basis and validity of Bruce's title.

On this critical point Mair makes his position quite clear after exploring the genealogical maze of the succession problem.[34] 'Robert Bruce alone, and his heirs, had and have an indisputable claim to the kingdom of Scotland.'[35] That claim did not rest, however, on the ground of hereditary right as such. Mair in effect cuts through the genealogical entanglement to reach the basis of hereditary right itself—indeed of any right whatever to political authority. In developing this argument, in fact, Mair gives us an important insight into the nature of his support for hereditary kingship. John Balliol, he acknowledges at least by implication, had had the superior hereditary title; but his conduct on the throne had demonstrated that he was 'unfit to rule' (*regno*

---

[32] *Historia*, fo. 74ᵛ; Freebairn edn., 171; Constable edn., 207. There are problems with Constable's rendering of this passage: to say that Balliol 'permitted the subjection of Scotland to the English king' is a less than adequate translation of 'Scotiam Anglo subdidit'. Again, for the phrase 'Scoti a regno eum eiiciunt', Constable has 'the Scots drove him from his place', implying some kind of deposition; but the words may mean no more than 'expelled him from the kingdom'. The point is not without ideological significance.

[33] *Historia*, fo. 75ʳ; Freebairn edn., 171–2; Constable edn., 207–9.

[34] *Historia*, fos. 75ᵛ–76ᵛ; Freebairn edn., 173–5; Constable edn., 209–13. In this discussion Mair correctly states the relationship between the Robert Bruce who became king and those who were, respectively, his father and grandfather. Subsequently, however, he appears to identify King Robert with his grandfather the claimant; and he also tends to telescope the events of Balliol's accession and reign with those of Bruce's successful rise to power from 1306 onwards.

[35] *Historia*, fo. 76ᵛ; Freebairn edn., 175; Constable edn., 213. 'Solus Robertus Bruseus & eius haeredes indubitatum ius in regno Scotiae habuerunt & habent.'

inidoneus). As a consequence, 'he and his line deservedly incurred deprivation by those to whom such action pertained. Now to take such action was a matter for the rest of the realm.'[36] This reference to the *reliquam partem regni* recalls of course the conciliarist view of papal authority in relation to the *reliqua pars ecclesiae*. Once again we see the force of Mair's 'communitarian' position. It is in the end the consent of the community that constitutes legitimate political power, and the withdrawal of that consent abrogates the ruler's authority. It is of course important to note and bear in mind that the 'community' here is the community of the realm incorporated in its 'princes, prelates, and nobles' (*principes, praelatos & nobiles*). It is their function to act on behalf, and in the interests of the *plebs*, the common people.[37] We shall see later just how hostile Mair is to any notion that plebeians might take it upon themselves to act politically. His 'free people' (*populus liber*) is an ordered hierarchy, acting always through its natural or accredited representatives.

So much for the community's right of resistance and their deposing power. It is also, however, their prerogative to elect and appoint a ruler where the ordinary processes for the transmission of power have, for one reason or another, broken down or been suspended. If it was the community of the realm that deposed John Balliol, it was the same body that raised Robert Bruce to the throne in his stead: 'thus the whole people agreed upon Robert Bruce as the man best deserving of the Scottish commonwealth.'[38] Mair the schoolman comes fully into his own here, arguing, for example, that Balliol himself and the other nobles 'were obliged to will that by which the security of the mystical body of which they were all parts might be preserved; and this could not well be achieved save by the expulsion of John Balliol and the rule of Robert Bruce as king'.[39] Mair concludes this part of the argument by making it clear that he is not concerned to deny Bruce's

[36] *Historia*, fo. 76ᵛ; Freebairn edn., 176; Constable edn., 215: 'Joannes Baliolus ex maiore filia natus, iuri suo cedens & ius omne suum Edwardo Anglo tribuens fuit regno inidoneus, & per consequens a iure suo & suorum merito per eos ad quos spectats priuandus: modo hoc ad reliquam partem regni spectabatur.'

[37] *Historia*, fo. 76ᵛ; Freebairn edn., 176; Constable edn., 215.

[38] *Historia*, fo. 76ᵛ; Freebairn edn., 176; Constable edn., 214: 'totus populus in Robertum Bruseum consensit de republica Scotica optime meritum.'

[39] *Historia*, fo. 77ʳ; Freebairn edn., 176; Constable edn., 214. Constable's translation here is mistaken, resting upon a suggested but unnecessary emendation of the text (214 n. 1).

hereditary claim; but he insists that the case he has stated is sufficient, independently of any claim of that kind.[40]

The ensuing chapter is devoted—again following the scholastic pattern—to stating and meeting possible objections to the proposed conclusion. Dealing first with the objection that Scottish kings were feudally subject to English suzerainty and that, specifically, Balliol had done homage to Edward I for his realm, Mair adopts both a historical and a theoretical stance. Historically, he says, it is clear on the face of the record that previous kings had done homage only for the lands they held in England. As for Balliol, even if he had acted freely (which Mair denies), he did not have legitimate right to the realm.[41] And in any case—here Mair's general principles come fully to bear—no king, however legitimate his authority, can, of his own mere will, confer that authority upon anyone else. We are confronted once more with the argument that royal *dominium* is not equivalent to an absolute right of ownership and free disposal.[42] Mair turns next to the argument that English supremacy would have been beneficial to the Scots and ought to have been accepted. He meets it in two ways. First, such expediency does not of itself mean that rightful independence should have been surrendered, any more than the interest of the state (as we might put it) should necessitate my handing over my house and furniture to someone else.[43] However, a more interesting point here lies in the encounter between what we may perhaps regard as Mair's two basic aims in respect of policy: his defence of Scottish independence and his belief in the long-term benefit of a union with England. His argument is simply that such

---

[40] *Historia*, fo. 77ʳ; Freebairn edn., 177; Constable edn., 215.

[41] *Historia*, fos. 77ᵛ–78ʳ; Freebairn edn., 177–8; Constable edn., 215–16. Mair's evident hesitation as to Balliol's title to the crown is reflected in a later retrospective reference (*Historia*, fo. 105ᵛ; Freebairn edn., 239–40; Constable edn., 287), where he argues that Balliol 'had been deprived of his right if he had any claim to it'. Constable's translation is significantly astray here, rendering 'a suo iure . . . destitutus erat' as 'had denuded himself of his claim'. This misses the point that *destituere* here has its common ecclesiastical sense, meaning 'to deprive' or 'to depose'.

[42] *Historia*, fo. 78ʳ; Freebairn edn., 178; Constable edn., 216: 'Reges enim non possunt regni sui iura secundum sua arbitria alteri conferre . . . Rex enim non habet ita liberum dominium in suo regno sicut tu in tunica tua . . .'. Cf. *Historia*, fo. 56ʳ; Freebairn edn., 130; Constable edn., 158 (apropos of king John's surrender of the English realm to the papacy): 'Ius regni a populo libero rex habet, nec contra populi voluntatem illud ius alicui concedere potest.' See also ch. 1 n. 104 above.

[43] *Historia*, fo. 77ᵛ; Freebairn edn., 178; Constable edn., 217.

a union will be beneficial only if it has a just and legitimate basis; and the obvious way of establishing such a basis is by matrimonial alliance.[44]

After this the discussion reverts more directly to Mair's fundamental theory of kingship. He defends the right of resistance and deposition against the charge that it must generate excessive disorder, by arguing that such measures are not to be taken lightly: only when the ruler is plainly incorrigible should he be deposed, and even then only after careful and dispassionate deliberation by the three estates of the realm.[45] Dealing with the argument that a king should after all have the same rights over his realm as a private owner has over his property, Mair introduces two important terms. He says first that a king—and indeed any ruler who governs a people for the common interest and advancement—is *persona publica*. As such he forfeits his position if he abuses his power to the detriment of the community. In any case—here we have the second of the terms introduced in this passage—the king's authority is merely *dominium gubernativum*, which does not make him, as the private owner is, *moderator et arbiter* over what is his.[46] This was to pick up a theme Mair had developed in his 1510 commentary on Book II of the *Sentences*. There, discussing the nature of a king's 'lordship' over his subjects' property, he had dismissed both the hypothesis that this was simple and straightforward ownership and the alternative view that it involved some kind of condominium with the private owner. Apart from the special case of the power to commandeer goods (as we would say) for the safety of the state in an emergency, the ruler has what Mair in this context calls *dominium regitivum*.[47] In effect, then, the king has only a power to exercise some kind of regulatory control over property: he has no right to interfere arbitrarily—save in a crisis—with property as such.

[44] *Historia*, fo. 78^r; Freebairn edn., 179; Constable edn., 217–18.

[45] *Historia*, fos. 78^v–79^r; Freebairn edn., 180; Constable edn., 219.

[46] *Historia*, fo. 79^r; Freebairn edn., 180; Constable edn., 220. Mair had earlier used the term *persona publica* in arguing that a king may not expose himself in war without the express or tacit consent of the people (*Historia*, fo. 44^r; Freebairn edn., 101; Constable edn., 125).

[47] *In secundum*, fo. 101^{r-v}. The concept of *dominium regitivum* was applied by Gabriel Biel to the pope's position as *dispensator* or steward of the goods of the church rather than *dominus*: see on this Burns, *Lordship, Kingship, and Empire*, 132. Mair shared that view (*Quartus*, 1509, fo. 142^v; *In quartum*, 1516; fos. 172^v, 175^v), but I have not found the term *dominium regitivum* applied by him in that context.

Finally, and briskly, Mair rounds off this part of his discussion in the *Historia* by disposing of the argument from the 'head and members' analogy. The pre-eminence of the head in a natural body does not imply similar pre-eminence in a 'mystical body': such arguments by analogy, as Mair had pointed out in his other writings, 'commonly limp'.[48]

It is not necessary here to follow Mair's account of Bruce's struggle to establish his claim to the throne and the independence of the realm, beyond noting that, at the very outset, he makes no great institutional point in regard to the coronation at Scone in 1306. In this, as we shall see, he differs from some later sixteenth-century writers. All he says is that Bruce 'with the support of his friends, went to Scone and assumed the crown'.[49] Things are different, however, when the seal is to be set on the victorious outcome of the struggle; and the difference will enable us to consider an important factor in Mair's historical account of royal government. 'After the terrible battle of Bannockburn had ended in victory,' Mair relates,

the Scots held at Ayr a great assembly such as the people of Britain call a Parliament, in which the three estates, representing the commonwealth just as a duly summoned council represents the church, came together. There it was unanimously concluded that Robert Bruce should continue as undoubted king of Scotland; and that, should he happen to pass away without male issue, his brother Edward should succeed him; and if both brothers were to die without sons Robert's daughter Marjory should reign. It is the business of the three estates, in a case of extreme difficulty, to provide authoritative clarification of doubtful issues regarding the kingship, and sometimes, where there are reasonable grounds, to depart from the common law.

Mair goes on to exemplify varying practices in regard to royal succession and to remark that such variations are only to be expected in the area of 'human positive laws', while insisting at the same time that the established law should not be too readily altered.[50]

This is not, of course, the first mention in Mair's *Historia* of the essential role of the parliamentary assembly: even in the less

---

[48] *Historia*, fo. 79ʳ; Freebairn edn., 180–1; Constable edn., 220.

[49] *Historia*, fo. 75ʳ; Freebairn edn., 172; Constable edn., 209: 'amicis suffultus Sconam adiuit, & regni diadema sibi vendicat.'

[50] *Historia*, fo. 87ʳ; Freebairn edn., 199; Constable edn., 242.

concrete context of the *In Matthaeum*, for that matter, the three estates had found a place.[51] And it is important to establish as clearly as possible what, according to Mair, the proper functions of that assembly are. We have just seen that the settlement of the crown and the succession, in situations where these matters may be in doubt, belongs to the estates. This makes it quite clear that the focus has shifted from the area of counsel—whether or not the advice given by counsellors is regarded as binding on the king— to an area of effective *power*. The point is consolidated when it emerges that the estates have authority to legislate, and the duty to do so on certain matters. Mair argues in particular that parliament should legislate to prevent royal alienation of the public domain, and that the king ought to consent to such a law.[52] This issue is closely connected with the problem of taxation, for safeguarding the domain was an essential means of limiting the need for taxes except for particular and extraordinary exigencies. This was, of course, precisely the kind of problem that had been posed in the parliaments of James III's reign and later. Mair is quite clear that taxes, when legitimately levied, must be paid as a matter of moral and civic duty; but he is equally sure that legitimate taxation cannot be based on the king's mere fiat. A particularly important point is that it is for the estates, and not for the king himself, to determine whether the situation faced by the realm does or does not constitute an appropriate occasion for levying a tax.[53]

It is clear then that, in Mair's view, the community, acting through the representative assembly of the estates of the realm, has a part to play in political life by no means confined to exercising the *ultima ratio* of deposition when tyranny has become extreme. Yet that ultimate power remains as the essential safeguard for the common good against misgovernment; and it is important to clarify what Mair has in mind in this regard. What he quite definitely did *not* envisage was anything in the nature of mass action by the populace at large. He shares to the full in the

[51] *In Matthaeum*, fo. 70ᵛ: 'in rebus arduis in quibus conuocantur tres status regni, qui regem in casibus ancipitibus habent dirigere.'

[52] *Historia*, fo. 58ᵛ; Freebairn edn., 135; Constable edn., 165–6.

[53] *Historia*, fos. 127ᵛ–128ʳ, 129ᵛ–130ʳ; Freebairn edn., 292–3, 296–7; Constable edn., 346–8, 350–2. The second of these passages makes the crucial point about the estates: 'Et necessitatem abstrusam & emergentem interpretari habent tres status, & non rex nec eius particulare concilium.'

predominant fear of the 'many-headed beast', and the concrete nature of his subject-matter in the *Historia* enables him to elaborate a theme already present in his other writings. Thus he expresses approval of the measures taken to suppress the Peasants' Revolt in England, 'for it is fitting to punish severely an unbridled people—that many-headed beast—rising against its head, in order that others may be deterred'.[54] Again, when he comes to Jack Cade's rising, he takes the opportunity to condemn not simply the *conspiratio* of the 'plebeians', but their *regimen* too. In this connection he also recalls the French Jacquerie, which he had already condemned vehemently in his 1510 commentary on Book II of the *Sentences*. Then, drawing on the account by Robert Gaguin, he had used such phrases as *insolens turba agricolarum*; now he argued that, in such cases, 'it is necessary to put down with the sword the insolent mob rebelling against the commonwealth, for otherwise they would bring disorder upon themselves and everything else'. There was surely, he had said in 1510, 'no worse plague for a polity than to be ruled by unbridled men of ignoble birth'.[55] The question of nobility will call for further comment later. For the moment it is worth noting that, even if we leave out of the reckoning the problem of popular rebellion, the concept of 'democracy' has, for Mair, an essentially pejorative connotation. If the rule of 'the many' has any legitimacy, it is only when it takes the form of 'timocracy' or *censupotestas*, where some kind of property qualification defines the group of those who have civic rights and wield political power.[56]

If it is not for the populace at large to take political action, however, neither is it, ordinarily at least, for the individual to take that responsibility upon himself. Mair had, in his earlier writings, taken a firm stand against any notion of legitimate tyrannicide. He did not deny that, once a tyrant had been duly and publicly condemned as such, an individual acting as the 'minister' of the

---

[54] *Historia*, fo. 111ʳ; Freebairn edn., 253; Constable edn., 302.

[55] *Historia*, fo. 139ʳ; Freebairn edn., 317; Constable edn., 375–6. Cf. *In secundum*, fo. 99ʳ⁻ᵛ.

[56] For the distinction between timocracy and democracy see *In secundum*, fo. 99ʳ; *Ethica Aristotelis*, fo. 134ʳ. What seems be a solitary instance of Mair's using the term 'democratic' in a less than hostile sense (*In quartum*, 1519, fo. 103ʳ) is almost certainly the result of a misprint in that edition. Even timocracy (*politia Timocratica ambitiosorum*) is firmly described as 'the worst of polities' (*In Matthaeum*, fo. 71ʳ; and cf. *Ethica Aristotelis*, fo. 134ʳ).

community might legitimately execute a capital sentence.[57] Nor did he rule out entirely the possibility that in some cases a tyrant might stand self-condemned as a public enemy and thus be liable to summary execution.[58] In general, however, his rejection of tyrannicide is decisive. In the *Historia* the question arises, once again, in an English rather than a Scottish context: the alleged attempt by a monk of Swineshead to assassinate King John. The death of a bad king may indeed, Mair acknowledges, be to the advantage of the community; but it cannot in any way be permissible for anyone—let alone a monk—to kill such a king on his own private authority.[59]

Despite all this it might still be expected that we should find Mair, given his general theory of kingship, endorsing with approval some specific cases of deposition. We cannot, unfortunately, know what view he took of the events of 1488 in Scotland—where he was then still living, as a young man of 20 or so. The handful of references he makes to James III hardly rise above faint praise: 'many kings have proved worse than James the Third, both at home and abroad.' [60] There is, however, nothing to suggest that Mair regarded James as a tyrant worthy of deposition. Two English cases in the previous century might also have seemed to come within the terms of Mair's 'resistance theory': Edward II and Richard II. Neither, however, is handled in quite that way. Mair does record the fact that 'the English, because he had heeded evil counsel, deprived Edward of Carnarvon of authority and anointed as king Edward the Third'; but he makes no comment on the fact. And when he narrates Edward II's captivity and death, he cries out at the treachery and wickedness of 'a crime not to be expiated by either time or punishment' perpetrated upon a king whose only fault was that he had followed the

[57] *Super tertium*, fo. 139ᵛ: 'Tu tanquam minister communitatis potes hunc tyrannum occidere, dum est licite condemnatus.' Mair also concedes the argument that in a 'just war' of self-defence against a tyrant it would be legitimate to kill him.

[58] This seems to be implied by his discussion (*In quatuor Euangelia*, 1529, fos. 130ᵛ–131ʳ) of the slaying of Eglon by Ehud (Judges 3: 12–25). Here the issues of usurpation and alien rule enter the argument; and although Mair argues that Ehud was in any case authorized to act as a *persona publica* by virtue of his position as *suae nationis apex*, he adds that even if this were not so—'si fuisset homo priuatus, fas illi fuisset publicum hostem & regni incubatorem de medio tollere'.

[59] *Historia*, fos. 56ᵛ–57ʳ; Freebairn edn., 132; Constable edn., 161.

[60] *Historia*, fo. 136ʳ; Freebairn edn., 210; Constable edn., 368, 'Jacobo tertio plerique reges tam domi quam foris deteriores inuenti sunt.'

counsel of wicked men; for otherwise, Mair says, Edward was 'both valiant in war and merciful within the limitations of his time—worthy therefore of comparison with great kings'.[61]

The other instance in which one might expect to find Mair's 'constitutionalist' principles being applied is the deposition of Richard II. Here Mair does acknowledge some degree of validity in the charges of misrule: Richard's unjust sentences of death or banishment upon some of the nobles, and his exploitation of the people in order to enrich himself. Yet he cannot approve—indeed he expresses his abhorrence of—what he calls the fickleness of both nobles and people in deposing a king 'on such flimsy grounds' (*in ita levi causa*). This is a sharp reminder of the caution and circumspection with which Mair advocates the 'right of resistance'. To invoke that right save in the most extreme circumstances is for him—as it was in this case—'to expose future rulers to the threat of sedition against the commonwealth; and such dreadful destruction, such a pernicious disaster, must be shunned'.[62]

These critical appraisals of actions directed against allegedly tyrannical rulers imply adverse judgements upon those who bear the responsibility, in Mair's theory, for taking such action: the *proceres regni*, the nobles, who—naturally and primarily, if not exclusively—represent the community of the realm. This is a crucially important theme not only for Mair but for all those who concerned themselves in this period with such a realm as Scotland. Now if Mair is unsparing in his condemnation of the 'many-headed beast' of plebeian power, this implies no automatic acquittal of the nobility on charges that are scarcely, if at all, less serious. The theme of nobility itself, with particular reference to the nature and basis of 'true nobility', was of course a central one for both schoolmen and humanists.[63] Mair himself had discussed the problem at some length in his *Sentences* commentary.[64] And he

[61] *Historia*, fos. 92^r, 95^{r-v}; Freebairn edn., 210, 216–17; Constable edn., 254 262–3.

[62] *Historia*, fo. 113^{r-v}; Freebairn edn., 258; Constable edn., 308.

[63] See on this Skinner, *Foundations of Modern Political Thought*, vol. i, *The Renaissance*, 45–6, 59–60, 81–2, 236–8, 257–9; also id., in C. B. Schmitt *et al.* (eds.), *The Cambridge History of Renaissance Philosophy* (Cambridge, 1988), 421–3, 428–9, 447–50.

[64] The relevant passage is translated, from the text in the 1521 *In quartum*, in the Constable edn. of Mair's *Historia*, 397–400. Cf. *In quartum*, 1516, fos. 174^r–175^r; and, for the earlier version of Mair's discussion, *Quartus*, 1509, fos. 141^r–142^r.

takes the matter up at an early stage in the *Historia*. Dealing with the accusation—the justice of which he does not deny—that the Scots in general were over-inclined to claim nobility of birth and to take pleasure in it, Mair offers an abridged statement of the dialectical argument he had used elsewhere. Either Adam was of noble birth—which would contradict the principle that no one is noble unless both his parents were so; or Adam was not of noble birth, in which case none of his descendants could claim such nobility. In truth, however, 'there is absolutely no true nobility apart from virtue and the acts that manifest it. What is commonly called nobility is no more than an empty form of words people use.'[65]

However, while Mair would evidently have agreed with Jeremy Bentham in seeing conventional 'nobility' as no more than 'factitious dignity', he had to live with the reality of a society in which those who claimed such dignity were in possession of real power and charged (he believed) with heavy responsibilities. Even in the *Sentences* commentary, the dialectic against inherited 'nobility' is followed by a careful statement of the Aristotelian view that 'nobility is ancient wealth'. And in that context Mair remarks that 'the common mode of speech', arbitrary though it may be, is not to be undervalued, while still insisting that 'not much respect is to be paid to what is commonly called nobility as compared with nobility of soul, unless'—and the proviso is significant—'greater advantage to the commonwealth is to be had in that way'.[66] The important question, therefore, is whether the nobles are discharging their responsibilities to the general advantage. In Scotland, Mair was quite sure, this was frequently not the case. For one thing, the nobles are too much inclined to internecine strife with their neighbours; and this is exacerbated by a second fault—their failure to educate their sons in such a way that, without losing any of the spirit they must display in legitimate warfare, they would learn to live together in peace and cease 'to stir up sedition in the commonwealth'.[67] That last point is critically important, for it raises the problem—

---

[65] *Historia*, fos. 14ᵛ–15ʳ; Freebairn edn., 70–1; Constable edn., 45–6. The position Mair takes may suggest either that 'scholastic' and 'humanist' views on this issue differed less than Skinner (n. 63 above) suggests, or that a late scholastic like Mair was significantly influenced by humanist ideas.

[66] *In quartum*, 1516, fos. 174ᵛ, 175ʳ; *Historia*, Constable edn., Appendix, 398, 400.

[67] *Historia*, fo. 15ᵛ; Freebairn edn., 33; Constable edn., 48.

inescapable in medieval Scotland, as in other realms—of 'over-mighty subjects'.

Neither the 'communitarian' basis of Mair's theory of political authority nor his conviction that the community could only act, when action was required, through its *proceres* led him to any degree of indulgence towards those who, for selfish or factious reasons, threatened the position of the crown. 'Mair, indeed,' it has been said, 'takes his place as the first in a long line of historians to interpret late-medieval Scottish history in terms of a continuous (and largely unsuccessful) struggle on the part of the crown to impose its will on over-mighty and irresponsible magnates.'[68] And he was perhaps particularly sensitive to the more recent manifestations of this problem. It is after describing James II's victory over the Douglases that Mair remarks: 'I am in the habit of telling my countrymen that there is nothing more dangerous than to exalt the power of great houses, especially if their strength lies on the borders of the realm.' He makes a point of illustrating the theme by referring to two episodes in his own lifetime: the forfeiture, in 1475, of John Macdonald, earl of Ross; and the similar fall of Alexander, Lord Home, in 1516.[69] The risk incurred by leaving such magnates unchecked is plain: 'those who are powerful do not fear to make war on their own authority; and if a number of nobles combine together with the commons, they are strong enough to resist the king when the need arises.'[70] Mair was, moreover, only too well aware of the ease with which the common people could be involved in such actions. If we look back from the latter part of the *Historia* to the general account of Scottish society in Book I, we find him saying that 'it would be better for king and commonwealth if subjects did not rise with their lords at a mere nod'.[71]

The remark just quoted occurs in close proximity to a brief statement by Mair of a favourite theme of his: the need for greater stability in Scotland's agrarian society, to be broadly based on security of tenure. It has been argued that this should be seen as, implicitly at least, a policy intended 'to squeeze . . . an

---

[68] Mason, 'Kingship, Nobility and Anglo-Scottish Union', 197.

[69] *Historia*, fo. 142ʳ; Freebairn edn., 324; Constable edn., 384.

[70] *Historia*, fo. 142ᵛ; 'Bellum enim potentes propria authoritate movere non verentur; & multi nobiles simul collecti cum vulgo sufficienter regi resistunt quando oportet.'

[71] *Historia*, fo. 10ʳ; Freebairn edn., 21; Constable edn., 31.

over-powerful aristocracy between a reinvigorated monarchy and a body of small landholding farmers released from the ties of economic and cultural dependency'.[72] The exploration of that hypothesis lies beyond the scope of the present investigation; but it should at least be noted that the aristocracy, however suspect in some respects, retains an absolutely essential place in Mair's understanding of the *politia regalis*. Nor is it by any means certain that he would agree with those historians who see the struggle to 'tame the magnates' as having been 'largely unsuccessful'. In an interesting passage reviewing the Stewart kings and their achievements, he sums up by observing: 'The Stewarts have preserved Scotland in peace and tranquillity [*in bona pace*] and maintained intact the realm bequeathed to them by the Bruces.'[73] That may have been, so far as peace and tranquillity were concerned, an over-generous verdict; but it does at least suggest that, in Mair's view, the magnates had not, in the final reckoning, had the best of it—nor, in that view, should they prevail, save in those rare and extreme cases when it was incumbent upon them to act, not for any sectional or factional purpose, but to safeguard the common good.

The nobles of Scotland—their functions, their culture, and their record—were also of crucial importance for the second of the two historians with whom this chapter is primarily concerned. That they cut a rather different figure in Hector Boece's *Scotorum Historiae* (1527) from what we have seen of them in John Mair is certainly true. The difference, moreover, is one that goes to the very heart of the two writers' conceptions of the nature of historiography and the role of the historian. Boece (*c.*1465–1536) was an almost exact contemporary of Mair and had undergone very much the same intellectual formation.[74] In the 1490s he and

[72] Mason, 'Kingship, Nobility and Anglo-Scottish Union', 204; and see pp. 200–5 for extended discussion. Mair's fullest critical examination of the tenure on which land was held by Scottish farmers is in *Quartus*, 1509, fo. 87[r-v]. See also the discussion of that passage by J. H. Burns, 'The Scotland of John Major', *Innes Review*, 2 (1951), 65–8.

[73] *Historia*, fo. 136[r]; Freebairn edn., 310; Constable edn., 368.

[74] On Boece's career see Macfarlane, *Elphinstone*, as index; J. Durkan, 'Early Humanism and King's College', *Aberdeen University Review*, 48 (1979/80), 259–79. There has in general been a somewhat surprising dearth of work specifically on Boece since W. D. Simpson (ed.), *Quatercentenary of the Death of Hector Boece, First Principal of the University of Aberdeen* (Aberdeen, 1937).

Mair had been arts faculty colleagues in Paris, teaching philosophy in the college of Montaigu. Boece's future, however, lay, not in the Paris theology faculty, but in Scotland: he was called back in 1497 by William Elphinstone, bishop of Aberdeen. The new university founded there two years before was to have Boece as a teacher in its arts faculty and later as its first principal. Much of the scholastic tradition survived, of course; but, from the beginning, there was also a strong element of humanism, owing much to Boece. It seems likely that it was his reputation as a classical Latinist and his friendship with Erasmus that prompted Elphinstone's invitation. Certainly Boece's *Historiae* was to be a book permeated by the humanist conception of the nature and purpose of historical writing. John Mair had not been untouched by the humanist current in the intellectual life of his time; but Boece—at least as a historian—may be seen as having committed himself entirely to it.[75] Mair's historiography was didactic in the dialectical mode of the schools: Boece's, equally didactic in purpose, adopted the mode of humanist rhetoric. The difference in style no doubt goes a long way towards explaining the fact that, by and large, it was Boece's version of the Scottish past, rather than Mair's, that prevailed and held the field. It is also necessary, however, to consider questions as to the more specific purposes with which Boece was concerned when he wrote his *Scotorum Historiae* in the mid-1520s.

To start with it must be noted that this was not Boece's first venture in historical writing—though hagiography may be regarded as a more appropriate description of his *Lives of the Bishops of Mortlach and Aberdeen*, published in Paris in 1522.[76] Two points may be mentioned in this connection. First, Boece refers in what have justly been called 'glowing terms' to Mair's achievement as

[75] See on these points J. MacQueen, 'Aspects of Humanism in Sixteenth and Seventeenth Century Literature' in id. (ed.) *Humanism in Renaissance Scotland* (Edinburgh, 1990), esp. 19–20. Interestingly, what is believed to be the only known portrait of Mair is used as the frontispiece of that book: Professor MacQueen criticizes the 'inadequacy' of the view of Mair as simply 'the last of the Schoolmen', while acknowledging that '[h]is style remained entirely that of an old-fashioned theologian'.

[76] *Hectoris Boetii Murthlacensium et Aberdonensium Episcoporum Vitae*: the text was reprinted by the Bannatyne Club (Edinburgh, 1825); and by the New Spalding Club, ed. with a translation by James Moir (Aberdeen, 1894; hereafter *Vitae*, Moir edn.).

a theologian.[77] Secondly, he mentions the fact that he himself was already at work on a history of Scotland.[78] That he had by then read Mair's *Historia* is possible, though perhaps unlikely; but we know that he did so at some stage. And it is hard to believe that he did not have his former colleague's work in mind as he wrote his own account. It is certainly tempting to suppose that the *Scotorum Historiae* was in some respects intended as 'a deliberate riposte' to Mair.[79] In general terms at least, it may well be the case that Boece, as a committed humanist, felt that the history of Scotland deserved to be told—and indeed celebrated—in a very different fashion from that which Mair had adopted. So great is the difference indeed that we may well agree with the view that 'it is more appropriate to place Boece in the tradition of panegyric oratory than history': the *Scotorum Historiae* thus becomes 'an extended rhetorical elaboration on a historical theme'.[80]

Yet the theme *is* historical, and it is necessary to consider whether Boece had purposes to serve, lessons to inculcate, going beyond the mere demonstration that attention to such classical models as Livy and Tacitus, together with careful cultivation of style, yielded a more effective piece of literature than applied scholasticism could hope to produce. As with Mair, so with Boece, questions must be asked in regard to political circumstances and their possible effect upon the historian. The period between the publication dates of Boece's *Vitae* and of his *Historiae* was one of considerable, if hardly constructive, change in the Scottish political scene. The regent Albany, after abortive attempts in 1522–3 to lead the Scots into war with England, withdrew again—and finally, as the event was to prove—to France in May 1524. His position as governor of the realm was undermined almost at once by the formal 'erection' of James V as king. Neither this nor the subsequent second 'erection' on 14 June 1526 could, with the nominal ruler no more than 12 or 13 years of age, be other than a

[77] *Vitae*, Moir edn., 89; and cf. Mason, 'Kingship, Nobility and Anglo-Scottish Union', 216 n. 10.

[78] See his account of Bishop Elphinstone's historical interests: *Vitae*, Moir edn., 99. Moir's translation, however, is somewhat misleading at this point: he makes Boece say, 'The bishop's writings I have largely followed in the history of Scotland . . . I have recently put in writing.' The Latin in fact means that Boece *is* following Elphinstone's lead in the history he has *begun* to write.

[79] Mason, 'Kingship, Nobility and Anglo-Scottish Union', 184.

[80] MacQueen, 'Aspects of Humanism', 25–6.

charade. Real power lay with those who, from time to time, con-
trolled the king's person: primarily the earl of Arran (next heir to
the crown after Albany) in the first instance, and certainly the earl
of Angus in the second. When Boece dedicated his *Scotorum
Historiae* to James V in an epistle dated 1 April 1526,[81] he cannot
have been unaware that the king was in the custody of Angus,
who had become chancellor of the realm by the time the book was
published. Archbishop James Beaton (of St Andrews since 1521),
to whom Boece addressed his second dedicatory letter on 1 May
1526, was to lose the office of chancellor less than three months
later. Both he and Boece's immediate patron in Aberdeen, Bishop
Gavin Dunbar, had been briefly imprisoned following what has
been called the *coup d'état* of 1524.[82] The problematic relationship
between royal power and magnate power could hardly be far
from the author's mind as the *Scotorum Historiae* was completed
and sent to the press.

On the other hand, the character of Boece's book is such that it
cannot be readily fitted into a 'political context' or identified with
a political cause or purpose, even to the extent that this can be
done with John Mair's concentrated and argumentative *Historia*.
There are, to be sure, concerns shared by the two writers.
Overarching both books is a firm belief in the stubborn independence of the Scots and a resolute rejection of English claims to
suzerainty over the realm of Scotland, even if Boece may have
been prepared to contemplate with some sympathy Mair's cher-
ished vision of an eventual (and peaceful) union of the two British
realms.[83] But the range of his interests (at least as evinced in this
context) was far wider than Mair's; and on some issues his views
are sharply different. Thus, it has been argued, we have in Boece
a far more favourable assessment than Mair's of the Scottish
Highlanders and their Gaelic culture. This is not a matter to be

---

[81] *Scotorum Historiae* (Paris, 1527; hereafter *Historiae*, 1527), sig. a iiii. The dates
of this letter and that to Archbishop Beaton mentioned below presumably account
for the fact that this edition, which has no date on the title-page and no colophon,
is often said (as in the British Library Catalogue) to have been published in 1526.
However, the letter addressed by Alexander Lyon, precentor of Moray, to the
nobility of Scotland which appears on the last page of the *Isagoge* preceding the
main text is dated 15 Mar. 1527.

[82] Donaldson, *James V to James VII*, 38–9.

[83] This is suggested by Arthur Williamson, *Scottish National Consciousness in the
Age of James VI: The Apocalypse, the Union and the Shaping of Scotland's Public Culture*
(Edinburgh, 1979), 190 n. 22. However, the references given there do not appear to
be directly related to this point.

pursued here, but it is connected with something that *is* relevant in the present discussion; for Boece valued the martial virtues of the 'wild Scots' of the Highlands as a touchstone for the qualities that must be regained by the nobility as a whole if their essential role in Scottish society was to be properly fulfilled.[84] There is, no doubt, room for some modification in the view of Boece's history as essentially 'martial' in tone.[85] Yet there can be no doubt as to his having commended 'chivalric' virtues in the nobility in a way Mair would have found quite unacceptable.[86]

At the same time, it is important to observe that Boece did, from the outset, recognize the threat posed by excessive magnate power. Already in his dedicatory epistle to James V he points to one crucial lesson his history will teach: 'No one who, relying on base and dishonourable grounds, has dared to attempt a revolution has failed to meet a disgraceful death.' This has been true of kings, he adds, 'but much more so of those of the nobility who, puffed up with unbridled power, have not been afraid to rise against their kings'.[87]

Yet, when we turn from the preamble to the story itself, it may well seem that the balance has shifted. The first six or seven books of the *Scotorum Historiae* are, notoriously, devoted to an account of early Scottish history which has little in common either with the medieval chroniclers or with Mair's *Historia*. Mair was indeed concerned, like Boece, to examine the various 'origin myths' that were current in the British historiography of their day. He is, however, seemingly little interested in any kind of 'foundation myth' for Scottish kingship.[88] Boece, in contrast, turns the bare fact—or alleged fact—of the establishment of the Scots in what was to become Scotland under Fergus, son of Ferchard, into an

---

[84] Williamson, *Scottish National Consciousness*, 120–1.

[85] See Durkan, 'Early Humanism', 266–7, on Erasmian affinities in Boece's work.

[86] Mason, 'Kingship, Nobility and Anglo-Scottish Union', 196–8.

[87] *Historiae*, 1527, sig. a iiii^v. It is of some interest to compare this with Boece's comment, in the part of the book published posthumously in 1574, on the problem posed by the Douglases in the reign of James II: 'Saepius dum magnatum quispiam opibus & gloria, Principi, paris suo in regno semper impatiens, sese aequare studet infestum se populo, & principem sibi infensum reddit' (*Scotorum Historiae . . . libri XIX* (Paris, 1574), hereafter *Historiae*, 1574, 368^r).

[88] Cf. *Historia*, fo. 18^v; Freebairn edn., 40–1; Constable edn., 56, where Mair remarks that Fergus laid only 'a weak foundation' for the kingdom. It is true, however, that when discussing the succession problem of the 1290s, he says: 'Populus liber primo Regi dat robur, cuius potestas a toto populo dependet; quia

elaborate account of Fergus's leadership and of how he became king—the first in an unbroken line of kings of Scots which, with James V, was well into its nineteenth century. The procedure is represented as one in which the Scots deliberated as to various forms of government, determined upon kingship, and appointed Fergus, who then, 'seated upon the fated stone chair' was acclaimed as king. Subsequently, and of their own motion, the people swore fealty to him and declared that they would never admit any form of government other than kingship or suffer anyone to be their king who was not of Fergus's lineage.[89] Succession within that lineage, however, was not by primogeniture: the crown (and an actual crowning is mentioned in the case of Fergus's immediate successor) was to pass to that male relative of the late king who was best fitted to rule. This implied, of course, an element of *electio* before *laudatio*;[90] and in fact Boece regularly mentions choice *omnium suffragiis* (or some such phrase) before the new king receives the *acclamationes* of the people. Usually—though there is less than complete uniformity on this point—the election is ascribed to the nobles, who thus, predictably, assume their key position in the supposed system of government.[91] And on the whole—here we have the shift in emphasis away from the problematic towards the positive aspect of aristocratic power—that function is seen as having been performed for the general good.

This is not to say that the choices made by the nobility proved uniformly happy in their outcome. Strikingly, indeed, the electors were quite often misled by placing too much confidence in heredity, only to find that 'of virtuous father virtuous son' was a far from infallible guide-line. In this or some other way, at all events, the Scots soon began to experience the evils of misrule—indeed of downright tyranny. Nothatus, the fifth king, having ruled tyrannically and oppressively, was overthrown and slain by a conspiracy of nobles. It is true that Boece may be somewhat

aliud ius Fergusius primus Rex Scotiae non habuit' (*Historia*, fo. 76ᵛ; Freebairn edn., 175; Constable edn., 213).

[89] *Historiae*, 1527, fos. 6ᵛ, 10ᵛ.

[90] These were the terms used, for instance, in medieval Castile: see A. MacKay, 'Ritual and Propaganda in Fifteenth-Century Castile', *Past and Present*, 107 (May 1985), 19–20.

[91] The elective process in one form or another is mentioned in regard to all but eleven of Boece's first eighty kings.

ambivalent in this passage, criticizing at least some aspects of the conspiracy.[92] But the pattern is one that recurs again and again, and the historian's approval is usually implied if not expressed. Of the first eighty kings in Boece's list, down to and including Kenneth III, two dozen were either tyrannical or morally depraved or both; and every one of them ended his life in that disgrace which was foreshadowed in the dedication of the book. Formal acts of deposition are, it is true, mentioned only occasionally: more often than not they are rendered unnecessary by the tyrant's suicide or his death in battle with those who have risen against his misrule. Nevertheless formal deposition is seen throughout as being available in reserve, and it is expressly recorded several times.[93]

Before considering Boece's work in periods when the light of a more authentic history can be brought to bear on what he says, it is important to review the earlier part of the book and assess its ideological implications. It was in his account of the reigns of the forty kings from Fergus I to Fergus II that Boece claimed to be drawing upon sources apparently quite unknown to earlier writers (or, for that matter, to his contemporary Mair), and in particular upon a chronicle allegedly written by Veremund, archdeacon of St Andrews, in the eleventh century. This is not the place to enter the intricate debate as to the nature and origins of Boece's 'vouchers' (as Thomas Innes called them in his swingeing critique).[94] What is in any case clear is that Boece both accepted

[92] See *Historiae*, 1527, fo. 17^{r-v}.

[93] e.g. in the cases of Evenus III (16th in Boece's series) and Conanus (24th); while Culinus (79th) was allegedly about to be deposed when he was assassinated. Imprisonment followed by 'death in custody' in one form or another is also mentioned several times, as is death in battle with the nobles who have conspired against the tyrant. It is proper to add that, in most cases, a new king is not said to have been installed until his predecessor (even if deposed, imprisoned, or exiled) was dead, regents or governors administering the realm in the interim.

[94] T. Innes, *A Critical Essay on the Ancient Inhabitants of the Northern Parts of Britain or Scotland* (1729), ed. with a memoir by George Grub (The Historians of Scotland, VIII; Edinburgh, 1885), 130–69. For the views of modern scholars see J. B. Black, 'Boece's *Scotorum Historiae*', in Simpson (ed.), *Quatercentenary of the Death of Hector Boece*, 30–53; T. D. Kendrick, *British Antiquity* (1950; New York, 1970), 65–8; M. Drexler, 'Fluid Prejudice: Scottish Origin Myths in the Later Middle Ages', in J. Rosenthal and C. Richmond (eds.), *People, Politics and Community in the Later Middle Ages* (Gloucester, 1987), 60–77; R. A. Mason, 'Scotching the Brut: Politics, History and National Myth in 16th-Century Britain', in id. (ed.), *Scotland and England 1286–1815* (Edinburgh, 1987), 60–84.

and elaborated upon what he found there.[95] It is impossible to believe that this highly educated scholar was a mere dupe, heedlessly repeating a story of which he failed to appreciate the implications. To adapt a celebrated formula, Boece must surely have known the nature and quality of what he was saying and believed that it was right. This is not to judge his historiography by anachronistically unfair criteria. Accepting the essentially rhetorical mode in which Boece wrote, we are both entitled and bound to ask what purposes his rhetoric was intended to serve. Of what truths did he wish his readers (James V included) to be persuaded? That what may be called broadly moral purposes were prominent in Boece's mind may be accepted without demur. [96] But the morality to be inculcated was, at least in one major respect, a political morality, a morality of government. We may agree that Boece sought the restoration, in the nobility of Scotland, of those warlike virtues, grounded in Spartan austerity and discipline, which had served the nation well in the long struggle to vindicate its independence. At the same time, however, the implication of his history is plainly that the nobles and people of Scotland had the right and had repeatedly demonstrated the power to call errant rulers to account and to punish their misdeeds. 'Resistance theory' may have had little or no lineage in the political culture of Scotland before the work of John Mair. Here, before Mair's ideas can have had much impact, the right of resistance was given emphatic and, as the event was to prove, enormously influential expression. This need not, and should not, be seen in terms of an 'inflammatory constitutional doctrine': the *Scotorum Historiae* is certainly not a 'radical political tract'. Nevertheless, if, in comparison with Mair, there is not much in Boece's *Scotorum Historiae* that could be called political theory, there is something that may be regarded as even more important: a powerful and dramatic political myth.[97]

Arguably, when the reader moves forward into periods when meaningful comparison between Boece and other historians is

[95] See MacQueen, 'Humanism in Sixteenth and Seventeenth Century Literature', 20–1.

[96] Durkan, 'Early Humanism', 267.

[97] On Scottish 'resistance theory'—or the lack of it—see R. A. Mason, 'Kingship, Tyranny and the Right to Resist in Fifteenth Century Scotland', *Scottish Historical Review*, 66 (1987), 125–51. For a critical account of the 'constitutionalist' interpretation of Boece see id., 'Scotching the Brut', where the phrases quoted above occur on p. 65; and cf. n. 30 (p. 79). Neither Mair nor Boece should (on the view taken here) be regarded as an advocate of anything resembling inflammatory radicalism.

possible, the picture may lose some of that dramatic clarity. At first, to be sure, during the long sequence of kings from Fergus II to Kenneth III, the pattern remains the same. Seven of these kings are said by Boece to have been punished for their tyranny; but, as Innes remarked,

Fordun, the only ancient Scottish historian who with his continuators contain[s] any account of these kings' reigns, hath not one word either of their bad administration or of their subjects exercising any power over them, but, on the contrary, gives a quite different account of such of them of whom he had found any particulars recorded.[98]

And Mair, in such of the half-dozen instances as he mentions, follows the earlier chroniclers. The only partial exception in the list is Culen, as to whose bad character all authorities agree; but Boece is alone in claiming that he was about to be deposed when he was slain by a nobleman whose daughter he had ravished.[99]

With Kenneth II (as we should more accurately designate the king who in Boece's sequence is 'Kenneth III') we come, in the third quarter of the tenth century, to an episode which was to be of some significance for sixteenth-century controversy. To quote a recent historian, 'we ought to take Fordun seriously when he claims that Kenneth II won a section of the Scottish magnates over to accepting new rules in the succession system.'[100] The somewhat intricate detail of what is now believed or conjectured to have been involved in the transaction need not detain us here. For Boece and those who followed his lead—Mair, perhaps surprisingly, does not refer to the matter—this was the point at which the Scottish monarchy became strictly hereditary on the basis of male primogeniture. The change, as Boece represents the episode, was not achieved without resistance,[101] nor—either in fact or in his narrative—were the new rules immediately effective in practice. None the less, it was to be important for the development of

[98] *Critical Essay*, 153.

[99] *Historiae*, 1527, fo. 232ᵛ. Cf. e.g. Mair, *Historia*, fo. 41ᵛ. Freebairn edn., 94; Constable edn., 117.

[100] A. P. Smyth, *Warlords and Holy Men: Scotland AD 80–1000* (London, 1984), 224; but cf. the discussion of royal succession in this period by A. A. M. Duncan, *Scotland: The Making of the Kingdom* (Edinburgh, 1975), 112–13.

[101] *Historiae*, 1527, fos. 238ᵛ–240ʳ. Boece sums up as follows: 'Hae tum leges nouae creandi Scotorum Regis, abrogatis veteribus, iubente Kennetho, maiorum autem compluribus tacentibus magis quam non probantibus: aliis tamen acclamantibus plausibiliter, rata fore quaecunque Rex sanciuit' (fo. 240ʳ).

'royalist' polemic that indefeasible hereditary right could from this point onwards be treated as the constitutional basis of Scottish kingship.

Such a system presented problems of its own; and it is now appropriate to consider what Boece made of the most acute problem of that kind faced by the realm of Scotland—the settlement of the succession in the period of the Great Cause of the late thirteenth century. For John Mair, as we have seen, this had presented an opportunity to apply a theory of monarchy already developed in his theological writings. In the case of Hector Boece we have no explicitly doctrinal material to consider. His understanding of kingship in this context as in that of the earlier stages of Scottish history must be inferred from the way in which he presents his narrative.

This is not by any means a straightforward task, though much of Boece's account of events is not particularly problematic. To start with, John Balliol, following Edward I's adjudication in his favour, went to Scone and was 'made king by the Scots in the customary manner'. Then, at Newcastle on 26 December 1292, he did homage to Edward 'against the will of the nobles', thus delivering himself and his realm into slavery. When, summoned by Edward to aid him against France, Balliol refused on the grounds that his submission had been invalid both because it had been made under duress and because it had lacked the necessary consent of the three estates, his defiance was futile. Defeated and abject, Balliol 'transferred all royal authority to Edward and abdicated as king'.[102]

It appears, however, that neither surrender nor abdication affected Balliol's status as, in Boece's view, *de jure* king of Scots. Nothing in his narrative of the ten years between the end of the *de facto* reign of King John and the beginning of the reign of King Robert contradicts this. Those who took the lead in resisting the English conquest did so in the name of King John. And when Balliol, having returned and found himself *persona non grata* in Scotland, went back to England and then withdrew to his French estates, he did so *sponte*—of his own free will: there was no question of his having been driven out of the realm. When Wallace 'was, by the voice of all, made commander to liberate his

[102] *Historiae*, 1527, fos. 304ʳ, 305ʳ.

country', he was 'commonly called governor under King John Balliol'.[103] On this basis the struggle against Edward was, so far as the crown was concerned, a struggle to restore effective authority to King John. The future King Robert plays an equivocal part in Boece's dramatic account. Alleged to have betrayed the Scots at Dunbar and to have sought the crown for himself under Edward's patronage, he is shown as reproaching Wallace after the battle of Falkirk for his presumptuous opposition to Edward's power and as being, in his turn, bitterly reproached as a traitor. Wallace, even after surrendering his public office, remains the heroic, and eventually the betrayed and martyred leader. And the guardianship of the realm, when it passed to John Comyn and Simon Fraser, was still exercised in Balliol's name.[104]

As to what happened in 1306, Boece's account is not particularly informative, nor does it offer any ideological *point d'appui*. There is indeed a close parallel with Mair's first, undeveloped reference to the matter: Bruce, Boece says, 'with the support of his friends, set out for Scone and seized the crown'. It is true that, in the *Scotiae Regum Catalogus* prefixed to the *Historiae*, he says that Bruce was 'proclaimed king of Scots' in 1306; but the fact remains that Boece, acknowledging that Bruce 'had few supporters in Scotland' at this stage, says nothing to indicate that his acquisition of the crown had any explicit constitutional authority. What happened at Scone was validated by its results: it was by defeating the English and restoring Scottish independence that King Robert vindicated his right to the crown.[105]

On the other hand, when Boece refers to the parliament held at Ayr after the victory at Bannockburn as having 'confirmed' the king's title (*rex confirmatus est*) and settled the succession in Bruce's family, there is an assumption that a title existed to be confirmed; and this in turn presupposes that Balliol's *de jure* claim had been superseded.[106] It is not, however, until a later stage in his narrative, and then in a context which appears to be wholly fictitious, that Boece gives any indication of how this had been brought about. He claims that Robert I sent Sir James Douglas to France in 1327 to secure from Balliol (who had by then in fact been dead for some fourteen years) a final renunciation of all rights to the crown of Scotland. Boece makes several points in this

[103] Ibid., fo. 304ᵛ. [104] Ibid., fo. 304ᵛ. [105] Ibid., fo. 310ᵛ.
[106] Ibid., fo. 325ᵛ.

connection. First, he argues that the mission was supererogatory; for (he says) it was universally recognized that King Robert's title was perfectly adequate and that Balliol, by abandoning the realm, had effectively abdicated. Moreover, by subjecting the Scottish people to Edward against the will of the estates of the realm, he had rendered himself unfit to rule (*inidoneum . . . publico . . . regimini*). In these circumstances, the people of Scotland, having rightly deprived Balliol of royal authority, had conferred it upon Bruce as the only saviour of the Scottish state. Characteristically, Boece presents all this in an almost proto-Shakespearian scene, in which Balliol, old, blind, and tired of life, acknowledges his faults and freely surrenders to Bruce and his heirs whatever right he might have had to the crown. If the drama reflects Boece the rhetorician, however, the doctrine is strikingly close to that of Mair (who, incidentally, makes no mention of the apocryphal Douglas mission). Even the language echoes the earlier writer: it is noteworthy that Boece uses here the less than classical word *inidoneum* precisely as Mair had used it, in the same connection, half a dozen years earlier.[107]

Before taking a retrospective view of the evidence surveyed so far in this chapter, there is another element in the pattern to be considered. Not the least important point about Boece's *Scotorum Historiae* is the promptness with which it became available in the vernacular. Quite soon, it seems, after assuming personal authority over the realm in 1528, James V commissioned not one but two versions of the book in Scots—one in prose, the other in verse. John Bellenden's prose rendering, which was printed in or about 1540, is both more and less than a translation from one language into another.[108] Himself a humanist in the same mould as Boece, Bellenden too saw the historian's task as essentially rhetorical.[109] This, as he confronted Boece's text, justified addition,

---

[107] *Historiae*, 1527, fo. 329ʳ.

[108] *The Hystory and Croniklis of Scotlande* (Edinburgh, n.d.; facsimile edn., The English Experience, Amsterdam, 1977; hereafter *Hystory*, 1540?). This edn. repr. as *The History and Chronicles of Scotland* 2 vols. [vols. i and ii in *The Works of John Bellenden*, 3 vols. (Edinburgh, 1821–2)]; hereafter *History*, 1821). An earlier version, written seemingly in 1531, has been printed by the Scottish Text Society: R. W. Chambers, E. C. Batho, and H. W. Husbands (eds.), *The Chronicles of Scotland*, 2 vols. (Edinburgh, 1938–41; hereafter *Chronicles*, 1531). The Appendix (ii. 413–16) provides the fullest account of Bellenden's life, by E. A. Sheppard.

[109] On Bellenden's humanism see MacQueen, 'Humanism in Sixteenth and Seventeenth Century Literature', 11–19.

subtraction, and variation as the translator saw fit; and 'fitness' here meant adaptation to a didactic or polemical purpose. Some of the consequences of this may be seen by examining Bellenden's version of the crucial episodes just considered in the context of Boece's original text.

Bellenden, it must be borne in mind, was working at the express command of a king who was now effectively and vigorously in power as the undoubted heir in a dynasty which might well take pride in its descent from a line stretching far back into the mists of time, but which also looked back, in a shorter but sharper perspective, to Robert Bruce as its heroic progenitor. Now Bruce, as we have seen, cuts an equivocal figure in Boece's narrative: if he emerges triumphantly as the heroic saviour of his country, the background out of which he emerges is deeply shadowed. Bellenden quite clearly saw it as his task to ensure that these shadows were not construed as stains on the character of James V's illustrious ancestor. To a certain extent this could be done by reducing still further the already low standing of Bruce's rival: Bellenden omits Boece's statement that Balliol was 'made king by the Scots' and presents him as having been, throughout, a mere creature of Edward I.[110] Yet the darker episodes in Bruce's story had to be faced—in particular, his alleged behaviour at Dunbar and at Falkirk. In the first version of his translation (of which the printed text is a revision and expansion) Bellenden retains some harsh comments on Bruce's 'treason'.[111] These are considerably softened in the final text, where, moreover, the supposed treason at Dunbar has become a Balliolite invention.[112] More significantly still, Bellenden inserts an elaborate apologia for Bruce, arguing that Balliol's hostility to his rival left Bruce 'na refuge in Scotland'; that he was 'an Inglisman born' who held lands in vassalage to the English king; and that he had Edward's promise to reverse the judgement in favour of Balliol 'and to make the said Robert kynge'. None of this may appear to do much for Bruce's heroic stature. Bellenden does better, perhaps, when he compares Bruce to St Paul, who from being 'ane gret scurge of crystyn pepyll' became 'the gretest pyllar of our faith'. In the same way, Bruce, having

[110] *Hystory*, 1540?, fos. 203ᵛ–204ᵛ, *History*, 1821, ii. 263; *Chronicles*, 1531, ii. 248.
[111] *Chronicles*, 1531, ii. 251–2, 256–9.
[112] *Hystory*, 1540?, fo. 207ʳ–ᵛ; *History*, 1821, ii. 366.

persewit the Scottis with gret cruelte for postponyng of hym fra his iust heritage & crown, zit fra he was maid kyng, he was the best prince that euir rang aboue the scottis. For thoucht he fand scotland in gret miserie and wois conquest be tyranny of Inglismen, zit he recouerit it be his singulare manheid and left it fre bot ony clame in gret tranquillyte.[113]

The road to Scone, where he was 'maid kyng', was thus Bruce's road to Damascus; but what precisely was the process of his conversion? Bellenden adds nothing to Boece's account of the critical moment in 1306, apart from the suggestion (withdrawn in the printed text, presumably because it tended to reduce the 'rags to riches' aspect of the story) that Bruce came to Scone with 'ane greta power of freindis'. Otherwise he repeats Boece's bald reference to the coronation and to the fact that 'the maist part of Scotland was aganis' Bruce. There is nothing to indicate that Bruce was 'maid kyng' by any process other than his assumption of the crown and going on to conquer the kingdom.[114] When it comes to the parliament at Ayr, again, Boece's reference to the 'confirmation' of King Robert's title is dropped, leaving only an account of how 'he gat the crown of Scotland tailzit to hym and ye airis gottin of his body', with reversion to his brother Edward and his male issue and then to his daughter Marjory and hers.[115] All this was enacted by the three estates; and Bellenden certainly acknowledges the constitutional role of that assembly. Thus, where Boece vaguely attributed Wallace's appointment as commander and governor *omnium suffragiis*, Bellenden explicitly refers—at least in one of the two contexts where the point arises—to the estates.[116] Neither in 1306 nor in 1314–15, however, is there any suggestion that Bruce's title was conferred or confirmed by a parliamentary or any other constitutional process. We are left to infer that, since Bruce was (Bellenden says) 'nerist be proximite to the crowne of Scotland', this was a case in which the rightful heir

---

[113] *Hystory*, 1540?, fo. 207ᵛ; *History*, 1821, ii. 374. It may be noted that the description of Bruce as 'an Inglisman born' contradicts an earlier reference to Scotland as 'his native cuntre' (*Chronicles*, 1531, ii. 248).

[114] *Hystory*, 1540?, fo. 210ʳ; *History*, 1821, ii. 381; *Chronicles*, 1531, ii. 264–5.

[115] *Hystory*, 1540?, fo. 214ʳ⁻ᵛ; *History*, 1821, ii. 393; *Chronicles*, 1531, ii. 278.

[116] *Hystory*, 1540?, fo. 207ʳ; *History*, 1821, ii. 372; *Chronicles*, 1531, ii. 256. In the other, earlier reference, *Hystory*, 1540?, fo. 206ʳ (*History*, 1821, ii. 359) has: 'he was chosin be general vocis . . . Gouernour of Scotland, in place of John Balioll'. *Chronicles*, 1531, ii. 253 does not have the last phrase. To say 'in place of John Balioll' implies, it may be observed, a position significantly different from Boece's 'gubernator sub Ioanne Baliolo rege'.

vindicated his claim by conquest and thus became at the same time 'the recouerer of Scotland'.[117]

That last phrase occurs at the beginning of Bellenden's rendering of the alleged mission to Balliol undertaken by Sir James Douglas. Now, although that rendering is somewhat more elaborate in the printed text than in the earlier draft, it significantly omits those elements in Boece which appear to acknowledge that there was an element of deposition or expulsion in the ending of Balliol's reign in addition to his having abdicated, or 'exonerit hym self' of the crown he was 'inabyll to iose [enjoy]'.[118] Taking this together with the other indications already considered, the conclusion seems inescapable that Bellenden, more particularly in the revised and expanded version of his *Hystory*, resolved the ambiguities in Boece's account in such a way as to minimize the 'constitutionalist' theme, while at the same time presenting Bruce in a less equivocal light as the upholder both of Scottish independence and of essentially hereditary kingship.

Much of this was paralleled and had perhaps been anticipated in the other vernacular version of Boece's *Historiae*, William Stewart's metrical chronicle.[119] This appears to be more or less contemporary with the first draft of Bellenden's translation and to have been undertaken likewise at the request of James V only a few years after his assumption of personal power in 1528. Stewart, engaged in versifying as well as translating, sat more loosely to his original than Bellenden had in general felt free to do. And in any case it seems clear that Stewart wished to set his own mark on the record he was presenting. Certainly there are distinctive features in his account of the issue between Balliol and Bruce. Doubtless Stewart's work, which did not appear in print until its inclusion in the Rolls Series in 1858, was a good deal less widely known and influential than either Boece's Latin or Bellenden's Scots prose. Yet it remains a document of some importance in the present investigation.

---

[117] For Bruce as 'nerist be proximite' see Bellenden's apologia for Bruce (*Hystory*, 1540?, fo. 207ᵛ; *History*, 1821, ii. 369). The term 'recouerour' (*Hystory*, 1540?, fo. 216ᵛ; *History*, 1821, ii. 403) replaced 'conquerour' in the earlier draft (*Chronicles*, 1531, ii. 286).

[118] *Hystory*, 1540?, fo. 216ᵛ; *History*, 1821, ii. 403.

[119] *The Buik of the Croniclis of Scotland: or a Metrical Version of the History of Hector Boece*, ed. W. B. Turnbull, 3 vols. (Rolls Series; London, 1858). For the identification of the author see vol. i, pp. vii–xiv.

Stewart's position is, to be sure, simple to the point of being simplistic. Bruce for him was the rightful heir kept out of his inheritance by an intruder backed by an English tyrant. All Bruce's actions, even the most apparently dubious, are to be explained and justified on that basis. In the Great Cause, 'King Edward decretit and gaif fals Sentence aganis Robert Bruce'. At the time of the battle of Dunbar, the agreement between Edward and Bruce was simply that the former would 'restoir' to the latter 'all his richt'; and Bruce's action in that battle was

> for to reskew his rycht
> Agane king Johne and for na vther thing.[120]

Rehearsing the argument a little further on, Stewart adds another point. Bruce had acted

> to reskew his kinrik and his croun.
> As euerilk man has ressone for his richt,
> For to exerce with power, strenth and micht
> Be way of deid his purpos to fulfill,
> Quhen he be ressoun can nocht cum thairtill.[121]

What Stewart presents is thus a firm *de jure* view of hereditary kingship, in which there can be little need for the king's 'right' to be validated by any kind of corporate action or constitutional procedure. Doubtless that right should be solemnized with due ceremony; and it is noteworthy that Stewart's one small addition to Boece's account of Bruce's assumption of the crown in 1306 is to emphasize the *solemnity* of the coronation— 'Solempnitlie . . . he crownit wes in Scone'.[122] He does say that the parliament at Ayr after Bannockburn was summoned by Bruce 'speciallie for to declair him king';[123] but that is the closest he comes to any suggestion that Bruce's kingship was conferred otherwise than by his undoubted hereditary right and his own actions to 'reskew' that right. Accordingly, it is not surprising to find that Stewart's chronicle makes no mention at all of the supposed Douglas mission to Balliol. The latter does not reappear after his humiliation by Edward, his exile in France, and his miserable death—

---

[120] Stewart, *Buik of the Croniclis*, iii. 144, 152, 153.   [121] Ibid. 155.
[122] Ibid. 201.   [123] Ibid. 241.

> With greit displesour that time endit he
> That put Scotland into perplexitie.[124]

One final point in worth adding. It is striking, and perhaps somewhat ironic, that it should be Stewart who gives us the most precise indication of the authority which was conferred upon William Wallace:

> The lordis all with their auctoritie
> Of Scotland maid him governour to be;
> With haill power baith for to heid and hing
> And justice gyde as he had bene ane king.[125]

It is natural to speculate as to the identity of the king in whose place and name Wallace is supposed to have exercised these powers. Balliol by then was presumably, in Stewart's view, no longer even *de facto* king, and king *de jure*, on that view, he had never been. It would seem to follow that Wallace was in effect regent for the rightful king, Robert Bruce—a conclusion which would throw an odd light on the encounter between the two at the time of the battle of Falkirk.[126]

Scottish historical writing in the reign of James V, considered in respect of its implications for the understanding of kingship in general and, specifically, of royal power in Scotland, has its complexities and doubtless its ambiguities. Some points are none the less clear. In the two most important works, Mair and Boece both present, each in his own way, a concept or image of kingship as an institution rooted and grounded in the 'mystical body' of the community. It follows that royal authority is to be wielded for the common good—for the security, well-being, and integrity of the community as a whole. To that end the king is invested with substantial and wide-ranging prerogatives; and the authority of which he disposes has, for the sake of stability and continuity, been converted into a hereditary institution. It remains in the end, however, a constitutional or limited authority; and, if it is intolerably abused by an incorrigible tyrant or an alien usurper, it may

---

[124] Ibid., 159.   [125] Ibid. 163.
[126] Ibid. 180–2. In Stewart's account the result of the confrontation is Bruce's repentance and conversion. Filled with remorse for the harm he had done 'Aganis Scotland to quhome he had sic richt . . . | Fra that da furth he did thame no mar deir [injury]'. It is noteworthy, however, that even here Stewart emphasizes Bruce's 'richt' to the crown.

be taken out of the hands to which it had been entrusted by those in whose interests that trusteeship had been established. The people, acting as an organized body through those persons and institutions whereby their corporate life is articulated, may legitimately resist misgovernment and take measures to bring it to an end.

At a time when both the concept and the practice of 'absolute monarchy' were gathering momentum, opposition to such ways of thinking about kingship was inevitably generated. In Scotland, the copious rhetoric of Boece's *Scotorum Historiae* lent itself to more than one interpretation; and already, in the vernacular versions discussed above, we can see the beginning of a process whereby the story could be told in ways more acceptable to rulers impatient of rigorous restraint. Both sides of the argument awaited further development in more critical circumstances; but those developments belong to later chapters. Before that, there are other modes in which 'political ideas' were expressed to be considered.

3

Satire and Complaint

WILLIAM STEWART'S *Buik of the Croniclis of Scotland* took us into the realm of verse, if scarcely of poetry; but there were to be—there had already been—vernacular works of greater significance and merit as literature in which political ideas, or at least political attitudes, found expression. In the reign of James V one major writer emerged; and his works will occupy a substantial part of the present chapter. Before Sir David Lindsay is considered, however, it will be useful to look at some earlier evidence of this kind. To do so will take us back to the reign of James III, where the present investigation began.[1] None of the evidence from that reign, to be sure, adds anything of great substance to our understanding of political thinking in the period. Yet both the anonymous *Thre Prestis of Peblis*[2] and the *Morall Fabillis* of Robert Henryson—specifically 'The Taill of the Scheip and the Doig' and 'The Taill of the Lyon and the Mous'[3]—are of more than literary interest. Within their largely conventional forms they contain matter which has, arguably, rather specific reference to conditions and problems in the Scotland their authors knew.[4]

Some of those problems are social or moral rather than political in any sense that is relevant here.[5] Others, however, lie very much

[1] The outstanding literary figure in the reign of James IV, William Dunbar, produced work that is rich in satire, complaint, and invective; but it does not seem to contribute to 'political thought' in any sense that is relevant to the present enquiry.

[2] *The Thre Prestis of Peblis how thai tald thar talis*, ed. T. D. Robb (Scottish Text Society; Edinburgh, 1920; hereafter Robb edn.).

[3] I have used the edition by H. Harvey Wood, *The Poems and Fables of Robert Henryson Schoolmaster of Dunfermline* (Edinburgh, 1933; hereafter Wood edn.).

[4] Recent literature on these points is conveniently listed in Macfarlane, *Elphinstone*, 197–8 n. 108. The last item in that list, R. L. Kindrick's 1979 article, may be regarded as one end of a spectrum in which the more sceptical end is represented by R. Lyall's chapter in N. Macdougall (ed.), *Church, Politics and Society: Scotland 1408–1929* (Edinburgh, 1983), 44–64.

[5] This is not, however, a distinction to be drawn too sharply: if it were, the attempt to bring the material examined in this chapter within the sphere of 'political discourse' would be self-defeating.

in the field of royal governance; and they are indeed problems inevitably met with in any account of the reign of James III. Justice, the administration, maladministration, or denial of justice, is a common theme throughout this material. In the first of the three tales told in the *Thre Prestis*, for instance, the king asks the nobility why the realm no longer has 'worthie Lords . . . full of fredome worship and honour'. The answer is that the fault lies in the arrogance and rapacity of the king's justices. This impoverishes the husbandmen who are both the lords' tenants and their followers in the king's service in time of war. The lords themselves, impoverished in their turn, 'sel thair Sonnes and aires for gold' in marriages with families that 'wist neuer yit of honour nor gentryse'. The king's response is to undertake that his itinerant justices shall in future be accompanied by a 'Doctour'

> That lufis God, his saul and our honour,
> The quhilk sal be and Doctour in the Law . . .

who will ensure that justice is administered equitably and without extortion.[6]

Another problematic aspect of criminal justice is one of the themes handled in the second tale in the *Thre Prestis*; and here the king is still more directly involved, for the issue is the use and misuse of the royal prerogative of pardon. The King is admonished by Fictus ('a Clark of greit science' disguised as a court jester) that by pardoning a murderer who goes on to commit the crime again twice over, he has rendered himself guiltier of the second and third crimes than the actual criminal. When this view is confirmed in parliament,

> The King sweir be his Sceptour and his Croun
> That he sould neuer gif mercie to nane
> That slauchter in his Realme committit than.[7]

In Henryson's 'Taill of the Scheip and the Doig', the theme is the perversion of civil justice. The sheep represents 'pure commounis, that daylie ar opprest'. The dog, who brings the action for recovery, is poor too; but his poverty cannot be seen as

---

[6] Robb edn., 9, 19–23. The suggestion (Macdougall, *James III*, 271) that the 'Doctour in the Law' of l. 343 'points unmistakably to Dr. John Ireland' is interesting in view of Ireland's judicial activity. There is of course the difficulty that Ireland's doctorate was in theology, not law; but Henryson, if he knew of Ireland, may not have been aware of that.

[7] Robb edn., 38, ll. 802–4.

having 'Justifyit the wrangous Jugement'. The substantive wrong was done, from the bench, by the wolf—'ane Schiref stout', who 'hes with him ane cursit Assyis about': his accomplices include the raven as 'Crownair', the fox as 'Clerk and Noter', the kite and the crow as 'Advocatis expert in the Lawis', and the bear and the badger as 'Arbeteris' to determine whether the sheep must answer before a hostile court. His plea against 'ane Juge suspect' is denied, judgement is given against him, and he is obliged to sell the wool off his back to pay what is held to be due to the dog. Henryson's indictment is plain enough, but he proffers no remedy other than prayer and resignation;

> We pure pepill as now may do no moir
> But pray to the, sen that we ar opprest
> In to this eirth, grant us in hevin gude rest.[8]

On broader issues of government and policy these vernacular writers also have something to say. In *The Thre Prestis of Peblis* there is even some institutional material, though it may be doubted whether much can be made of this on such technical points as the functioning of parliament and the king's council.[9] The subject of counsel, however, is a recurrent one, and there appear to be fairly clear references to what some saw as James III's deficiencies in this respect. The second tale in *The Thre Prestis*, one element in which has already been considered, is much concerned with the evils that follow when a king is guided, not by 'sad counsel or sage' but by 'yong counsel'. And the fact that these evils include his addiction to 'sport and play'—including the delights of 'Lamenry' or wenching—suggest strongly that the writer has in mind the charges that were levelled, justly or otherwise, against James III.[10] The political if not necessarily the moral remedy is, of course, that the king should turn to his natural counsellors. Thus the abuses of the prerogative of pardon are set right in parliament; and the estates (where the 'concordant vnitie' of the realm is to be found) are to determine

> Quhat man in hous war meit with him to dwell
> Of wisdome for to gif him counsel.[11]

---

[8] Wood edn., 42–8.
[9] For an attempt to develop such points see T. D. Robb's introduction to his edn., pp. xxxii–xxxix.
[10] Ibid. 38–44.   [11] Ibid. 38, ll. 797–8.

Yet to counsel was not to command. Command, *imperium*—the 'fre impyre' asserted in the name of James III in 1469—was proper to the king alone. In Henryson's 'Taill of the Lyon and the Mous' it is the lion who represents the king, whose power may at times lie dormant—as when the lion sleeps and the mice can play freely over him—without, however, losing thereby any of its force or the fear it should inspire. Even—the captive mouse is sternly told by the now waking lion—even if what appeared to be his sleeping body had been no more than his skin stuffed with straw,

> Because it bare the prent off my persoun,
> Thow suld ffor ffeir on kneis have fallin doun.[12]

It may be building too much upon a narrow base to suggest that this imagery implies a 'divine right' view of kingship; and in any case such a formulation may lack adequate precision.[13] Certainly, however, Henryson seems to be concerned to emphasize the power and majesty, the 'excellence' and 'Celsitude' of the king. Yet he also acknowledges that this power may be abused. When 'the Lyon held to hunt . . . And slew baith tayme and wyld' (perhaps a reference to James III's alleged harrying of *Scoti domestici* and *Scoti sylvestres* alike) he became 'This cruell Lyon'. Here we have tyranny and oppression, not by the king's judges or other officers, but by the king himself: what is to be done about it?

The answer, in Henryson's fable, is that 'the pepill fand the way'—a way to capture and tie up the lion; and that is what they did. This, however, is no simple allegory of 'resistance theory': the mice, led by him whose life had been spared by the royal prerogative of pardon, release the lion from his bonds.[14] The ambiguities are scarcely resolved by the *moralitas* Henryson appends to the fable. The king is rebuked in so far as he 'lyis still in lustis, sleuth, and sleip'; but so too are his subjects—

> Wantoun, unwyse, without correctioun:
> Thair Lordis and Princis quhen that thay se
> Of Justice mak nane executioun,
> Thay dreid na thing to mak Rebellioun . . .

And the fact that a king 'May be overthrawin, destroyit, and put

---

[12] Wood edn., 52, ll. 1452–3.

[13] J. MacQueen, *Robert Henryson: A Study of the Major Narrative Poems* (Oxford, 1972), 172; and cf. Macdougall, *James III*, 273.

[14] Wood edn., 54–6.

doun' is attributed to Fortune, 'quhilk of all variance Is haill maistres'.[15] That Henryson in all this had in mind James III and his vicissitudes in 1482 is more than likely; but his attitude to those events is a good deal less than unequivocal.[16]

The image of kingship in these late fifteenth-century texts is thus a complex and perhaps at times an ambiguous one. Yet it may not be too far from 'the substance of things hoped for' by articulate Scots as they looked towards the throne. The king they hoped (or perhaps in some cases feared) to see was 'ane strang Lyoun', whose power might indeed be abused (and might *in extremis* have to be restrained), but who could yet cause even more harm by sloth and negligence, by misplaced leniency, and by failing to give effect to law and justice. To ensure the due exercise of his authority such a king needed wise counsel; and this he should seek especially from the estates of the realm in parliament, where above all the 'concordant vnitie' of the realm could be expressed.

From the pen of Sir David Lindsay of the Mount (1486–1555) we have a substantial series of works written over a quarter of a century and more and spanning both the personal reign of James V and the first dozen years of his daughter's minority. Judgements as to the literary quality of these works will inevitably vary, though current opinion would doubtless incline more towards the view of Lindsay as 'the greatest makar of his day' than towards that which dismissed his work as 'verse rather than poetry'.[17] What is of more immediate concern here is the fact that Lindsay was so largely concerned with public issues—with the social and political problems of his native country and the means by which these problems might be solved. It is also important to bear in mind that the views he expressed were those of one who, from early manhood onwards until at least the last decade or so of

[15] Ibid. 56–7.

[16] The attempt by Nicholson (*Later Middle Ages*, 509) to establish a very precise parallelism may be contrasted with Wood's brusquely dismissive judgement: 'Attempts to identify these lines with any particular historical events have been, and are bound to be, futile' (Wood edn., 243). The truth probably lies between the two extremes.

[17] The former view is that of Wormald, *Court, Kirk, and Community*, 65; the latter, that of J. Craigie, *Chambers's Encyclopaedia*, 1955 edn., viii. 744 (s.v. 'Lyndsay'). On Lindsay's career see esp. D. Hamer (ed.), *The Works of Sir David Lindsay of the Mount 1490–1555*, 4 vols. (Scottish Text Society; Edinburgh, 1931–6, hereafter Hamer edn.), i, pp. ix–xl.

his life, was close to the summit of public life. As tutor to the young James V, as diplomat, as Lyon King of Arms, Lindsay was at least as close to the person of his king as John Ireland had been (and for a longer period) and much more intimately concerned with issues of policy and governance. It need come as no surprise, therefore, to find him, from the outset, handling themes similar to those we have encountered in his vernacular predecessors, but handling them in a perspective of broader experience, and with correspondingly greater depth and elaboration.

Already in 1528, when James V, now 16, was just beginning to exercise something like effective personal authority, *The Dreme of Schir Dauid Lyndesay* took up the crucial issue of justice and its effective execution. Why do the Scots 'want Iustice and polycie More than dois France, Italie, or Ingland?' The reason is found 'in to the heid'—

> For, quhen the heddis ar nocht delygent
> The membris man, on neid, be necligent.

The fault lies with the 'Prencis', who, charged with 'the Gubernatioun . . . of the peple', should have the execution of justice as their constant preoccupation. The use of the plural here does, to be sure, suggest that the target is not so much the young king as those 'infatuate heidis Insolent' who have ruled during his nonage. But the contrasting portrayals of 'the sleuthful hird' and 'the gude hird' suggest that the king's essential role as *pastor* and *rector* is also in Lindsay's mind.[18] When the text moves on to the complaint of 'Ihone the comoun weill', again, Lindsay seems to 'look before and after'. On the one hand, 'polecey is fled agane in France', and

> I se, rycht weill, that prouerbe is full trew,
> Wo to the realme that hes ouir young ane king.[19]

The hope, however, is that James will henceforth rule the realm in unity and peace; and the *Dreme* ends with an 'Exhortation to the Kyngis Grace', in which, perhaps, one passage stands out amid the predictable injunctions to cultivate the cardinal virtues and 'Do equale Iustice boith to gret and small':

---

[18] Hamer edn., 30–1. On the king as *pastor* and *rector* see J. H. Burns, *Lordship, Kingship, and Empire*, 154.

[19] Hamer edn., i. 34, ll. 1010–11.

> Remember of thy freindis the fatell end,
> Quhilks to gude counsall wald not condiscend,
> Tyll bitter deith, allace, did thame persew.

It is at least tempting to see in this an ominous reference to the fate of the king's grandfather, James III.[20]

The reign of James III is in any case unequivocally touched on in Lindsay's next major work, *The Testament of the Papyngo*, which dates from 1530. It is there indeed that Lindsay makes his contribution to the 'legend' of James's 'low-born favourites' and their malign influence.[21] It is there that he gives graphic expression to the disaster at Sauchieburn—

> At morne, ane king with sceptour, sweird, and croun;
> Att ewin, ane dede deformit carioun.

In the present context, however, nothing is added to the familiar point that James's downfall came about because 'prudent Lordis counsall wes refusit'.[22] Even James IV—who was, for Lindsay, 'the glore of princelie gouernyng'—was ruined 'be his awin wylfull mysgouernance' in rejecting wise counsel. Yet, flawed though his achievement was by the fatal misjudgement which led to the catastrophe at Flodden, James is still Lindsay's ideal of what a king—and specifically a king of Scots—should be. He was, for Lindsay, 'that rycht redoutit Roye, That potent prince'—

> Duryng his tyme so Iustice did preuaill
> The Sauage Ilis trymblit for terrour;
> Eskdale, Euisdale, Liddisdale, and Annerdale
> Durst nocht rebell, douting his dyntis dour[23]

The picture of a strong king, enjoying the 'perfyte fauour' of the nobility and maintaining a court of which 'throuch Europe sprang the fame', is sharply contrasted with the situation during his son's minority. Then 'Diuers rewlatris maid diuers ordinance', with the result

> That few or none stude of ane vther aw.
> Oppressioun did so lowde his bugyll blaw.[24]

---

[20] Ibid. 37, ll. 1114–16. The reference could, however, be to James IV and the ill-advised Flodden campaign.
[21] See on this Macdougall, *James III*, 278–9.   [22] Hamer edn., i. 69–70.
[23] Ibid. 70–1.   [24] Ibid. 71–2.

There was, then much to be amended in the government of Scotland when James V began to rule as well as reign, and we may suppose that Lindsay had great expectations in this regard. We can be sure that he heartily endorsed much of what James attempted and achieved: the firm, even severe, enforcement of order (a policy of which the hanging of Johnnie Armstrong in 1530 was a forceful opening statement); the regular administration of justice; and, generally, those aspects of James's character and conduct which led to his being seen as 'the carlis king'.[25] On the other hand, if Lindsay had criticisms of royal policy he might have hesitated to voice them. It was one thing to rail mockingly at James's personal morals (as in *The Answer to the Kingis Flyting*, written in 1535 or 1536); to censure his conduct of affairs, as Lindsay had retrospectively censured previous kings and those who ruled during James's minority, might have been another matter. In fact we do not have all the evidence on this point that we might have had. The text of the first version of Lindsay's masterpiece, *Ane Satyre of the Thrie Estaitis*, performed at Linlithgow on the Feast of the Epiphany in 1540, has not been preserved. The two texts we do have—to be considered presently—date from the early 1550s; and by then, other considerations apart, Lindsay was preponderantly concerned with the reform of abuses in the church. That this was already prominent among his concerns in the reign of James V is, to be sure, entirely clear. Yet the account of the 1540 *Thrie Estaitis* given to Sir William Eure and reported by him to Thomas Cromwell may suggest that the balance in that text was somewhat different. There can be no certainty as to this. However, bearing in mind the fact that, as Eure's letter to Cromwell makes clear, the primary purpose of the communication was to emphasize what was believed to be James V's commitment to 'reformacion of spiritualtie',[26] it is remarkable how much attention is paid to temporal matters in the account of Lindsay's 'interluyde'. Something approaching half of the report of the 'hevie complaynte' made by the 'poor Man whoe did goe vpe and downe the scaffald' is concerned with his having

[25] The tradition that saw James V as 'the poor man's king' is viewed sceptically by e.g. Donaldson, *James V to James VII*, 56 (who none the less acknowledges that 'James's very severity to malefactors may have made him loved by the law-abiding'). It is of some interest that the phrase 'the carlis king' is preserved by William Barclay in his *De regno et regali potestate* (Paris, 1600), 229.

[26] Hamer edn., ii. 5. For the 1540 version generally see ibid. 1–6.

been, in common with 'many thousaund in scotlande', oppressed and impoverished by 'the courtiours taking his fewe [feu] in one place and also his tackes in an other place'. And for this, he continued, 'thair was noe remedye to be gotten, for thoughe he wolde suyte to the kingis grace, he was naither acquainted with controuller nor treasurer, and withoute thaym myght noe man gete noe goodenes of the king'.

It is also noteworthy—although the precise significance of the point may be debatable—that Lindsay evidently took care to distinguish between the king in the audience and the king on the stage. The king before whom the complaint is laid was, the poor man insisted, 'not the king of scotlande, for ther was an other king in scotlande that hanged John Armestrang with his fellowes . . . and many other moe, which had pacified the countrey and stanched thifte'. This provides the cue to introduce the theme of ecclesiastical reform; for this was the thing that James had neglected. Yet, however we are to interpret this passage, it is hard to resist the conclusion that, albeit indirectly, Lindsay *was* criticizing adversely some aspects at least of James's governance—certainly, but perhaps not only, his backwardness in dealing with the faults of the church.

Not for a dozen years after the performance at Linlithgow do we have further evidence to consider; for Lindsay's writings in that period are not concerned with issues that are relevant here. It is true that in his substantial poetic essay in 'universal history', known as *The Monarche*, dating from the years 1550–2, there are, so to speak, political *obiter dicta*. More than that, there is a fairly elaborate attack on the temporal power of the papacy.[27] Themes that concern us, however, are resumed at length only with the two versions of *Ane Satyre of the Thrie Estaitis* performed, at Cupar and Edinburgh respectively, in 1552 and 1554.[28]

The change in circumstances over the dozen years between the first and second performances of Lindsay's play had of course

[27] Ibid. i. 325–46. It is perhaps just worth emphasizing that when *Ane Dialogue betuix Experience and ane Courteour, Of the Miserabyll Estait of the Warld* is referred to as *The Monarche*, the noun is equivalent, not to 'Monarch', but to 'Monarchy'. Lindsay's universal history is presented in the traditional framework of the four 'monarchies' that have successively ruled, the world, with the usurped power of the papacy as the fifth.

[28] Parallel texts of the 1552 and 1554 versions are printed on facing pages, Hamer edn., ii. 8–405. References below are throughout to the fuller, 1554 text.

been dramatic, England had moved to a decisively Protestant religious settlement; but, so far as Scotland was concerned, the project of an enforced marriage between the child queen Mary and her English cousin Edward VI had been defeated. The queen was now in France, on whose military aid against England the realm was again dependent. On the other hand, the movement for reform of the church, tending increasingly towards Protestant doctrine as well as long familiar anti-clericalism, had gathered strength; and, as regents, neither the earl of Arran nor the queen dowager, Mary of Guise (who succeeded him in April 1554), could be said to have been wholly unambiguous in their attitudes towards the religious issue. Lindsay himself, it seems clear, had become increasingly preoccupied by abuses in the church. In consequence, much of the expanded version of his *Thrie Estaitis* is given over to anti-clerical satire which does not contribute to the present investigation. Other issues are dealt with, however, and certainly these texts are too substantial to be ignored, even though the discussion of them here will necessarily be selective.

The king, in this developed presentation of Lindsay's *Satyre*, is no longer the silent and formal figure of the 1540 version. As *Rex Humanitas*, he is the pivot on which the action turns. It is true that the work as a whole is essentially a series of loosely linked episodes, ranging in character from moral allegory to the grossest of low comedy. Yet it does have a central theme, if hardly a plot. The theme is the transformation of the king from the plaything of Solace and Wantonnes and the dupe of Flatterie, Falset [Falsehood], and Dissait [Deceit] into the client of Gude-counsall, the instrument and ally of Divyne Correction. In counterpoint with this, in the parts of the text where the full thrust of Lindsay's satire is to be felt, we have the figure of Johne the Commoun Weill and the spectacle of the Thrie Estaitis, who at first appear '*gangand backwart led be thair vyces*'.[29] The problem, then, is not simply to induce the king to heed wise counsel and use his power to correct abuses: the abuses affect all the estates of the realm, and the king is urged—

> Syne them reforme as ye think best
> Sua that the Realme may liue in rest,
> According to Gods lawis.[30]

---

[29] Hamer edn., ii. 225.
[30] Ibid. 229, ll. 2349–51.

The foundation for reform has already been laid by Divyne Correctioun, heralded by his Varlet and welcomed by Gude-counsall. The moment is marked by a clear statement of the nature and purpose of kingship:

> Quhat is ane King? nocht but ane officiar,
> To caus his Leiges liue in equitie:
> And vnder God to be ane punischer
> Of trespassours against his Maiestie.[31]

These lines are spoken by Divyne Correctioun; and the sermon is continued by Gude-counsall, now admitted to the royal presence:

> The principall point Sir of ane kings office,
> Is for to do to euerilk man iustice,
> And for to mix his iustice with mercie,
> But rigour, fauour or parcialitie.[32]

It is noteworthy that Lindsay represents the king as no more than an 'officiar'; but of course his office is divinely ordained:

> For ye ar bot ane mortall instrument
> To that great God and King Omnipotent,
> Preordinat be his divine Maiestie,
> To reull his peopill intill vnitie.[33]

This phase of the action ends when Diligence, the king's herald, summons 'all members of Parliament, Baith spirituall stait and Temporalite' to 'speid them to the Court'.[34] After the interval, the king greets the assembled estates:

> Welcum to me my prudent Lord[i]s all,
> Ye ar my members suppois I be your head:
> Sit doun that we may with your iust counsall,
> Aganis misdoars find soueraine remeid.
> We sall nocht spair for fauour not for feid,
> With your avice to mak punitioun,
> And put my sword to executioun.

Against this programme, however, the Spiritualitie object—

---

[31] Ibid. 167, ll. 1605–8.

[32] Ibid. 187, ll. 1882–5. To refer to these speeches as sermons seems entirely apt: both Divyne Correctioun and Gude-counsall begin with scriptural texts—respectively, *Beati qui esuriunt & sitiunt Iustitiam* (Matt. 5: 6) and *Initium sapientiae est timor Domini* (Ps. 111: 10; Prov. 9: 10). One is reminded of the Gerson sermons drawn upon by John Ireland.

[33] Hamer edn., 187, ll. 1878–81.   [34] Ibid. 189.

> For quhy? the peopill of this Regioun
> May nocht indure extreme correctioun.

But Divyne Correctioun insists 'That euerilk man opprest geif in his Bill'; and that is the cue for 'Iohne the common-weil of fair Scotland' to make his entrance.[35]

The burden of the 'Bill' of complaint is that 'the common-weill hes bene overlukit' because 'the thrie estaits gangs all backwart'. This in turn is because there has been misguidance at every turn and on all levels. The Spiritualitie 'ar led be Couetice and cairles Sensualitie'. The Temporalitie (that is to say, the nobles) 'hes lang tyme bene led be publick oppressioun'. As for the third estate, 'Falset and Dissait' are the 'Leiders of the merchants and sillie crafts-men'. Meanwhile 'Flattrie . . . wes guyder of the Court', so that 'we gat litill grace'.[36] The first task, accordingly, is to drive these vices from their entrenched positions. Only when they have been put in the stocks can the estates (or two of them, at all events: the spiritual estate is represented throughout as stubbornly opposed to reform) turn to Gude-counsall for guidance in drafting

> Sic actis that with gude men be praysit,
> Conforming to the common law.[37]

At the same time the 'poor Man' of the 1540 text reappears as Pauper (or Poverte) and adds his voice to those of Gude-counsall and Johne the Common-weill. All agree in urging a reform of land-tenure to ensure that 'husband-men may . . . hald thair awin', as they cannot do at present. This is coupled with vigorous condemnation of 'idill men . . . strang beggers' and, inevitably,

> thir great fat Freiris,
> Augustenes, Carmleits and Cordeleiris,
> And all vthers that in cowls bene cled,
> Quhilk labours nocht and bene weill fed.[38]

Lindsay's vehement anti-clericalism is unflagging throughout this part of the *Satyre*, but the church does not monopolize his attention. 'The misusing of Iustice airis' is also condemned, on the ground that petty thieves are hanged, while

> he that all the warld hes wrangit,
> Ane cruel tyrane, ane strang transgresour,

[35] Hamer edn., 231, 233.   [36] Ibid. 237, 239.   [37] Ibid. 245, ll. 2518–19.
[38] Ibid. 247, 249, 251.

> Ane common publick plaine oppressour,
> By buds [bribes] may he obteine fauours
> Of Tresurers and compositours[39]

Divyne Correctioun promises 'reformatioun', urging the temporal lords to 'Expell oppressioun', the merchants to shun 'Dissait', and the spiritual estate to

> Set in few [feu] your temporall lands,
> To men that labours with thair hands
>
> .   .   .   .   .   .
>
> Quhair throch the policy may incresse.[40]

To all this the two temporal estates agree (subject, on the part of the nobles, to the king's granting 'ane remissioun' for their past offences), and, as the stage direction states, '*Heir sall the temporal staits, to wit, the Lords and merchands imbreasse Iohne the Commoun-weill*'.[41]

The Spiritualitie, needless to say, will have nothing to do with reform, claiming in any case 'exemptioun, | For all your temporall punicioun'. Strikingly, Divyne Correctioun's response is to exclaim, 'ye think to stryue for stait'.[42] And a prominent theme in what follows is a strong insistence on the king's right and duty to take order with the church. Whatever is to be made of Lindsay's own religious position at this late stage in his life, there can be no doubt that he here anticipates what was being said only a few years later by such Protestant leaders as John Knox. Where Knox, however, had (as we shall see) grave doubts as to whether effective action could be expected from the crown, it is entirely in that direction that Lindsay's hopes lie. He recognizes, to be sure, and indeed insists on the fact that royal power had sometimes been abused in this respect. In a celebrated passage he attacks the misguided 'devotioun' of David I in lavishly endowing religious foundations—

> King Iames the first Roy of this Regioun
> Said that he was ane sair Sanct to the croun.

The true function of the king, however, guided by the 'rype advisement' of the estates, is to bear in mind that

---

[39] Ibid. 253, 255.   [40] Ibid. 255, ll. 2671–88.   [41] Ibid. 259.
[42] Ibid. 257, ll. 2699–700, 2702. The use of the term 'stait' here is of some interest, with its clear implication that what is at issue is, as we might say, the 'sovereignty' of 'the state'.

> Ane Bischops office is for to be ane preichour,
> And of the law of God ane publick teachour.
> Rycht sa the Persone vnto his parochoun
> Of the Evangell sould leir them ane lessoun.[43]

Only those properly qualified for these duties should be promoted to ecclesiastical office; and it is clearly implied that these appointments are to be in the king's hands. The proposal is

> That the Kings grace sall gif na benefice
> Bot to ane p[r]eichour that can vse that office;

and also

> . . . that thir kings man take it in thair heid
> That thair be giuen to na man bischopries,
> Except thay preich out throch thair diosies.[44]

Abuses of ecclesiastical power are firmly laid at the king's door:

> Alace, alace, quhat gars thir temporal Kings
> Into the Kirk of Christ admit sic things?[45]

And what the king has, for whatever reason, allowed to go amiss he must evidently undertake to set right.

Expert assistance in the work of reform is summoned, when Diligence is dispatched to

> . . . seik out throw all towns and cities
> And visie all the vniuersities,
> Bring us sum Doctours of Divinitie,
> With licents in the law and Theologie[46]

and returns with 'ane Doctour of Divinitie' and 'twa Licents' and the comment

> I heare men say thair conversatioun,
> Is maist in Divine Contemplatioun.[47]

Yet the essential responsibility remains with the king. Divyne Correctioun gives him 'baith counsel & Command' to 'vse exercitioun'—to put his royal power into effect:

---

[43] Hamer edn., 281, ll. 2976–7; 275, ll. 2899–902.
[44] Ibid. 287, ll. 3035–6, 3044–6.   [45] Ibid. 297, ll. 3153–4.
[46] Ibid. 297, ll. 3163–6.   [47] Ibid. 309, ll. 3309–12.

> Ye ar the head sir of this congregatioun,
> Preordinat be God omnipotent
>
> .   .   .   .
>
> And quha saever beis inobedient,
> And will nocht suffer for to be correctit,
> They salbe all deposit incontinent,
> And from your presence they sall be deiectit.[48]

The general principle here is duly applied in practice: the three bishops representing the spiritual estate are 'deprivit' and replaced by the 'thrie cunning Clark[i]s sapient'. Having vainly protested that 'sic reformatioun . . . Into Scotland was neuer hard nor seine', the deprived prelates first *'pas to Sensualitie'* and finally *'depairts altogidder'* with the abbot, the parson, and the prioress.[49] Their disgrace is in contrast with the fate of Johne the Commonweil, whose rags are replaced by 'ane new abuilyment, | Of Sating, Damais or of the Velvot fyne' and who—significantly—is given 'place in our Parliament'.[50] The scene is now set for the solemn proclamation of 'The Nobil Act[i]s of our Parliament', of which fifteen are promulgated. Only a few points in this 'legislation' call for notice here. 'The Kirk of Christ and his Religioun' are to be defended. It is laid down that 'the Act[i]s honorabill | Maid be our Prince in the last Parliament' are to be faithfully observed: it is not clear what Lindsay had in mind here, but at least the provision underlines the point that for him law is made by the king 'in parliament'. The third act prescribes that 'all the Temporall lands | Be set in few [feu] efter the forme of France'.[51] There are highly specific arrangements for the organization of the judiciary. Permanent courts, each with sixteen 'senators', are to sit in Edinburgh and, for 'all the Norther Airtis', in Elgin or Inverness. The judges are to be

> Chosen without partiall affectioun
> Of the maist cunning Clarks of this Regioun:
> Thair Chancellar chosen of ane famous Clark,
> Ane cunning man of great perfectioun[52]

The remaining acts, taken up largely with the reform of the church, need not be examined closely here. What is striking about

---

[48] Ibid. 311, ll. 3329–30, 3333–6.   [49] Ibid. 341, 343, 345.
[50] Ibid. 345, ll. 3770–2.   [51] Ibid. 347.   [52] Ibid. 349, 351.

them, however, is, once again, the extent to which Lindsay sees
this as a legitimate and indeed essential use of the royal power of
legislation. He does not deny that there is a place for spiritual
judges and jurisdiction; but he allows no room for the kind of
clerical immunity or ecclesiastical independence that had prevailed in the past. Here we have a king in parliament envisaged as
legislating against plurality in the holding of benefices,

> Twa Prelacies sall na man haue from thence
> Without that he be of the blude Royall . . .[53]

where one may wonder whether realism or satire inspired the
second line. Legislation is also to keep bishops in their dioceses
and priests in their parishes, where—again with legislative sanction—priests and bishops alike have the king's

> licence and frie libertie
> That thay may haue fair Virgins to thair wyfis
> And sa keip matrimoniall Chastitie
> And nocht in huirdome for to leid thair lyfis.[54]

There may be no explicit reference to 'royal supremacy' over the
church; but the substance of such an authority is emphatically
present, and indeed central, in what Lindsay's *Satyre* recommends as the remedy for the ills he has diagnosed.

With the ceremonial process of lawmaking completed, the remainder of the play is given over to more or less black comedy:
the hanging, at Pauper's request, of the vices; and the final encounter between the King and his herald on the one hand and, on
the other, Folie—who asks, mockingly,

> The King, quhat kynde of thing is that?
> Is yon he with the goldin Hat?[55]

Only two points from these closing scenes need be noted here.
First, when Falset is about to be hanged, he seeks to draw along
with him all the many characters who have employed falsehood;
and among others—

> Cum follow me all catyfe covetous Kings,
> Reauers but richt of vthers Realmis and Ringis [Reigns],
> Togidder with all wrangous conquerours
> And bring with yow all publick oppressours.[56]

---

[53] Hamer edn., 353, ll. 3895–6.   [54] Ibid. 353, 355, ll. 3924–7.
[55] Ibid. 379, ll. 4316–17.   [56] Ibid. 373, ll. 4206–7.

Again, when Folie has been given leave 'to speik of Kings', he uses the opportunity to condemn 'princelie and imperiall fuillis':

> The pryde of Princes withoutin faill
> Gars all the warld rin top ovir taill.
> To win them warldlie gloir and gude,
> They cure nocht schedding of saikles blude.

Scotland and England, France and the Empire, Spain, the Pope— all stand condemned:

> They leird nocht this at Christis Scuillis;
> Thairfoir I think them verie fuillis.[57]

Thus kings who are usurpers or conquerors or who otherwise stir up conflict and bloodshed are condemned. Otherwise, however, it is clear that Lindsay's criticism of rulers is directed, not at their positive and oppressive misrule, but at their indolence, their self-indulgence, their appetite for flattery, their disregard of wise counsel. The tyrants who are repeatedly mentioned and condemned in the *Thrie Estaitis* are not kings to be resisted and deposed: they are those within the realm whose excessive power, greed, and cruelty rage unchecked by the king, so that the commonwealth is neglected and the king's humble subjects are reduced to penury. The remedy for this is good governance; and that is the focal point in Lindsay's picture of kingship. Given the nature of his work, with *Ane Satyre of the Thrie Estaitis* as its culminating achievement, it is indeed a *picture* we find there, and neither a theory of government nor an analysis of institutions. The picture is no doubt conventional enough, even if the colours in which it is painted are more vivid than those to be found in more pedestrian 'mirrors of princes'. Yet there may be a little more to be said in the present context before leaving this part of the subject.

There is, after all, an institutional dimension to Lindsay's work; and while this may be of secondary importance in literary terms, yet (like the architectural detail in the background of some paintings of the period) it has a degree of real interest. It is clear, for one thing, that Lindsay had certain specific views as to the administration of justice and the organization of the judiciary.[58] And if there is nothing so explicit in regard to the conciliar element in

---

[57] Ibid. 401, ll. 4560–3, 4584–5.   [58] Ibid. 349–51.

government (Gude-counsall remaining a purely symbolic figure), the recurrent insistence on the role of the estates is not significant only for the pageantry of the play. Lindsay clearly regards the parliamentary assembly as the embodiment of the community of the realm. The king is, of course, its head, and there is no suggestion that anyone but the king could give 'exercitioun' to the powers of government. Nor, however, is there any suggestion that the major reforms Lindsay is urging could be brought about except 'by and with the advice and consent' of the estates. The consent, it is true, need not be unanimous. The obdurate refusal of the spiritual estate to accept 'correctioun' is met, strikingly, by the assertion of a form of 'majority rule', when Temporalitie declares:

> Wee set nocht by quhidder ye consent or nocht:
> Ye ar bot ane estait and we ar twa,
> *Et vbi maior pars ibi tota.*[59]

The devaluing (or worse) of the spiritual lords necessarily enhances the importance of the third estate; and it is worth considering briefly the part they play in Lindsay's account.

The medieval Scottish answer to the Abbé Siéyès's question, *Qu'est-ce que le Tiers Etat?* was straightforward: the third estate consisted of burgh representatives—specifically and all but exclusively, representatives of royal burghs. Even on this basis representation of the 'commons' had been limited, and it has been argued that the burgesses as a parliamentary force were under pressure and had suffered some decline during the reign of James III.[60] It would doubtless be going too far to suggest that Lindsay seeks to advance the claims of the burgesses. Yet, as has been pointed out, their importance for him is emphasized by the default of the spiritual estate; and they are certainly given their fair share in the debate Lindsay portrays. Their representative is a 'Merchand', and it is above all the trading interests of the towns that he voices:

> Sir we ar heir your Burgessis and Marchands.
> Thanks be to God that we may se your face,
> Traistand wee may now into diuers lands
> Convoy our geir with support of your grace:

---

[59] Hamer edn., ii. 269, ll. 2834–6.   [60] Nicholson, *Later Middle Ages*, 452–3.

> For now I traist wee sall get rest and peace.
> Quhen misdoars ar with your sword overthrawin
> Then may leil merchands liue vpon thair awin.[61]

Their interests, however, involve a sharp clash with the corrupt interests of churchmen; and the Merchand is given a considerable say in the attack on the abuse of the temporal wealth of the church and upon the flow of money to the papal court—

> For we merchants I wait within our bounds,
> Hes furneist Preists ten hundreth thowsand punds.[62]

Again it is the Merchand who voices one of the sharpest attacks on the failure of bishops and priests to discharge their spiritual responsibilities:

> The sillie sauls that bene Christis scheip
> Suld nocht be givin to gormand wolfis to keip.[63]

When we consider, further, that, in comparison with the other estates, the deficiencies of the burgesses are somewhat lightly touched on, we may well conclude that the third estate carries its full weight in Lindsay's conception of a well-ordered realm.

It remains to comment on the dramatic moment when '*thay cleith Iohne the common-weil gorgeouslie and set him doun amang them in the Parliament*'.[64] This is not, of course, to be interpreted as a symbolic appeal for 'parliamentary reform' in the sense of organic changes in the structure of the estates. Similarly, the role ascribed to Pauper, the poor man, while crucially important, does not, needless to say, imply that Lindsay would have recommended, or could indeed have conceived of, the direct representation in parliament of the 'poor commons'. Yet there is another sense in which representation *is* here seen as subject to reformation—to a process which will restore it to its true character and function. That it is conceived of as *virtual* representation is certainly true, but the essential point remains unaffected. The 'common weil', which includes the interests and welfare of the poor, of 'laboreris with thair hands', of all the king's subjects, is now incorporated into the assembly of the estates. The *res publica* is to be inseparably part of the *corpus mysticum regni*. The three estates, properly understood, are not merely, in Lindsay's vision, estates of the

---

[61] Hamer edn., ii. 229–30, ll. 2366–72.   [62] Ibid. 271, ll. 2849–50.
[63] Ibid. 287, ll. 3036–7.   [64] Ibid. 345.

realm, *status regni*: they are also, more fundamentally, *status reipublicae*. 'Johne the common-weil', gorgeously attired, is not an additional member of the body politic: he is the animating princi-ple giving it life and purpose, and the king is the divinely or-dained 'officiar' to put that purpose into effect.

To turn from Lindsay's *Satyre of the Thrie Estaitis* to *The Complaynt of Scotland* (almost certainly the work of Robert Wedderburn), which antedates by some three to five years the later versions of the *Satyre*, is obviously to move to a very different literary genre.[65] Yet for present purposes there is at least a degree of common ground between the lively if lengthy verse dialogue and the pro-lix prose of the *Complaynt*. In both works the three estates are central: a suggested subtitle for the *Complaynt* is *ane Exortatione to the Thre Estaits to be vigilante in the Deffens of their Public veil*.[66] Here, however, the estates do not figure in their parliamentary role, but simply as the constituent parts of a body politic weakened by their deficiencies at a time when it is threatened by the over-whelming power of 'oure ald enemeis . . . the cruel volffis of ingland'. The shadow of English invasion and the Scottish de-feat at Pinkie (September 1547) hangs heavily over the author. It does not, however, obscure other concerns. There is 'uniuersal pestilens and mortalite'; and—above all for our purposes here—'the contentione of diuerse of the thre esstaitis of scotland' means that 'the uniuersal pepil ar be cum distitute of iustice policie ande of al verteus bysynes of body ande saule'.[67] There is no need here to pursue the intriguing byways into which the text entices the reader. The real and earnest business of the book is resumed with the complaint of 'Dame Scotia' against her three sons, the three estates. The burden of that complaint is that the divisions and dissensions among the estates weaken the realm as a whole so that it is disabled in the struggle against English invasion and

[65] *The Complaynt of Scotland* (c.1550) *by Mr Robert Wedderburn*, ed. A. M. Stewart (Scottish Text Society; Edinburgh, 1979; hereafter Stewart edn.). Earlier editions, still worth consulting, are by J. Leyden (Edinburgh, 1801); and by J. A. H. Murray (Early English Text Society; London, 1872–3, repr. 1891). Stewart (pp. viii–x, xvi–xx) sets out the case for Wedderburn (c.1510–c.1553) as the author and provides (pp. xi–xvi) an account of his life. He also examines (pp. xxi–xxviii) a subject not considered here—Wedderburn's use of his sources, and in particular the question of his extensive 'borrowings'. The problems are analogous to those encountered in regard to the Gerson material in Book VII of Ireland's *Meroure of Wyssdome*.
[66] On the 'subtitle' see *Complaynt*, Stewart edn., p. viii.   [67] Ibid. 1.

oppression. Strikingly, neither the nobility nor the church is given any opportunity for defence or rebuttal of the charges brought against them. The third estate is given a substantial voice; and it is worth noting both the way in which that estate is envisaged and the kind of defence that is proffered.

To start with, it is noteworthy that, in the *Complaynt*, the third estate is emphatically not identified with the burgesses or merchants. It is designated 'Laubir [Labour]' and consistently described as consisting of 'lauberaris to burgh ande land'—those who, in both town and country, work for their living, especially in 'mecanik craftis'. Mercantile activity is mentioned too; but it certainly does not hold the predominant place it had in Lindsay's account of the third estate. This does not mean that the importance of that estate is underrated. It is indeed 'ane notabyl membyr of ane realme, vitht out the quhilk the nobillis & clergie can nocht sustene ther stait nor ther lyif'. As such, the commons deserve better than the 'taxationis, violent spulye [spoliation], and al vthyr sortis of aduersite, quhilk is onmercifully execut daly' by their temporal and spiritual superiors alike.[68] The Romans, we are reminded,

in ald tymes prouidit prudentlie for the deffens of the comont pepil contrar the nobillis, the senat, and al vtheris of grit stait or dignites, and contrar ther extorsions, for thai institut ane nobil man of office, callit tribunus plebis, quha deffendit the fredum and liberte of the comont pepil . . .

'bot allace', Laubir exclaims, 'it is nocht nou of that sort vitht me'. The other estates, while professing to be 'brethir and defendouris' of the commons are in fact 'vrangous oppressouris' more to be feared than the power of England.[69] The grievances detailed in the substantial fifteenth chapter of the *Complaynt* are very much the same as those we have encountered in Lindsay's satire and before him in John Mair's account of Scotland: in particular, the insecurity of tenure and the exaction of constantly increased 'fermis'.[70] And yet, the argument goes on, the estate suffering these wrongs is not only (as we would say) the economic base on which the other estates necessarily depend: it was prior to them and laid the foundation of the entire polity. Commonly regarded as the junior partner—the youngest brother—Laubir claims to be in

[68] Ibid. 97–8.   [69] Ibid. 98.   [70] Ibid. 97.

truth the eldest, 'gottyn and borne lang befor' either the nobles or the spiritual estate—

it vas i that first instituit there [their] faculteis. for the pollice that vas inuentit be me & my predecessouris . . . hes procreat the stait of my brethir. the faculteis and the begynnyng of nobillis and spiritualite, hed bot pure lauboraris to there predecessouris.

Now, upstarts as they are, they hold 'al lauberaris to be rustical and inciuile, ondantit [untamed], ignorant, dullit slauis'.[71] At least, however, the abject condition of the third estate invalidates (Laubir argues) any charge against them of treason such as others have committed; for 'it is nocht possibil that ane pure man can haue oportunite til exsecut ane traisonabil act contrar ane prince'.[72]

This, to be sure, is only one side of the case; and in fact the plea on behalf of the third estate is brusquely and harshly rejected by Dame Scotia. Chapter XVI of the *Complaynt* is a vehement account of plebeian vices:

as sune as ye that ar comont pepil ar onbridilit and furtht of subiectione, your ignorance, inconstance, ande inciuilite pulcis [impels] you to perpetrat intollerabil exactions. for al the insurrectionis that euyr occurrit in ony realme contrar the prince & the public veil, hes procedit of the ignorance & obstinatione of the comount pepil. There for none of you suld haue liberte, bot rather ye suld be daly dantit & haldin in subiectione, be cause that your hartis is ful of maleis ignorance variance & inconstance.[73]

Nor are matters improved when plebeians become wealthy and seek to rise above their station in society; for then

thai be cum mair ambitius ande arrogant, nor ony gentil man, sperutual or temporal . . . and there [their] childir . . . for falt of educatione and eruditione . . . be cum vane, prodig, and arrogant . . . There is nocht ane mair odius thyng in this varld as quhen the successour of ane indigent ignorant mechanyk lauberar ascendis tyl ony dignite abufe his qualite, for incontinent eftir his promotione, he myskennis god ande man.[74]

Paradoxically, then, the third estate, having been allowed to enter a plea in self-defence, fares in some respects worse than either of the others. It is true that when Dame Scotia turns to 'hir

---

[71] Stewart edn., 100–1.   [72] Ibid. 102.
[73] Ibid. 110.   [74] Ibid. 111–12.

eldest sonne callit the nobilis and gentil men', she allows Laubir
the excuse of ignorance—essentially because that excuse is to be
denied to the nobility.[75] And, in a further paradox, a substantial
part of the charge against the first estate is based on a ground
already stated in the plea entered by the third. Arguing on lines
we have already encountered in Mair's writings and elsewhere,
Wedderburn questions the whole basis of hereditary 'nobility'.
Virtue alone—and it is above all martial virtue that is at issue
here—constitutes true nobility, which cannot be inherited: 'ane
person may succeid to heretage and to mouabil gudis of his
predecessours, bot no man can succeid to gentreis nor to vertu':[76]
'ye professe you to be gentil men,' the Scottish nobles are told,

bot your verkis testifeis that ye ar bot inciuile vilainis. ye vald be reput &
callit vertuous & honest, quhou be it that ye did neuyr ane honest act . . . I
see no thing amang [our] gentil men bot vice.[77]

And the denunciation ends with a brisk injunction: 'correct your
selfis of the artiklis of this accusation'.[78] Only in that way can they
earn the honour they claim and discharge their filial obligations to
their native country.

Wedderburn then turns (in a chapter considerably shorter than
that which dealt with the nobility) to the spiritual estate of which
he was himself a member. He gives Dame Scotia two principal
themes. The first, preceded by an emphatic insistence that the
clergy, of all people, can have no plea whatever on the ground of
ignorance, is that the 'lang abusione' which sets the lives of
churchmen at variance with the doctrine they teach must be corrected. Failing such correction, 'scismatikis' will proliferate despite 'statiutis, lauis, punitions, bannessing, byrnyng, hayrschip
[and] torment'.[79] And the spiritual estate have even more reason
than the other two to fear the 'ald enemeis'; for English conquest
would bring upon them the fate suffered by their brethren under
Henry VIII. This, in turn, leads on to the second main theme:
namely, that churchmen—at least 'sa mony . . . that ar defensabil
men'—must not scruple to go to war in person in defence of the
realm. The latter part of the chapter is devoted to satisfying

[75] Ibid. 113: 'the vice of thy yongest brother suld be supportit be rason of his
ignorance and of his pouerte bot thou can haue na excusatione to collour thy
mischeuous conuersation ande the violent extorsions that thou daly committis
contrar thy tua brethyr, lauberaris & clergie.'
[76] Ibid. 119.   [77] Ibid. 122.   [78] Ibid. 123.   [79] Ibid. 125–7.

'scrupulus consciens' on this point, especially by reference to the provisions of the canon law; '& than doutles your faculte sal nocht be spulyeit fra the liberte that it possessis'.[80]

The final chapter, with its review of the self-destructive divisions prevailing in a country plagued by every kind of war known to the ancient Romans, and its desperate appeal for 'ane faythful accord' among the three estates, need not be more closely examined here. What is needed is rather to look back at the *Complaynt* as a whole and to locate it in relation to the other examples of political discourse considered here so far. This is by no means a straightforward task. For one thing, if we ask what part is played in this text by kings and kingship, the answer will be limited and largely negative. Kings are indeed mentioned repeatedly; but, when they are not the kings of ancient history, cited for exemplary purposes, they are mostly the kings of England, figuring of course as the villains of the piece. By the same token, when tyranny is mentioned, it is above all the usurping tyranny of unjust English invaders. The problems with which Wedderburn is concerned are indeed problems of 'misgovernance'; but it is, so to speak, the self-misgovernance of nobles, churchmen, and commons alike, in their various ways, that creates the problems. Nor is the solution to be found in 'good governance' from above; it lies in individual and collective self-reformation from within. If there is to be leadership—and the commons especially are depicted in such a way as to suggest that there must be—then it may be said to take one of two forms. A reformed nobility and gentry would presumably be responsible for maintaining discipline over the volatile and untrustworthy plebeians; and—this is perhaps especially important—a reformed (but still Catholic) church would lead by example as well as by precept.

It is hard not to see this, in its mid-sixteenth-century setting, as *Hamlet* without the Prince of Denmark. And indeed the existence of a prince (or princess) is assumed and recognized as an essential part of a community which is, after all, envisaged throughout as a *realm*. Yet here the prince (the king or queen) does not play the part—or any of the parts—commonly attributed to sovereigns in early-modern political discourse. For this there are, no doubt, circumstantial reasons. Scottish kingship was in abeyance, so to

---

[80] Stewart edn., 127–30.

speak, or in commission when the *Complaynt* was written. The authority of the crown, with a child queen absent in France, was represented by a regent, the earl of Arran. And there is in fact one reference in the text to that fact: it is 'my lord gouuernour' whom 'the nobil lordis and barrons of scotland', together (Wedderburn hopes) with warrior churchmen, are to follow into battle 'contrar the . . . ald enemeis of ingland'.[81] The book, however, was dedicated, not to Arran, but to his great and eventually successful rival for political power, the queen dowager Mary of Guise. It is clear that this was the direction in which the author looked for leadership in Scotland's crisis: his panegyric dwells upon Mary's 'magnanime auansing of the public veil of the affligit realme of scotlande', on her 'heroyque vertu', on her descent from ancestors illustrious above all for having 'deffendit the liberte of ther subiectis'.[82] He refers too with admiration to Mary's 'regement and gouernyng'; but he could not, in the end, have ignored the fact that however effective her power may already have been, legitimate authority to rule was not yet in her hands.[83] Wedderburn's *Complaynt* was laid before 'the Margareit and Perle of Princessis',[84] but he could not, as matters stood, look to her as the head of a body politic to which firm government would bring the order and coherence he sought. Though the point is not explicitly made in the text, one may surmise that some at least of its readers would draw two conclusions: that effective royal authority was the missing factor without which the moral suasion of *The Complaynt of Scotland* was unlikely to prevail; and that the queen dowager offered the best available hope of establishing that authority in the immediate future.

Mary of Guise, in the event, replaced Arran (or Châtelherault as he had by then become) as regent in April 1554. In August the final version of David Lindsay's *Satyre of the Thrie Estaitis* was

---

[81] Ibid. 129.   [82] Ibid. 1–3.

[83] Ibid. 1. To say (Stewart edn., p. xiv) that 'after the 1544 meeting of the Estates Mary of Lorraine was "de facto" Regent' is surely to overstate the case—and, consequently, to underrate the skill and pertinacity with which Mary pursued her goal. By the time Wedderburn wrote the *Complaynt* her position was indeed strong and becoming stronger; but it was perhaps only after her visit to France (she returned to Scotland in Nov. 1551) that Arran's 'continued tenure of the office of governor became little more than camouflage' (Donaldson, *James V to James VII*, 81).

[84] Stewart edn., 1.

performed before her in Edinburgh. On the occasion of her proclamation as regent on 12 April, however, the script for the
dramatic entertainment which formed part of the celebrations
came from the pen of a much less celebrated and now largely
forgotten writer. Yet William Lauder (c.1520–72) has some claim
to consideration here. His *Compendious and Breue Tractate concern-*
ing ye Office and Dewtie of Kyngis, Spirituall Pastoris, and Temporall
Iugis, published in Edinburgh in 1556, can provide both a coda to
the present chapter and a bridge to the next. When it was published, the full force of the 'uproar for religion' in Scotland still lay
some time ahead; but, as we shall see in due course, the years
during which Mary of Guise governed as regent were increasingly dominated by the developing conflict over ecclesiastical
reform; and some at least of Lauder's preoccupations are similar
to those of Knox and other Protestants, just as they echo some
notes that can be detected in Lindsay's *Satyre*. Lauder himself,
while he remained about the court until at least the summer of
1558, was plainly moving towards a Protestant stance, if indeed
he had not already adopted such a position by the time he wrote
his *Tractate*. After the establishment of the reformed kirk, probably in the early 1560s, he became minister of Forgandenny in
Perthshire; and there he died, having added to his earlier work a
group of religious poems, with which we need not here concern
ourselves.[85]

The primary message of Lauder's 1556 *Tractate* is the by now
only too familiar one that a king's essential 'Office and Dewtie' is

> To minister, and cause ministrat be,
> Iustice, to all, with equitie.

True, his subjects must recognize that he is

> To be dred, seruit, and obeyit,
> And as thair maister to be weyit;

but he, for his part, must acknowledge that he is 'bot constitute, |

---

[85] *Ane Compendious and Breue Tractate concernyng ye Office and Dewtie of Kyngis,*
Spirituall Pastoris, and Temporall Iugis: laitlie compylit be William Lauder, for the
Faithfull Instructioun of Kyngis and Prencis (1556), ed. F. Hall (Early English Text
Society; London, 1864, rev. edn. 1869; hereafter Hall edn.). For particulars of
Lauder's life supplied by David Laing see Preface, pp. v–xi; also Laing's
additional notes in the Preface to *The Minor Poems of William Lauder*, ed. F. J.
Furnivall (Early English Text Society; London, 1870), pp. v–viii.

Vnder God, as ane Substitute'. And this divine 'constitution' implies that justice must always be 'Gratiously mixit with mercye'.[86]
Mercy, however, is not to be confused with that kind of dispens-
ing with strict justice which is corruptly purchased and leads to
the impoverishment of the poor commons. This is the outcome,
kings are warned,

> Geue [if] ye neclect your Prencelie cure,
> And becum Auaricious,
> Parciall, cruell, or Couatus;
> With sum dispensand for pure pakkis,
> That they may brek your Prencelie actis;
> Raisand gret derth, exorbitent
> Aganis your actis of Parliament;
> Oppressand your Communitye,
> And bryngand thame to povertie.[87]

The king's responsibilities are spiritual as well as temporal. To
maintain that 'ane godlie kyng' should so rule as to ensure that
every subject knew his duty 'To lufe and feir' the law of God was,
to be sure, traditional doctrine; but Lauder gives the king the
specific responsibility for choosing preachers and pastors who
will conscientiously perform their duty—

> For to Instruct the cristin flok,
> And, with exempyll of thare lyfe,
> To edefye Man, Maid, and wyffe.[88]

Failing this, it is the king who will ultimately bear the blame—

> . . . geue [if] thay haue the floke abusit,
> Ye, Kyngs, sall be for that accusit.[89]

The pattern is repeated when Lauder turns, at even greater
length, to 'the Election off the Temporall Iugis'. The choice is
again the king's responsibility; and he is strictly enjoined to make
it carefully and prudently. 'Goddis worde' is once more given
priority; for if a judge

> . . . knawis nocht god, nor yit his law;
> And so of hym he stands no aw,
> In Court, in Parliament, or Cessioun,
> Planelie for to commit Oppressioun.[90]

---

[86] Hall edn., 3.   [87] Ibid. 8, ll. 100–8.   [88] Ibid. 12, ll. 300–2.
[89] Ibid. 13, ll. 331–2.   [90] Ibid. 15–16, ll. 417–20.

Lauder, however, also has more specific concerns. In an interesting passage he reports that

> Gret murmour is, and mony sayis
> That sum Solistars, now thir dayis,
> Vincusis Lawers in thare cause,
> For all thare ledgin of the lawis.
> Suithlie, I thynk sic Solistatioun
> Gret myster [need] hes of Reformatioun;
> Because it smellis, vnfenyeitlie,
> To verray percialytie;
> Quhilk Percialytie smoris doun [smothers]
> Iustice in euery land and toun.[91]

However, although 'ledgin of the lawis' (legal learning) may not guarantee justice it is none the less indispensable in the king's 'temporall officiaris':

> Thay suld haue knawlage of boith the Iuris,
> Als weill the Canone as Ciuile law:
> Thay suld thame vnderstand and knaw.
> For blynd men (as I haue feill)
> Can nocht decerne fair colours weill:
> No more can Iudgis Illiturate
> Discus ane mater (weill I wat).[92]

Yet, supported though he may and should be, by the expertise of his 'officiaris', Lauder's king still bears the inescapable final responsibility for all that goes on, well or ill, in the 'haill Regioun and ryng' he has in his 'gouernyng'. Should he fail in his duty he will be punished; but the punishment, while it may take such temporal forms as the loss of his realm (and as it will certainly take the form of penalties in the world to come), is exacted by God and not by any human authority. Human agency may indeed be used by God to vindicate his law; but there is no suggestion here of any kind of 'resistance theory'.[93] Indeed, to review the material

---

[91] Hall edn., 16, ll. 425–33.

[92] Ibid. 16, ll. 448–54, where ll. 451–2 may indicate that Lauder was colourblind.

[93] Cf. ibid. 9, ll. 191 ff.; 11, ll. 261–2, and perhaps esp. the following (17, ll. 472–8): 'Except your Iugis Iustlie Iuge ǀ The causis of all Creaturis, ǀ Boith of the ryche and of the puris, ǀ Your Crown, Sworde, Ceptour, & your wand, ǀ Thay sall be tane out of your hand, ǀ And geuin to vtheris, frome yow and youris, ǀ That wyll do Iustice at all houris.'

considered in this chapter, from the 1480s to the 1550s, is to be struck by the virtually complete absence of a kind of political thinking which had been expressed, however cautiously, by John Mair and which, by the 1550s, was beginning to find more vehement expression in Protestant polemical writing. The development in Scotland of such themes as the right (and perhaps the duty) to resist 'tyrannical' rulers is the subject, in part, of the next chapter.

4

Reformation and Resistance
John Knox

THE figure of John Knox imposes itself upon the scene as the enquiry moves, in this chapter and the next, into the formative decades of the Scottish Reformation. That is not to say that we need or can accept without qualification the heroic stature he has been accorded in a good deal of the historiography of the subject. And the requisite caution is in large part a matter of refusing to take the man at his own valuation. Knox was no mean self-publicist, and the shadow of his remarkable *History of the Reformation in Scotland* lies heavily across the path of historical interpretation.[1] It can certainly be argued that Knox's share in shaping both events and attitudes was less than he doubtless believed and certainly wished his readers to believe.[2] Yet for the purposes of the present investigation it is far from easy to cut Knox down to a size that fails to tower over the surrounding landscape. His writings, even without the *History*, ensure by their scope and character his predominant place in any attempt to understand the 'political ideas' of Reformation Scotland.[3] There are, to be sure, other factors and influences to be considered; but, as in all historical undertakings, we must work with the evidence we have, and in the present context much of our evidence necessarily comes from Knox.

---

[1] The text of the *History* is in the 1st 2 vols. of *The Works of John Knox*, ed. D. Laing, 6 vols. (Wodrow Society; Edinburgh, 1846–64; hereafter Laing edn.). A modernized, annotated, and invaluably indexed text is *John Knox's History of the Reformation in Scotland*, ed. W. C. Dickinson, 2 vols. (Edinburgh, 1949; hereafter Dickinson edn.).

[2] See on this e.g. G. Donaldson, 'Knox the Man', in D. Shaw (ed.), *John Knox: A Quatercentenary Reappraisal* (Edinburgh, 1975), 23–4.

[3] Besides the texts in the Laing edn. cited below, there are several modern reprints: see *The Political Writings of John Knox*, ed. M. A. Breslow (Washington, 1985); and, esp., *John Knox: On Rebellion*, ed. R. A. Mason (Cambridge Texts in the History of Political Thought; Cambridge, 1994; hereafter Mason edn.).

Another preliminary problem calls for consideration. For one reason and another there is a certain tendency to think of Reformation political thinking in the period when Scotland was moving to the adoption and establishment of Protestantism as, essentially, Calvinist political thinking. Specifically, we are apt to have in mind the development of what Quentin Skinner has called 'the Calvinist theory of revolution'. In fact, as Skinner shows, that theory was very far from being 'Calvinist' in any direct or unqualified sense.[4] There can indeed be no doubt that from the mid-sixteenth century onwards Calvin's was the primary influence in the dynamic development of Protestant doctrine; and Scotland has traditionally been regarded as one of the areas where 'Protestantism' came to be more or less identified with 'Calvinism'. Yet it is far from easy to determine precisely when and how Calvin's teaching was first known to Scottish Protestants; and even when that teaching had been disseminated so as to become the primary factor in shaping the reformed Scottish church, it is not to be assumed that other doctrinal views simply disappeared. Nor, again, is it correct to suppose that John Knox, by then indeed a committed Calvinist, monopolized the process of formulating doctrine and order.[5]

Protestant doctrines began to appear in Scotland in the mid-1520s, travelling mainly along the North Sea trade routes.[6] It is possible, though the matter remains (and will perhaps always

[4] Q. Skinner, 'The Origins of the Calvinist Theory of Revolution', in B. Malament (ed.), *After the Reformation* (Manchester, 1980), 309–30.

[5] See, among much else on a theme extending far beyond the scope of the present enquiry, the editions of the 1560 *Confession of Faith* by T. Hesse (Munich, 1938) and G. D. Henderson (Edinburgh, 1937); W. I. P. Hazlett, 'The Scots Confession 1560: Context, Complexion and Critique', *Archiv für Reformationsgeschichte*, 78 (1987), 287–320; R. Kyle, 'John Knox and the Purification of Religion: The Intellectual Aspects of his Crusade against Idolatry', *Archiv für Reformationsgeschichte*, 77 (1986), 265–80; R. L. Greaves, *Theology and Revolution in the Scottish Reformation: Studies in the Thought of John Knox* (Grand Rapids, Mich., 1980), esp. 111–25; M. Taylor, 'The Conflicting Doctrines of the Scottish Reformation', in McRoberts (ed.), *Essays on the Scottish Reformation*, 245–73, esp. 256–62; J. Durkan, 'The Cultural Background in Sixteenth-Century Scotland', ibid. 274–331, esp. 295–8, 303–14.

[6] See, on the period down to the early 1540s, I. B. Cowan, *The Scottish Reformation: Church and Society in Sixteenth-Century Scotland* (London, 1982), 89–99. It was not only the direct North Sea routes that were important: Cowan points out (p. 92) that '[t]he sea-port of Ayr constituted an obvious gateway into western Scotland'—an area destined to be especially important for Protestant development. See also Durkan, 'Cultural Background', 298–303, on influences from England.

remain) obscure, that their influence mingled with surviving traces of the 'Lollard' tendencies which were still in evidence a generation or so earlier.[7] It is true that some of the views attributed to the 'Lollards of Kyle' might have been unacceptable to Luther and to the other 'magisterial' reformers of the sixteenth century. Knox, indeed, anxiously and angrily dismisses the alleged article, 'That Christ at his coming has taken away power from kings to judge' as

the vennemouse accusatioun of the ennemyes, whose practise has ever bene to mack the doctrin of Jesus Christ suspect to Kingis and rewllaris, as that God thairby wold depose thame of thair royall seattis whare, by the contrair, nothing confermes the power of magistratis more than dois Goddsi wourd.[8]

Yet most of the thirty-four articles of the indictment are such as would have presented little or no difficulty to the emergent Protestants of the 1520s. What we know of the beliefs of Patrick Hamilton, the proto-martyr of the Scottish Reformation, based on the document which appears in Knox's *History* as 'Patrick's Places', indicates a positive concern to advocate the doctrine of justification by faith: nothing is said directly in the negative vein which characterizes the Kyle articles, though it may be inferred that Hamilton would have rejected much that the Lollards rejected, and perhaps more. There is, in any case, nothing in 'Patrick's Places' that could be described as being in any sense political doctrine.[9]

Before turning to the next substantial piece of evidence—the articles alleged against George Wishart—it will be useful to glance at the case of Alexander Seton, the first of several Dominicans to figure prominently in what we may term the prehistory of Scottish Protestantism. In or about 1536, Seton, after preaching an essentially Lutheran doctrine, had fled to Berwick. From there he

---

[7] For the 'Lollards of Kyle' see Knox, *History*, Laing edn., i. 7–11; Dickinson edn., i. 7–10. Cf. Macdougall, *James IV*, 105–7. John Ireland (*Meroure*, i. 164), addressing James IV in 1490, says that 'in thi realme has bene, and yit, as I wndirstand, are, Errouris and heresiis lurkand'. Ireland's witness has perhaps been insufficiently noticed; but see Wormald, *Court, Kirk, and Community*, 91–2.

[8] Laing edn., i. 8–9; Dickinson edn., i. 8. It is, incidentally, far from clear that Dickinson is correct in suggesting (p. 8 n. 5) that 'to judge' here refers only to judgement 'in matters of religion' and that Knox 'seems to confuse the issue'.

[9] Laing edn., i. 19–35; Dickinson edn., ii, Appendix I, 219–29.

wrote to James V a letter in which several points are worth noting. First, the king is warned that his 'power and authoritie to exercise justice' within the realm is in danger of being usurped by 'the Bischoppis and Kirkmen' as though 'thei war rather King, and thow the subject (quhilk unjust regiment is of the selfe false, and contrair to holy Scripture and law of God)'. Moreover, Seton claims, the bishops are seeking to turn James against the 'temporale Lordis and liegis'; and 'when thy baronis ar putt doun, what arte thow bot the King of Bane?' Only if James will 'tack hardiment and authoritie, quhilk thow hes of God' to resist this usurpation, will he have 'thy liegis' hartis, and . . . tranquilitie, justice, and policie in thy realme'. Given the later alliance between Protestant preachers and at least some important elements in the nobility, this suggestion that the godly prince should work together with his 'barons' to repress clerical usurpation is not without some interest.[10]

In the account of the trial of George Wishart for heresy in 1546 there are perhaps some echoes of the attitude reflected in Seton's letter. Certainly Wishart seems to have attempted to have his case transferred from the exclusive jurisdiction of Cardinal Beaton to that of the earl of Arran, then governor of the realm on behalf of the child queen. Arran, he claimed, would be 'ane indifferent and equall judge'. Pressed on his attitude to Beaton, he argued that he did not 'refuise' the cardinal as a judge; 'but I desyre the word of God to be my judge, and the Temporall Estate, with some of your Lordschippis [the bishops] myne auditoures; because I am hear my Lord Governouris prisoner'. Implicit in this, as in Seton's letter, is the claim that temporal rulers—the 'godly prince' and the temporal lords who are associated with him in his government— have authority to judge in spiritual causes.[11]

Interestingly, the first of the eighteen articles alleged against Wishart was itself concerned with the status of temporal power; for it claimed that he had been guilty of contempt of the Governor's authority: 'when thow preached in Dundye, and was charged be my Lord Governouris authoritie to desist, nevertheles thow woldest not obey, but persevered in the same.' Wishart's answer was the classic one:

[10] Laing edn., i. 48–52; Dickinson edn., ii, Appendix II, 230–2.
[11] Laing edn., i. 154–5; Dickinson edn., ii, Appendix III, 235–6.

My Lordis, I have red in the Actes of the Apostles, that it is not lauchfull for the threattis and minacinges of men, to desist from the preaching of the Evangell. Tharefoir it is writtin, 'We shall rather obey God then [than] men.'[12]

Beyond that unexceptional and unexceptionable point, the evidence regarding Wishart throws no light on the 'political ideas' of the first Scottish Protestants. The natural inference is that they shared the general view in which Christian duty enjoined obedience and submission to those endowed by God with temporal authority, save only when that authority sought to impose conduct believed to be contrary to the revealed will of God.

Such an inference seems to be confirmed by the next available piece of evidence. This is the treatise on justification by faith written in 1548 by Henry Balnaves of Halhill.[13] Balnaves was among the 'Castilians' besieged in St Andrews after the murder of Beaton and subsequently imprisoned in France. During his captivity in Rouen, he wrote this exposition of an essentially Lutheran doctrine of justification. It includes the following passage on temporal society:

The Politike or Civill Justice is, the obedience which every subject and inferiour estate of man giveth to their prince and superiour, in all the worlde. The which proceedeth of the lawe of nature, and is a good worke; without the which obedience (to the punishment of the wicked and defence of the just) no common-weale might bee conserved and kept in rule and order, but all would run to confusion. Therefore are princes and higher powers commanded of God to be obeyed, as his good worke, for they ar the ministers of God unto good.[14]

Having said this in his twelfth chapter, Balnaves later, in the twenty-fifth, takes care to emphasize the heavy responsibilities borne by rulers, who are reminded that God will surely punish any default in that regard. There is, however, nothing to suggest that subjects may resist or seek to control their ruler: he is to be 'feared, reverenced, and also loved'; for rulers 'are as it were gods, and so called in the Scripture, by reason of participation of the power of God'.[15]

[12] Laing edn., i. 155–6; Dickinson edn., ii. 236.
[13] Balnaves's treatise was posthumously published in 1584, together with Knox's *Briefe Sommarie* (discussed below) as *The Confession of Faith, conteining how the troubled man should seeke refuge in his God* (Edinburgh, 1584): it is reprinted in the Laing edn., iii. 431–542. For Balnaves (?1502–70) see Laing's account, ibid. 405–30.
[14] Ibid. 462.   [15] Ibid. 529.

During the St Andrews siege John Knox had, at a celebrated moment, responded to what he took to be God's call by preaching his first sermon. He had joined the Castilians in April 1547, at about the time when papal absolution for Beaton's murder arrived: the rejection of that pardon was followed by the second phase of the siege. Knox's preaching had political implications, at least so far as the polity of the church was concerned. He rejected completely the claims made for the papal monarchy, citing with indignant contempt the absolutist language used by canon lawyers in its defence.[16] It is, however, harder to evaluate the temporal implications of his position at this early stage. It has been suggested, reasonably enough, that by identifying himself with the Castilians he was giving tacit approval to what was unquestionably an act of rebellion against constituted authority. To go on from this, however, to argue that Knox regarded those who killed Beaton as 'civil magistrates', authorized in that capacity to slay idolaters, would seem to stretch the evidence beyond what it will bear.[17] Even in Knox's retrospective account, some twenty years after the events in question, there is nothing to indicate that he saw 'his best beloved Brethren of the Congregation of the Castle of St Andrews' in quite that light. Beaton's death was, to be sure, a manifestation of divine justice, and Knox would not condemn 'such as oppose themselves to impiety, or take upon them to punish the same, otherwise than laws of men will permit . . . let us not damn the persons that punish vice (and that for just causes)'. This, however, is a very different matter from ascribing civil authority to such instruments of God's vengeance.[18]

At all events, the first explicit indication of Knox's political position does not reveal any concern with such matters, despite the fact that it belongs to the period when he was himself enduring the harsh temporal consequences of associating with rebels. Sometime in the latter part of his captivity, in a galley lying at Rouen, Knox received, read, and revised a copy of Balnaves's treatise on justification. He later referred to his *Briefe Sommarie* of the text as 'containing the sum of his doctrine, and confession of his faith', which was 'sent . . . to his familiars in Scotland'. His purpose, according to the accompanying epistle, was 'not so

[16] Ibid. i. 190–1; Dickinson edn., i. 85–6.
[17] Cf. Greaves, *Theology and Revolution*, 127, 134.
[18] Laing edn., i. 234; Dickinson edn., i. 112.

much to illustrate the Worke ... as ... to give my Confession of the article of Justification therein contained'.[19] We may certainly regard the 'political' statements in the *Sommarie* as a true expression of Knox's views at this time. He writes, in the twelfth chapter,

The justice of man is devided in politick and ceremoniall. Politicke justice is an obedience which the inferiour estate giveth to their superiour: which should be keept, because it is the command of God that Princes be obeyed.[20]

And, in the twenty-fifth chapter, while there may be a special emphasis on the ruler's paramount duty to preserve purity of worship, there is nothing in this that is particularly striking or distinctive.[21]

Released from the galleys in February 1549, Knox was permitted to make his way, not to Scotland, but to England. There for the remainder of Edward VI's reign he lived and worked. In his *History* he was (perhaps understandably) somewhat dismissive about this part of his career, devoting only a sentence of his narrative to it, and observing in one of his conversations with Mary Queen of Scots that he had lived in England 'onlie the space of fyve yearis'.[22] They were crucial years, however, during which Knox not only had his first extended experience of ministry and preaching but also came for the first time into contact with the world of politics. All this was in a country where he remained, technically, an alien. Yet, in a period when the church of England was moving for the first time into an unequivocally Protestant position, he was to wield not inconsiderable influence and to reach a point at which he was offered, though he refused, a bishopric. All this serves to justify the claim that Knox was, during these years and beyond, in his years of exile, an Englishman by adoption; and it has led to the further suggestion that we need—not least in the context of political ideas—to think of two John Knoxes, reacting differently to circumstances differing

[19] Laing edn., iii. 9.

[20] Ibid. 17–18. Greaves (*Theology and Revolution*, 127; and cf. also p. 112) observes that Knox 'deliberately added a statement to his summarization of Balnaves' treatise exempting Christians from obeying higher powers when they commanded things opposed to divine law'. It is hard to see this restatement of standard Christian doctrine as contributing to the development of 'resistance theory'.

[21] Laing edn., iii. 25–6.

[22] Ibid. i. 231 (cf. ii. 280); Dickinson edn., i. 110 (cf. ii. 15).

sharply on the two sides of the Border.[23] We need not, however—
and indeed must not—take too schizoid a view of the matter.
Even if we leave aside psychological factors (and it was, after all,
the same individual who confronted the two national situations),
the fortunes of Protestant reform in England and in Scotland were
too closely interwoven to be rent asunder without doing some
violence to our historical understanding. At all events, it is clear
that even an essentially Scottish enquiry like this cannot safely
ignore Knox's English concerns.

It is true, nevertheless, that those concerns began to have
decisive political consequences only after Knox had left England
early in the reign of Mary Tudor. While Edward VI lived and the
Protestant settlement of the church remained intact, Knox had
no reason to question the doctrine of Christian obedience to
established temporal power. That is not to say that his attitude
during these five years was one of easy compliance. He could not
regard the ecclesiastical settlement represented by the 1549 Act of
Uniformity and the associated Prayer Book as satisfactory,
though he found it possible to conduct his ministry in Berwick
and Newcastle without coming into open conflict with the authorities. And the 1552 revision of the Prayer Book represented a
considerable advance from Knox's point of view. Yet it was at this
juncture that events manifested both Knox's growing influence
and the possibility of his falling out with the establishment.
Kneeling to receive communion was for Knox an unscriptural
custom which tended dangerously towards 'the idolatry of the
Mass'. It seems clear that he was one of those who secured the
addition to the Prayer Book of the so-called 'black rubric', which
explicitly denied any kind of 'real presence' of Christ in the eucha-
ristic elements. Yet kneeling was still enjoined, and Knox felt
obliged to urge compliance upon his congregation. In so doing he
strongly emphasized the Christian duty of obedience, admonish-
ing his brethren to remember

always ... that due obedience be given to magistrates, rulers and
princes, without tumult, grudge or sedition; for how wicked that ever

[23] This theme is developed by J. E. A. Dawson, 'The Two John Knoxes: England,
Scotland and the 1558 Tracts', *Journal of Ecclesiastical History*, 42 (1991), 555–76. For
Knox's years in England see J. Ridley, *John Knox* (Oxford, 1968), 84–170. For Knox
as 'an Englishman by adoption', see J. H. Burns, 'John Knox and Revolution 1558',
History Today, 8 (1958), 566.

themselves be in life, as how ungodly that ever their precepts or commandments be, ye must obey them for conscience sake; except in chief points of religion; and then ought ye rather to obey God nor man; not to pretend to defend God's truth or religion (ye being subjects) by violence or sword, but patiently suffering what God shall please be laid upon you for constant confession of your faith and belief.[24]

It was precisely what Protestants saw as the 'chief points of religion' that were threatened when Edward VI's premature death was followed by the accession of Mary Tudor. Within a few months of that ominous event Knox was in exile; and, though he was never to return to live permanently in England, it was the situation in his adopted rather than in his native country that preoccupied him for at least the early years of this new phase in his career. It may well be the case that he had always foreseen a return to Scotland; but, if so, this cannot be explained by the argument that 'his roots were in the revolutionary Protestantism of Scotland, not in the authoritarian Protestantism of England'.[25] For one thing, 'revolutionary Protestantism' did not in any substantial sense exist in Scotland at this time; and, in any case, there is every reason to think that Knox would have welcomed 'authoritarian Protestantism' if only the right authority could have been found to impose the right kind of doctrine, whether in Scotland or in England. The problem he faced in the early months of 1554 was that the established authority in England was being used to reintroduce a religion he believed to be idolatrous and blasphemous.

The first evidence we have of Knox's response to this challenge dates from the very beginning of his exile. Writing from Dieppe before the end of January 1554 to 'the faithfull ... within the realme of England, that luffeth the cumming of oure Lorde Jesus', Knox insists above all that they must 'avoyd all fellowship with idolatry, and with the maintainer of the same'. He appeals, in an important passage, to the league betuixt God and us, that he alone sall be oure God, and we salbe his pepill': obedience 'im matteris of religioun' is required by God 'of all thame that be within his league ... For all that be in this league ar one bodie ... Then

<hr>

[24] Quoted by Ridley (*Knox*, 110) from the text printed by P. Lorimer, *John Knox and the Church of England* (London, 1875), 259. This 'Epistle to the Congregation of Berwick' (Oct. 1552) is not in the Laing edn.

[25] Ridley, *Knox*, 118.

plaine it is, that of one bodie thair must be one law.' Obedience to God may entail disobedience to those—'be thay Kingis or be thay Quenis'—who 'intendis to drawe us frome God'. Disobedience, however, does not imply active resistance:

now sall sum demand, What then? Sall we go and slay all ydolateris? That wer the office, deir Brethrene, of everie Civill Magistrate within his realme. But of yow is requyreit onlie to avoyd participatioun and company of thair abominationis . . . it is plane, that the slaying of ydolateris appertenis not to everie particular man.[26]

Two points call for further comment. First, by introducing the concept of a 'league' or covenant between God and the community of believing Christians and by arguing that in the 'one bodie' of such a covenanted community there can be only 'one law', Knox had assumed a position pregnant with theological and political possibilities. How far he was as yet prepared to propose the actualization of these potentialities may be another matter. The second point for comment is related to that last remark. It has been suggested that Knox's reference to the 'office' or duty of the civil magistrate in regard to idolatry need not and should not be interpreted restrictively as applying only to the sovereign ruler. It has even been claimed that Knox was in effect saying that 'it was the duty of every "Civill Magistrate" in England to "slay all ydolateris"'.[27] There are several reasons for questioning this view. First, Knox's reference is to 'everie Civill Magistrate *within his realme*'; and the last three words seem to point decisively towards the sovereign as *the* magistrate in question. Again, the statement is cast in the subjunctive, not the indicative mood; and this may suggest that Knox's point *would* apply—but would apply only—to a civil magistrate who was part of a covenanted community. Thirdly, there is really little or nothing in Knox's later and more developed writings about the 1554 situation in England to indicate anything as drastic as the suggested duty of subordinate magistrates there to extirpate idolatry.[28]

At all events, between the writing and the printing of his January letter Knox journeyed from Dieppe to Switzerland.

---

[26] Laing edn., iii. 192–4.
[27] Greaves, *Theology and Revolution*, 134; and cf. pp. 171–2, where the point is perhaps restated more strongly (see also p. 117).
[28] See the discussion of the *Faythfull Admonition* below.

There, in his own words, he 'travellit through all the con-
gregationis . . . and reasonit with all the Pastouris and many
other excellentlie lernit men upon sic matters as now I can not
commit to wrytting'.[29] These 'matters' included the question of
political obedience and the right to resist. Knox went initially to
Geneva, where he had his first meeting with Calvin. Calvin sent
him on with a letter of introduction to Pierre Viret in Lausanne;
and from there Knox proceeded to Zurich, where, with Heinrich
Bullinger, he had the best documented of these consultations. In
the full perspective of Knox's career, the encounter with Calvin
must take first place; for it was to be in Geneva—'the most godlie
Reformed Churche and citie of the warld'—that Knox would
spend the most crucial years of his exile.[30] In the present more
limited context, however, Calvin was perhaps the Protestant
leader least likely to encourage Knox in developing any kind of
'resistance theory'. Yet it is clear that the political issue was, for
Knox at this stage, at least as urgent as any other.

As for Bullinger, whether or not he 'was obviously not trying to
discourage Knox from considering armed rebellion', his cautious
responses can scarcely be described as amounting to positive
*en*couragement.[31] Some of Knox's questions were easily disposed
of. Thus there was no difficulty in confirming, retrospectively,
the hereditary succession of a minor—'Edward VI of blessed
memory'. As for Mary's title, while God's law certainly placed
women as such in a subordinate position, it might still be the case
that the laws of a particular realm allowed or even enjoined
female succession: such laws are not abrogated by the Gospel and
it would be dangerous for the faithful to oppose them. Knox had
also asked—obviously with Mary's proposed Spanish marriage
in mind—whether a queen regnant might transfer her authority
to her husband. To this Bullinger would reply only that the issue
was one to be resolved by those skilled in the laws and customs of
the realm in question. Knox then introduced the problem of
'idolatry'. If this were imposed by the magistrate, was he (or she)

[29] Laing edn., iii. 235.

[30] The phrase about Geneva is from Knox's letter of 10 Apr. 1559 to William
Cecil (ibid. ii. 16; Dickinson edn., i. 283). Earlier, he had described Geneva as 'the
maist perfyte schoole of Chryst that ever was in the erth since the dayis of the
Apostillis' (Letter to Anne Lock, 9 Dec. 1556: Laing edn., iv. 240).

[31] Cf. Greaves, *Theology and Revolution*, 129.

to be obeyed; or could the leading men (*proceres*), having military power at their disposal, defend themselves and those subject to them against 'such ungodly violence' (*vim istam impiam*)? Bullinger replied, of course, that impious commands must never be obeyed, whatever the cost of disobedience. As for resistance, he observed that Eusebius and Evagrius both record cases of such action against established rulers without condemning those who rebelled. The Bible indeed allows and even commands 'just and necessary defensive action' (*justam necessariamque defensionem*). But he adds a caution: such ostensibly righteous action may easily be used as a pretext for the pursuit of quite different ends. No certain judgement in such cases can be pronounced except on the basis of a thorough knowledge of the circumstances; and no action of the kind should be undertaken except with wise counsel and after earnest prayer. Pressed by Knox as to which side the faithful should support if 'religious nobles' (*religiosi Proceres*) took such action, Bullinger would only repeat his warning about the risk of contaminated motives and his insistence that the decision must be taken by those fully apprised of all the relevant facts.[32]

The missing term in this series of Knox's contacts is the meeting with Pierre Viret. We may assume that Knox presented his letter from Calvin in Lausanne, and it is highly probable—one could say virtually certain—that the problem of Christian obedience was discussed. Frustratingly, no record of the interview has survived. This is peculiarly unfortunate for present purposes because Viret would have been much more inclined than either Calvin or Bullinger to take a positive view of the legitimacy of active resistance, and in particular of the role of 'lesser magistrates' in that connection. In 1547 he had advocated these opinions in his *Remonstrances aux fidèles*, and it is a fair surmise that he would communicate them to Knox. If this is correct, we can regard Knox's third and fourth questions to Bullinger as reflecting in some measure his Lausanne conversation; and this in turn would imply that Bullinger's response

---

[32] Laing edn., iii. 221–6, where the Latin text is printed with the translation by H. Robinson from id. (ed.), *Original Letters Relative to the English Reformation*, 2 vols. (Parker Society; Cambridge, 1846–7), ii. 745–7. Cf. Calvin, *Opera* [*Corpus Reformatorum*, vols. xxxix–lxxxvii] (Brunswick, 1863–1900), xv [xliii], 90–3 (Bullinger to Calvin, 26 Mar. 1554). Calvin's earlier response to Knox's questions is indicated in his letter to Bullinger of 29 Apr. 1554 (ibid. 125).

may have tended to check whatever encouragement Knox had derived from Viret.[33]

However this may be, Knox returned to Dieppe resolved to continue and expand his advice to the increasingly afflicted and apprehensive Protestant congregations he had left in England. Writing on 10 May 1554, he raised the question of the condign punishment of 'the tirantis of Ingland' and declared his certainty that both temporal and eternal penalties awaited them; but—'To determinate unto thame a certaine kynde of warldlie punishment it aperteaneth not to me ... Let us pacientlie abyd ... the tyme that is apoyntit to oure correctioun.'[34] Three weeks later he returned to the theme and urged his readers:

two things ye must avoid. The former, that ye presume not to be revengers of your own cause, but that ye resigne your vengeaunce unto Him, who only is able to requite them ... Secondly, that ye hate not with any carnal hatred these blinde, druel, and malicyous tiraunts ...

adding, however, that there was 'a spiritual hatred', with which 'earnestly may we praye for theyr destruction, be they Kynges or Quenes, Princes or Prelates'.[35]

The fierce rhetoric to which this 'spiritual hatred' could lead is well illustrated by the most extensive of Knox's writings on English affairs: *A Faithfull Admonition ... vnto the Professours of Gods truthe in England*, written at Dieppe between the end of May and 20 July 1554 (the date in the colophon of the first edition). Here Knox indulged in violent invective directed not only against the Catholic bishops—'wyly Wynchester, dreaming Duresme, and bloudy Bonner', but against Mary Tudor—'I finde that Jesabel ... that cursed idolatress ... never erected half so many gallowes in al Israel as myschevous Mary hath done within

---

[33] See, on Viret, Greaves, *Theology and Revolution*, 132–3, 175–6. Greaves (p. 132) interprets Viret as having reaffirmed his views on resistance 'in works published in the 1560s and 1570s'. Skinner, however (*Foundations of Modern Political Thought*, ii. 209, 303) contrasts Viret's 1547 exposition of 'the constitutional theory of resistance' with his horrified rejection, in 1563 of 'any idea of popular revolution'. The fullest treatment is by R. D. Linder, *The Political Ideas of Pierre Viret* (Travaux d'Humanisme et Renaissance, lxiv; Geneva, 1964), esp. ch. 7: see in particular pp. 137–42 on the 1547 *Remonstrances* (reprinted in 1559 as part of Viret's *Traités divers*) and on Viret's possible influence. Linder argues that Viret's support for resistance was always heavily qualified: in particular, the argument in the *Remonstrances* was intended to apply only to societies where there were specifically constituted 'lesser magistrates'.

[34] Laing edn., iii. 234–5.   [35] Ibid. 244–5.

London alone.'[36] To Mary's idolatry, moreover, was now to be added the projected marriage which would 'brynge in a straunger, and make a proude Spaniarde kynge'. And it was in this connection that Knox, for the first time, introduced an essentially political argument as distinct from his more characteristic scriptural vein of prophetic denunciation. The consequences of the Spanish marriage would indeed—and of course—include 'the overthrowe of Christianitie and Goddes true religion'; but this is now only one entry in a catalogue of half a dozen items, the list culminating in 'the utter subversion of the whole publicke estate and commonwealth of Englande'. And Knox rests his case upon 'the juste lawes of the Realme': it is the 'auncient lawes and actes of Parliament' that 'pronounceth it treason to transferre the Crowne of Englande into the handes of a forreyn nation' and it is by these criteria that Mary is 'an open traitoresse to the Imperiall Crown of England'. Only when he declared that 'the usurped government of an affectionate woman is a rage without reason' did Knox, in this passage, break out of the 'constitutional' framework in which he had evidently decided to place his argument.[37]

It is fairly clear that, in adopting this approach, Knox was both responding to the advice he had received from Bullinger, with its emphasis on the established laws of particular political systems, and seeking to broaden the basis of his attack on Mary Tudor's government. Yet it is noteworthy that he refrains from drawing political conclusions from his political argument. If Viret had alerted him to the possibility of appealing to 'lesser magistrates' as instruments for the enforcement of 'auncient lawes' against the 'treason' of a ruler who disregarded them, Knox was not yet ready to take up the idea in any overt way. Instead he has recourse to impassioned prayer: 'God, for his great mercies sake, stirre up some Phineas, Helias, or Jehu, that the bloude of abhominable idolaters may pacifie Goddes wrath, that it consume not the whole multitude. Amen.'[38] And this was to say no more than he had already said in May. To say that '[d]uring the spring and summer of 1554, Knox developed the theory that the subjects

[36] Ibid. 294. As Laing (ibid. 294–5 n. 3) points out, the 'gallowes' were those erected for the execution of supporters of Sir Thomas Wyatt's abortive rebellion.

[37] Ibid. 295–6.

[38] Ibid. 309; and cf. the longer prayer, in the same vein, later in the *Admonition* (ibid. 328).

of a Catholic sovereign were lawfully entitled to overthrow their sovereign by armed revolution' is perhaps to be as wide of the mark as it is, in such matters, possible to be.[39] It is true, certainly, that Knox had laid, or begun to lay, foundations on which such a 'theory' might be erected. He was sure that 'all is not lawfull or just that is statute be Civill lawis, neither yet is everie thing syn befoir God, quhilk ungodlie personis alledgeis to be treasone'; and again that 'Goddes worde draweth his electe after it, against worldlye appearaunce, agaynst natural affections, and agaynst cyvil statutes and constitutions'.[40] How far it might and should 'draw' them was a question Knox had not yet resolved.

Not for almost two years after this do we have any substantial evidence for the development of Knox's thinking in regard to political authority; and, when the evidence resumes, it is, as we shall see, in a Scottish rather than an English context. The intervening period, however, had continued the English dimension of Knox's career, embracing as it did his involvement in 'the troubles at Frankfurt' and the early stages of his association with the English exile community in Geneva. The vehemence of his 1554 *Admonition* embroiled him with the more moderate exiles; and the mounting violence of persecution in England was certainly intensifying the heat of Knox's indignation against Mary. At this stage, however, there is no explicit indication of further development in his 'political' doctrine. He shared, at Frankfurt, in the drafting of a 'forme of prayers' which was to be adopted by the English congregation in Geneva and in which the Confession of Faith included the following passage:

And besides this Ecclesiasticall censure, I acknowlage to belonge to this church a politicall Magistrate, who ministreth to every man justice, defending the good and punishing the evell; to whom we must rendre honor and obedience in all thinges, which are not contrarie to the Word of God.[41]

This was not a doctrine from which Knox would have dissented at any stage in his career: it was the implications of the last clause that remained problematic.

[39] Ridley, *Knox*, 171.
[40] The first phrase is from the letter of 10 May 1554 (Laing edn., iii. 236); the second from the *Admonition* (ibid. 312–13).
[41] Ibid. iv. 172–3. For Knox's involvement in 'the troubles at Frankfurt' in the latter part of 1554 see ibid. 1–68; Ridley, *Knox*, 189–214.

In the autumn of 1555 Knox returned, after an absence of more than eight years, to Scotland (perhaps venturing briefly into England, though this is doubtful). The reasons for his visit were, it seems, primarily personal rather than pastoral. Sometime before leaving England early in 1554 he had precontracted marriage with Marjory, daughter of Richard Bowes, Captain of Norham Castle, and niece of Sir Robert Bowes, Warden of the East and Middle Marches. It was in response to an appeal from his mother-in-law (who had perhaps by then sought refuge in Scotland) that Knox returned to solemnize the marriage.[42] However, the situation he found in Scotland induced him to remain until the following summer; and during those months his preaching did much to establish him as a leading figure among the Scottish Protestants, whose cause was advancing under the ambiguously tolerant policy of the queen regent, Mary of Guise. From this point onwards it is impossible to discuss Knox's ideas in isolation from the views of what was to become, at the end of 1557, 'the Congregation'. And it is important to recognize that these views were not by any means consistently identical with Knox's teaching. It is convenient, in analysing the political position of the Protestant party, to consider, first, in continuity with what has gone before, Knox's writings between 1556 and 1558, reserving the corporate views of the Congregation for examination at the start of the next chapter. It must be borne in mind, however, that there is, throughout, a dialogue here, sometimes explicit, sometimes implicit, but always an important factor in the process of development.

Political issues were brought back to the forefront of Knox's mind towards the end of his Scottish sojourn both by the company he was keeping and by the response of the church authorities to his preaching. Those who heard him preach and 'so approved his doctrin, that thei wissed it to have bein publict' included such magnates as the queen's half-brother Lord James Stewart (later earl of Moray) and the earls of Argyll and Glencairn, together with important representatives of the gentry or lesser nobility like John Erskine of Dun (Knox's principal patron at this stage).[43] Knox now appeared to the episcopal hierarchy sufficiently important to be summoned to 'compear' at the

---

[42] For Knox's movements at this time see Ridley, *Knox*, 223–5; and for the earlier history of his relations with Marjory Bowes and her mother, ibid. 130–44.

[43] *History*, Laing edn., i. 245–50; Dickinson edn., i. 118–21.

church of the Blackfriars in Edinburgh on 15 May 1556. 'Butt', in Knox's words, 'that dyet held nott': he was not, in the event, called upon to answer for his teaching.[44] That Mary of Guise may (as Knox believed) have intervened to stay the proceedings is certainly possible—even probable—given the tendency of her policy at this time. At all events, Knox's aristocratic supporters— specifically, the earl of Glencairn and the Earl Marischal—'willed the said Johne to wrait unto the Quein Regent somewhat that mycht move hir to heir the word of God'. This was the origin of Knox's letter 'To the excellent Lady Mary Douagire, Regent of Scotland'.[45]

The tone of the letter, notably deferential and conciliatory, showed that the Protestants, including Knox, could be as 'politic' as the queen regent herself when that course promised advantageous possibilities. Not that we need doubt Knox's sincerity in referring to 'the honor that God commandeth to be geven to Magistrates, which, no doubte, if it be trew honor, conteyneth in itself, in lawfull thinges obedience, and in all thinges love and reverence'. Lawful obedience he had never denied or questioned; and if love and reverence had been somewhat lacking in his attitude to Mary Tudor, he might plausibly have pleaded extreme provocation as his excuse. In any case, the policy of conciliation did not lead Knox to abate the demands his teaching made upon rulers. 'I am compelled to say,' he told the queen regent, '[o]neles [unless] in your regiment and using of power, your Grace be found different from the multitude of Princes and head rulers, that this pre-eminence wherein ye ar placed shal be your dejection to torment and payn everlasting.' Nor can it be argued that religious policy is not the concern of the civil ruler. 'No, no,' Knox exclaims, 'the negligence of Bishoppes shall no lesse be requyred of the handes of Magistrates . . . then [than] shall the oppression of fals judges.'[46]

---

[44] Laing edn., i. 251; Dickinson edn., i. 122.

[45] Laing edn., i. 251–2; Dickinson edn., i. 122–3; and for the text of the *Letter*, Laing edn., iv. 75–84; Mason edn., 48–71. That text includes the Additions made by Knox in 1558. The original text was first printed in 1556 as *The copie of a letter, sent to the ladye Mary Douagire, regent of Scotland, by John Knox*, together with Knox's 'Vindication of the Doctrine that the Mass is Idolatry'.

[46] Laing edn., iv. 78–9; Mason edn., 55. Pending appropriate action by the 'Magistrates', Knox reminded his followers that 'Within your own houses . . . in some cases, ye are bishoppes and kinges': as such they both might and should

Such hopes as the Protestant party may have had of this approach were disappointed; nor did the church authorities fail to resume the proceedings against Knox they had suspended in May 1556. Later that year he was burnt in effigy at the Cross of Edinburgh; and, as he subsequently learnt, his letter to the queen regent had been treated as 'a pasqwill'—a mere lampoon.[47] He himself had left Scotland in July and by September was back in Geneva with his wife and mother-in-law. The first year or so of his second period of exile yielded little if anything to indicate further political reflection. If the long letter 'To his Sisteris in Edinburgh' dates, as seems likely enough, from those months, it suggests that the problem of female government was fermenting, so to speak, in his mind. The subject of women's dress drew Knox into a significant digression:

gif wemen, forgetting thair awn weaknes and inabilitie to rule, do presume to tak upon thame to beir and use the vestementis and weaponis of men, that is, the offices whilk God hath assignit to mankynd onlie, they sall not eschaip the maledictioun of Him who must declair himself enemy, and a seveir punisser of all thois that be malicious perverteris of the order establissit be his wisdome.

Recollecting, however, that his correspondents were unlikely to be greatly tempted by either transvestism or tyranny, Knox decided to 'omit further declaratioun of the same for this present'.[48]

Meanwhile developments of greater importance were proceeding in Scotland. Before Knox's departure for Geneva, indeed, there were signs of the rising tension generated by the queen regent's attempt 'to drive an ill-yoked team in double harness . . . to unite the interests of Scotland with the service of the house of Guise'.[49] The proposal to support a standing army by means of a tax based on a comprehensive record not only of lands

ensure that the members of the household were 'partakers in readyng, exhorting, and in makyng common prayers'; for 'of you it shalbe requyred howe carefullye and dylygentlye ye have alwayes instructed theym in Goddes true knowlege' (Laing edn., iv. 137: from 'A most Wholesome Counsell how to behave ourselves in the midst of this Wicked Generation', dated 7 July 1556).

[47] *History*, Laing edn., i. 252; Dickinson edn., i. 123; and cf. Laing edn., iv. 457 for Knox's comment in 1558.

[48] Laing edn., iv. 228. The letter was probably written in the autumn of 1556.

[49] A. I. Cameron (ed.), *The Scottish Correspondence of Mary of Lorraine* (Scottish History Society; Edinburgh, 1927), 371.

but of the names and 'qualities and habilitie of everie manis person and quantitie of thair substance and gudis movable and immovabill', brought forward in May 1556, met with stubborn and successful resistance. The opposition was led not by the nobles alone (and certainly not by the magnates generally) but by those whom Lesley calls 'the baronnis and gentill men'—that lesser nobility from whom Protestant leadership was also emerging. The policy for which the projected army would have been an instrument was essentially one of supporting France against Spain; but when, a year or so later, England was drawn into the Habsburg–Valois conflict on the Spanish side, an extension of the Anglo-Scottish truce was negotiated.[50]

Scottish reaction against the diplomatic and military policies of Mary of Guise was not, it must be emphasized, either exclusively or even primarily Protestant in inspiration. Nor, of course, were the motives of the regent's opponents simply patriotic or 'nationalist', though the appeal to 'the ancient custom, laws, and liberty of the realm' and to the traditional notion that the king (or queen) was properly designated as being 'of Scots', not 'of Scotland' was no doubt sincere as far as it went.[51] Yet for an increasing number of those concerned, alienation from the established church and commitment to the new religious teachings was combining with secular motivation, whether patriotic, sectional, or simply selfish. By March 1557 a group of the nobles who had been favourably impressed by Knox's preaching a year earlier were ready to invite him back. In doing so, they assured him of their willingness 'to jeopard their lives and goods, for the setting fordward of the glorie of God', and indicated that, while the religious policy of 'the Magistrats' in Scotland had not changed, there had been 'no farther crueltie . . . than was before'. Moreover 'the Friers' were, they suggested, 'in lesse estimation, both with the Queen's Grace, and with the rest of the Nobilitie'.[52] Knox

---

[50] Donaldson, *James V to James VII*, 87–8; John Lesley, *The History of Scotland from the Death of King James I in the Year MCCCCXXXVI to the Year M.D.LXI* (Bannatyne Club; Edinburgh, 1830), 254–5. Lesley refers contrastingly to the support offered by 'sum of the lordis of the nobilitie for plesour of the Queen [Regent]'.

[51] Lesley, *History*, 255.

[52] Laing edn., iv. 257; Mason edn., 133–4. Laing's text was based on 'a collation of the MSS of Calderwood's History' (p. 258 n. 1). It differs slightly from the text given by Knox in his *History* (Laing edn., i. 267–8; Dickinson edn., i. 132) and described by him as 'the true copy of the bill'. One variant may be worth noting:

received this letter in May; and, after considerable hesitation, but strongly urged by Calvin and others, he left Geneva in September. At Dieppe, however, he was checked by 'contrare letters'.[53] We can only speculate as to the reasons that had prompted second thoughts on the part of those who had pressed Knox so strongly in March to return, though the likeliest explanation may lie in their having realized that they had simply overestimated the support they could hope to enlist. Certainly when—perhaps responding to Knox's urging—they drew up the document which marks the formal inauguration of 'the Congregation', it attracted fewer signatures than its sponsors must have expected.[54] This 'commoun Band' is dated 3 December 1557; and by then there had been important political developments which must have affected the attitudes of the reform party.

The queen regent's anxiety to bring about a Scottish attack on England which might relieve the pressure on France became more urgent with the heavy French defeat at St Quentin (10 August 1557). Forces for an invasion were indeed assembled in the autumn; but the nobles who commanded the army refused to proceed. William Robertson long ago pointed out that 'this first instance of contempt for the Regent's authority can, in no degree, be imputed to the influence of the new opinions in religion'.[55] And when Mary of Guise pursued her pro-French policy by taking steps towards the marriage of her daughter to the Dauphin, she was able to enlist Protestant as well as Catholic support. The eight ambassadors appointed to undertake the negotiating mission to France included such committed Protestants as Erskine of Dun; and one name in the list—conspicuously absent from the 'First Band' just eleven days earlier—was that of Lord James Stewart, who had, with Erskine, participated in the March invitation to Knox.[56]

in Knox's version the reference to 'the forward setting of the glorie of God' is followed by the words (missing in the Calderwood version), 'as he [God] will permitt tyme'.

[53] *History*, Laing edn., i. 269; Dickinson edn., i. 133; Mason edn., 134.

[54] Donaldson (*James V to James VII*, 89) points out that this 'First Band', apart from its five signatories, 'failed to attract the many others for whose signatures ample space was provided'.

[55] *History of Scotland*, 2 vols. (Edinburgh, 1791), i. 93. Cf. Lesley, *History*, 260–1.

[56] The eight 'commissioners' were appointed in parliament on 14 Dec. 1557 (*APS* ii. 501–2): they are listed by Cameron, *Scottish Correspondence*, 411 n. 5.

Knox himself, lingering at Dieppe between late October and the turn of the year, responded to these events in a somewhat complex fashion. His initial frustration at being checked in a mission which he had undertaken with some difficulty and perhaps some reluctance was vented in two letters, one (which does not survive) to the Scots nobility at large, the other to the four who had invited him to come back to Scotland. In this surviving letter (dated 27 October 1557) Knox implicitly taunted the four signatories of the March invitation with their professed readiness 'to jeopard their lives . . . for the . . . glorie of God', urging them now that 'yow awght to hasard your awin lyves, (be it against Kingis or Empriours,)' for the deliverance of their afflicted 'subjectis' and 'brethrein'. In developing this admonition Knox for the first time clearly invoked the concept of 'lesser magistrates' with specific responsibilities:

for only for that caus ar ye called Princes of the people, and ye receave of your brethrein honour, tribute, and homage at Goddis commandiment; not be reasson of your birth and progenye, (as the most parte of men falslie do suppose,) but by ressoun of your office and dewtie, which is to vindicat and deliver your subjectes and brethrein from all violence and oppressioun to the uttermost of your power . . .

and he adds, emphatically: 'your conscience shall one day be compelled to acknowledge, that the Reformatioun of religioun, and of publict enormities, doth appertene to mo then to the Clargie, or cheaf reularis called Kingis.'[57] This may well be regarded, especially in view of Knox's reference (vague though it is) to 'publict enormities' as well as to 'the Reformatioun of religioun', as the most significant development so far in his 'political thought'.

Yet Knox showed no inclination as yet to develop these ideas in a more 'radical' direction. When he next wrote, on 17 December, to the Protestant lords (still unaware, of course, of the 'commoun Band' signed a fortnight earlier), there was a distinct note of caution and reserve. And the reason is soon made clear: 'I will . . . advertise yow of sic brut [rumour] as I heir in this partis uncertanlie noysit; whilk is this, that contradictioun and

---

[57] *History*, Laing edn., i. 272; Dickinson edn., i. 135; Mason edn., 137. Knox has a marginal note to the effect that the general letter to the nobility had been 'lost by negligence and trubles'.

rebellioun is maid to the Auctoritie be sum in that realme.' The rumours undoubtedly referred to the refusal to prosecute the planned invasion of England in November; and it is also clear that what chiefly alarmed Knox was the involvement of Châtelherault—'him wha in the beginning of his autoritie and government [as regent] began to profess Chrystis treuth, but suddanlie slyding back, became ane cruell persecutour of Chrystis memberis, a manifest and oppen oppressour of all trew subjectis, and a manteaner of all mischevous men'. It is natural to suppose that Knox was mindful here, in his warning against the danger of contamination by political and dynastic ambition, of the caution recommended by Bullinger (and no doubt by Calvin) a few years before. And his own strenuous recommendation now is

that nane of yow that seik to promote the glorie of Chryst do suddanlie disobey or displeas the establissit Autoritie in thingis lawfull . . . But in the bowellis of Chryst Jesus I exhort yow, that with all simplicitie and lawfull obedience, joynit with boldnes in God, and with open confessioun of your faith, ye seik the favouris of the Autoritie, that by it (yf possibill be) the causs in whilk ye labour may be promotit, or at the leist not persecuted.

Only if and when this policy has failed, will it be lawful to proceed to

the extreamitie, whilk is, to provyd, whidder the Authoritie will consent or no, that Chrystis Evangell may be trewlie preachit, and his halie Sacranentis rychtlie ministerit unto yow, and to your brethren, the subjectis of that Realme. And farther, ye lawfullie may, yea, and thairto is bound to defend your Brethrene from persecutioun and tiranny, be it aganis princes or empriouris, to the uttermost of your power . . .

This was to reiterate the message of his October letters; but Knox now took care to add, 'provyding alwayis . . . that nether your self deny lawfull obedience, nethir yit that ye assist nor promot thois that seik autoritie and pre-eminence of warldlie glorie'. He realized that this caution might seem to accord ill with his reference, in the autumn, to 'the warre begun' between Protestants and the Catholic authorities; but he insisted that there was no contradiction: 'for a greit difference thair is betuix lawfull obedience, and ane feirfull flattering of princes, or ane injust accomplischment of thair desyres in thingis whilk be requyrit or devysit for the distructioun of a commoun-welth. But this article I omit for this present.'[58]

That last sentence suggests a degree of hesitation on Knox's part, an unwillingness to develop more explicitly the consequences of the 'greit difference' to which he had referred. And something of the same ambiguity perplexes the reader of another, almost exactly contemporary document from Knox's pen. A group of French Protestants had been imprisoned in Paris since September 1557, and Knox (who was to visit French congregations in, probably, the early months of 1558), translated the *Apology* which had been published on their behalf and made some additions to the text which are relevant here. He rebuked the 'blindness' of rulers who failed to see that the greatest threat to their authority did not come from Protestants; for 'we affirme that na power on earth is above the power of the Civill reular; that everie saule, be he Pope or Cardinall, aught to be subject to the higher Poweris. That thair commandementis not repugnyng to Godis glorie and honour, aught to be obeyit, evin with great loss of temporall thingis.' The real threat to royal authority came from the 'generatioun of Anti-Chryst'—the popes, cardinals, and bishops, with their claims to clerical immunities and ecclesiastical supremacy. Against this Knox upheld the doctrine of Tertullian, 'that the Emperour and everie Prince within his awn dominiouns, hath his haill autoritie of God, and is inferiour to none but to God onlie'. At the same time, however, Knox was persuaded that 'the regement of Princes is this day cum to that heap of iniquitie, that na godlie man can bruke office or autoritie under thame'; and consequently it was necessary 'that either Princeis be reformit, and be compellit also to reforme thair wickit lawis, or els that all gud men depart fra thair service and cumpany'.[59] He did not, however, give any indication as to how such reforms might be brought about.

---

[58] Laing edn., iv. 284–6; Mason edn., 147–8. A fortnight earlier, on 1 Dec., Knox had written 'To his Brethren in Scotland' about the problems posed by 'the dissolute lyfe of suche as haif professit Chrystis halie Evangell' (Laing edn., iv. 262). That letter (itself an expansion of an earlier one which may have miscarried and has not survived), though important for his ecclesiology and his views on predestination and election, does not touch on issues that are relevant here. It does, however, include (ibid. 277) the interesting *obiter dictum* that 'seldome it is that opin tiranny doith utterlie suppres in any realme or province the trew religioun ernistlie ressavit be a multitude'.

[59] Laing edn., iv. 324–5, 327. Knox's translation is dated (ibid. 347) 'In haist, from Deip, the 7th of December 1557'.

There is thus a pervasive ambiguity in Knox's 'political thought' at this stage in its development. He is now certain that the lesser magistrates, the 'Princes of the people', have the right and duty to seek religious reform and, if this is not carried out by 'the Authoritie', to ensure, on their own initiative, the establishment of sound doctrine and order. He suggests, further, that this corrective power may extend to the wider area of 'publict enormities'—of 'thyngis whilk be requyrit or devysit for the distructioun of a commoun-welth'. At the same time, however, he wishes both to retain for Protestants the political advantage of their being perceived as the consistent defenders of the doctrine of Christian obedience and yet to avoid the risk that the cause of 'Chrystis trewth' may be polluted by worldly motives.

Events were now to bring Knox closer to a decisive resolution of such uncertainties. Several factors would probably, at the end of 1557 and early in 1558, have combined to turn his mind increasingly towards the 'heap of iniquitie' and the problems it posed for the 'gud' and the 'godlie'. He would surely, in Dieppe, have had further news of the continuing persecution in England; he may have heard from Scotland, belatedly, of the queen regent's derisive reception of his letter to her; and he could have learnt of the first steps being taken towards the marriage of the young queen of Scots and the projected grant to her husband of the crown matrimonial.[60] By the time he returned to Geneva, perhaps in early March, Knox was in the state of mind which generated, through the spring and summer of 1558, the most vehement of all his 'political' writings.[61]

The earliest of these pamphlets was also to be the most notorious. What ensured that reputation for *The First Blast of the Trumpet against the Monstrous Regiment of Women* was not the underlying principle or precept on which its argument was based. Most if not

[60] Donaldson, *James V to James VII*, 88–9; Wormald, *Court, Kirk, and Community*, 114–15; Cameron, *Scottish Correspondence*, 377–8.

[61] The dating of these pamphlets, and especially of *The First Blast of the Trumpet*, presents some problems. There does not seem to be any specific evidence for Laing's statement that the *First Blast* 'was probably written at Dieppe towards the end of 1557' (Laing edn., iv. 352). Knox had returned to Geneva by 16 Mar. 1558—when he wrote to Janet Henderson or Guthrie (ibid. 248)—and he had by then visited La Rochelle and probably Lyons on his way back to Switzerland (Ridley, *Knox*, 261–3). By 18 May *The First Blast* had been in print long enough for John Foxe in Basle to have received a copy and written the letter to which Knox replied on that date (Laing edn., v. 3–6). The pamphlet must in any case have been completed and revised in Geneva, where it was published by Jean Crespin.

all of Knox's contemporaries would have accepted the substance, however uneasy they might have felt with the expression, of his essential thesis:

> To promote a Woman to beare rule, superioritie, dominion, or empire, above any Realme, Nation, or Citie, is repugnant to Nature; contumelie to God, a thing most contrarious to his reveled will and approved ordinance; and finallie, it is the subversion of good Order, of all equitie and justice.[62]

That Knox's immediate 'target' was Mary Tudor and his immediate aim her overthrow may be granted readily enough. That he did not have in mind also the situation in Scotland is harder to square with what he in fact says.[63] In any case, he not only takes care to express his argument in general terms: he also endeavours, more than anywhere else in his writings, to cite in support authorities other than that which was for him still, as always, paramount—the Bible. The classical authority of both Aristotle and the civil law is invoked; and, perhaps most importantly, Knox turns to the great tradition of natural law: 'men illuminated onlie by the light of nature, have seen and have determined, that it is a thing most repugnant to nature, that women rule and governe over men.'[64] Nature itself, however, is of course the work of God's creative will; and consequently for Knox there is a 'second part of Nature, in the whiche I include the reveled will and perfect ordinance of God'.[65] The order of nature is the order of God's creation; and political order—'the election of a kinge and apointing of judges'—'did flowe frome the Morall lawe', which, in turn, is 'the

[62] Laing edn., iv. 373; Mason edn., 8. The suggestion (Ridley, *Knox* 267) that in adopting this view Knox had 'decided . . . to pander to popular prejudices which he personally did not really share' has neither evidence nor probability to support it. There is an interesting analysis of the pamphlet by W. I. P. Hazlett, ' "Jihad" against Female Infidels and Satan: Knox's *First Blast of the Trumpet*', in W. van H. Spijker (ed.), *Calvin: Erbe und Auftrag* (Kampen, 1991), 279–90. See also Greaves, *Theology and Revolution*, 157–68.

[63] The English 'targeting' is emphasized by Dawson, 'The Two John Knoxes'. Scotland is mentioned, explicitly or implicitly, seven or eight times in *The First Blast*. The most striking reference is to 'Scotland, by the rashe madnes of foolish Governers, and by the practises of a craftie Dame, resigned . . . under title of mariage, in to the power of France' (Laing edn., iv. 411; Mason edn., 39). This passage, it may be worth noting, was obviously written when Knox was well informed as to the negotiations with France: it occurs, admittedly, within a few pages of the end of the pamphlet.

[64] Laing edn., iv. 374–6; Mason edn., 9–11.

[65] Laing edn., iv. 377; Mason edn., 11.

constant and unchangeable will of God, to the which the Gentil is no lesse bounde then [than] was the Jewe'.[66] This means that, willing though Knox may be to broaden the basis of his argument, he cannot allow what would have been the commonest justification of female rule—that it was grounded in established law and custom or in the consent of the community. Knox will have none of this: 'nether may the tyrannie of princes, nether the foolishnes of people, nether wicked lawes made against God, nether yet the felicitie that in this earthe may hereof issue, make that thing laufull which he by his Word hath manifestlie condemned.'[67]

Here, for many readers, was where the trouble started—with the implied subversion of the established order. Worse was to come. Knox insisted that in a realm afflicted with the government of a woman, patient endurance was not enough:

they must studie to represse her inordinate pride and tyrannie to the uttermost of their power.
The same is the dutie of the Nobilitie and Estates, by whose blindnes a Woman is promoted . . .
The same is the dutie aswell of the Estates as of the People that hath bene blinded. First, They oght to remove from honor and authoritie that monstre in nature . . . Secondarilie, if any presume to defend that impietie, they oght not to feare first to pronounce, and then after to execute against them the sentence of deathe.[68]

That Knox had in mind above all the application of this doctrine to the England of Mary Tudor may be both true and obvious; but his argument was deliberately expressed in alarmingly general terms. Nor was it, in its nature, an argument that could be applied specifically and exclusively to the case of female rule. This was only the *First Blast*: others were certainly in Knox's repertoire, as he himself was to make clear enough within a few months of the (anonymous) publication of his pamphlet.

In the *Appellation*, published in the summer of 1558, Knox was, as we shall see presently, concerned mainly with the situation in Scotland. Yet he went out of way to reaffirm, if anything still more sharply, the message of the *First Blast*: 'I fear not to affirm, that it had bene the dutie of the Nobilitie, Judges, Rulers and People of

[66] Laing edn., iv. 377, 397, 399; Mason edn., 11, 29, 30.
[67] Laing edn., iv. 413; Mason edn., 41–2.
[68] Laing edn., iv. 415–16; Mason edn., 43–4.

England, not only to have resisted . . . Marie, that Jesabel, whome they call their Queen, but also to have punished her to the death.' And that duty, he now claimed, had been theirs as soon as the suppression of 'Chrystes Evangil' and the restoration of 'divellish idolatrie' had begun.[69] He went further, however. He appended to the new pamphlet an outline of his intended argument in the *Second Blast* (which he never in fact completed). These four 'Propositions' merit careful consideration as being, arguably, Knox's boldest generalizations in regard to political issues.

The first proposition states that lawful royal power over a Christian people depends, not on 'birth onely, nor propinquitie of blood', but on 'election' in accordance with 'the ordenance, which God hath established in the electioun of inferiour judges'. Secondly, 'No manifest idolater, nor notoriouse transgressor of God's holie preceptes, oght to be promoted to any publike regiment . . . in any realme, province, or citie, that hath subjected the self to Christe Jesus'. Neither, the third proposition adds, 'can othe nor promesse bynd any such people to obey and maintain Tyrantes against God'. The consequence, expressed in the fourth proposition, is that if any such 'wicked personne' has been rashely . . . or ignorantly' appointed to rule and subsequently 'declareth himself unworthie of regiment . . . moste justly may the same men depose and punishe him, that unadvysedlie before did nominate, appoint, and electe' him.[70]

Bold as these propositions are, they are stated with a crucial limitation. They apply to 'any realme, province, or citie, that hath subjected the self to Christe Jesus'. This, in Knox's eyes, was true of England by virtue of the settlement made under Edward VI and subverted by Mary. It was not yet true of Scotland; and this makes a significant difference to the course of action Knox advocates in his *Appellation* and the accompanying *Letter to the*

[69] Laing edn., iv. 507; Mason edn., 104. The *Appellation* was published in Geneva in 1558, sometime after 14 July (the date of Knox's 'Letter to the Commonalty': Laing edn., iv. 538; Mason edn., 127). The volume also included (besides the 'Propositions', discussed below, intended for development in Knox's *Second Blast*) *An Admonition to England and Scotland* by Anthony Gilby—which underlines the Anglo-Scottish concerns of Knox and his associates at this period.

[70] Laing edn., iv. 539–40; Mason edn., 128–9. The 'Propositions' are headed 'John Knox to the Reader', so that Knox himself ended the short-lived anonymity of his *First Blast*.

Commonalty of Scotland. That he regarded his strictures on female government as fully applicable to the queen regent is certain. With the conclusion of the marriage treaty, Mary of Guise had become for Knox the 'craftie Dame' by whose 'practises', together with 'the rashe madnes of foolish Governers', Scotland had been 'resigned . . . in to the power of France'.[71] And when, in the summer of 1558, he expanded his 1556 letter to the regent, he told her bluntly that her power was merely 'borrowed, extraordinarie, and unstable', held only 'by permission of others; and', he added 'seldom it is that Women do long reigne with felicitie and joy'.[72] He also sharpened his teaching as to obeying God rather than man and, to the accusation that this might lead to 'sedition' and 'tumultes', replied that 'everie tumult and breach of publike order' was not 'contrarie to Goddes commandement'. The prophets had 'feared not to breake publike order established against God'.[73] The implied threat is unmistakable. Yet Knox was not quite ready to treat Mary of Guise as he would have wished Mary Tudor to be treated. The text of the original letter still stood: the appeal is still that the regent should use her authority—no matter how 'extraordinarie' and 'unstable'—in the cause of religious reform.

Knox can have had few illusions as to the response to his appeal. The letter had become a mere appendage to more important themes; for he was now ready to clarify his 'political' message to those who had embraced 'Christ's truth'. His *Appellation* is above all 'his supplication and exhortation to the nobilitie, estates, and communaltie' of Scotland.[74] So far as the nobility and estates are concerned he advocates positively what, nine months or so before, he had described as 'the extreamitie'. They must now, as 'Heades of your commune welth' provide for the instruction of their subjects in true religion, defend them 'from all oppression and tirannie', and see to it that those who 'blynde and deceave the people' or 'robbe and oppresse the flock, may be removed and punished as God's Law prescribeth'. They are 'Magistrates': God has 'marked' them as such 'by his owne seall'.[75] Knox goes on to

[71] Laing edn., iv. 411; Mason edn., 39.
[72] Laing edn., iv. 452; Mason edn., 65.
[73] Laing edn., iv. 441–2; Mason edn., 56–7.
[74] See the title-page of the original edn., reproduced by Laing, iv. 465.
[75] Laing edn., iv. 481–2; Mason edn., 83.

elaborate the argument that 'the Reformation of religion in all points' is one of the duties of civil rulers—a duty incumbent not only upon kings but upon 'Nobils and Estates' as 'Judges and Princes'.[76] Now, however, the argument is taken a significant step further.

Already in the *Appellation* Knox made the point he developed fully in the *Letter to the Commonalty*. The duty of establishing and maintaining true religion falls not only on the sovereign, not only on the nobility and estates: it is also the duty of 'the whole bodie of that people, and . . . every membre of the same, according to the vocation of everie man, and according to that possibilitie and occasion which God doth minister to revenge the injurie done against his glorie, what time that impietie is manifestly knowen'.[77] In the *Letter* Knox relates this explicitly to the equal dignity of all Christians:

Beloved Brethren, ye are Goddes creatures, created and formed in his owne image and similitude, for whose redemption was shed the most pretious blood of the onlie beloved Sonne of God . . . [T]he gospell . . . of the kingdome truelie preached, is the power of God to the salvation of everie belever, which to credit and receave, you, the Communaltie, are no less adetted then [than] be your Rulers and Princes. For albeit God hath put and ordened distinction and difference betwixt the King and subjects, betwixt the Rulers and the commune people, in the regiment and administration of Civile policies, yet in the hope of the life to come he hath made all equall.[78]

It followed that

ye, althoghe ye be but subjectes, may lawfully require of your superiours, be it of your King, be it of your Lordes, rulers, and powers, that they provide for you true Preachers, and . . . expell such as . . . devoure and destroy the flock . . . And if in this point your superiours be negligent, or yet pretend to maintaine tyrantes in their tyrannie, most justly ye may provide true teachers for yourselves . . . Ye may, moreover, withhold the frutes and profettes which your fals Byshopes and Clergie most injustly receyve of you.[79]

And failure to discharge what Knox plainly saw (despite the permissive language in the passage just cited) as a duty, would

---

[76] Laing edn., iv. 490, 494–5; Mason edn., 90, 94.
[77] Laing edn., iv. 501; Mason edn., 99.
[78] Laing edn., iv. 526–7; Mason edn., 118.
[79] Laing edn., iv. 533–4; Mason edn., 123–4.

mean that the people would be 'criminal and gyltie . . . of the same crimes' as their 'Princes . . . Rulers' and 'Byshoppes'.[80]

Yet caution is still necessary in establishing the precise import of Knox's political doctrine. No doubt he was ready to invoke the power of the 'commonalty', but only as the *ultima ratio* in situations that would otherwise be desperate. He may well by now have finally abandoned whatever hope he had had of persuading 'the Authoritie' to become the instrument of reform; but, for the remedy, he turned in the first place and above all to the 'Princes of the people'. Having pointed, in the *Appellation*, to the responsibility of 'the whole bodie' of the realm, he again addressed the nobility: 'if this be required of the whole people, and of everie man in his vocation, what shall be required of you, my Lordes, whome God hath raised upp to be Princes and Rulers above your brethren . . . yea, whome he hath appointed to be as bridels, to represse the rage and insolencie of your Kinges . . . ?'[81] In that last phrase Knox was of course associating himself with a powerful element in 'constitutionalist' thinking—illustrated, for instance, in Seyssel's *Monarchie de France*, and soon to be radically exemplified in the Scottish context by George Buchanan.[82] It would, however, be a mistake to ascribe to Knox any such wide-ranging 'political theory'.

Knox did, to be sure, manifest an awareness of broader political issues and of the reality of 'constitutional' principles and practices. For him, however, such matters are always, at best, subordinate to the imperatives—the divine imperatives—of religious truth and purity. In the *Appellation*, specifically, there is not even the kind of passing reference to 'publict enormities' outside the area of religion that can be found, occasionally, in his earlier writings. He was both profoundly convinced that merely political considerations must never be allowed to prevail over the demands of God's law and profoundly concerned to safeguard the integrity of religious purposes against the infection of worldly ambition. It cannot be doubted that by the summer of 1558 he was advocating revolution and tyrannicide in England and, in Scotland, at least direct intervention by the nobility and estates,

---

[80] Laing edn., iv. 535; Mason edn., 124–5.

[81] Laing edn., iv. 504; Mason edn., 102.

[82] Claude de Seyssel (ed. J. Poujol), *La Monarchie de France et deux autres fragments* (Paris, 1961), 119, 154–5; and for Buchanan see Ch. 6.

backed by the commonalty, in the crucial area of religious policy. The first of these programmes was rendered unnecessary by the death of Mary Tudor. The second was to be carried out; but the process of doing so was to be a more complex matter than Knox's dogmatic simplifications implied.

5

Congregation, Kirk, and Crown

WHATEVER influence John Knox's polemics in 1558 may have had—and we have no firm evidence as to the reception of his pamphlets in Scotland—cannot have been a major factor in the shaping of events during the first critical phase of the Scottish Reformation. Knox's preaching in 1555–6 had no doubt been seminal; his admonitions in the latter part of 1557 may, despite their ambiguities, have acted as a catalyst; but the revolution which came to a head in 1559–60 was not produced, though it may have been fostered, by pamphleteering. This is not, of course, to say that the revolution could or did dispense with ideology. Nor need it be doubted that Knox contributed, both before and during the crisis, to the making of the requisite ideology. What must be emphasized, however, is that the nature of the revolutionary movement was such as could not be sustained solely by a diet of biblically inspired prophecy and denunciation. The political ideas of the Congregation in the struggle which led to the establishing of the kirk contained Knoxian (or similar) elements, but the arguments that were used had a broader basis and their appeal was directed to a wider audience—even, in the end, to an audience extending furth of Scotland itself.[1]

Initially, it is true, the Congregation sought to make a virtue of steering clear of political as distinct from essentially religious issues. The steps taken immediately after the 'first Band' of December 1557 seem to have been directed towards building up a framework for Protestant prayer and worship without precipitating a direct confrontation with the authorities. And although, according to Knox, some 'Headis . . . concernyng the Polecy' were agreed upon at the same time, there is no indication as to what these political issues were, nor do they appear to have been

---

[1] See R. A. Mason, 'Covenant and Commonweal: The Language of Politics in Reformation Scotland', in N. Macdougall (ed.), *Church, Politics and Society: Scotland 1406–1929* (Edinburgh, 1983), 97–126.

pursued at this stage.[2] When, in the spring of 1558, the bishops
questioned the behaviour of the earl of Argyll in maintaining
a Protestant preacher in his household, the earl stood his
ground and declared at the same time, 'I will serve my Princess
with bodye, harte, goodis, strenth, and all that is in my power,
except that whilk is Goddis dewitie, quhilk I will reserve to him
self alone.'[3] The burning for heresy of the aged Walter Myln in
April might suggest a more vigorous policy on the part of the
ecclesiastical authorities, though it may at the same time have
gained some increase in sympathy for the Protestant cause. In any
case Protestant progress was irregular and uneven, with no indication of any major change in the religious situation during the
summer.

Meanwhile a political situation in which dynastic considerations were always prominent and sometimes paramount was
entering a period of almost kaleidoscopic transformation. With
the marriage of the queen of Scots to the Dauphin in April 1558
one major object of her mother's policy was achieved. Not until
December, however, did the Scottish parliament finally grant
Francis the crown matrimonial. This, together with the somewhat
open 'secret' provisions of the marriage treaty threatened the
interests of the house of Hamilton, though a further nine months
were to elapse before Châtelherault concluded that those interests
required his adherence to the Congregation.[4] Already in November 1558, however, only a week or two before the estates met, new
prospects for the Protestants had opened—though the width of
the opening was to remain far from clear for many months. The
death of Mary Tudor and the accession of Elizabeth meant that
the Congregation might attract the English support which was
ultimately to be decisive in securing the victory of 1560.

Yet the moment for resolute political commitment still lay in
the future. Sometime in the autumn of 1558 the Congregation
had made a further approach to the queen regent, attributing to
her, in her 'grave Counsell', a desire to bring about 'a publict
Reformatioun, alsweall in the religioun as in the temporall

[2] Knox, *Works*, Laing edn., i. 276; Knox, *History*, Dickinson edn., i. 138.
[3] Laing edn., i. 284; Dickinson edn., ii. 250–1.
[4] Châtelherault was, though not unchallengeably, heir-presumptive to the
crown until the birth of James VI in 1566. For his position at this period see
Dickinson edn., i. 230 n. 2.

government'. This 'first Oratioun, and Petitioun' does refer to 'defaultes in the Temporall regiment'; but its specific concerns are exclusively with religious issues—access to the Bible 'in our commoun toung'; the right to interpret Scripture 'in oure... conventionis'; the administration of baptism in the vernacular; communion under both kinds; and the reform of 'the wicked, sklanderous, and detestable Lyiff of Prelates, and of the State Ecclesiasticall'.[5] When, in late November or early December, the matter was raised in parliament—with a view, in particular, to suspending the doctrinal jurisdiction of the ecclesiastical authorities—two points were emphasized. First, it was recognized that 'tumult or uproare' might now be unavoidable in the pursuit of religious reform: but this should not be imputed to the Protestants, 'who most humlie do now seak all thinges to be reformed by ane ordour'. Secondly, the petitioners insist that their 'requeastis, proceeding from conscience, do tend to none other end, but to the Reformatioun of abuses in Religioun onlie': it is as 'faithfull and obedient subjectis' that they seek the protection of 'the Sacred Authoritie'.[6]

The queen regent's response to this situation was, it seems, to urge the archbishop of St Andrews, equipped as he was with the powers of a *legatus a latere*, to summon a provincial council of the Scottish church. This assembly, meeting in March and April 1559, has been called 'the final instalment of Mary's policy of conciliation'.[7] By the time it met, indeed, diplomatic developments had eroded such motivation as that policy had hitherto had. The Franco-Spanish truce of October 1558 ripened into the treaty of Cateau-Cambrésis (March–April 1559), in which England and Scotland were included. Free, at least for the time being, of any fear of English intervention, the regent turned to deal more resolutely with a movement in which she doubtless saw danger at least as much from 'sedition' as from heresy.[8] Knox points to Easter (26 March) as the turning-point; and in a different perspective Ninian Winzet experienced a decisive change in Linlithgow

---

[5] Laing edn., i. 302–6; Dickinson edn., i. 149–52.
[6] Laing edn., i. 309–14; Dickinson edn., i. 154–8.
[7] Donaldson, *James V to James VII*, 91.
[8] See e.g. Laing edn., i. 324, 329; Dickinson edn., i. 163, 167. The second passage, citing a letter addressed 'to those of the Nobilitie who than [then] persecuted us', refers to the view of the Protestants as 'Heretickis, seditious men, and trubilleris of the commoun wealth'.

between Easter and Pentecost.[9] By coincidence it was near the end of the paschal season that Knox himself returned finally to Scotland. The situation in which he at once became involved was already one of 'tumult' and indeed, though on a modest scale, of civil war. In such circumstances it was less and less possible for the Congregation to eschew politics. Yet they still sought studiously to maintain that, if they were 'compelled to tak the sweard of just defence against all that shall persew us for the mater of religioun, and for our conscience saik', this would not imply any withdrawal in other respects of their 'accustomed obedience . . . to our Soverane Maistres, to hir Husband, and unto your grace Regent'. Now, however (writing to Mary of Lorraine on 22 May 1559), they added that, if persecution continued, they would take their case to a larger tribunal, appealing not only 'to the King of France . . . but also to the Princes and Counsall of everie Christiane Realme' in justification of their 'revolt'.[10]

From France, needless to say, they could hope for no favour. England might be another matter. In May the Acts of Supremacy and Uniformity had firmly established the direction to be taken by Elizabeth's religious policy. Both the queen's dislike of rebellion, however, and the desire to safeguard England's dwindling hopes of recovering Calais by avoiding action prejudicial to French interests restricted the prospects of English support for the Scottish Protestants. Circumstances changed yet again with the premature death of Henry II in July. This brought Francis II and Mary Stewart to the throne of France as well as Scotland, and their armorial quarterings heralded the intention of asserting Mary's claim to the English crown as well.[11] So far as Scotland was concerned, Mary's new status made it at least highly probable that she would never return to reign in person: the realm would become a French appanage, destined by the marriage treaty to pass to Francis and Mary's heirs. All this was reflected in the belated return to the Protestant fold of Châtelherault, nearest heir to the crown; in the project of a marriage between his son Arran and Elizabeth; and in the increasingly political programme adopted by the Congregation.

[9] Laing edn., i. 315–16; Dickinson edn., i. 158–9. Cf. Ninian Winzet, *Certane Tractatis for Reformatioun of Doctryne and maneris*, in J. K. Hewison (ed.), *Certain Tractates*, etc., 2 vols. (Scottish Text Society; Edinburgh, 1888, 1890) i. 53.

[10] Laing edn., i. 26–7; Dickinson edn., i. 164–5; *Knox: On Rebellion*, Mason edn., 149–50.

[11] *Cal. Scot. Pap.*, i, no. 509.

By the time the news, first, of the French king's wound and then of his death reached them, the Protestants had occupied Edinburgh, though their hold on the capital was precarious and was to be surrendered before the end of July. At the beginning of the month, faced with a royal proclamation in which their 'seditious tumult' was denounced and they themselves were branded as 'manifest traytouris', they once again protested that their

mynd and purpose was and is to promote and sett furth the glorie of God, maynteane and defend the trew poreacharis of his word; and . . . abolish and put away idolatrie and false abusis . . . For as to the obedience of our Soveraneis authorotie in all civile and politick matteris, we ar and shalbe als obedient as ony uther your Gracis subjectis within this realme.[12]

Yet, as the proclamation had pointed out, they had already 'violentlie intrometted with, taikin, and yot withhaldis the irnis of our Cunzie hous [the royal mint], quhilk is ane of the cheife pointis that concernis our Crown'. Such actions, it was argued, 'declaired, that it is na religioun, nor any thing thairto perteaning, that thai seak, but onelie the subversioun of our authoritie, and usurpatioun of our Crown'.[13] The rejoinder, so far as the coining-irons were concerned, certainly indicated that the Congregation's concerns extended beyond strictly religious issues: the justification of the seizure was 'that the commoun wealth was greatlie hurt by corrupting of our money'. As for the charge of usurpation—'we war borne counsalouris of this realme, sworne to procure the proffit of the same' and as such it was for them a matter 'of dewetie and of conscience' to prevent whatever 'should turne to the detriment of the hole body of this realme'.[14]

The charge of sedition and usurpation went further, however. Privately (according to Knox), the queen regent 'abused' Châtelherault by 'perswaiding unto him, and unto his freindis, that the . . . Erle [of Argyll] and Priour [of St Andrews: Lord James Stewart] had conspyred, first to deprive our Soverane . . . of hir authoritie, and thairefter the Duke and his successioun of thair titill to the Crown of Scotland'.[15] Publicly, the proclamation of 1 July linked the charge of 'subversioun' with the allegation that the Congregation 'daylie receave Inglismen with messagis unto

[12] Laing edn., i. 365–6; Dickinson edn., i. 194–5.
[13] Laing edn., i. 364; Dickinson edn., i. 193.
[14] Laing edn., i. 372; Dickinson edn., i. 199.
[15] Laing edn., i. 368 (cf. 420); Dickinson edn., i. 196 (cf. 234).

thame, and sendis siclyk in Ingland'.[16] That there were contacts
with England is neither doubtful nor surprising, though it may be
that these had not so far been at the highest level. Soon, however,
there was a change in that respect. On 19 July, just nine days
after Henry II's death, letters (penned by Knox, then acting as
secretary) were addressed by the leaders of the Congregation
both to Elizabeth herself and to Cecil, her principal adviser.
Argyll, Glencairn, Lord James, and their colleagues still represented their 'hole and onlie purpos' as being largely concerned
with 'the glory of Christ Jesus' and those things which, in their
view, conduced directly to the advancement of that cause; but
they also declared their determination 'to maintean the libertie of
this oure countrey from the tyranny and thraldome of strangearis
as God shall assist us'.[17] Elizabeth vouchsafed no direct reply; but
Cecil responded promptly enough, though circumspectly. Writing on 28 July, he raised 'doubts whether all sorts of men' might
take the kind of action the Protestant nobles envisaged, 'or some
only'.[18] These doubts Argyll and Lord James sought, in a letter
dated 13 August, to dispel: 'our consciences are fully persuaded it
not only appertains to us as part of the nobles and council, to
provide that the ancient liberties of the realm be freed from the
tyranny of strangers, but also to abolish (God assisting us)
all manifest idolatry and [its] maintainers.'[19] By the end of the
month there were indications that this policy might entail drastic
measures.

In a memorandum dated 31 August 1559 and endorsed by
Cecil, the possibility of replacing Mary Queen of Scots on the
throne by 'a Scotsman in blud' was envisaged and the claims of
the house of Hamilton were recognized. If Mary and Francis
would not agree to the establishment of a council to govern in the
queen's absence, with the suppression of 'idolatry' as one of its
objectives, then 'the Estates shall commit the government to the
next heir'. That situation was interpreted as implying that 'Al-
mighty God is pleased to transfer from her the rule of that
kingdom for the weale of it'; but plainly the instrument of that
divine transference was to be an act of deposition by the Scottish
parliament. [20]

---

[16] Laing edn., i. 364; Dickinson edn., i. 193.
[17] *Cal. Scot. Pap.*, i, nos. 493, 494.   [18] Ibid., no. 506.   [19] Ibid., no. 525.
[20] Ibid., no. 537.

In Scotland meanwhile the rival parties wrangled and manœuvred over the 'Appointment' in terms of which the Congregation had left Edinburgh.[21] The climax came with a proclamation by the regent on 28 August and the retort this evoked. In the proclamation 'sum Prechearis of the Congregatioun' were accused of provoking 'seditioun and tumult' by attacking 'Princeis in generall ... and ... the obedience to the hiear poweris', and those in authority throughout the realm were urged 'to tak ordour ... that ... the Prechearis ... use thame self mair modestlie ... and ... not to mell [meddle] sa mekle with civill policie and publict governance'.[22] The Congregation's response was certainly the most overtly 'political' statement yet made by them. Addressed 'To the Nobilitie, Burghis and Communitie of the Realme of Scotland', it referred even in its heading to 'the advancement ... of the Commonwealth' as well as 'the glorie of God'; and its opening appeal was to '[t]he love of oure natyve cuntrey'. Only towards the end of a lengthy document is the religious issue directly raised; and when it is, a point is made of urging even those not 'perswaidit' by that consideration not to 'cast ... away the cair you aucht to have ower your communwelth' and to 'remember your deir wyffis, children, and posteratie, your ancient heretageis and houssis'. All these interests, they are warned, are endangered by the regent's sinister policy, directed as it is to the bringing in of 'strangearis'. The threat posed by French troops, which had been at the heart of the Congregation's anxieties throughout the spring and summer, was now intensified; but it is expressed here in the context of a comprehensive attack on the queen regent's administration.[23]

What we have here is in fact a political manifesto; and the political content may be identified as exhibiting at once the traditional discontents of feudal magnates, the anxieties of a gentry class then achieving greater political awareness and significance, and the commercial interests of the burgesses. The last of these points is plainly reflected in the elaborate attack on the debasement of the coinage, with the attendant risk that 'the haill exchange and traffique to be had with forane natiounis (ane thing

---

[21] Laing edn., i. 376–97; Dickinson edn., i. 202–17 (and cf. the lengthy index entry under 'Leith, Appointment at the Links of', Dickinson edn., ii. 437).

[22] Laing edn., i. 399; Dickinson edn., i. 218–19; Mason edn., 158–9.

[23] Laing edn., i. 400–8; Dickinson edn., i. 219–26; Mason edn., 159–65.

maist necessarie in all commun-wealthis,) sall thairby be utterlie extinguissitt'.[24] More generally, there is a strong emphasis on the endangered private and family rights of property and inheritance, and a pointed reference to 'unaccustomit and exhorbitant taxatiounis' and the associated 'inquisitioun tane of all your gudis'.[25] Running throughout, there is an appeal to 'our ancient lawis and liberteis', violated already by actions 'done without the avise or consent of the Nobilitie and Counsall of this realme'.[26] In effect an 'ancient constitution' was invoked against an arbitrary and (literally as well as figuratively) alien abuse of royal power.

As the Congregation saw things, the 'serpent lurking in the breist of our adversareis' was the intention 'to bring yow and us baith under the perpetuall servitude of strangearis'. In opposition to this they demanded, in the latter part of September 1559, that the queen regent should 'joyne to hir ane Counsall of naturall Scottismen': if this were granted, along with 'permitting the religioun to have fre passage', they still claimed that 'than [then] sould nane in Scotland be mair willing to serve hir Grace than sould the Lordis and Brethren of the Congregatioun be'.[27] There may be an echo here of the proposal in the memorandum at the end of August for a council to act on behalf of the absent queen; but there is now no hint of any attempt to depose her. That strategic objective may well have persisted in some minds, but the tactical aim for the time being was to subvert the regent's authority. It was with this in view that the Congregation, early in October, addressed the princes of Christendom at large in a Latin manifesto. Their emphasis here was principally upon the usurpation of the chief offices of state by Frenchmen. They traced the whole history of Mary of Guise's regency, making, among other points, the extraordinary claim that the Protestants had been

[24] Laing edn., i. 402–4; Dickinson edn., i. 221–2; Mason edn., 160–1. There is an interesting reference in this passage to the alleged activities of James III's favourite Thomas Cochrane (Laing edn., i. 402 at n. 1; Dickinson edn., i. 261 at n. 4; Mason edn., 161). For the development of the Cochrane 'legend' down to this period, see N. Macdougall, ' "It is I, the Earle of Mar": In Search of Thomas Cochrane', in id. and R. A. Mason (eds.), *People and Power in Scotland: Essays in Honour of T. C. Smout* (Edinburgh, 1992), 28–49.

[25] Laing edn., i. 402; Dickinson edn., i. 221; Mason edn., 160.

[26] Laing edn., i. 402, 406; Dickinson edn., i. 220, 224; Mason edn., 160, 161, 163–4.

[27] Laing edn., i. 405, 415; Dickinson edn., i. 223, 230.

encouraged by her French advisers to attack abuses in the church
and so put themselves in a false position. [28] The charges of debas-
ing the coinage and bringing in foreign troops to subjugate the
country are rehearsed. In fine, the manifesto claims, no rebellion
is involved, but only a just defence of the ancient liberty (*pristina
libertas*) of the realm. There is, for obvious reasons, given the
audience that is being addressed, no reference here to the advancement of 'Christ's truth'.[29]

In Scotland the Congregation were by now preparing the way
for the deposition of the queen regent. She for her part, prompted
by the archbishop of St Andrews, issued a proclamation on
2 October accusing the Congregation, and specifically its two
most notable recent recruits, Châtelherault and his son Arran, of
using 'the pretendit quarrell of religioun' to further their political
ambitions. Their aim, she declared, was nothing less than 'to
pervert the haill obedience' of the queen's subjects by themselves
'usurping the Authoratie'.[30] This evoked a lengthy reply, the details of which need not be examined here; but there are ideological
points in it of some interest. Rebutting the charge that their aim
was 'the subversioun and overthraw of all just authoritie', the
Lords claim that they 'thocht na thing but that sick authoratie
as God approvis by his word, be establischeit, honourit, and
obeyit'.[31] This has the authentic Knoxian resonance. So does the
subsequent avowal of the intent to 'brydill [the regent's] blynd
raige, in the quhilk sche wald erect and mantene idolatrie, and
wald murther oure brethren quha refuses the same'. She thus
'dois utterlie abuse the authoratie establischeitt by God'.[32] Such
language is strikingly reminiscent of a letter written about three
weeks after Knox's return to Scotland, in which those members of
the nobility hostile to the Congregation were admonished that
'[t]he name and the cloke of the Authoritie, whiche ye pretend,
will nothing excuse yow in Godis presence'; for 'thair is a great
difference betuix the authoritie quhiche is Godis ordinance, and
the personis of those whiche ar placit in authoritie'. The divinely
ordained authority 'can never do wrang ... But the corrupt

[28] A. Teulet (ed.), *Papiers d'état relatifs a l'histoire de l'Écosse au XVIe. siècle*, 3 vols.
(Paris, 1852–60), i. 422–3.

[29] Ibid. 425–8.   [30] Laing edn., i. 421–4; Dickinson edn., i. 235–7.

[31] Laing edn., i. 424; Dickinson edn., i. 238.

[32] Laing edn., i. 428; Dickinson edn., i. 240.

Persone placed in this authoritie may offend'.[33] Four months later
this doctrine was being brought to bear upon 'the Quene Regent
and hir perverst Counsall'.

Yet, concerned though they were to claim that it was 'nothing
ellis, bot the zeall of the trew religioun quhilk movis us to this
interpryse', the Lords of the Congregation were not acting simply
as 'professors of Christ's truth'. In this same 'Declaratioun', they
insist that 'God hes maid us counsallouris be [by] birth of this
realme', bound by nature 'to luiff our awin cuntrey' and by oath
'to be trew to this commune-wealth'.[34] And their 'interpryse'—or
this phase of it—was now to culminate in a resolutely political act.

On 21 October, once more in occupation of the capital and
assembled in the Tolbooth, 'The Nobilitie, Baronis, and Broughes
convenit to advise upoun the affairis of the commoun-weall' ordained the suspension of the queen regent's 'Commissioun',
claiming to do this 'In name and authorite of our Soverane Lord
and Lady'—from whom, of course the commission of regency
had emanated. The declared grounds of this act were entirely
temporal, the religious issue being barely mentioned in the document. Mary of Guise 'and certane strangearis her Prevey
Counsallouris' are charged by the assembly with 'the interprysed
destructioun of thair said commoun-weall, and overthrow of the
libertie of thair native cuntree'. This, it is said, would 'mak us and
our posteritie slaves to strangearis for ever; Whiche, as it is
intollerable in commounn-wealthis and free cuntreis, sa is it
verray prejudiciall to our Soverane Ladye, and her airis
quhatsumever, in caise our Soverane Lord deceise butt [without]
airis of her Grace's persone'. There is vehement condemnation of
'ane strangear in ane of the greatest offices of credite within this
realme'—Yves de Rubay's appointment as Keeper of the Great
Seal (or vice-chancellor)—with a particularly interesting reference
to his having 'introducit a new captiouse styill and forme
of . . . pardonis and remissionis', with the alleged attendant risk
of 'the haill subversioun and alteratioun of the remanent lawis of
this realme'. This and the regent's other 'wicked interprises' had
been carried out 'against the express will of the Nobilitie and
Counsall'; and all endeavours had failed to induce her to 'joyne
her self to us, to consult upoun the effaris of our commoun-weall,

[33] Laing edn., i. 331–2; Dickinson edn., i. 168; Mason edn., 153–4.
[34] Laing edn., i. 432; Dickinson, i. 243.

as we that be borne Counsallouris to the same, be [by] the ancient lawis of the realme'.[35] And so, the Lords informed Mary of Guise in a letter written two days later, 'as your Grace will not acknawledge us, our Soverane Lord and Ladyis liegis, trew barones and liegis, for your subjectis and Counsall, na mair will we acknawledge yow for any Regent or lauchfull Magistrat unto us'.[36] When, on 24 October, the Congregation 'summoned the towne of Leyth'—held by the regent and her French troops—they did so 'in name of oure Soverane Lord and Lady, and of the Counsall presentlie in Edinburgh' and again 'in our Soveranmis and thair said Counsallis namis'.[37] The form of a 'provisional government' had been established: how much substance it might have remained to be seen.

It is possible to see in these proceedings 'the transfer of power from an "ungodly prince" to what may be called a "godly council"—a "great council of the realm," under the duke [of Châtelherault]'s presidency'.[38] Yet the Congregation had to navigate a hazardous passage among rocks and shoals of several kinds. 'Godliness' alone would not serve their purposes; and the taint of rebellion might wreck their best (indeed their only) hope—the support of the queen of England. The decision on 21 October was taken after consulting the principal preachers— John Willock and John Knox, now colleagues in the ministry of what was about to become the High Kirk of Edinburgh. It was Willock who stated the 'godly' grounds for depriving the queen regent of her authority: the power of rulers was 'bounded and limited by God in his word'; subjects owe obedience, but rulers are commanded by God 'to give some dewitie to the subjectis'; though rulers are God's 'lieutennentis on earth', their divine commission was never such 'but that for just causses thei mycht have bene depryved'; and finally 'in deposing Princes . . . God did nott alwayis use his immediate poware; but sometymes he used other meanis whiche his wisedome thocht good and justice approved'. Willock's conclusion was that Mary of Guise might justly be deprived of authority inasmuch as she had failed to administer justice impartially, to preserve her subjects' 'liberties from

[35] Laing edn., i. 444–8; Dickinson edn., i. 251–5; Mason edn., 171–4.
[36] Laing edn., i. 450; Dickinson edn., i. 255.
[37] Laing edn., i. 451; Dickinson edn., i. 256.
[38] Donaldson, *James V to James VII*, 97.

invasioun of strangearis, and to suffer thame have Godis word freelie and openlie preached amanges thame'. She was besides 'ane open and obstinat idolatress, a vehement manteanare of all superstitioun and idolatrie; and finallie . . . sche utterlie dispysed the counsall and requeistis of the Nobilitie'.[39] Reassuring as all this may have been to some consciences, remarkably little—indeed virtually nothing—of the 'godly' case against the regent appeared in the act of deprivation itself.

Knox for his part had, while endorsing Willock's doctrine, struck a somewhat cautious note, insisting that 'the iniquitie of the Quene Regent, and mysordour owght in nowyis to withdraw neather our heartis, neather yitt the heartis of other subjectis, from the obedience dew unto our Soveranis'. They would not 'escheap Godis just punishment' if they were guilty of deposing the regent 'rather of malice or private invy, than for the preservatioun of the commoun-wealth, and for that her synnes appeared incurable'. Further, any sentence of deprivation should be reversible 'upoun her knawin and oppen repentance, and upoun her conversioun to the commoun-wealth, and submissioun to the Nobilitie'.[40]

These circumspect views are consonant with much of Knox's thinking during the half-year since his return to Scotland. Concerned, even before that, to undo the damage done to his reputation by the extremities of the *First Blast*, he had come to terms, in his own way, with Elizabeth's succession. Writing to Cecil from Dieppe on 10 April 1559, he neither denied the authorship nor retracted the doctrine of the pamphlet which had so incensed the English queen. He declared that he was no 'ennemye to the Persone or yet to the Regiment of her quhome God hath now promoted'; but he insisted that her authority was the result of 'the miraculouse wark of God, comforting his afflicted by ane infirme veschell'. It would be 'foolishe presumpcioun' for Elizabeth to 'ground . . . the justnes of her title upoun consuetude, lawis, or ordinances of men'.[41] Not surprisingly, Knox was denied the permission he then sought to visit England. Back in Scotland and deep in the counsels of the Congregation, he wrote two further letters to Cecil, with the second of which he enclosed a letter (dated 20 July 1559) addressed 'To the verteous and godlie

[39] Laing edn., i. 442–3; Dickinson edn., i. 250; Mason edn., 169–70.
[40] Laing edn., i. 443; Dickinson edn., i. 250–1; Mason edn., 170–1.
[41] Laing edn., ii. 20–1; Dickinson edn., i. 285–6.

Elizabeth, by the Grace of God Quein of England'. It cannot have done much to advance the claims of the Congregation to Elizabeth's favour; for Knox made it clear that, in his view, the divine grace by which she reigned did not operate through her birth, which she must '[f]orgett', nor by way of 'the consent of people, the process of tyme, nor multitude of men'. It was due entirely to 'the dispensatioun of [God's] mercie, which only maketh that lauchfull to your Grace, quhilk nature and law denyeth to all women'.[42]

Yet misconceived as these letters manifestly were in the circumstances, they did genuinely reflect Knox's endorsement of what he regarded as truly lawful authority. So far as Scotland was concerned, letters he wrote in late June and early July repeatedly stressed the Congregation's readiness 'to serve the Authoritie among us established in all things not plainlie repugning to God, to his commandement, and glorie'.[43] 'We meane no tumult, no alteratioun of authoritie,' he declared; and again—'non that professeth Christ Jesus usurpeth any thing against the authoritie'.[44] 'Persuaid yourself , and assure otheris,' Sir Henry Percy was urged, 'that we mean neyther sedition, neyther yit rebellion against any just and lauchfull authoritie, but onlie the advancement of Christes religion, and the libertie of this poore Realme.'[45] Even when Mary of Guise had been 'suspended', Knox could write to her in respectful terms. Recalling his 'Letteris [*sic*] and Additioun to the same, now printed', he insisted yet again that he had sought to 'perswaid and obteane that [her] authoritie and regiment should be obeyed of us in all thingis lauchfull'. That, however, had become impossible now that she had shown herself to be an 'open ennemye to this commoun-wealth'—an enmity manifested above all in her 'malice against Christ Jesus, his religioun, and trew ministeris'. Knox could still pray, in a postscript, that God might move Mary's 'harte yitt in tyme to considder, that ye fight nott against man, but against the eternall God'; but he cannot be supposed to have had much confidence in a positive answer to that prayer.[46]

[42] Laing edn., ii. 29–30; Dickinson edn., i. 292–3.
[43] Laing edn., vi. 23–4 (Knox to Anne Locke, 23 June 1559).
[44] Laing edn., vi. 30 (Knox to William Cecil, 25 June 1559); ibid. 32 (Knox to Cecil, 28 June 1559).
[45] Laing edn., vi. 36 (Knox to Sir Henry Percy, 1 July 1559).
[46] Laing edn., i. 435–6; Dickinson edn., i. 245–6.

In any case, it was to the needs of the conflict 'against man'—
military and, above all, diplomatic necessities—that the leaders of
the Congregation now had to attend. Acting in effect as 'regents',
with Châtelherault at their head sometimes referred to as
'Governor', they manœuvred during the winter of 1559/60 for the
essential assistance of England to overthrow the power of France
in Scotland.[47] Politics, as understood by, for instance and perhaps
above all, William Maitland of Lethington, took the foremost
place; polemics, such as Knox had engaged in over the years,
retreated. There were still, to be sure, ideological factors to be
borne in mind. Elizabeth's deep-seated distrust of anything like
political subversion had to be allayed; and it can be argued that,
'to conciliate Elizabeth', at least 'from the time of the Treaty of
Berwick the Scottish insurgents put their emphasis more on religious and less on political objectives'.[48] Yet the declared aims of
that agreement, reached on 27 February 1560, were entirely political, rendered acceptable to Elizabeth by the prospective expulsion
of French forces from Scotland and by the Congregation's explicit
disavowal of any intended rebellion against constituted authority: neither

the said Duck [of Châtelherault], and all the Nobilitie . . . joyned with
him . . . nor any of thame, meane by this compt to wythdraw any dew
obedience to thair Soverane Lady, the Quene, nor in any lefull thing to
withstand the French King, hir husband and head, that during the marriage shall nott tend to the subversioun and oppressioun of the just and
ancient liberties of the . . . kingdome of Scotland; for preservatioun
whereof, boyth for thair Soveranis honour, and for the continuance of the
kingdome in ancient estait, thei acknowlege thameselfis bound to spend
thair guidis, landis, and lyves.[49]

When, on 27 April, the 'Last Band at Leith' was drawn up, pride
of place was, it is true, given to the religious issue: 'We . . . sall sett
fordwart the Reformatioun of Religioun, according to Goddes
word.' The signatories, however, included 'dyveris utheris that
joynit with' those 'professing Chryst Jesus in Scotland'; and accordingly the 'Band' referred also to 'the misbehaviour of the

---

[47] *Cal. Scot. Pap.*, i, no. 566 (10 Nov. 1559).

[48] Donaldson, *James V to James VII*, 101.

[49] Laing edn., ii. 51; Dickinson edn., i. 306–7. Cf. *Cal. Scot. Pap.*, i, no. 665, where
the word 'compt' has been read as an abbreviation of 'compact': this is possible,
but Dickinson's modernized rendering as 'account' is more probable.

Frenche Ministeris heir; the intollerabill oppressiouns committit be [by] the Frenche men of weir [war] upon the poore subjectis of this Realme, by meyntenance of the Quene Dowager, under collour and pretence of authoritie'. The remedy was the 'recovery of oure ancient fredomis and liberteis; to the end, that in tyme cuming, we may . . . be onlie rewllit be [by] the lawis and customeis of the cuntrey, and borne men of the land'. And these purposes were to be pursued 'under the obedience of the King and Quene our Soveranis'.[50] Again, in a letter addressed on the following day to Mary Queen of Scots, the lords protested that they meant only 'to do the duty of your loving natural subjects' and 'to preserve your realm in the state of a kingdom'.[51]

It was not, then, simply Protestant purposes or merely a Protestant faction that achieved, with English aid, the victory signalized by the treaty of Edinburgh (6 July 1560). The death of Mary of Guise less than a month before had, as it were, drawn a line across a page on which the text was already complete; but that text had to do with diplomatic and constitutional issues, not with the religious question. French forces were to be withdrawn from Scotland, and Francis and Mary recognized Elizabeth's title to the English crown. In the 'Concessions' annexed to the treaty the king and queen met some of the political demands of their rebellious Scottish subjects. In particular, a council of twelve or fourteen was to be appointed from a list of twenty-four names drawn up by the estates, five or six nominated by the king and queen, seven or eight by parliament. Again, 'in tyme cuming the King and Quene sall not depute any stranger [foreigner] in the administratioun of the civile and criminall Justice; and in lykwyise in the office of Chancellarie, Keipar of Seall, Treasurer, Comptrollar, and uther lyk officis . . . but sall be content with their awin subjectis borne in this realme.'[52] Besides all this, and much more of an essentially political character, 'certane Articles concerning the Religioun . . . war presentit'; but for one reason and another, 'that mater was delayit'.[53]

[50] Laing edn., ii. 61–2; Dickinson edn., i. 314–15.

[51] *Cal. Scot. Pap.*, i, no. 765.

[52] Laing edn., ii. 73–82; Dickinson edn., i. 323–30. On the status of these 'Concessions' see Dickinson edn., i. 323 n. 1, where the conclusion reached is that they 'may be regarded as an annex to the Treaty of Edinburgh'.

[53] Laing edn., ii. 82–3; Dickinson edn., i. 330–1. The final phrase quoted is from Lesley, *History*, 292: cf. *De origine* (1675), 529.

The delay was brief. The 'Concessions' annexed to the treaty of 6 July had included the important provision that the estates should be convened immediately. It was indeed intended that there should be no parliamentary consideration of religious issues, apart from the appointment of a delegation to wait upon the king and queen, by whom issues of such 'wecht and importance' were to be 'recognoscit and decidit'. The event was to be quite different. When the estates assembled in August, those present included—despite the provision in the July 'Concessions' that 'all they that hes usit to convene' should attend—a substantial number of lairds who had not been so 'usit'; and the ban on discussing religious issues was ignored.[54] What was achieved (though without royal approval or ratification) fell, it is true, a considerable way short of the effective establishment of a reformed church. Steps in that direction were taken, however, and the relevant documents are of interest here because of the light they throw on the way in which Scottish Protestants then envisaged temporal, and specifically royal, authority.

The first of these indications comes in the Confession of Faith approved by the estates on 17 August 1560. The document was the work of a group of leading preachers, probably those who, as we shall see, had produced the first draft of what became the first Book of Discipline. That Knox played a major part need not be doubted; but the Confession was certainly not his alone.[55] It was drafted, if Knox is to be believed, in only four days after 'the Barronis and Ministeris' who had petitioned for parliamentary action on the religious issue had received the estates' 'commandement' to prepare it.[56] There seems to have been only

[54] Laing edn., ii. 78–9; Dickinson, edn., i. 328. In his introduction, Dickinson (ibid. 1) describes the August 1560 parliament as being 'thronged by Protestant lairds'. Cf. Donaldson, *James V to James VII*, 102: 'the parliament . . . was attended by a large number of lairds or "barons" below the rank of lords of parliament, who were not "in use to be present".'

[55] Knox included the text of the Confession in his *History*: Laing edn., ii. 95–120; Dickinson edn., ii. 257–79. There are two modern edns.: by G. D. Henderson (Edinburgh, 1937); and by T. Hesse, in the series (ed. W. Niesel) *Bekenntnisschriften und Kirchenordnung der nach Gottes Wort reformierten Kirche* (Munich, 1938). See also K. Barth (trans. J. L. M. Haire and I. Henderson), *The Knowledge of God and the Service of God According to the Teaching of the Reformation: Recalling the Scots Confession of 1560* (London, 1938); and, esp., W. I. P. Hazlett, 'The Scots Confession 1560: Context, Complexion and Critique', *Archiv für Reformationsgeschichte*, 78 (1987), 287–320.

[56] Laing edn., ii. 92 (and cf. 89–92); Dickinson edn., i. 338 (and cf. 336–8).

limited debate and less than half-hearted opposition in parliament; but the endorsement of the Confession was not achieved entirely without difficulty. In particular, the chapter or article that is of most interest here, 'Of the Civile Magistrat', seems to have undergone close scrutiny and, probably, revision before the Confession was approved. The document as a whole, besides what was presumably the normal procedure of submission to the Lords of the Articles, was referred, for further consideration, to Lethington and to John Winram (one of the less radical ministers).[57] They, Randolph subsequently reported to Cecil, although they 'coulde not reprove the doctrine, yet dyd thei mytigate the austeritie of maynie wordes and sentences'. Specifically, he added,

The autor [sic] of thys worke had also put in thys treatie a tytle or chapter of the obediens or dysobediens that subjectes owe unto their magistrates: yt contayned lytle les mater in fewe wordes than hath byne otherwyse wrytten more at large. The surveyors of this worke thought yt to be an unfeet [unfit] matter to be entreated at thys tyme, and so gave their advise to leave yt owte.[58]

Laing concluded that this advice had been ignored or overruled, since the Confession as adopted does include the article in question;[59] but it seems much more probable that what appears there represents a significant amendment to the original draft. Nothing whatever is said about 'dysobediens'. The duty of submission to 'Kingis, Princes, Reullaris, and Magistratis' is strictly enjoined: they are 'the lieutennentis of God', and those who 'resist the Supreme power (doing that thing which apperteanis to his charge) do resist Goddis ordinance, and thairfoir can not be gyltless'.[60] There was, to be sure, a loophole, so to speak, by virtue of the parenthetical qualification; but it is hard to see how even the English queen, hypersensitive as she was in such matters, or her nervous advisers, could have taken serious exception to this lapidary statement of the doctrine of Christian obedience.[61]

[57] *Cal. Scot. Pap.*, i, no. 902 (Randolph to Cecil, 7 Sept. 1560). Winram (c.1492–1582) was a late convert to Protestantism; and Donaldson (*James V to James VII*, 110) points out that he was one of those 'who had come under Lutheran or Anglican influence and had never been near Geneva'.

[58] *Cal. Scot. Pap.*, i, no. 902 (pp. 477–8).   [59] Laing edn., vi. 121 n. 1.

[60] Laing edn., ii. 118–19; Dickinson edn., ii. 271.

[61] None the less, when Lethington wrote to Cecil on 13 Sept. (*Cal. Scot. Pap.*, i, no. 903), he asked to be informed if there was anything in the Confession that was

There was, nevertheless, a problematic element in the doctrine as stated in 1560; and the problem was one which may well be said to have dominated Scottish thinking about ecclesiastical polity for the rest of the century—and indeed, in one way or other, to have become for three hundred years and more an almost obsessive concern of Scottish Protestantism. What did, and what did not, 'appertain to the charge' of the civil magistrate in matters ecclesiastical? The Confession of Faith was forthright:

Moreover, to Kingis, Prince, Reullaris, and Magistratis, we affirme that cheiflie and maist principallie the [conservatioun] and purgatioun of the Religioun apperteanes; so that not onlie thei are appointed for civile policey, but also for mantenance of the trew Religioun, and for suppressing of idolatrie and superstitioun whatsomever.[62]

This still left open, however, crucial questions as to the relationship between even the 'godly' civil power here envisaged and the visible institutional church in the society ruled by that power. And the Scottish Protestants were now in a position to constitute and organize that church.

Preparations for that moment had begun several months before the 'Reformation Parliament' met—before, indeed, there was any certainty that such a meeting would become possible. At the end of April 1560, 'the Great Counsall of Scotland' (that is, the 'provisional government' established after the suspension of the queen regent in October 1559) commissioned six of the leading preachers to draw up 'a Buke . . . tuiching the Reformatioun of Religioun'. This—in effect a draft constitution for the reformed church—had been completed three weeks later, on 20 May.[63] Nothing, of course, could be attempted by way of implementation until after the treaty of Edinburgh and the assembly of the estates; and even then no positive action was taken. The Confession of Faith and acts prohibiting the celebration of mass and abolishing

'misliked' at the English court, so that 'it may eyther be changed (if the matter will so permit) or at leist in some thyng qualified, to the contentation of those which otherwyse might be offended'.

[62] Laing edn., ii. 118; Dickinson edn., ii. 271. The text as given by Knox has 'reformatioun' for 'conservatioun'; but the latter is the reading in the text adopted by the estates in 1560 (and confirmed in 1567).

[63] Laing edn., ii. 183–4, 285–7; Dickinson edn., ii. 280, 323. Knox reproduces the Book (Laing edn., ii. 183–257; Dickinson edn., ii. 280–323), and this text has been followed here; but see also J. K. Cameron (ed.), The First Book of Discipline: With an Introduction and Commentary (Edinburgh, 1972).

papal jurisdiction completed the legislative work of the 'Reformation Parliament'.[64] The matter was still, of course, on the
agenda; but it was only in January 1561 that the 'Booke of Common Reformation' became, with at least some kind of public
sanction, though still without the full parliamentary authority it
was never in fact to acquire, the first Book of Discipline.[65]

The details of church organization need not be explored here.
The points that matter for the purposes of this investigation are,
on the one hand, the essential concept of 'discipline' itself; and, on
the other, the relationship between that ecclesiastical discipline
and the authority of the civil ruler. In these respects the crucial
'Head' in the Book is the seventh, which begins by drawing an
explicit parallel with temporal society:

As that no Commoun-Wealth can flourishe or long indure without gude
lawis, and scharpe executioun of the same, so neathir can the Churche of
God be brocht to puritie, neathir yit be retained in the same, without the
ordour of Ecclesiasticall Discipline, which standis in reproving and cor-
recting of these faltis, which the civill sweard doeth eather neglect, eather
may not punische.

There are 'crymes capitall, worthie of death' which 'aucht not
properlie to fall under censure of the Churche; becaus all suche
oppin transgressouris of Goddis lawis aucht to be tackin away be
[by] the civill swearde'. These crimes, it must be noted, include
blasphemy as well as adultery, murder, and perjury. There is a
division of spheres of authority, then; but at the same time it is
made clear that both are concerned with the 'scharpe executioun'
of 'Goddis lawis'.[66] The discipline of the church is to be administered by 'the Minister, Elderis, and Deaconis': here and elsewhere
the first Book of Discipline is concerned primarily with the church
at its basic congregational level. At all levels, however, the principle of discipline is pervasive. On the crucial topic of 'Persons
subject to Discipline', the authors were absolutely clear: 'To Discipline must all Estaitis within this Realme be subject, yf they offend, alsweil [as well] the Reullaris as thay that are reulit.' There
was, to be sure, a special concern to insist that 'the life and

[64] *Cal. Scot. Pap.*, i, no. 891 (Randolph to Cecil, 25 Aug. 1560). The text of the two
acts is given by Knox (Laing edn., ii. 123–5; Dickinson edn., i. 340–1).

[65] Laing edn., ii. 257–8; Dickinson edn., ii. 324, where Knox gives the text of an
'Act of Secreit Counsall', subscribed by twenty-six lords on 27 Jan. 1561.

[66] Laing edn., ii. 227; Dickinson edn., ii. 306.

conversatioun of the Ministers aucht most diligentlie to be tryed';
but there can be no doubt that temporal rulers were to come fully
within the scope of the Kirk's disciplinary censure and control.[67]
There need be no conflict between this and the exalted view of
temporal rulers in the Confession of Faith: it was, after all, the
office that was divinely ordained, not the particular incumbent.
Not only might he or she 'offend': the offence might be all the
more heinous in view of the character of the office. None of this is
explored in the first Book of Discipline. The text was, nevertheless, being revised, discussed, and endorsed at a time of political
crisis and uncertainty, when there must have been grave doubt as
to whether the new church would or would not find itself working with a 'godly magistrate'.

The crisis was caused by another royal death in France: on
5 December 1560 Mary Queen of Scots, still only 18, was wid-
owed. It must from the first have seemed likely, and it soon
became certain, that she would return to Scotland and rule there
in person for the first time. The possibility of a Protestant viceroy-
alty vanished. Yet there was no certainty as to what might replace
it. Mary and Francis had, it was true, refused to give their royal
assent to the legislation of August 1560. Yet Knox for one may
have entertained the notion that Mary, married to Châtelherault's
heir, the earl of Arran, might reign as a Protestant sovereign; and
the urgency with which the Book of Discipline was promoted
seems to reflect an anxiety to consolidate the position of the kirk
as much as possible before the queen's return.[68] The prospect of a
Protestant marriage soon dissolved; but even when Mary did
come back, in August 1561, her policy was not one of instant
Catholic reaction against the still insecure Protestant establishment, now just a year old. Her inaugural proclamation forbade
any attempt to alter the 1560 settlement until such time as the
estates had taken definitive order in the matter. On the other
hand, it was plain that the queen herself had no mind to change
her religion; and the celebration of mass at court, while 'politic'
leaders like Lord James Stewart and Lethington might accept it as
a necessary gambit in their diplomatic and dynastic strategy, was

---

[67] Laing edn., ii. 233; Dickinson edn., ii. 309.
[68] Laing edn., ii. 137–8; Dickinson edn., i. 351. Cf. Donaldson, *James V to
James VII*, 104, 107–9.

inevitably an abomination in the eyes of the Protestant ministers and their followers.[69]

This is the background to the series of 'set-piece' confrontations in which we can best trace the development of 'political ideas' during the earlier part of Mary's six-year personal reign. These included, to start with, Knox's meetings with the queen. In the first of these, which took place just over a fortnight after Mary's return, she began by challenging Knox as to his doctrine in the *First Blast*, which she saw as 'a book against hir just authoritie'. Once again Knox declined to recede from his position: yet on this occasion he seems to have been prepared to treat it as belonging to the realm of ideas rather than practice. He drew an explicit parallel with Plato's *Republic*,

in the whiche he dampneth many thingis that then war manteaned in the warld, and required many thingis to have bene reformed; and yitt, notwithstanding he lived evin under suche policies, as then war universallie receaved, without farther trubling of any estait. Even so, Madam, am I content to do . . . Yf the Realme fyndis no inconvenience frome the regiment of a woman, that whiche thei approve, shall I not farther disallow, then [than] within my awin breast . . .

and Knox added, with his customary tact, that he would, on this basis, be 'alse weall content to live under your Grace, as Paull was to lyve under Nero'. When the queen turned to the charge that Knox had 'taught the people to receave ane other Religioun, than thair Princes can allow', the reply was of course immediate: it was not 'frome worldly Princes, but frome the Eternall God alone' that 'rycht Religioun' had its authority; and scriptural examples demonstrated how that authority must be preferred to all others. Mary objected that 'nane of thai men raised the sweard against thair Princes'. This, according to Knox, was only because 'God . . . had not gevin unto thame the power and the meanes'; but '[y]f . . . Princes exceed thair boundis . . . and do against that whairfoir they should be obeyed, it is no doubt but thei may be resisted, even by power'. This was not to argue, as Mary suggested, 'that my subjectis shall obey you, and not me': Knox maintained that his concern was 'that boyth princes and subjectis obey God'.[70]

---

[69] Laing edn., ii. 272–7; Dickinson edn., ii. 9–13.
[70] Laing edn., ii. 277–83; Dickinson edn., ii. 13–17; Mason edn., 175–9.

It is unnecessary here to pursue the inevitable subsequent argument as to how God's will was to be ascertained, the queen relying on 'the Kirk of Rome' which was for her 'the true Kirk of God', Knox insisting that 'God planelie speaketh in his word.' which was 'plane in the self'. With the principle of *sola acriptura* so boldly asserted there could be no compromise; and the conversation ended in that predictable impasse.[71]

Yet the Protestant party was less monolithic than Knox would have wished in its attitude to the queen. When the elaborate celebration of mass on All Saints' Day (1 November 1561) provoked vehement protests by the ministers, a meeting was held at which a clear division of opinion emerged on the question 'Whitther that subjectis mycht put to thair hand to suppresse the idolatrie of thair Prince?' Four of 'the principall Ministeris', including Knox, found themselves at odds with lay magnates and officials, who argued 'That the subjectis mycht not lauchfullie tack hir Messe frome hir'. It was resolved that advice should be sought from Calvin (to whom Knox, though he concealed the fact, had already written on the same subject on 24 October); but Lethington, who undertook to write, carefully refrained from doing so.[72] There was also a significant difference of view as to the extent to which the kirk—specifically, the General Assembly—could act independently of the crown, Knox insisting that 'the libertie of the Churche' must not 'stand upoun the Quenis allowance or dysallowance'.[73]

The next encounter to be considered took place, probably, in mid-April 1563.[74] At Easter (11 April), according to Knox, Catholics 'in diverse partis of the Realme, had erected up that idoll, the Messe . . . The brethren universallie offended . . . determined to

---

[71] Laing edn., ii. 283–6; Dickinson edn., ii. 17–20; Mason edn., 179–81.

[72] Laing edn., ii. 291–2; Dickinson edn., ii. 23–4. Knox's letter is printed, with a translation and facsimile, in the Laing edn., vi. 133–5. When the matter was raised in the General Assembly of 1564, and Knox 'wes commandit . . . to wryte to Mr Calvin, and to the leirnit in uther Kirkis, to knaw thair jugementis in that question, he refuissit', claiming that he already had 'the jugementis in this . . . of the moist godlie and the moist leirnit that be knawin in Europe'; but he again said nothing about his approach to Calvin in 1561 (Laing edn., ii. 460–1; Dickinson edn., ii. 134).

[73] Laing edn., ii. 294–7; Dickinson edn., ii. 25–7.

[74] The meeting that took place in mid-December 1562, following Knox's criticism of the queen for having 'daunced excessivelie till after mydnycht' (Laing edn., ii. 330–5; Dickinson edn., ii. 43–6), did not give rise to anything that need be considered here.

put to thair awin handis, and to punishe for example of otheris.'
The queen, in consequence, summoned Knox to appear before her
at Lochleven to enlist his support in checking this usurpation of
her authority: 'Will ye', she demanded, 'allow that thei shall tack
my sweard in thair hand?' In reply, Knox repeated much that he
had said before, which need not be repeated here. He did, however, invoke more explicitly than he had done elsewhere the
'contractual' view of the relationship between ruler and subjects,
urging the queen

to considder what is the thing your Grace's subjectis lookis to receave of
your Majestie, and what it is that ye aught to do unto thame by mutuall
contract. Thei ar bound to obey you, and that not but in God. Ye ar bound
to keepe lawis unto thame. Ye crave of thame service; thei crave of you
protectioun and defence against wicked doaris. Now, Madam, yf ye shall
deny your dewtie unto thame, (which especialle craves that ye punishe
malefactouris) think ye to receave full obedience of thame? I feare,
Madam, ye shall not.[75]

This was a time of considerable Protestant anxiety, for diplomatic moves were afoot to bring about Mary's marriage to Don
Carlos, son of Philip II of Spain. During the meeting of parliament
in late May and early June, Knox preached 'befoir the most parte
of the Nobilitie' and took the opportunity both to defend the
legality of the 'Reformation Parliament' and to denounce the
projected marriage between the queen and 'ane infidell (and
all Papistes are infidels)'. As a result he was summoned to appear before the queen to answer her demand 'what have ye
to do . . . with my mariage? Or what ar ye within this
Commounwealth?' 'A subject', Knox replied,

borne within the same . . . And albeit I neather be Erle, Lord, nor Barroun
within it, yitt hes God made me, (how abject that ever I be in your eyes)
a profitable member within the same: Yea, Madam, to me it apperteanes
no lesse to forewarne of suche thingis as may hurte it . . . then [than] it
does to any of the Nobilitie; for boyth my vocatioun and conscience
craves playnes of me. And thairfoir, Madam, to your self I say that
whiche I speak [spoke] in publict place: Whensoever that the Nobilitie of
this Realme shall consent that ye be subject to an unfaythfull [i.e. infidel]
husband, thei do as muche as in thame lyeth to renunce Christ, to banishe
his treuth from thame, [and] to betray the fredome of this Realme.[76]

[75] Laing edn., ii. 372–3; Dickinson edn., ii. 71–2.
[76] Laing edn., ii. 384–8; Dickinson edn., ii. 80–3.

The stormy scene that followed had more to do with passionate conviction on one side and passionate indignation on the other than with political ideas. Two points about Knox's position are worth noting, however. First, his anxieties about the royal marriage mirror precisely those he had expressed almost ten years earlier in regard to Mary Tudor; and, once again, those anxieties were not only spiritual but temporal (the threat to 'the fredome of this Realme'). Secondly, he may be seen as invoking not only his 'vocatioun' as a preacher but his right as a subject, the latter being (it seems) of equal status with that of the aristocratic 'born counsellors of the realm'.[77]

The matters at issue between Knox and the queen were now to move from the relative privacy of the court on to the public stage. A letter written by Knox on 8 October 1563 'to the Brethren in all quarteris' led to his being summoned formally before the queen in council in mid-December. The charge he faced was that his having urged 'the Brethren' to assemble in Edinburgh on the date set for the trial of two Protestants accused of violent acts when mass was celebrated (in the queen's absence) at Holyrood in August amounted to 'treasonable convocatioun of the Quenis liegis'.[78] The charge was found not proven; but the underlying issues were soon to be debated more fully and more publicly still, and in an ecclesiastical rather than a temporal forum—the General Assembly of the kirk itself.

When the Assembly met in December 1563, it is true, the only development was that Knox was again exonerated and indeed formally enjoined 'to adverteis the Bretherin in all quarteris as oft as evir dainger appeirit'.[79] Only when the Assembly next met, in June 1564, was there a major debate on the kirk's attitude to the queen and her authority. Appropriately, though no doubt accidentally, Knox's elaborate account of this debate constitutes the conclusion of his *History of the Reformation*.[80] It would be disproportionate here to follow that account at length; but there are important points to note both in regard to Knox's dialectic with

[77] However, when Mary raised the point again, in December, Knox evidently put more emphasis on 'the office whairintill it hes plesit God to place me' as 'ane watchman, bayth over the Realme, and over the Kirk of God gatherit within the same' (Laing edn., ii. 409–10; Dickinson edn., ii. 98).

[78] Laing edn., ii. 395–411; Dickinson edn., ii. 88–99.

[79] Laing edn., ii. 415; Dickinson edn., ii. 101.

[80] Laing edn., ii. 425–71; Dickinson edn., ii. 108–34; Mason edn., 182–209.

Lethington and in regard to views expressed by other members of the Assembly.

Lethington opened the debate in what Knox calls 'the harangue'. Having set out the issues as he saw them—the Protestants' indebtedness to the queen for 'libertie of religioun'; the importance of convincing Mary of their good will towards her; and the danger of expressing divergent views regarding her rule—he made a direct appeal: 'especiallie we maun craif of you our brother Johne Knox, to moderat your self, als weall in form of praying for the Quenis Majestie, as in doctrine that ye propose tuyching hir estait and obedience.' This gave rise to a prolonged and essentially scriptural disputation, the upshot of which, on Knox's side, may be summed up in the words of the last of five conclusions he claimed to have established:

That Godis pepill hes executit Godis law aganis thair King, having no farther regaird to him in that behalf, than gif he had bene the maist simpill subject within this Realme.

And thairfoir . . . I am assureit that nocht onlie Godis pepill [may], but also, that thai ar bounde to do the same whair the lyke crymes ar committit, and when he gevis unto thame the lyke power.[81]

This, Lethington had argued in the course of the debate, was to 'mak subjectis to controlle thair prynces and reuleris'; and Knox in reply had demanded

What harm . . . shoulde the Commounwelth ressaif, gif that the corrupt effectiounis off ignorant reuleris were moderatit, and so brydillit be [by] the wisdome and discretioune of godlie subjectis, that thai soulde do wrang nor violence to no man?[82]

Confronted by Lethington with the rejection of the right of resistance by 'Luther, Melanchton . . . Bucer, Musculus, and Calvin', Knox retorted that the first two had been concerned with the anarchism of the Anabaptists—'quhilk opinioune I no less abhore than ye do'—while the others had had in mind oppressed Christians 'so dispersed that thai haif no other force but onlie to sobbe to God for delyverance. But my argument', he goes on,

hes ane uther grounde; for I speik of the pepill assembled togidder in one bodie of ane Commounewelth, unto whome God hes gevin sufficient

---

[81] Laing edn., ii. 453; Dickinson edn., ii. 129; Mason edn., 204.
[82] Laing edn., ii. 440; Dickinson edn., ii. 120; Mason edn., 194.

force, nocht onlie to resyst, but also to suppres all kynde of opin idolatrie: and sik ane peopill, yit agane I affirme, ar bound to kepe thair land clene and unpollutit.[83]

When Lethington suggested that 'ye sall nocht haif monie lernit men of your oppinioun', Knox replied, first, that 'the treuthe ceisses nocht to be the treuthe, howsoevir it be that men [either] misknaw it, or yit ganestand it'; but he then added, 'I lack nocht the consent of Godis servandis in that heid', and produced in support of his claim 'the Apologie of Magdeburgh'.[84]

At this point, after a disagreement over procedure, other opinions were sought. John Douglas, rector of St Andrews University, and John Winram, superintendent of Fife—both of whom had taken part in drawing up the first Book of Discipline—agreed in arguing that, if the queen were to 'oppone hir self to oure religioun . . . the Nobilitie and Estaitis of this Realme, professouris of the trew doctrine, may justlie oppone thame selfis to hir'; but they doubted whether it would be legitimate to deprive the queen of 'hir awin Messe' by violence.

A view at once more decisive and more interesting here was expressed by 'Mr Johne Craig, fellow-minister with Johne Knox in the Kirk of Edinburgh'. Craig, a former Dominican, recalled a 'Conclusioun' he had heard debated ten years previously in the University of Bologna. The issue had been precipitated by the alleged 'disordour and tyrannie attemptit be [by] the Paipes Governouris', exercising in the city the temporal power of the Pope, 'who was King of that cuntrie'. The 'conclusion' was, in Craig's rendering of the Latin text, that

All Reuleris, be thay supreame or be thay inferiour, may and aucht to be reformed or deposed be [by] thame be [by] whom thay ar chesin, confirmed, or admitted to thair office, as oft as thay brak that promise maid be [by] the oath to thair subjectis: Because that thair Prince is no less bound be [by] oath to the subjectis, then [than] is the subjectis to thair Princeis, and thairfoir aucht to be keipit and reformed equallie, according to the law and conditioun of the oath that is maid of [either] partie.[85]

---

[83] Laing edn., ii. 442–3; Dickinson edn., ii. 121–2; Mason edn., 195–6.

[84] Laing edn., ii. 453-4; Dickinson edn., ii. 129–30; Mason edn., 204. For the *Bekentnis Unterricht und Vermanung der Pfarrhern und Prediger der Christlichen Kirchen zu Magdeburgh* (Magdeburg, 1550), see Skinner, *Foundations of Modern Political Thought*, ii. 207–10.

[85] Laing edn., ii. 456–7; Dickinson edn., ii. 131–2; Mason edn., 206–7—where Knox also gives the Latin text. Craig's translation is correct, but in the Laing edn.,

To Craig's application of this principle to the case in hand it was objected that the Scots were 'ane kingdome', whereas the Bolognese were 'but ane Commounwelth'. Craig's rejoinder was striking: 'my jugement is, that everie kingdom is, or at leist, sould be ane Commounwelth, albeit that everie Commounwelth be nocht ane kingdom'. He went on to say that, in Bologna, the issue had been 'disputed [to] the utermoist', and that the result had been in favour of the view that the thesis under discussion represented

what aucht to be done in all Kingdomis and Commounwelthis, according to the law of God, and unto the just lawis of man. And gif be [by] the negligence of the peopill, or be [by] tyrannie of Princes, contrair lawis haif bene maid, yit may that same peopill, or thair posteritie, justlie craif all thingis to be reformed, according to the originall institutioun of Kingis and Commounwelthis.[86]

Craig's contribution to the 1564 debate foreshadowed much that was to be said in the ideological sequel to the deposition, three years later, of Mary Queen of Scots. That sequel belongs to the next chapter. Here it will suffice to say that the response of Knox and other Protestant zealots to the catastrophe of Mary's personal reign was predictable in its scriptural denunciation. Preaching less than a week before Mary's enforced abdication, Knox (it was reported) 'did inveygh vehemently against the quene, and perswaded extremytye towardes her'.[87] A month later, in a letter to an English correspondent, he described Mary as 'that vile adulteresse, and cruell murtherer of her owne husband'. 'No soverane lady is shee to me,' Knox said of the then exiled queen in March 1571, 'nor yit to this realme'.[88]

By the time Knox wrote the words just quoted he and his colleagues were aware that in delivering them from an idolatrous adulteress as their ruler God had not yet led them into the Promised Land. Stubborn problems remained in regard to the full establishment and endowment of the kirk and its relationship to the temporal power. That power was, it is true, now wielded,

the penultimate word appears as 'other' (for *utraque*): Dickinson's emendation to 'either' has been followed here.

[86] Laing edn., ii. 458–9; Dickinson edn., 133; Mason edn., 207–8.
[87] Laing edn., vi. 553 (Throckmorton to Elizabeth, 19 July 1567).
[88] Laing edn., vi. 566, 588.

formally, by a godly, though still an infant prince, and in substance by regents whose commitment to the Protestant faith was
as genuine as the enthusiasm of their response to the zealots'
demands was variable. It was in these uneasy circumstances—
while the deposed queen still had substantial support and the
possibility of her return could not be confidently ruled out—that
the kirk struggled to work out its true position and embody that
position in definitive institutions. This is the background to the
drafting of the second Book of Discipline (1578).[89] The details of
that document and much of the scholarly controversy to which it
has given rise need not concern us here.[90] It does, however, deal
more closely and more extensively than the first Book had done
with issues that are certainly relevant in the present context and
which will retain their relevance when we come to deal with
political ideas in the Scotland of the adult James VI. While he was
still a child, a theory of 'church and state' was developed which
he was to see in time as an unacceptable challenge to royal authority; and that theory may be regarded as having been enshrined
in the second Book of Discipline. It can indeed be argued that the
theory in question was in no real sense a novel one; that the
principles enunciated in the second Book would have been entirely familiar and acceptable to those who had drafted the first;
and that those principles 'can be said to represent . . . the logical
extension of earlier ideals'.[91] Yet logic can, after all, be more or less
compelling according to circumstances; and we need to know at
least why and how the implications were now spelt out.

   In the late summer of 1571, government appointments to the
archbishoprics of St Andrews and Glasgow and to the see of
Dunkeld clearly raised alarm as to the direction of the regent
Mar's ecclesiastical policy; for there had been no reference to, nor
any consultation with the church authorities. A compromise was
worked out before the end of the year and subsequently ratified
by the General Assembly. It involved an oath which referred to
the sovereign as 'supreme Governour of the realme, as well in
thinges temporall as in the conservatioun and purgatioun of
religioun'.[92] That last phrase echoed what had been stated in the

---

[89] For which see J. Kirk (ed.), *The Second Book of Discipline: with an Introduction
and Commentary* (Edinburgh, 1980; hereafter Kirk edn.).

[90] Cowan, *Scottish Reformation*, 123–30, provides a helpful summary.

[91] Kirk edn., 40.   [92] Cited, Kirk edn., 40.

1560 Confession of Faith; and yet the juxtaposition of the title 'supreme Governour' and the implicit reference to the discipline and 'policy' of the church could be interpreted as pointing along paths many were unwilling to follow. Nor was such reluctance likely to be lessened by developments under the forceful regency of the earl of Morton. It was against this background that the authors of the second Book of Discipline—including, but not (contrary to what has been received wisdom) dominated by, Andrew Melville—set to work.[93]

Not only did the text they produced include a section expressly entitled 'Of the Office of ane Christiane Magistrat in the Kirk': already in the very first section the issue of spiritual and temporal power and jurisdiction was confronted:

This power and policie ecclesiasticall is different and distinct in the awin nature fra that power and policie quhilk is callit the civille power and appertenis to the civile government of the commoun welth, albeit thay be bayth of God and tend to ane end gif thay be richtlie usit, to wit, to advance the glorie of God and to have godlie and gud subjectis.[94]

The spiritual power was derived 'immediatlie frome God and the Mediatour Chryst Jesus': it did not have 'any temporall heid on erth but onlie Chryst, the onlie spirituall king and governour of his kirk'. To be sure, the members of 'the ecclesiasticall estait' were 'subject to the magistrat civile'; but by the same token 'the persone of the magistrat' should be 'subject to the kirk spirituallie and in ecclesiasticall government'. The two powers—'the power of the sword' and 'the power of the keys'—could not (at least 'ordinarilie') be exercised by the same person.[95]

Yet, separate and distinct as they are, the two powers serve, each in its own way and within its own sphere, the same ultimate purpose; and indeed each has a positive as well as a negative controlling function in regard to the other:

The civile power sould command the spirituall to exercise and do thair office according to the word of God; the spirituall reularis sould require the Christiane magistrat to minister justice and punishe vyce and to maintene the libertie and quyetnes of the kirk within thair boundis . . .

---

[93] Kirk edn., 45: 'The all but universal belief which insists on attributing the second Book of Discipline to Andrew Melville is simply not supported by the facts of history, and its abandonment is long overdue.'
[94] I. 9: Kirk edn., 166.   [95] I. 10, 14–15: Kirk edn., 166, 169–70.

The magistrat aucht to assist, mantene and fortifie the jurisdictioun of the kirk; the ministeris sould assist thair princes in all thinges aggreable to the word [of God].⁹⁶

These points are further developed in the section devoted specifically to 'the Office of ane Christiane Magistrat'. There a strict obligation 'to advance the kingdome of Jesus Chryst' is laid upon 'Christiane princes, kingis and other magistrats'. In particular, they are 'to sie that the publick estait and ministrie' of the church 'be mantenit and sustenit'—a matter, it need hardly be recalled, which had throughout been the most contentious issue between the ministers and their aristocratic patrons. In regard to the discipline of the kirk, rulers were called upon to 'punishe civilie thame that will not obey the censur of the same'—an injunction, however, hedged by the requirement that it be obeyed 'without confounding alwayis of the ane jurisdictioun with the other'. As legislator, the ruler is '[t]o mak lawis and constitutions aggreable to Goddis worde for the advancement of the kirk and policie thairof without usurping ony thing that pertenis not to the civill sweard'. And the authoritative dignity of the ecclesiastical estate is resoundingly proclaimed:

quhair the ministrie of the kirk is anis lauchfullie institut, and thay that ar placed do thair office faythfullie, all godlie princes and magistrats aucht to heir and obey thair voice, and reverence the majestie of the sone of God speiking be [by] thame.⁹⁷

It may be true to say that there are 'not even slender foundations for the belief that the second Book of Discipline significantly altered the church's political doctrine', and that what it did was simply to 'provide . . . a succinct summary of earlier strands of thought'.⁹⁸ By doing even that, however, the authors of the Book may perhaps be said to have so woven those strands together as to give the Kirk a 'political doctrine' which had not till then been fully articulated. And this in turn prompts questions as to the nature and coherence of the doctrine now propounded. That it was, as Melville was to tell James VI in a celebrated remark, a doctrine according to which there were 'two Kings and

---

⁹⁶ I. 17, 22: Kirk edn., 170–2.   ⁹⁷ X. 1, 3, 5, 8, 9: Kirk edn., 213–16.
⁹⁸ Kirk edn., 65.

two Kingdoms in Scotland' is doubtless clear enough.[99] Yet the
duality that had perplexed the medieval church was as problematic as ever; and the doctrine of the second Book of Discipline
might also be interpreted as implying, in the end, a rejection of
duality. *Both* jurisdictions served the same purpose—a purpose
defined by the word of God in the Bible; and it was through the
spiritual estate that 'the majestie of the sone of God' spoke to his
subjects.

On the other hand, it is possible to detect a pervasive ambiguity
in the attitude of the Scottish Protestants of the sixteenth century
towards the authority of the temporal ruler. Over against, and yet
in some sense coexisting with, the view that kings and magistrates were to be seen as subjects of ecclesiastical authority, there
was a view notably expressed by John Knox in the sermon he
preached on 19 August 1565, three weeks after the queen's marriage to Darnley. It was a sermon which, with the new king as an
indignant member of the congregation, embroiled Knox yet again
with the court.[100] Yet it embodied an exalted view of royal power:
'it is evident,' Knox declared,

that it is neither birth, influence of starres, election of people, force of
armes, nor, finally what soever can be comprehended under the power of
nature, that maketh the distinction between the superior power and the
inferior, or that doth establish the royall throne of kings; but it is the
onely and perfect ordinance of God, who willeth his power, terror, and
Majestie in a parte, to shine in the thrones of Kings, and in the faces
of Judges ... so that who soever would study to deface the order of

[99] Commenting (Kirk edn., 58) on the point that, in his words, 'the Book
postulated the existence of two parallel, divinely ordained jurisdictions, separate
and distinct, yet co-ordinate', Kirk draws attention to a letter addressed by the
Congregation to the queen regent on 6 May 1559, in which they say: 'Sa
vnderstand yourself maist nobill princess in Christis kingdome to be ane servand
and na quein, haveand na preheminence nor authoritie aboue the kyrk' (*Miscellany
of the Maitland Club*, iv (Aberdeen, 1839), 89). This letter, which Knox does not
mention or record, is dated just two days after he joined the Congregation in
Dundee, and may well have been drafted without his collaboration.

[100] The sermon (Laing edn., vi. 227–73) was printed (probably in London) in
1566, entitled *A Sermon preached by Iohn Knox Minister of Christ Iesus in the Publique
audience of the Church of Edenbrough, within the Realme of Scotland, vpon Sonday the 19
of August, 1565. For the which the said Iohn Knoxe was inhibite preaching for a season*:
Knox's preface is dated 19 Sept. 1565. For the sequel see Laing edn., ii. 497–8;
Dickinson edn., ii. 159–60: this passage is in the fifth book of the *History*, probably
written, not by Knox, but by a continuator.

regiment that God hath established, and by his holy worde allowed, and bring in such a confusion as no difference should be betwyxt the upper powers and the subjects, doth nothing but evert and turne upside down the very throne of God.

True, the divine origin of royal power carried with it both obligation and limitation. The ruler, Knox, says, must 'considder that he is appoynted Lieutennant to one, whose eyes continually watch upon him, to see and examine howe he behaveth himself in his office'. Again, 'Kings . . . have not an absolute power in their regiment what pleaseth them; but their power is limitted by God's word'.[101] Other ways of envisaging and enforcing the limitations of royal power were to be asserted and denied in the strenuous controversy provoked by the deposition of Mary Queen of Scots; and to that controversy the next chapter is devoted.

[101]   Laing edn., vi. 236, 238.

6

Politics, Humanism, History
George Buchanan and his Critics

ON 24 July 1567, ten weeks after her scandalous marriage to the earl of Bothwell, Mary Queen of Scots abdicated in favour of her infant son. Bereft for the time being of both military and political support, a prisoner since mid-June in the hands of implacable enemies, she yielded to what was for the moment inevitable. Five days later James VI was crowned and (despite John Knox's opposition) anointed king. Even in an age of vehement controversy and violent conflict, these were dramatic developments. To many minds they seemed to subvert the foundations of royal authority and thus of the social order; and they gave rise, accordingly, to vigorous ideological debate, in which rival principles were deployed and both the general nature of kingship and the historical development of the particular realm of Scotland were contested. Much of this took place in a broad European context. Events in Scotland were from the first of European concern. Mary Stewart, after all, had been 'queen in three kingdoms'.[1] Her cause as queen of Scots was by no means lost; in France, as queen dowager, she retained patronage if not political power; and in England she might yet claim the inheritance from Elizabeth, still unmarried and barren. The high tide of ideological debate came, it is true, only a dozen years later, when developments elsewhere—in particular, the wars of religion in France—had broadened its scope. It was then, in 1579, that the most important Scottish contribution was made, with the publication of George Buchanan's *De iure regni apud Scotos*.[2] That

---

[1] The phrase was used for the collection of articles on Mary published in the *Innes Review*, 38 (1987), and subsequently reissued as M. Lynch (ed.), *Mary Stewart: Queen in Three Kingdoms* (Glasgow, 1987).

[2] *De Jure Regni apud Scotos, dialogus, authore Georgio Buchanano, Scoto* (Edinburgh, 1579). On this and other early edns., see *George Buchanan: Glasgow Quatercentenary Studies* (Glasgow, 1906), 451–3; and cf. I. D. McFarlane, *Buchanan* (London, 1981), 512–13. For later edns. see below n. 28.

dialogue—which has been called, doubtless with some degree of hyperbole, 'the most influential political essay of the sixteenth century'[3]—had, however, been written twelve years or so earlier, probably no more than a few months after the midsummer crisis of 1567. It was part of the controversial ferment produced by that crisis; and there are even earlier stages in the controversy to be considered here first.[4]

Pamphleteering evidently began immediately after the queen's surrender at Carberry in mid-June. Before the end of the month a broadsheet *Exhortation to the Lords* had been printed by Robert Lekprevik, in which the leaders of what was to become 'the king's party' were urged to keep the queen closely confined.[5] A month later sterner measures were advocated in *Ane Declaratioun of the Lordis iust quarrell*.[6] Published anonymously like so many other pamphlets of the time, this 'tragical dialogue' (as Sir Nicholas Throckmorton called it in his letter to Cecil of 19 July) anticipates strikingly so much of Buchanan's argument in the *De iure regni* that one might be tempted to identify that 'prince of poets of his age' as its author. Buchanan could certainly (though his mother-tongue was Gaelic, not Scots) write to some effect in vernacular prose; but we have no example from his pen of vernacular verse with which to compare the *Declaratioun*, and the matter remains entirely in the realm of surmise.[7]

In any case, what matters here is the substance, not the

[3] H. J. Laski (ed.), *A Defence of Liberty against Tyrants* (London, 1924), intro., 5.

[4] Thomas Maitland, Buchanan's interlocutor in the dialogue, is represented as referring to the events of the spring and summer of 1567 as fairly recent; but the earliest evidence we have of the work's being in existence is a letter, no longer extant, dated 11 Mar. 1569 from Mary's agent in London, John Betoun (Innes, *Critical Essay*, 204). See the discussion by H. R. Trevor-Roper, *George Buchanan and the Ancient Scottish Constitution* (*English Historical Review, Supplement 3*, 1966), 15–16 and n. 1.

[5] *Cal. Scot. Pap.*, ii, no. 520 (June 1567).

[6] J. Cranstoun (ed.), *Satirical Poems of the Time of the Reformation*, 2 vols. (Scottish Text Society; Edinburgh, 1891), i. 57–64. The lines quoted below are on pp. 61–2.

[7] *Cal. Scot. Pap.*, ii, no. 565 (Throckmorton to Cecil, 19 July 1567); and cf. Trevor-Roper, *George Buchanan*, 17 n. 1, where Throckmorton's account of the 'tragical dialogue' is said (with more than a little exaggeration) to be 'a perfect description of *de Jure Regni*'. This ignores, for one thing, the point that Buchanan's dialogue as we have it was not a 'demand . . . for Mary's deposition' but an *ex post facto* justification of it. So far as Buchanan's possible authorship of the *Declaratioun* is concerned, it is important to bear in mind that the ideas it expressed were common enough in both the humanist and the scholastic tradition: Buchanan was by no means the only educated Scot to whom they would have been familiar.

authorship of the piece, in which the crucial passage begins with an account of the origins and basis of political authority:

> Philandrius sayis: 'Brother, than [then] consider
>   How fyrst began all dominatiounis
> Quhen rude pepill assemblit thame togidder,
>   And maid thair Kingis be [by] creatiounis.
> In votis than war variatiounis.
>   I trow rycht few was chosin be the haill,
> But he was King quhais pairtie did preuaill.

Kingship, then, is essentially an elective office; and what has been established by the community may likewise be revoked:

> Rycht sa gif Princes sa thame self abuse,
>   That of force subiectis man [must] put to thair hand,
> Guid men sould nocht than to reforme refuse,
>   Thocht all at ainis concur not on thair band;
> Naimly, gif Iustice on thair partie stand,
>   And maist consent gif quha wald rackin rycht,
> Sen God hathe gein to thame baith strenth and mycht.

Particularly noteworthy here is the insistence that 'maist' is to be construed as 'rycht'—as, in effect, the *maior et sanior pars* of medieval thinking, which we shall encounter again when Buchanan considers the point. Next, the author of the *Declaratioun* spells out more directly the implications of his doctrine:

> Yea, thocht it war [were] ane King for to depose,
>   For certaine crymis, I think the subiectis may,
> Or fylthy faultouris fast in prisone close,
>   Rather than lat ane haill countrie decay.

And the point is driven home by a direct reference to Scottish history:

> As gif ane King his pepill wald betray,
>   And him and thame baith bring to seruitude,
> He sould in this reformit be, I say,
>   Naimly be Nobillis and be men of gude.
> The Baliols cause—considder how it stude:
>   Quhat rycht had Robert Bruice him to expell?
> Because to Ingland he subiect him sell.[8]

---

[8] For varying interpretations of 'the Baliols cause' see Ch. 2; Buchanan's view of the matter is discussed below.

And although (as Throckmorton put it) this might 'seeme to procede from a poettes shoppe, the haill number here (I feare me) and the lordes also, do thynk as ys conteynyd theyryn, and do meyne to performe the effecte'.[9]

Five days after Throckmorton wrote, the 'effecte' was indeed 'performed'. Those who brought about its performance, followed by the coronation of the infant king, cannot have remained for long in any doubt as to the alarm and hostility their proceedings would arouse. Not only did their radical measures destroy such unity as had prevailed among those who had combined with a view to dissolving the queen's marriage to Bothwell. Even more seriously, the effective deposition alienated the queen of England. Within three days of Mary's enforced abdication Elizabeth was writing to Throckmorton with orders to demand of those responsible what warrant they had for their action: no such warrant, she insisted, was to be found either in the Bible or in the 'civil laws' of any realm in Christendom.[10] There was plainly a need for a more considered and sophisticated defence of what had been done than vernacular pamphleteering could provide, and it seems likely that those concerned turned almost at once to someone well equipped for such a task. George Buchanan had indeed, following his return to Scotland in 1561, after many years in continental Europe, been Mary's tutor and court poet. By then, however, his conversion to Protestantism was firm, whatever the ambiguities of earlier years: he had become principal of St Leonard's College at St Andrews in 1566, and in the very year of Mary's deposition he was to be Moderator of the General Assembly of the kirk. Again, his loyalty, as a Lennox man, to the family of the murdered Darnley can only have fuelled his bitter hostility to the queen.[11] Our concern here, however, is not with Buchanan's fierce invectives against Mary, but with the dialogue in which he sought to persuade the educated public, with whom, throughout Europe, his reputation as a Latinist was unrivalled, that her deposition was in full accord both with the basic principles of political

[9] *Cal. Scot. Pap.*, ii, no. 565 (punctuation slightly modified).

[10] Ibid., no. 577 (Elizabeth to Throckmorton, 27 July 1567).

[11] *De Maria Scotorum regina . . . historia* and its translation *Ane detectioun of the duinges of Marie Quene of Scottes* were both published in London towards the end of 1571. For the complex bibliography of these writings see McFarlane, *Buchanan*, esp. 340–4. There is a modern translation by W. A. Gatherer in *The Tyrannous Reign of Mary Stewart: George Buchanan's Account* (Edinburgh, 1958).

society and with the specific norms of the Scottish constitution—
the *ius regni apud Scotos*.

That Buchanan's dialogue on these themes was written in the
latter part of 1567 seems (as noted above) probable enough. To
what extent it corresponded to the text eventually printed in 1579
or to the version which evidently circulated quite widely in
manuscript during the intervening years we have no way of
knowing. There is, however, at least one document from those
years which *may* give some indication of Buchanan's thinking and
which certainly affords important evidence for the ideological
position adopted by the party to which he by then firmly adhered.
This is the 'wryting delyvered by the Erle Morton to the Commissioners for the Queen's Majesty' on 28 February 1571.[12] The
context for this was the situation created by Mary's flight into
England in May 1568 and her subsequent detention there. Elizabeth was still by no means satisfied as to the legitimacy of what
had been done in Scotland in July 1567, and this 'wryting' was a
further attempt—predictably ineffectual—to persuade her of it. It
is possible—but no more than possible—that Buchanan had a
hand in drafting the document. Certainly there are some quite
close parallels between elements in the argument and the theory
he was to expound (or had perhaps already expounded) in the *De
iure regni*. The text, however, is something of a patchwork, and it
cannot be said to bear, as a whole, the imprint of a single mind.
Thus it begins with a technical juristic refutation of the argument
that Mary's abdication was invalid because she was under duress
at the time. This is evidently the work of someone with a closer
and more extensive knowledge of civil and canon law than we
have any reason to suppose that Buchanan possessed.[13] Next
there is an elaborate narration, avowedly based on Boece's
Scotorum Historiae, of cases illustrating the authority said to have
been wielded by the people of Scotland (usually through their
aristocratic leaders) over tyrannical and immoral kings. Some of

[12] Printed, from BL MS Cotton, Caligula C.II, fos. 520–526b, by Trevor-Roper,
George Buchanan, 40–50.

[13] Perhaps (Dr John Durkan has suggested) Edward Henryson, 'doctour in the
Lawis' and a classical scholar of some note, who was active in the publication of
Scottish laws in the mid-1560s (*APS* i. 29). See on him Cairns, Fergus, and
MacQueen, 'Legal Humanism', in MacQueen (ed.), *Humanism in Renaissance
Scotland*, 48–52; and Durkan, 'Cultural Background', in McRoberts (ed.), *Essays on
the Scottish Reformation*, 292.

these instances were, to be sure, cited in the *De iure regni* and all
were rehearsed in Buchanan's own *Rerum Scoticarum Historia*; but
this in itself hardly supports the case for his authorship of the
1571 'wryting'.[14] The same may be said of the brief references to
examples from 'other realmes and commonw[ealths]', some of
which recur in Buchanan's dialogue, though it is arguable that the
classical instances in the list reflect strongly the humanist culture
in which he (though by no means he alone) was steeped.[15]

The 1571 document may be said to be at its closest to
Buchanan's way of thinking (and writing) when the argument
turns to 'the lawe of God and Nature'.[16] Yet here again the case is
stated in ways that seem significantly different from what we
shall find in the *De iure regni*. There are passages drawing heavily
upon Melanchthon and upon Calvin's *Institutes*; and there is
further reference to both civil and canon law in ways that do not
seem characteristic of Buchanan. There is, besides, another consideration, which may carry more weight. At two separate points
the 'wryting' invokes emphatically the authority of custom—
'commoun and ancient conswetude, unreprovit, agaynsaid or
abrogat, quhilk inducis lawe'.[17] Now it has been pointed out that
Buchanan, in the *De iure regni*, takes a much less favourable view
of custom, criticizing the tendency for its 'tyranny' to prevail over
rational considerations.[18] This is indeed only one illustration of
the fact that the 1571 document manifests a different pattern and
balance of argument from that which is found in Buchanan's
dialogue. The 1571 pattern is indeed that of an argument based
essentially on the appeal to an 'ancient constitution', in which
custom and the historical record preponderate, with a technical

[14] Trevor-Roper, *George Buchanan*, 42–7. For references to later Scottish events in
the 'wryting', see nn. 64, 124, below.

[15] Ibid. 48: 'Pisistratus and Theseus in Athens; Damaratus, Pausanias,
Cleomenes and Nabis in Lacedemon'. It may just be worth noting that Edward
Henryson had been involved in editing Plutarch, an important source for several
of these instances.

[16] Ibid.: 'This cause of Scotland . . . is not onely lawfull by the resones before
specified, but also of the lawe of God and Nature and the cyvill and imperiall lawe
the same is allowable and worthily don . . .'.

[17] Ibid. 42. The phrase is repeated, almost verbatim, at the very end of the
document, on p. 50.

[18] Cairns, Fergus, and MacQueen, 'Legal Humanism', 61–2, 64–5; and see
Buchanan, *De iure regni*, 68–9; LX–LXI. (References to the *De iure regni* are to the
(Arabic) page-numbers of the first edn. and to the (Roman) numbers of the chap-
ters into which the text is divided in the most accessible later edns.)

juristic backing at certain points. These elements are, to be sure, present in Buchanan's theory; but they are secondary and instrumental in relation to a central argument of another kind, which makes no more than a perfunctory appearance in the 'wryting'. That argument must now be examined.

Before embarking upon a close scrutiny of the 'resistance theory' which Buchanan finally committed to print in 1579, it is necessary to give some consideration to the career and development of the author. This is not, of course, the place for a comprehensive or detailed account of a life in which there are a number of problematic phases.[19] Some points do however call for attention in the context of Buchanan's political thought. That he had been John Mair's pupil both at St Andrews and in Paris is obviously significant, though the degree of its significance for present purposes is not easy to determine. In any case it is sufficiently clear that, at an early stage, Buchanan repudiated Mair's scholasticism with all the contempt which, from the standpoint of a committed humanist, the learning of the schools merited. That he none the less carried over some traces of that learning into his account of political society and the authority of rulers is doubtless true enough; and we shall encounter at least one point where his interpretation of Scottish history may have owed more to Mair than to Boece (his usual authority, though one whose exuberance Buchanan was constrained to chasten in certain respects). The obvious fact remains that it was as a humanist and above all as a master (both in prose and verse) of classical Latin that Buchanan achieved his European renown; and with his work we encounter for the first time in this enquiry a fully realized humanist political theory.[20]

[19] McFarlane, *Buchanan*, is the fullest and most detailed account; but P. Hume Brown, *George Buchanan Humanist and Reformer: A Biography* (Edinburgh, 1890), is still worth consulting, as are several of the essays in *George Buchanan: Glasgow Quatercentenary Studies 1906*.

[20] On Buchanan's political ideas see Skinner, *Foundations of Modern Political Thought*, ii. 339–48; R. A. Mason, '*Rex Stoicus*: George Buchanan, James VI and the Scottish Polity' in J. Dwyer, R. A. Mason, and A. Murdoch (eds.), *New Perspectives on the Politics and Culture of Early Modern Scotland* (Edinburgh, 1982), 9–33; J. H. M. Salmon, 'An Alternative Theory of Popular Resistance: Buchanan, Rossaeus and Locke', in *Diritto e Potere nella Storia Europea: Atti del quarto Congresso Internazionale della Società Italiana della Storia del Diritto, in onore di Bruno Paradisi* (Florence, 1982), 824–49. Among older accounts, the most thorough, still well worth consulting, is by W. S. McKechnie, '*De Jure Regni apud Scotos*', in *George Buchanan: Glasgow Quatercentenary Studies*, 211–96.

Two questions in particular are posed as we approach that theory, exhibited in its maturity only three years before Buchanan's death. The first question is concerned with his experience of and his response to the great controversies and conflicts of his age—the framework in which political thinking necessarily took place. Buchanan's experiences in this regard had certainly been less dramatic than those which had helped to shape John Knox's attitude to authority. That is not to suggest, however, that he had had an easy passage through the stormy decades of the early Reformation. Embroiled with the religious orders, and in particular with the Franciscans, in the Scotland of the 1530s, accused of heresy together with some who, in 1539, paid for their beliefs and practices with their lives, Buchanan probably owed his escape at this time to the royal patronage he enjoyed as tutor to one of James V's bastard sons. He found refuge, first, in the England of Henry VIII. No Protestant as yet, however, he spent the next two decades as scholar and teacher in France and Portugal. It was during this period that he began to build in the humanist 'republic of letters' the reputation of which he had laid the foundations in the Paris of the late 1520s and early 1530s. It was not, however, to be a time of untroubled tranquillity. In particular, it was marked (and marred) in its middle years by Buchanan's protracted trial for heresy before the Lisbon Inquisition.[21]

It was in 1547—probably towards the end of the year—that Buchanan went to teach in the College of Arts at Coimbra, of which his friend André de Gouvea had become principal by royal appointment. Two years later, Gouvea having died in June 1548, the first inquiries began which were to lead to charges of heresy against Buchanan and two of his Portuguese colleagues. The three were arrested in August 1550; and it was not until the end of February 1552 that Buchanan, who had abjured on 29 July 1551 the heresies to which he had confessed, was released from penal detention in the monastery of San Bento. The intricate details of the proceedings against him need not be examined here; but there are certain points to be noted. First, the accusations both revived the charges against Buchanan in Scotland a dozen years or so earlier and added allegations regarding his brief sojourn in

---

[21] On this see esp. McFarlane, *Buchanan*, 131–51; also J. M. Aitken, *The Trial of George Buchanan before the Lisbon Inquisition including the text of Buchanan's Defences with a Translation and Commentary* (Edinburgh, 1939).

England. In the latter connection, secondly, issues were raised
that have a bearing on his political thinking. Buchanan claimed,
for instance, that one of the matters on which he differed from the
opinions held in the England of the late 1530s was the question of
obedience to human laws—even the laws 'of profane magistrates'. That obedience he claimed to have upheld—though
against what precise contrary view he upheld it is far from clear.
Perhaps more significantly, Buchanan also claimed that he had
'always professed' papal supremacy in the church, though 'with
the proviso that I declared the Pope to be subordinate to the
Council'.[22] No doubt this reflects the Parisian conciliarism expounded by Mair and others during Buchanan's student years.

The second question to be considered at this stage is whether
these experiences find any reflection in Buchanan's writings before the *De iure regni*; and, more generally, whether there is any
evidence as to his political ideas before the crisis of 1567 and its
sequel. On both counts there is perhaps only one document of any
substance. The *Baptistes*—the first of Buchanan's Latin plays to be
written, though the last to be printed—was evidently first performed in Bordeaux very early in the author's sojourn there, and
thus quite soon after his exile from Scotland and his brief stay in
England. In this play the fate of John the Baptist at the hands of
Herod is presented as (in Buchanan's own words) 'an image of
the tyranny of that time'. Specifically, the tyranny he had in mind
was (he told the Inquisitors in 1550) the treatment of Thomas
More by Henry VIII.[23] Whether this is to be taken at its face value
or treated as a politic manœuvre in the situation Buchanan then
faced need not concern us. The play is certainly concerned, to
a very large extent, with tyranny; and strong claims have
been made for its significance as evidence for Buchanan's
political thinking. It has been called 'the poetical draft of ... *De
Jure Regni*', and described as reflecting, in comparison with other
'Renaissance neo-classical tragedies ... a more "democratic"
view of kingship'.[24] In truth the text lends little support to such
claims. The issues dealt with in the play turn (in McFarlane's
words) 'on the refurbished commonplace of the King as opposed
to the Tyrant'; and Buchanan's 'refurbishing' adds little if

---

[22] Aitken, *Trial of George Buchanan*, 22–3.
[23] Ibid. 24–5.
[24] Hume Brown, *George Buchanan*, 124; McFarlane, *Buchanan*, 387.

anything to the theme. It could indeed be argued that the most interesting point in the *Baptistes* is Buchanan's development of what may be termed his anti-Machiavellian position. Both the queen and her daughter—but especially the former—urge the king to put aside 'common duty' and to 'judge nothing to be shameful that is to his advantage as ruler'; and these are views Buchanan plainly rejects.[25]

One other piece of evidence remains to be considered—admittedly antedating by only a year or so the first draft of the *De iure regni*, yet certainly written before the crisis which evoked Buchanan's more radical political ideas. This is the poem entitled *Genethliacon Jacobi Sexti Regis* but written soon after the birth of the infant prince. Here, while we can scarcely be said to have in 'the concluding lines' what 'may be regarded as a brief summary of the teaching of the *De Jure Regni*',[26] we do have some fairly clear anticipations of the views expressed in the dialogue. Buchanan advances, for instance, the argument that a good king provides an essential and effective pattern for his people to imitate. Again, he declares that such a king, while prepared to be merciful towards offenders, should be rigorous in maintaining his own subjection to the laws he has prescribed. Yet, though he does insist in the closing lines on the point that divine retribution will surely overtake a king who defaces by vicious or tyrannical behaviour the image of God he should exhibit to his subjects, neither here nor in the *Baptistes* is it 'distinctly implied . . . that kings exist by the will . . . of the people'.[27] That crucial doctrine was reserved for *De iure regni apud Scotos*.[28]

By the time the dialogue was published, Buchanan (now in his seventies) had been tutor to the young king of Scots for the best

[25] *Baptistes*, vv. 1203–31, esp. 1225–7: 'Diadema quisquis induit capiti semel, | Vulgaris omnes ponat officii gradus. | Nil arbitretur turpe, quod regi utile.'

[26] Hume Brown, *George Buchanan*, 198.

[27] Ibid. 197.

[28] Besides the early edns. (n. 2 above) the dialogue was included in the 1715 (Edinburgh) and 1725 (Leiden) edns. of Buchanan's *Opera Omnia*. It was also reprinted in the second (Edinburgh, 1583) and later edns. of Buchanan's *Rerum Scoticarum Historia*. There is a facsimile reprint of the first edition of the *De iure regni* (Amsterdam, 1969). There are two modern translations: *The Powers of the Crown in Scotland*, ed. C. F. Arrowood (Austin, Tex., 1949); *The Art and Science of Government among the Scots*, ed. D. H. MacNeill (Glasgow, 1964). Neither can be recommended: the translations below are my own. For the form of references here see n. 18 above.

part of a decade; and its publication, like the belated publication of *Baptistes* two years earlier, was evidently connected with that position and Buchanan's conception of his tutorial responsibilities. Both works were intended to serve, in their different ways, the purposes of a *Fürstenspiegel*. At the same time, the original polemical purpose of the *De iure regni* was not to be ignored. Though the civil strife in Scotland between the king's party and the queen's had ended half a dozen years before, the stability of the political situation there could not by any means be taken for granted. The firm rule of the earl of Morton—the fourth successive regent to hold office since the crisis of 1567—had been interrupted, if only briefly, in the spring of 1578; and the forces which eventually brought about his downfall in 1580 were, in part at least, motivated by support for the exiled queen and (if only in a political sense) the Catholic cause.[29] On the European scene a more thoroughgoing (and, from a Protestant point of view, thoroughly alarming) Catholic upsurge had marked the years since the St Bartholomew's Day massacre of 1572 and the rise of the League. The reaction against this had produced a counter-blast of what William Barclay was to call 'monarchomach' pamphleteering. It was the high tide of what has been termed 'the Calvinist theory of revolution', and barriers against its advance were already being erected in such works as Adam Blackwood's *De conjunctione religionis et imperii* (1575). Buchanan's contribution to the controversy appeared belatedly in print in the same year as Duplessis Mornay's *Vindiciae contra tyrannos*, so that the issues raised in Scotland over the previous twenty years were now fully incorporated into the European debate.[30] The retort to Buchanan came, as we shall see, primarily from fellow Scots—but from Scots whose careers had taken them permanently into continental Europe and whose works were to be published as far from Scotland as Poitiers, Paris, and Ingolstadt. Yet the argument still

[29] Donaldson, *James V to James VII*, 171–5. It may be worth noting that, following Morton's return to power, the leaders of the house of Hamilton (to whom Buchanan was bitterly hostile) were forfeited and banished, while Esmé Stewart, proximate male heir of the Lennox family, returned to Scotland from France in September 1579.

[30] On the 'debate' generally see J. H. M. Salmon in Burns and Goldie (eds.), *Cambridge History of Political Thought 1450–1700*, ch. 8; for 'the Calvinist theory of revolution' see Q. Skinner in B. C. Malament (ed.), *After the Reformation*, 309–30.

revolved around the treatment of a Scottish queen twenty years and more earlier.

From the first, however, the European context was fully present in the minds of Buchanan and his readers. The argument is placed immediately in relation to European opinion. Whether or not there had been an actual conversation between Buchanan and Thomas Maitland (Lethington's brother)—and Maitland was later to repudiate the views attributed to him—the scene is set by his recent return from France and the account he gives of the scandal caused there by the proceedings against the queen. Buchanan's task is to defend and justify those proceedings in ways that will commend themselves to the kind of company Maitland has been keeping. This, together no doubt with Buchanan's own inclinations and interests, is what gives his theory such a different character from most other Protestant writings of the period. The readers at whom the dialogue is directed were not to be satisfied—many of them could only have been repelled—by the biblical rhetoric of a Knox or a Goodman. Nor would the need have been met by the amalgam of juristic learning and a simple appeal to an 'ancient constitution' we have seen in the 'wryting' of 1571. It was, first and foremost, to Cicero and to Seneca, and behind them to Aristotle, that Buchanan would look for his arguments. To be sure, the element of Stoic rhetoric in the text is likely to have been enhanced by the revision Buchanan doubtless undertook in his role as James VI's 'pedagogue'; but we have no reason to doubt that this was from the first the essential idiom in which his argument was couched.

Certainly it is with Aristotelian and Ciceronian themes that the argument effectively begins. The crucial issue being to distinguish legitimate kingship from tyranny, Buchanan approaches it by way of an enquiry into the origin of government, which in turn presupposes an understanding of the origin of human society. There was, he suggests (with Homeric authority for the hypothesis), what in later terminology would be called a pre-social state of nature: 'men lived in huts or even in caves . . . without laws or settled habitation [they] wandered as nomads . . . And [they] came together according as they were moved by the desires of their hearts or as some convenience and common advantage [*utilitasque communis*] united them.' Yet a settled social life is more agreeable to nature (*naturae magis consentaneum*) than such a

wandering and solitary existence. And mere 'utility' will not suffice to bring about a social order: it might indeed, as directed to
self-interested ends, dissolve rather than sustain such an order. It
is, rather, 'a certain force of nature' that brings and binds men
together in communities. This natural impulse may be, as with
animals, purely instinctive; but with mankind it is inseparably
associated with rationality—'the light infused by divine provi-
dence into our souls' (*lucem animis nostris diuinitus infusam*).
Nature, reason, wisdom, the evangelical command to love God
with all one's heart and one's neighbour as oneself—all these
speak with one voice; and God is the true 'author' of human
society.[31]

If we pause at this point to ask where the inspiration of
Buchanan's social theory so far is to be found, we may certainly
identify Stoicism as the general source, with specific reference to
Cicero. It is true that the Ciceronian passage that seemingly
underlies the account of the 'state of nature' comes from an early
work, *De inventione*, which Cicero later viewed with some embarrassment.[32] And Buchanan goes out of his way to reject the
hypothesis in that text which attributed the establishment of society to the skill of an 'orator'. On the other hand, he invokes
Cicero's support, in *De re publica*, for the view that nothing in the
world of human achievement is more pleasing to God than the
societies 'that are called states [*civitates*]'.[33] Those societies, again,
are characterized by an essentially organic unity: 'their parts aim
at maintaining the same kind of coherence as is found among the
members of our bodies.' The underlying Aristotelian element in
Buchanan's Stoicism is fully in evidence here: God and nature
alike propel mankind into ordered societies, where reason and
wisdom may realize common purposes, so that mutual duties
may be recognized and shared interests jointly pursued.[34]

Yet if the state of nature was not a golden age to be regretted,
the state of society is not, in itself, a utopia: it brings with it

[31] *De iure regni*, 8–12; VIII–XI.
[32] See on this Salmon, 'An Alternative Theory', 829–30.
[33] Cf. *De re publica*, VI. xiii. 13: Buchanan gives a close paraphrase of Cicero's
words rather than an exact quotation.
[34] *De iure regni*, 11; XI *ad fin.*, where the phrase translated in the text above reads,
'Harum ciuitatum partes similiter inter se junctas esse volunt, atque cuncta
corporis nostri membra inter se cohaerent'. (The 1579 reading of the last word is
correct, rather than the *cohaerere* adopted by some later edns.)

problems to which government and law provide the only solution. The organic analogy is essential to this stage in the argument; for Buchanan's contention is that the conflict of interests he
sees as inevitable in a society made up of people of 'different
kinds, ranks, conditions, and characters' will produce results
analogous to the diseases of the natural body—'disorders and
intestine disturbances'. As in the one case so in the other, a physician must be found to set matters right; and the physician of the
body politic is, of course, the ruler, whose function it is to maintain, restoring when necessary, that balance among the various
elements which constitutes health.[35]

This is to accord a decisive role to the king; for it is with
kingship that the dialogue is, *ex professo*, concerned throughout.[36]
Yet at the same time it is made clear that the king is instrumental
to the needs of his subjects: 'Kings were appointed not for themselves but for the people.'[37] And they were—they are—indeed
appointed. There seems to be no place here for any authority, any
right to rule, inhering in an individual or in a lineage independently of the community. Again the title *king* as such had no
particular aura for Buchanan. The ruler he envisages may be
called, like Aeneas, 'Father' or, like Agamemnon, 'Shepherd of his
people'; he may be designated Duke or Prince or Governor: the
nomenclature is a matter of indifference, since what counts is the
recognition that the ruler's authority is to be used for the good of
the community.[38] It will be used, above all, to establish and maintain justice—'that restraint which is applied in matters of common concern and in men's dealings with one another'.[39] With this
in view, it was reasonable for our forefathers, in appointing their
kings, to look for a man of outstanding ability, or at least for one

[35] *De iure regni*, 12; XII.

[36] Mason observes ('*Rex Stoicus*', 15) that 'Buchanan is not interested in the
merits of the various forms of government classified by Aristotle . . . but only [in]
monarchy and its degenerate form, tyranny'; and cf. ibid. 15 and n. 12, for the use
by Buchanan and others of the title *De regno* for the dialogue. It is, however,
arguable that Mason, seeking (justifiably) to correct an overemphasis by other
scholars on Buchanan's 'radicalism', may himself somewhat overemphasize the
role of 'Buchanan's ideal king, the prudent ruler impervious to the demands of his
passions' (ibid. 19).

[37] *De iure regni*, 13; XII *ad fin.*: 'reges non sibi, sed populo creatos esse'.

[38] Ibid. 12–13; XII.

[39] Ibid. 15; XIV: 'illa moderatio, quae in rebus communibus, & hominum inter se
commerciis, posita est, commodissime mihi nomine iustitiae intelligi posse
videatur.'

who was notable for nobility of birth, for his wealth, or for his prowess in war. After all, Maitland remarks, 'it is the people's right to confer authority on whomsoever they wish'. This how-ever, poses a problem if we adhere to the medical paradigm; for we assess a physician by his learning and practised skill in the art of medicine, not by his electoral popularity. If there is an art of government (and Buchanan is positive that there is) how are its essential criteria to be reconciled with that elective process with-out which (he is equally positive) we can never have a properly constituted king?[40]

It is at this point that Buchanan introduces the concept of law. Every art is defined by its rules; and the rules of the art of govern-ment (*regiae artis praecepta*) are found in 'the civil laws'.[41] Yet it is not enough to have, as we might express it, a purely theoretical or academic knowledge of those rules: properly understood, the art of government, like every other art, consists in the prudent prac-tical application of the rules. Practical wisdom (*prudentia*) is thus the essential characteristic of the ruler. If we were to find an individual perfectly endowed with that quality we should have to call him 'a king by nature, not by virtue of election'; and to such a ruler 'unrestrained and all-embracing power' would have to be granted.[42] It is abundantly clear, however, that Buchanan regards this as an extremely rare and improbable contingency. And it is when, in the absence of such a paragon, the community turns instead to someone who only approximates to the ideal, that the problems arise in which (it seems fair to say) Buchanan is primar-ily interested.

It is in fact to the inevitable imperfections even of a ruler who displays at least 'the image of a true king' that Buchanan immedi-ately turns: 'lest he lack the firmness necessary to resist the passions which may—and usually do—turn [men] away from the true path, we shall establish law as his colleague, or rather as a restraint upon his desires.'[43] This is a critical point in the

---

[40] Ibid. 15–17; xv–xvi.   [41] Ibid. 16–17; xvi.

[42] Ibid. 17–18; xvii–xviii; 'Haec [prudentia] . . . si summa & perfecta in quopiam esset, tum natura, non suffragiis, regem esse diceremus; liberamque rerum omnium potestatem ei traderemus.' (It is possible that *tum* should read *eum*, though this is not suggested in any edn.)

[43] Ibid. 18; xviii: 'quoniam aduersus animi affectiones, quae possunt, & plerumque solent, auertere a vero, ne satis firmus sit timemus, legem ei, velut collegam, aut potius moderatricem libidinum, adjiciemus.'

argument. Laws, previously introduced as the rules of the art of government, guide-lines for the ruler in his task of maintaining justice, now become—and remain for much of the dialogue—rules intended above all to govern the ruler himself, to counteract the universal tendency for 'the authority established for the public weal to turn into arrogant despotism'.[44] Buchanan is concerned, in this passage, to refute Maitland's charge that he is being 'rather unfair to kings' (*subiniquus regibus*) and that this reflects his admiration for the republics of the ancient world and for contemporary Venice. Buchanan's rejoinder is in effect an elaboration of a point he had already made: it does not matter whether we do or do not call the ruler a king; what matters is that he should be, in Cicero's phrase, 'the voice of the law'. At the same time, however, law itself is to be 'a dumb king'.[45] Buchanan goes on, in a passage which we may readily suppose to have been added, for didactic purposes, to the original polemical dialogue, to argue against the erroneous conception of kingship as an office that should be marked by magnificence and splendid ceremony: rather, it should be characterized by the austere dignity of *antiquitas illa sancta & sobria*.[46]

The majesty that counts is the majesty of the law. Yet law itself has its problematic aspects even for Buchanan, as we discover in a rather intricate passage after a brief recapitulation of the argument thus far.[47] He initiates a closer examination of the analogy between government and medicine, the upshot of which is that in neither case can all eventualities be provided for by fixed rules. We are given, indeed, a vigorous restatement of the classic case *against* the rule of law, with its rigidity, its inability (general as it is) to adjust to the needs of particular cases, its inherent rigour. To remedy these defects seems to require a discretionary power which we may happily allow to our physicians but which remains stubbornly problematic in the case of the ruler. Since he (Maitland

---

[44] *De iure regni*, 20; XIX: 'Sed (ut humana sunt omnia) statu rerum in peius prolabente, quod publicae utilitatis causa fuerat constitutum imperium, in superbam dominationem vertit.'

[45] Ibid. 19–20; XIX *ad fin.* Buchanan is paraphrasing Cicero, *De legibus*, III. i. 2, where the text has 'magistratus', not 'rex', but where the 'sovereignty' of law is succinctly asserted: 'ut enim magistratibus leges, ita populo praesunt magistratus'.

[46] *De iure regni*, 20–4; XIX–XX. The passage includes (23; XX) a lengthy quotation from Cicero, *De officiis*, II. xii. 41–2.

[47] *De iure regni*, 25–32; XXI–XXVII.

is persuaded to acknowledge) 'may not be freed from the restraints of law, who . . . is to propose the law which we are to give
him as his schoolmaster?'[48] Maitland's own answer is that only
the ruler himself, the professional defining the rules of his profession, should make law. To this Buchanan inevitably replies that
there is no difference between such an arrangement and leaving
the ruler free of all legal restraint. It is for the people, from whom
the ruler derives his authority, to define the laws in accordance
with which that authority shall be exercised over them.[49]

This fundamental proposition is expounded in a passage easily
misconstrued and hard to elucidate with confidence.[50] Buchanan
is quick to rebut Maitland's charge that he wishes to give authority to 'the many-headed beast'. It was not his intention to leave
so important a matter 'to the judgement of the people at large'
(*uniuersi populi iudicio*). What he has in mind is that 'more or less
in accordance with our custom, selected men from all the estates
should meet in council with the king. Then, once they had formulated a proposed law, it should be submitted to the judgement of
the people.'[51] Now, if the reference to 'our [Scottish] custom' is
to be taken seriously, the *selecti* must be equated with the com-
mittee of the articles which drafted proposals for consideration by
the three estates; and it is that assembly whose judgement is
identified as the decisive *populi iudicium*. If so, however, we must
suppose that Buchanan is drawing a distinction between the
uniuersus populus, whose judgement he repudiates, and the

[48] Ibid. 31; xxvi *ad fin.*: 'Quando igitur regem soluere legibus non licet, quis
tandem erit legis lator, quam ei tanquam paedagogum dabimus?' This is the
reading of the 1579 edn., where the list of corrigenda indicates that *quam* should
read *quem*. Later editors made this change and also, without authority, substituted
legislator for Buchanan's more classical *legis lator*. In fact, the original uncorrected
reading (followed in the translation here) is defensible and may be preferable:
quam refers back to *legis*, and it is *the law* not the lawgiver that is the 'schoolmaster'.
The distinction is not a merely trifling one.

[49] Ibid. 32; xxvii: 'populo, qui ei imperium in se dedit, licere volo, ut eius imperii
modum ei praescribat.'

[50] Some earlier suggestions of my own, in 'The Political Ideas of George
Buchanan', *Scottish Historical Review*, 30 (1951), 64, are such as I must now regard
with an embarrassment similar to that with which the mature Cicero is said to
have regarded *De inventione*. Even when anachronistic distortion is avoided, however, there is still room for divergent views: see Mason 'Rex Stoicus', 20; and cf.
Salmon, 'An Alternative Theory', 831–2. The view taken here is closer to Mason's
than to Salmon's; but the latter still carries weight.

[51] *De iure regni*, 32; xxvii. Buchanan uses, for the proposed law, the Athenian
term προβούλεμα.

populus, who are to be regarded as present in the parliamentary assembly.[52] In any case, 'popular' judgement is defended along essentially Aristotelian lines, summed up when Buchanan says, 'The judgement of the many is usually, in all respects, better than individual opinion.'[53]

Accepting this reluctantly, Maitland asks what function, then, is left for the king in Buchanan's scheme of government. His role in lawmaking seems to be, at most, consultative; and at an earlier stage in the discussion it had been agreed that justiciable issues should be referred to the judges before whom advocates would argue the case. In the same passage, the question of what we might term policy decisions—issues awaiting resolution in the future, just as judicial issues concerned what was already past— had been briskly disposed of by the bland statement that kings did not in such matters act without the counsel of wise men.[54] Yet, Maitland now argued, there remained a need still unprovided for: in doubtful cases the law required interpretation to ensure the fulfilment of its true purpose, the good of all citizens. Buchanan's immediate response seemed to acknowledge that the king should meet this need by applying the maxim *Populi salus suprema lex esto*. Yet, he insisted, this must not involve granting the king such a power of interpreting the law as would, in effect, free him from its restraint.[55] He elaborates the point by a lengthy attack on the notorious abuse of such a power by the papacy.[56] It is not in that dangerous area, then, that the proper office of a king is to be found.

Buchanan will not admit that the king he envisages is either merely ornamental or paralysed by restrictions that leave him no real function in the community. It is here—in a long passage which must surely represent a didactic expansion of the original

[52] This point is made by Mason, *'Rex Stoicus'*, 20; but it has to be acknowledged that Buchanan's terminology is problematic: for one thing, the term *universus* would, in juristic language, tend to suggest the corporate character of what is being described, and that is surely what is intended when Buchanan refers to the final 'judgement of the people' on legislative proposals.

[53] *De iure regni*, 33; XXVIII: 'multitudo fere melius, quam singuli, de rebus omnibus iudicat'.

[54] Ibid. 26–7; XXIII. So far as legislative power is concerned, Maitland, while accepting Buchanan's argument that this should be vested in the people, remarks (33; XXVIII) that this leaves kings as no more than *tabulariorum custodes*—keepers of the archives.

[55] Ibid. 32–6; XXVIII–XXIX.   [56] Ibid. 36–9; XXX–XXXII.

text—that we have his most elaborate presentation of the ideal Stoic king. Such a king has a moral function of the most essential importance. He is indeed to ensure due observance of the law; but not by exercising legislative, judicial, or executive power in what were to become their recognized forms (arguably beginning to take shape in this very period). Buchanan's ruler is to fulfil his role in society by the sheer force of example. Set, as he necessarily was, upon a public stage, in full view of his subjects, the king was to purge society of its moral ills by exhibiting a model of virtue too potent for its attractive force to be resisted.[57]

Such a view would undoubtedly have carried weight with Buchanan's readers, nor should it be discounted in our attempt to understand his doctrine historically. Not, obviously, that there is anything distinctive or original in themes that were woven into the very fabric of *speculum principis* writing. What is striking in Buchanan's theory is, in the end, not what he expects of his king but what he seeks to bar the king from doing. Of course a medieval or sixteenth-century king was expected to give his people a moral example; but he was also expected to rule them in ways that Buchanan's Stoic king must either leave to others or perform within bounds far more narrowly prescribed than most contemporaries would have accepted as reasonable, necessary, or practicable. In the end it is the fear of tyranny that preponderates in Buchanan's thinking; and it is to that critically important aspect of his *De iure regni* that we must now turn.

This phase of the discussion begins with themes that need not be pursued closely here. The linguistic history of the word 'tyrant' is explored in order to explain its decline from an honourable or at least neutral sense to one that is entirely pejorative.[58] The Aristotelian account of tyranny is summarized, with special emphasis on the point that kingship is rule exercised over free men who willingly submit to it, while tyranny is the rule of a master over slaves. Buchanan acknowledges that such absolute despotic

---

[57] Ibid. 41–50; XXXIV–XL. The hypothesis that this passage is a 'didactic expansion' is supported by the references to royal education in Maitland's long speech towards its close (48–9; XL). It is also arguable that this passage may be reflected in James VI's political writings, esp. in *Basilikon Doron*, where the king cites the same lines from Claudian as Buchanan does (44; XXXVII: cf. Craigie edn., i. 53) and twice uses the analogy between the king and one set on a public stage (ibid. i. 53 and 105).

[58] *De iure regni*, 50–2; XLII–XLIV.

power may be usurped and yet used beneficially and that it may be expedient to tolerate it.[59] The true tyrant, however, is an enemy to human society; and whether he is so by nature or has degenerated into what is essentially an inhuman state, he may properly be treated as if he were a noxious beast.[60]

Maitland then brings the discussion back to its immediate focus. It may indeed be the case that, under elective monarchy, a tyrannical ruler can, in one way or another, be got rid of; but the Scottish monarchy is hereditary and based upon an original transfer of all authority to the king analogous to the Roman *Lex Regia*. Buchanan expresses reservations as to the Roman precedent, but accepts that it is now necessary to relate his principles to the Scottish constitution. After an 'overture', so to speak, foreshadowing themes—notably the fate of James III—to be resumed later, he argues that what had been an elective monarchy became strictly hereditary only in the reign of Kenneth III, and that the *quid pro quo* received by Kenneth's subjects was the firm subjection of royal authority to the restraints of the law.[61] The intention is clearly to counter the argument that hereditary kingship carries with it emancipation from control by the community. It does not, Buchanan maintains: the cases of early kings whose tyranny was punished by deprivation combined with death or banishment are precisely matched by instances in more recent times.[62] Thus Balliol 'was rejected by the nobility because he had subjected his realm to the authority of Edward king of England, and Robert I was chosen in his place'.[63] And when Buchanan returns to the case

[59] *De iure regni*, 52–3; XLV–XLVI. One of the instances of 'benevolent despotism' cited by Maitland is the rule of Cosimo de' Medici in Florence. Buchanan had previously made the point that absolute power may be conferred on a ruler with the people's consent: thus the Roman dictators were 'tyranni legitimi' (ibid. 52; XLIII).

[60] Ibid. 53–9; XLVII–XLIX.　　　[61] Ibid. 59–62; XLIX *ad fin.*–LII.

[62] Ibid. 61, 81; LII, LXXIII. The early instances specifically cited (61; LII) are those of Culen and Ewin III, and their names, together with that of Ferchard I, are used generically (81; LXXIII): '. . . si Culenos, Evenos & Ferchardos commemorem . . .') in the context of Buchanan's claim that he 'could list twelve kings [of Scots], or even more, who, for their crimes and shameful deeds, were condemned to perpetual imprisonment, or escaped in exile or by suicide the just punishment of their offences'.

[63] Ibid. 65; LVI, where Buchanan refers to the replacement of Balliol by Bruce as having taken place 'fere 260 abhinc anno'—indicating that this part of the dialogue at least was written in or about 1567. It may also be noted that Buchanan, like the author of *Ane Declaratioun of the Lordis iust quarrell*, is following a version of events similar to that given in Mair's *Historia*: cf. p. 65 above.

of James III he asserts that 'all the Estates in public assembly gave judgement that he had been justly slain for his extreme cruelty to his subjects and his scandalous depravity'.[64]

The context for this vehement statement of the case against James III is Buchanan's concern to rebut the objection that his account of the Scottish monarchy is derived from the remote past. The 'constitution' to which he appeals is doubtless 'ancient'; but what matters more than its antiquity is its contemporary vitality. And indeed—for, in the end, Buchanan devotes relatively little specific attention to Scottish institutions as such—what matters most of all is that those institutions conform to his general theory of kingship. He is, to be sure, concerned also to establish that his position is consistent with Scripture. He argues, in this connection, that tyrants are accorded no biblical exemption from the punishment of sin: reverence for authority does not extend to the unworthy wielder of that authority. (The canonists' distinction between 'the pope' and 'the man who is pope' is invoked at this point.) Admitting that he cannot cite a scriptural instance of a king's punishment by his subjects, Buchanan argues that Old Testament history, dealing as it does with kings appointed directly by God, is irrelevant to the argument.[65] The essential point remains valid: where royal authority is derived from the community, the people have the same authority over the king as he does over each of his subjects.[66] And Buchanan proceeds to elucidate the relationship of people, law, and king by drawing a parallel with that of king, magistrate, and dempster or crier in a criminal court. As the magistrate's authority comes from the king so does the king's come from the people; and as the dempster merely pronounces a sentence determined by the magistrate, so the king acts only as the voice of the law. It follows that it is for the people to call the king to account if he breaks the law.[67]

[64] *De iure regni*, 81; LXXIII. This, it may be observed, is a much harsher statement than the reference to James III in the 1571 'wryting': 'the doings of king James [the] third were after his death disallowed by parliament, and suche as took parte with hym during certein tyme before his d[eath] tooke remyssion and fyned therefore' (Trevor-Roper, *George Buchanan*, 47–8).

[65] *De iure regni*, 68–81; LX–LXXII.

[66] Ibid. 60; LXXII: 'Nos autem id contendimus populum, a quo reges nostri habent, quicquid iuris sibi vendicant, regibus esse potentiorem; iusque idem in eos habere multitudinem, quod illi in singulos e multitudine habent.'

[67] Ibid. 85–6; LXXVII.

How is this collective authority to be exercised? How, indeed, are we to understand the term 'the people' in regard to such action? First, Buchanan argues, it is 'the greater part of the people' (*maior pars populi*) whose decision must prevail. Maitland raises the classic objection that people in general, if they are not blindly conservative, are intimidated or corrupted in one way or another: for the most part, indeed, they are a mere rabble 'glutted with blood and plunder'.[68] Buchanan's reply is critically important. He admits that many people will, to be sure, come within the scope of Maitland's condemnation; but he denies that most will. Those who yield to the pressures or the inducements of a tyrant are not to be regarded as citizens at all, for they betray society itself. True citizens are those 'who obey the law, who defend human society, who would, for the well-being of their fellow-countrymen, undergo every hardship and every peril, rather than, through cowardice, grow old in dishonourable ease'. If citizenship is reckoned by these criteria, then 'not only the better, but the greater part will stand up for liberty, for virtue, and for security' (*pro libertate, pro honesto, pro incolumitate, stabit*).[69]

This vividly evokes the humanist ideal of republican citizenship; but, as always, the interpretation of the ideal is problematic. As with the medieval *maior et sanior pars*, as with the *valentior pars* of Marsilius of Padua, we have the difficult task of evaluating the quantitative and the qualitative element in the concept. It has been suggested, but also denied, that Buchanan was 'simply employing a variant of the well-known Marsilian formula of the *valentior pars*'.[70] There may in fact be an unresolved ambiguity in what he says. He does, certainly, appear to begin his reply to Maitland on this point by claiming that 'most' people are guiltless of the charges brought against the 'rabble'; yet he also says that the citizen-body is to be reckoned 'not by numbers' but by

[68] *De iure regni*, 87–8, 89; LXXVIII, LXIX.

[69] Ibid. 89–90; LXXX. The collocation of *libertas* and *incolumitas*, it may be noted, is Ciceroniam: see e.g. *De re publica*, I. xxxii. 49—a particularly relevant passage, since Cicero is there putting the argument that 'free popular government ought not to be entirely rejected on account of the excesses of an unbridled mob'.

[70] Mason, '*Rex Stoicus*', 23; and cf., for a similar view, F. Oakley, 'On the Road from Constance to 1688: The Political Thought of John Major and George Buchanan', *Journal of British Studies*, 2 (1962), 1–32, at 18–19, 24–6. This interpretation is rejected by Salmon, 'An Alternative Theory', 832–3.

reference to civic virtue.[71] It seems safe at least to agree that Buchanan is neither 'anticipating modern democratic procedure' nor advocating 'the Lockean precept of a purely quantitative majority'.[72]

In any case, the problem of the procedure for dealing with a tyrannical ruler is not yet solved. In some sense 'the people' are to act; but Buchanan recognizes that this must in practice mean action by 'those to whom the people, or the greater part of the people, have transferred that power'.[73] As the discussion proceeds, however, the identity of the recipients of this transferred authority remains frustratingly vague. It seems at first as though our attention is to be directed to 'the ordinary judicial process' (*ad ordinaria judicia*). If the king is in unjust possession of an individual's property, or is guilty of some other civil wrong, he may be sued—admittedly through his agent (*procuratorem eius*); but Buchanan regards this as a formality which does not affect the substantive situation. How much more, then, should the king be answerable to the courts for the far greater wrongdoing that constitutes tyranny![74] And Buchanan goes on to argue that there is no affront to the king in his being subjected to such judicial procedures, citing from ecclesiastical history the case of John XXIII's deposition and submission to Martin V, together with the decree of the council of Basle subordinating papal to conciliar authority.[75] He invokes, too, a classic authority for the principle that rulers should be subject to the law—the *Digna vox* of the joint emperors Theodosius and Valentinian.[76] Very soon, however, we

---

[71] *De iure regni*, 89–90; LXXX, where Buchanan begins by claiming that Maitland's 'multitude' of the depraved and corrupt will be 'Magna profecto: nec tamen maxima', but also goes on to say that citizenship is to be reckoned by worth, not by numbers: 'si cives non e numero, sed dignitate, censeantur . . .'. It may also be noted that, at the end of this passage, he uses the term *plebs* rather than *populus*.

[72] Mason, 'Rex Stoicus', 23; Salmon, 'An Alternative Theory', 833.

[73] *De iure regni*, 88; LXXIX: 'In uniuerso . . . populo, aut in maiore eius parte. Illud etiam amplius tibi largior, in iis, in quos populus, aut maior pars populi, eam potestatem transmiserit.'

[74] Ibid. 90–1; LXXXI.

[75] Ibid. 91; LXXXII. Buchanan in fact calls the deposed pope 'Ioannes vigesimus secundus'; but he plainly has in mind the anti-pope (as he would now be reckoned) John XXIII. This slip misled Arrowood (*The Powers of the Crown in Scotland*, 136 n. 84) into using the reference as a link between Buchanan and 'the tradition of William of Occam'.

[76] Ibid. 92; LXXXII. The *Digna vox* (Cod. 1. 14(17). 4) is also quoted, more accurately, in the 1571 'wryting' (Trevor-Roper, *George Buchanan*, 48). Buchanan's

find that 'due process' will not meet the case. The tyrant is at least as unlikely as a strongly armed robber to submit voluntarily to trial, and force may have to be used. To the objection that this will violate the subjects' oath of allegiance Buchanan responds with a succinct recapitulation of his basic position. True, subjects are bound by their oath; but the ruler is equally bound by *his* promise to govern justly: 'There is thus a mutual pact between the king and the citizens.' The tyrant, by breaking this pact, declares himself a public enemy, against whom war may justly be levied; and in a just war not only the people as a whole but individual citizens have a right to kill the enemy. It follows that anyone is entitled to kill a tyrant (*cuivis Tyrannum occidere licebit*).[77]

Thus contract theory and tyrannicide meet at the climax of Buchanan's argument. This surely has more to do with the ideology—or mythology—of civic humanism than with 'a rationalization of the under-developed political culture of early modern Scotland'.[78] Yet it has to be acknowledged that it is towards that culture that Buchanan eventually turns as he endeavours to muffle the impact of a theory which (Maitland objects) threatens to precipitate 'universal disorder'.[79] At first Buchanan seeks to rebut this by claiming that his concern is to explain 'what may or should be done in situations of this kind', not to urge actions which call for 'deliberation in the undertaking, discretion in the attempt, and courage in the execution'.[80] At the very end of the dialogue, however, he seems to retreat even from the theoretical exposition of general principles. He insists, somewhat petulantly, that, whatever foreigners may think of the matter, all he has done is to exhibit the institutions by means of which Scotland—'a kingdom, small indeed, but free these two thousand years from the sovereignty of foreign nations'—has 'from the outset appointed constitutional rulers' (*Reges legitimos*) and maintained the rule of law. Whatever may be the case elsewhere—and certainly the Scots are

---

version lacks the crucial pronoun *nobis* near the end of the quotation; and, remarkably, he omits altogether the important clause in which the emperors say, 'Indeed our authority depends on the authority of the law'.

[77] *De iure regni*, 96–9; LXXXV–LXXXVIII.

[78] Mason, '*Rex Stoicus*', 25.

[79] *De iure regni*, 99; LXXXVIII, where Maitland exclaims: 'Nam si cuiuis tyrannum occidere licebit, vide ... quantum ... omnibus omnium rerum perturbationem immittas!'

[80] Ibid. 100; LXXXIX.

not alone in living by such principles—this is, Buchanan insists, the *ius regni apud Scotos*.[81]

That claim was to be challenged by Buchanan's critics; and we shall in due course have to consider how far he himself sustained it in his *Rerum Scoticarum Historia*. For the moment it is the challenge that concerns us: specifically, the replies to the *De iure regni* by three expatriate Scots—Ninian Winzet, Adam Blackwood, and William Barclay. The positive doctrine expounded in their writings, more especially in the works of Blackwood and Barclay, will also be our concern when the discussion turns, in the next chapter, to the kind of 'royalist' theory of which James VI was the most prominent if not the ablest upholder. Here the emphasis will be on the more specific aspects of the case against Buchanan, with particular reference to his claim to have given an account of the Scottish constitution.[82]

With this in mind it is appropriate to begin with Winzet; for, while his little-known work hardly figured in the general development of royalist theory, he was more substantially concerned than his younger colleagues with Buchanan's account of the Scottish past. He was closely associated with John Lesley, bishop of Ross, whose Latin history of Scotland, published in 1578, was intended to paint a picture of that past in tone, so to speak, with the principles of monarchy as the queen's party understood them. Winzet, abbot of the *Schottenkloster* at Regensburg since 1577, resumed in his *Flagellum Sectariorum* the polemic against heresy he had begun in his vernacular pamphlets of the early 1560s. His *Velitatio in Georgium Buchananum* was in effect an appendix to the *Flagellum*, published with it in 1582 and provoked by Winzet's having read, in the spring of 1581, the second (1580) edition of the *De iure regni*.[83] Winzet's work thus provides a bridge between the earlier and later stages of the controversy generated by the

[81] Ibid. 101–4; XCI–XCII.

[82] For a fuller account of the three respondents than is possible here, see J. H. Burns, 'George Buchanan and the Anti-Monarchomachs', in R. A. Mason (ed.), *Scots and Britons: Scottish Political Thought and the Union of 1603* (Cambridge, 1994), 138–60; or, in an abridged and modified version, N. Phillipson and Q. Skinner (eds), *Political Discourse in Early Modern Britain* (Cambridge, 1993), 3–22.

[83] *Flagellum Sectariorum ... Accessit Velitatio in Georgium Buchananum ...* (Ingolstadt, 1582). The two works have continuous pagination. The *Flagellum* is dated 31 Jan. 1581, the *Velitatio* 15 May 1581. Winzet refers (*Velitatio*, 215) to the fact that he is writing in Lent.

Scottish Reformation. He had engaged directly in controversy
with John Knox; and when he resumed the conflict twenty years
later Knox· was still very much in his thoughts: the *Flagellum
Sectariorum* includes a Latin version of the propositions Knox had
intended to develop in *The Second Blast of the Trumpet*.[84]

Throughout, Winzet argued as a theologian—an amateur in
his early writings, a professional (albeit one who qualified late in
life) in his Latin works.[85] In the latter his concern is, to be sure,
predominantly with political theology—with false and true
understandings of the nature of authority in a Christian society.
He is therefore particularly anxious to maintain the *sacred* character of kingship. Even a king who has turned tyrant is shielded
by his anointing from impious 'touching' by violent hands.
Buchanan's attempt to justify tyrannicide accordingly fails the
most essential test of legitimacy.[86] Yet kingship, for all its divine
sanction and consecration, is a human institution, and Winzet
argues that Buchanan has misrepresented it at this level also.

It is important to recognize that Winzet does not question—
indeed he asserts—the role of the community in the political
process. What he rejects is what he calls the *regnum populare*
advocated by his opponent, involving as (he claims) it does the
surrender to the *promiscua plebs* of authority that belongs to the
king alone. The king himself, however, does (under God) owe his
possession of that authority to 'the people'. Winzet's *populus* is (as
we shall see) an organized body acting, and capable of legitimate
action, only through the agency of the three estates. That agency
could be effective both in the establishment of royal authority and
in the situation created by a king guilty of serious misgovernment. Such a ruler would, by his tyranny, have deprived himself
of legitimate authority, and the community would be both

[84] *Flagellum*, 20–1. The propositions are also mentioned twice in the *Velitatio*: in
the dedicatory epistle to the duke of Bavaria, and again in the main text (p. 208).

[85] The vernacular works are reprinted in Ninian Winzet, *Certain Tractates together with the Book of Four Score Three Questions and a Translation of Vincentius
Lirinensis* . . . ed. J. K. Hewison, 2 vols. (Scottish Text Society; Edinburgh, 1888,
1890; hereafter Hewison edn.). Winzet disclaimed theological skill in his early
work: 'As a theologe I profes me to be nane' (Hewison edn., i. 62). He evidently
began his formal study of theology in Paris between 1566 and 1574, but completed
it at the recently founded university of Douai, graduating there in July 1575.

[86] Winzet refers several times to David's refusal to use violence against Saul—
to 'touch the Lord's anointed': see *Velitatio*, 177, 276, and cf. *The Buke of Four Scoir
Three Questionis*, q. 30 (Hewison edn., i. 95).

entitled and obliged to take whatever corporate action might be necessary to set matters right.[87] All this would be in accordance with what Winzet calls the *leges politicae*. These 'politic laws'—foreshadowing in some sense the *droit politique* and 'constitutional law' of later thinking—are essentially customary in their origin and basis. They can indeed be changed; but if this is to be done the process must be one in which both the community and its ruler have a share.[88] And, in the last resort, it is the people's share that is preponderant. It is both true and, for Winzet in his case against Buchanan, crucially important that, in the normal processes of government, authority belongs to the king. It is from the king that every other power in the realm 'flows as from its source'.[89] When, however, normal processes collapse in the face of tyranny, the ruler's forfeited power 'returns to the people from whom it originally issued'.[90]

In all this Winzet is arguably clearer and more consistent than Buchanan as to the kind of polity he has in mind; and what he says may also be regarded as reflecting more accurately the 'political culture' of the Scotland he knew. At many essential points he makes it clear that the collective action he envisages is action by the estates of the realm. Two especially notable instances should be singled out. The first occurs when Winzet is discussing the imposition of new laws—or indeed of any new proposal affecting the 'public estate' of the realm. For this, he says, the king must have the consent of the people—'by which I mean the better part of the people: that is to say, the three estates or those who are summoned from the estates to the public assembly'.[91] Again, when dealing with conduct by the ruler in breach of the *leges politicae*, Winzet says that such cases will be judged 'by

[87] *Velitatio*, 248 (*regnum populare*); 274 (*promiscuam plenem*); 260, 269, 275 (on the problems of tyranny).

[88] Ibid. 274 (*leges politicas*); dedicatory epistle, sig. xx 3ᵛ: 'non posse magis populum probatas iam olim regni leges non consentiente Rege damnare & abrogare, quam posse Regem renitente populo, siue tribus regni ordinibus nouas leges imponere.'

[89] Ibid. 266: 'tu nescire non potes in regno esse solum Regem, a quo tanquam a fonte omnis in politicis rebus potestas dimanat.'

[90] Ibid. 269: 'totum ius regni siue principatus . . . ad populum, unde profluxit, redire.'

[91] Ibid. 256: 'populi autem nomine intelligo, meliorem populi partem, tres nimirum regni ordines, siue qui ex iis ad publica comitia vocantur.' It is not clear whether Winzet applies this stipulation to legislation in general or only to legislation affecting the 'public estate' of the realm.

God and sometimes by the three estates of the realm, not by the
common people indiscriminately [*promiscuam plebem*], nor by one
or other of the estates on its own, nor by a few rebels who, for
their own advantage and not that of the commonwealth, usurp
the authority of the estates'.[92]

That last phrase resounds with echoes of the Scottish past,
including what was to Winzet the very recent past; and it may
thus serve to introduce what he himself has to say, in his rebuttal
of Buchanan's view, about the history and institutions of his
native country. With the remoter past Winzet displays little concern. For him the government established by the Scots under
Fergus was a firmly monarchical and strictly hereditary system,
with no place for the elective principle or for constitutional limits
enforced by a right to resist and depose defaulting sovereigns.[93]
For Buchanan's *mutua pactio* Winzet substitutes a treaty (*foedus*)
between king and people, the essential effect of which is to ensure
that the king shall exercise jurisdiction over his subjects, not the
subjects over the king.[94] He agrees with Buchanan as to the
importance of the law of succession adopted under Kenneth III,
but not as to its significance: it did not introduce the hereditary
principle but regulated its application. The suggestion that the
people received as a *quid pro quo* the king's acceptance of legal
restraints on his power is dismissed as a 'frivolous conjecture'.[95]
The settlement of the crown during the interregnum of the 1290s
shows, Winzet argues, that no trace of elective monarchy then
existed: both Balliol and, after the latter's admittedly ignominious
surrender of the realm to Edward I, Bruce succeeded by strict
hereditary right.[96]

The most interesting case for Winzet, however, was that of
James III. Flatly rejecting Buchanan's condemnation of the king
and justification of his treatment in 1488, he offers an account of
James's character and conduct which, while not uncritical, is

[92] *Velitatio*, 274: 'iudicem habere affirmo . . . Deum & tres aliquando regni
ordines, non autem promiscuam plebem, aut ex ordinibus unum aut alterum, aut
ex his paucos seditiosos, qui sui non Reipub. causa se illorum nomine obtrudant.'
[93] Ibid. 160–1, 242. In the second passage Winzet dismisses such cases as those
of Culen and Evenus as 'irrelevant to the present question regarding the *ius regni*'.
[94] Ibid. 237: 'Videor mihi ex his videre foedus inter Reges & populum iam
initum, regnum feliciter inceptum, atque in eo Regem ius populo dicere, non
populus Regi . . .'.
[95] Ibid. 242–3, 245, 246.
[96] Ibid. 254–6.

broadly favourable.[97] James was no tyrant; and—this is crucially important for Winzet—the action taken against him had no legality, nothing of 'due process' about it. If Buchanan claims that the king was condemned by the *maior et sanior pars*, that assertion is contradicted by the evidence that 'by far the greater and the better part of both nobility and people adhered to their King'. Nor could there have been any legitimate condemnation when the accused was not present, the case was not heard, and there was no due appointment of place, day, time, or judge.[98] In fact (Winzet sums up in a later reference), 'James III was made away with, not by a sentence passed by the nobles, but by the envy of a few conspirators'.[99]

Scotland thus embodies for Winzet the true character of legitimate kingship. It is a system in which the king, succeeding by hereditary right, is consecrated by anointing, and this protects him against personal violence even if he lapses into tyranny. His task is to *rule*; and while he may delegate certain governmental functions, the governing authority is always his. That authority, however, is to be wielded for the good of the people he rules; and the community of the realm has a role both in its establishment and in certain aspects of its exercise. The community finds its voice, so to speak, and its will in the three estates of the realm— estates not so much represented by as deemed to be present in 'those who are summoned to the public assembly'. One further aspect of Winzet's thought remains to be considered. He accepts, as we have seen, the idea that king and people are bound to one another by a treaty (*foedus*). To this, however, he adds a crucial if somewhat cryptic clause: the duty to uphold the *ius regni*, he says, is one in which both king and people are, by oath, 'bound to the realm itself' (*uterque ipsi regno est astrictus*).[100] The precise meaning of that phrase may be obscure; but it is clear at least that Winzet sees the political community as an entity which is not at the free

[97] Ibid. 238–41. Winzet refers directly to Giovanni Ferreri's continuation of Boece's *Scotorum Historiae* (published in 1574); and we may also assume that he had discussed the subject with Lesley when the latter was working on his *De rebus gestis Scotorum*. However, there are distinctive features in Winzet's account, which may merit closer scrutiny than it has received.

[98] *Velitatio*, 240. There are interesting parallels here with the attack by Rodrigo Sánchez de Arévalo on the proceedings at Avila in 1465 against Enrique IV of Castile: see J. H. Burns, *Lordship, Kingship, and Empire*, 89–91.

[99] *Velitatio*, 254.

[100] Ibid. 283.

disposal either of its ruler or of its constituent members at any given time.

There is naturally a good deal of common ground shared by Winzet with Buchanan's other Scots critics. Thus both Blackwood, who preceded Winzet in the controversy, and Barclay, who followed him, share, as Catholics, his concern to associate the Protestant heresy with the seditious subversion of temporal authority.[101] Both, however, approached the task of refuting Buchanan as jurists, not theologians; and this different perspective naturally affects the way in which they argue the case. Again, in the context of the present enquiry, we are dealing, in these two writers, with major contributors to the main stream of royalist thinking at a critical time. Some elements in their work belong therefore more to the next chapter than to this. It remains important, however, to take account of their ideas in the more limited context of the debate over the *ius regni apud Scotos*.[102]

Blackwood is especially concerned, in his *Apologia*, to argue that his adversary's dialogue does not, in fact, give an account of the *ius regni apud Scotos* at all. The system Buchanan describes is one in which supreme power lies, not with the king, but with the people; and his use of alleged analogies with Denmark or with Venice simply confirms the irrelevance of his argument to the Scottish case.[103] In a particularly striking passage, Blackwood contrasts the most celebrated example of elective monarchy with the truly royal power that prevails in such a realm as Scotland:

[101] Blackwood, like Winzet, had faced the problem before encountering Buchanan's theory, in his *De conjunctione religionis et imperii* (Paris, 1575). Barclay's position was complicated by the fact that, by the time he completed his *De regno et regali potestate* (Paris, 1600), the 'monarchomach' position he both labelled and condemned had been adopted by Catholic as well as Protestant propagandists.

[102] Blackwood, *Adversus Georgii Buchanani dialogum, De iure regni apud Scotos, pro regibus apologia* (Poitiers, 1581; hereafter *Apologia*); 2nd edn., Paris, 1588. This seems to have been the only reply to the *De iure regni* of which Buchanan himself had any knowledge: Elie Vinet, writing to Buchanan on 9 June 1581 (see Buchanan, *Opera*, 1725 edn., ii. 767) promises to send a copy 'as soon as it is published in Poitiers', but we do not know whether this was done. Barclay's *De regno et regali potestate adversus Buchananum, Brutum, Boucherium, & reliquos monarchomachos*, though not published until 1600, had been begun at much the same time as Winzet and Blackwood's replies to Buchanan. The first two of its six Books are largely concerned with the *De iure regni*; but the work was laid aside and subsequently resumed on the larger scale indicated by its title.

[103] *Apologia*, 27.

The Senate and People of Rome had a certain authority over [the emperor]: the Senate and People of Scotland have no authority over [their king]. The emperor had a limited power over the people: our kings have free and full power. The sovereignty [*imperium*] of the latter has always been pure and absolute [*merum . . . ac solutum*]: that of the former depended on the will of others [*ex alieno nutu*]. The first kind of lordship [*dominium*] is called kingship [*regnum*], the second principate [*principatus*].[104]

Kingship, thus understood, is a divinely constituted hereditary power, consecrated by the king's anointing.[105] The king holds the *summam imperii*, which includes plenary power over the laws. *Regia potestas* in this sense is indeed a requisite in every political society, but it is much better placed in the hands of a true king than in those of a dependent magistracy such as Buchanan's theory entails. Blackwood analyses that theory dialectically with the aim of showing that it implies a contradictory division of power that is in its nature indivisible.[106]

Leaving for consideration in the next chapter some further implications of Blackwood's formidable conception of royal power, we may now look briefly at some of his more specific applications of the theory to the Scottish case. His rigorously hereditary principle means that there was and is no place for an elective element in the Scottish monarchy. The *ius regni* derives entirely from the original oath which bound the Scots in allegiance not simply to Fergus but to his heirs in perpetuity.[107] Consequently, Blackwood's interpretation of 'the Baliols cause' is essentially the same as Winzet's: Balliol abdicated, and Bruce succeeded him not *populi suffragiis* but by force of arms in vindication of his indubitable hereditary right.[108] The community, having no say in the succession to the crown, has *a fortiori* no right to depose a king who has come to the throne by legitimate succession. Blackwood will not, accordingly, entertain any suggestion that James III's fate exemplified the punishment of tyrants.[109]

Otherwise, in Blackwood's handling of Scottish themes, it is not so much his juristic skill as his command of rhetoric that is called

---

[104] Ibid. 51.   [105] Ibid. 71–3.
[106] The analysis is in ch. 33 of the *Apologia* (293–307).
[107] Ibid. 159–62.   [108] Ibid. 188.
[109] Ibid. 188–9.

into play. His concern is so to exalt the ancient, hereditary, absolute kingship of the Scots as to suggest that Buchanan stands self-condemned for his impious and futile attempt to subvert it.[110] The same view of Scottish history prevails in Barclay's *De regno*, where indeed the author shows little interest in arguing over such matters as the issue between Balliol and Bruce. The warlike valour of the Scots—exemplified above all in Wallace, the Gideon of his nation—is to be celebrated, together with the stubborn loyalty of his fellow countrymen to their royal house and their refusal to endure alien rule.[111]

Both in respect of its scope and having regard to the date of its publication, Barclay's *De regno* and the position adopted by 'that great Assertor of the Power and Sacredness of Kings'[112] belong more to the next chapter than to this. There is, however, one aspect of his theory which calls for notice here, arising as it does directly from the controversy with Buchanan and supported by Barclay from the text of Winzet's *Velitatio*. This was precisely the element in Barclay's argument that was seized upon by Locke in order to demonstrate that '*Barclay* the great Champion of Absolute Monarchy, is forced to allow, That a King may be *resisted*, and *ceases to be a King*'.[113] It is unquestionable that Barclay does allow for legitimate resistance. On the one hand, there was, in the civil-law tradition to which he adhered, an ineradicable natural right of self-defence; and this could be invoked by a people suffering intolerable oppression.[114] On the other hand—and this was where Barclay drew heavily upon Winzet—there was the argument that tyrannical misgovernment deprived a ruler of legitimate authority and exposed him to justified resistance by his aggrieved subjects. Barclay will not allow that such action can be taken through the ordinary courts; but he does allow for recourse to arms—for what Locke was to call the 'appeal to Heaven'.[115] In one way or another, it seems (and there were differences between Barclay and Winzet as well as between both of them and

---

[110] *Apologia*, 306.   [111] *De regno*, 121, 213, 297.

[112] John Locke, *Two Treatises of Government*, ed. P. Laslett (Cambridge Texts in the History of Political Thought; Cambridge, 1988), 419.

[113] Ibid. 424.

[114] *De regno*, 159. It is important to note that Barclay rules out both the notion of any element of *punishment* in the community's self-defence and Buchanan's claim that an individual subject may take the task of resistance upon himself.

[115] Ibid. 212–14.

Buchanan), it was hard in the late sixteenth century to see Scottish kingship in simple terms of passive obedience and non-resistance.

By the time his critics were preparing their attacks on the *De iure regni*, Buchanan himself must, during the last year or two of his life, have been at work on the completion and final revision of the work which has been regarded as a massive *pièce justificative* in support of his political theory.[116] Yet the *Rerum Scoticarum Historia* seems to have been the fruit of many years' interest in the subject; and its origins and development present many problems lying beyond the scope of the present enquiry. What can hardly be doubted is that the political principles expounded in the *De iure regni* pervade and colour much of the *Historia*. This is particularly true of Books IV and V together with the early chapters of Book VI, where Buchanan traces the history of Scotland from the supposed establishment of the monarchy under Fergus to the change in the law of succession under Kenneth III. Buchanan (like most of his Scottish contemporaries) accepts Boece's account of the first forty kings. He modifies that account in some respects and the text as we have it may indeed represent a revision undertaken after the posthumously published work of Humphrey Lhuyd, with its contemptuous dismissal of the whole farrago as entirely fabulous.[117] Buchanan resolutely adheres to the picture of an elective monarchy under which misrule was subject to punishment by the community in the form of deposition, exile, or death. At times, as Thomas Innes pointed out, he even adds to Boece's version.[118] If it is the case that 'Renaissance historiography grows up in a context of ideological intensity',[119] the ideological thrust in Buchanan's case seems plain enough.

Yet closer inspection suggests that matters are not quite so straightforward. There are crucial points at which Buchanan not only misses what look like obvious pegs on which to hang his

[116] *Rerum Scoticarum Historia auctore Georgio Buchanano Scoto* (Edinburgh, 1582): reprinted in the first volume of the 1715 and 1725 edns. of Buchanan's *Opera Omnia*. The fullest discussion of the *Historia* is in ch. 12 of McFarlane, *Buchanan* (416–40). See also Trevor-Roper, *George Buchanan*, esp. 16–39; and Mason, '*Rex Stoicus*', esp. 24–30.

[117] See on this esp. Trevor-Roper, *George Buchanan*, 25–31.

[118] Innes, *Critical Essay*, 219. The whole of Innes's critique of Buchanan (ibid. 176–223) is still important: see Trevor-Roper's comments, *George Buchanan*, 1–2, 19 n. 2, 38–9.

[119] McFarlane, *Buchanan*, 425.

ideological argument but also seems to retreat from positions he had adopted in the *De iure regni*. The constitutional transaction in the reign of Kenneth III is a case in point. In the *De iure regni* Buchanan had argued that the establishment of hereditary monarchy was balanced by the subjection of royal power to legal restraints—a conjecture for which earlier accounts afforded no warrant, and which has disappeared entirely from the *Historia*. It is true that Buchanan now suggested that the new law of succession did not, as he had previously assumed, have the consent of the community (at least of the nobles): it had been imposed by force. Yet, whereas he had maintained in the dialogue that *if* the change had been brought about by force or fraud it would have been invalid, he refrains in the history from drawing that conclusion.[120] He does, to be sure, do what he can to emphasize vestiges of the elective principle, and is particularly concerned to stress the role of the estates. Thus the parliament at Scone after the death of Alexander III had before it the *appointment* of a new sovereign; the consent of the estates to the marriage of Marjorie Bruce was to be an essential condition of her children's right to succeed; and when Buchanan repeats Boece's fiction of the mission sent to France to induce John Balliol to surrender his right to the crown, he takes care to insist that, in any case, the declaration of the estates alone (as in the 1315 parliament at Ayr) confers a fully adequate title.[121]

Even more striking is the shift in Buchanan's attitude to the case of Balliol himself. In the *De iure regni*, evidently following Mair's interpretation, he saw this as a clear case of the setting aside of an unsatisfactory ruler by the community of the realm. In the *Historia*, however, he says nothing to suggest that he regarded the episode as an apt illustration of the king's subordination to the community.[122] In the same connection it is noteworthy that when Buchanan records Morton's speech in parliament reporting on the negotiations in England in February 1571, he omits any reference

---

[120] *Historia*, 1582, fos. 67ᵛ–68ʳ; 1725 edn., 185–6; cf *De iure regni*, 61–3; LII–LIV.

[121] *Historia*, fo. 73 (sig. R i)ʳ, 1725 edn., 232; fo. 82 (sig. S [vi])ʳ⁻ᵛ, 1725 edn., 259; fo. 84 (sig. T ii)ʳ, 1725 edn., 264. (The leaves are misnumbered in the 1582 edn., fos. 73–85 being duplicated.)

[122] The omission is all the more striking since the relevant part of the *Historia* is one where Buchanan explicitly refers to Mair's work as a source: ibid., fo. 77 (sig. S i)ᵛ; 1725 edn., 245. It is noteworthy that Buchanan refers to Wallace as 'regent and Balliol's lieutenant' (*Prorex . . . & tanquam Ballioli Legatus*): ibid., fo. 76 (sig. R [v])ᵛ; 1725 edn., 243–4.

to 'the Baliols cause'.[123] Yet he was evidently drawing on the 'wryting' submitted by Morton to Elizabeth's commissioners; in which we read that

John Balliol was by the nobilitie and estates of Scotland deposed . . . and Robert Bruce, nixt of the bloode roiall, promoted to the crowne and kingdom, which deposition and depryvacion was never annulled . . . wherein the nobilitie and people of Scotland, defending their auncient and laudable custome and their lawe, rather spent their blode than they wold suffer their libertie fall and decaye.[124]

The omission of anything of this kind from the *Historia*, on either of the two occasions when the Balliol case was, or could have been, mentioned, is perhaps the most striking, though by no means the only, evidence that Buchanan, by the time he completed his history was inclined to mitigate the 'radicalism' of the *De iure regni*.[125]

Yet if a tactical retreat may be discernible at some points, there is no question of a total withdrawal. James III, though not ill-disposed by nature, became, through the vicious influence of 'men of the basest kind', 'a pernicious king' and the nobles (*proceres*) who took arms against him were benefactors of their country. 'James's death was branded with such infamy that the Estates, in the next parliament, decreed that he had been justly slain'.[126] For Lesley, we may note by way of contrast, while his account of James's reign is by no means favourable to the king, those who killed him were 'savage and cruel murderers'.[127]

It is of course in regard to the crisis of Mary's reign that Buchanan's ideological position bears most strongly upon events in his native country. The details of his strongly partisan account of those events are not our concern: what matters here is his interpretation of them.[128] It may be worth noting first, however,

---

[123] Trevor-Roper (*George Buchanan*, 8) is thus quite mistaken in saying 'Both [the 1571 'wryting' and Buchanan's version of Morton's speech] dwell on the competition of Balliol and the Bruce.'

[124] Ibid. 47.

[125] Trevor-Roper (ibid. 36) refers, in a wider context, to 'the gradual, shamefaced and yet disingenuous retreat of the old revolutionary'. In respect of Buchanan's 'revolutionary' political theory at least, that is something of an overstatement.

[126] *Historia*, fos. 142^v–143^r; 1725 edn., 437–9.

[127] *De rebus gestis Scotorum* (1675), 316. Cf. also Winzet's view, discussed above.

[128] See for a detailed commentary Buchanan, *Tyrannous Reign of Mary Stewart*, ed. Gatherer, intro., and the footnotes to Gatherer's translation of the relevant parts of the *Historia* (down to Mary's flight into England).

that he had taken earlier occasions to associate himself with that hostility to female sovereignty which was so strongly marked in Knox's thinking. The proposed or actual appointment of queen regents in the minorities of James III, James V, and Mary herself afforded opportunities which Buchanan seized upon eagerly and, especially in the first case, exploited fully.[129] And if a queen regent was bad, a queen regnant behaving as Mary (in Buchanan's view) had behaved must be a great deal worse. Even before his narrative reaches the final crisis, Buchanan makes his polemical position clear. At the grim moment of the murder of Riccio in 1566, he has the haggard figure of Ruthven reading the queen a lecture on constitutional morality: her authority could be legitimately exercised only in accordance with the law and with the advice and consent of the nobility.[130] The same point is made when Buchanan portrays the queen, in the parliament of April 1567 (two months after the murder of Darnley), as revealing her previously concealed 'lust for tyrannical power' (*tyrannidis cupiditatem*)—heedless of the fact that 'the Scots have no laws other than acts of parliament' and foreshadowing a regime in which 'the prince's will would be regarded as law'.[131] When he reaches the crisis of July 1567, Buchanan refrains from alleging any formal act of deposition, preferring to treat Mary's abdication as the voluntary result of persuasion by the 'avengers' of Darnley's murder; but he is careful to insist that Moray was 'elected as regent'.[132] Again, when recording Moray's defence, at the York conference of October 1568, of the proceedings against Mary, Buchanan ascribes to him the claim that these had, throughout, been 'rightful, in accordance with the laws and ancient practice of the nation, and conducted in public assembly'.[133] And the argument is, of course, elaborated in Buchanan's final reference to the matter, in the

[129] *Historia*, fos. 131ᵛ–133ᵛ, 1725 edn., 403–9 (James III); fo. 153ᵛ, 1725 edn., 466 (James V); fo. 186ʳ, 1725 edn., 554–5 (Mary).

[130] Ibid., fo. 211ʳ; 1723 edn., 611.

[131] Ibid., fo. 216ᵛ; 1725 edn., 636–7.

[132] Ibid., fo. [222]ᵛ; 1725 edn., 655–6 (the 1582 foliation is defective, '223' being duplicated). It may be worth noting that Buchanan begins his account of Moray's regency with the phrase *Rege creato* (ibid., fo. 224ʳ; 1725 edn., 657). Gatherer (*Tyrannous Reign*, 151) renders this as 'The King having been crowned'; but this loses something of the force of Buchanan's words, which suggest that James had been 'made king' in the sense of being elected or appointed.

[133] *Historia*, fo. 227ᵛ; 1725 edn., 667–8: 'Nihil a Regiis, nisi iure & legibus, & e vetustis gentis institutis, idque in conuentu publico actum.'

speech he attributes to Morton in the parliament following the negotiations of February 1571.[134]

However we are to interpret the relationship between that speech, the 'wryting' which it certainly echoes, and Buchanan's own exposition in the *De iure regni*, we can at least be sure that the leading Scottish humanist of the Renaissance had laid, both in the dialogue and in the *Historia*, the basis for a great deal of later ideology. The edifice built on those foundations was one in which Buchanan's royal pupil steadfastly and strenuously refused to be confined. James VI's preferred doctrinal habitation must be surveyed in the next chapter.

[134] Ibid., fos. 242ᵛ–244ᵛ; 1725 edn., 711–16.

7

Free Monarchy
James VI

THREE months before the infant James VI came to the throne, his mother, in the parliament of April 1567, 'formally took the reformed church under her protection'.[1] It was an act, whether judged against the background of what had gone before or in the light of what was to follow, heavy with irony. By the time Mary died on the scaffold twenty years later, her son, now ruling as well as reigning, was deeply embroiled with the kirk of which he was, according to one view of the oath prescribed in 1571, 'supreme Governour'.[2] Nor, remarkably effective though his government was in time to become, can it be claimed that James, despite his firm and sincere Protestant commitment, ever found a wholly peaceful *modus vivendi* with the Scottish church. One element in that church, always prominent and at critical moments predominant, was shaped by the 'second reformation' of the 1570s and after, its goals inscribed in the *Second Book of Discipline* adopted by the General Assembly in 1578.[3] However we are to assess the influence on that document of Andrew Melville, there can be no doubt that his was the main intellectual force in ecclesiastical affairs between his return to Scotland from Geneva in 1574 and his detention in 1606 (followed by banishment from 1611 until his death in 1622). The doctrine of the 'two kingdoms' with which his name is inseparably associated, may have been less novel and less exclusively 'Melvillian' than has sometimes been supposed. What is surely beyond question is that the confrontation between Andrew Melville and James VI involved a clash between irreconcilable ecclesiologies, each with immediate and important implications for the way in which royal power was to be conceived.

[1] Donaldson, *James V to James VII*, 128. [2] Ch. 5 at n. 92.
[3] Ch. 5 n. 89.

At the heart of Melville's teaching lay a rigorous insistence on the parity of ministers in the church, with the consequential rejection of all forms of episcopacy and the assertion, in its place, of church government by means of a hierarchy of courts from the kirk session at the base of the pyramid to the General Assembly at its apex. A particular bone of contention was the introduction, between the levels of session and synod, of the district presbyteries which were to lend their name to the term by which this form of church polity has come to be known. It was the suppression, by the so-called 'Black Acts' of 1584, of the nascent presbyterian order in the Kirk that precipitated the first phase of conflict with the young king. James, then 18, was not yet quite his own man. Formal regency had ended with the fall of Morton at the end of 1580; but the ascendancy of Esmé Stewart, created duke of Lennox in 1581, and, following the crisis of the Raid of Ruthven (August 1582), that of James Stewart, earl of Arran, between the summer of 1583 and the autumn of 1585, were such as to preclude our regarding the king himself as being in control of the government during those years.[4] Yet we have no reason to doubt his full approval of the ecclesiastical policies which led to Melville's flight to England and the passing of the 'Black Acts'. Arran's fall was not the prelude to any significant relaxation of the government's opposition to the Presbyterians. Whether or not it is the case that Morton had held out to the young king the prospect of becoming a 'frie King and monarche, having the rewell and power of all Esteates', there can be little doubt that James found such possibilities alluring.[5] He himself declared, a month after his escape from the Ruthven Raiders in June 1583, his determination 'to be known to be a universal king'—independent of faction, seeking unity and peace under his unchallenged authority.[6] And a Melvillian general assembly plainly embodied a threat to that kind of kingship.

The first ten years or so of James's personal rule were marked by successive crises. The execution of his mother in 1587 was followed by the threat of the Armada; and even the failure of 'the enterprise of England' (which must inevitably have affected

---

[4] See Donaldson, *James V to James VII*, 148–50, 197–9.

[5] *The Autobiography and Diary of Mr James Melvill*, ed. R. Pitcairn (Wodrow Society; Edinburgh, 1842), 61.

[6] *Cal. Scot. Pap.*, 6, 523.

Scotland too) did not end Protestant Europe's anxieties. To James 1589 brought Elizabeth's revelation of treasonable correspondence with Spain by Huntly, Errol, and other lords committed or inclined to the Catholic cause. Four years later the affair of the 'Spanish Blanks' caused fresh alarm.[7] By then, indeed, the uneasy situation had provided the Presbyterian party in the kirk with an opportunity to undo some of the damage their cause had suffered by the 'Black Acts'. The 'Golden Acts' of 1592 did not, it is true, embody a total retreat on the king's part, though there had already been, from the mid-1580s onwards, a considerable relaxation of the intended rigour of 1584. Presbyteries had continued to develop, the role of bishops had continued to decline. Yet even in 1592 the episcopal order was not abolished; nor— casting its long shadow across centuries of later church history— was lay patronage. And above all, 'on the central issue of ecclesiastical independence there was no capitulation to Andrew Melville'.[8] The annual General Assembly was to continue, but the date and place of its meeting were to be in the hands of the king (a point of which the significance would not have escaped the conciliarists and papalists of the fifteenth century). Again, the composition of the Assembly fell short of the standards set by the *Second Book of Discipline*, for the ministers (the *Book*'s 'ecclesiastical persons') were still to sit together with lay members. Nevertheless, the 1592 acts were regarded 'as the Magna Carta of presbytery'.[9]

James could not rest content with such a settlement, though his power to change it was, for the moment, severely restricted. Fear of a Catholic conspiracy, combined with the popular odium the king incurred for his supposed complicity in the slaying by Huntly of 'the bonnie earl of Moray' in 1592, had to be met by an alliance, however unpalatable, with Melville and his party in the kirk. Only the voluntary exile accepted by Huntly and Errol in March 1595 (they returned in June of the following year), and then their reception into the kirk and the reversal of their forfeiture (June, November 1597) ended the threat of political Catholicism.[10]

---

[7] See Donaldson, *James V to James VII*, 189–90 and n. 25.

[8] Ibid. 199. One factor in the decline of episcopacy at this period was the 1587 Act of Annexation, whereby all the temporalities of the pre-Reformation church were transferred to the crown. Neither the bishops nor the Presbyterians stood to gain by this appropriation.

[9] Donaldson, *James V to James VII*, 200.   [10] Ibid. 190–6.

Meanwhile ultra-Protestant pretensions had reached new heights. In September 1596, at Falkland, Melville told the king that, in the kingdom of Christ, he was only 'God's sillie vassall'.[11] Three months later, in mid-December, an anti-popish riot in Edinburgh gave James the opportunity to halt the advance of Protestant extremism. By the end of 1597 he had gained enough ground to have legislation adopted for the royal nomination of bishops who would have seats in parliament.[12] The struggle was far from over; but the king who wrote, in 1597 and 1598, *The True Lawe of Free Monarchies* and the *Basilikon Doron*[13] was neither of a mind to yield to Melville's interpretation of the 'two kingdoms' nor in a political situation which constrained him to do so.

Before examining the political ideas expressed in James VI's writings of the late 1590s it will be useful to pause and consider the general state of thinking about kingship in late sixteenth-century Europe. Something of this has already been reviewed in the course of the last chapter; for the challenge of 'monarchomach' doctrine, promulgated by Buchanan and others, elicited, by way of reponse, much polemical writing in defence of hereditary 'absolute' kingship.[14] Both Adam Blackwood and William Barclay merit some further consideration in a context broader than that of their dialectics against the *De iure regni*. It was a context in which writers on the problems of political authority had available to

---

[11] Melville, *Autobiography*, 370. James Melville (1556–1614), Andrew's nephew, was present with him on this occasion. Perhaps more telling than the notorious phrase quoted above was the elder Melville's statement that in Christ's 'kingdome, the Kirk . . . King James the Saxt is . . . nocht a King, nor a lord, nor a heid, but a member!'

[12] Donaldson, *James V to James VII*, 195, 201–2. See also Wormald, *Court, Kirk, and Community*, 128–9.

[13] In the case of *The True Lawe*, I have used the original 1598 spelling of the title: the now commonly adopted *Trew Law* (and not, as the editors of James's *Minor Prose Works* suggest—p.203 n. 1—*Treue Lawe*) was first used in the 1616 collection of James's *Workes*. As for *Basilikon Doron*, the now standard transliteration from the Greek letters used consistently in the MS and all early edns. was adopted by C. H. McIlwain in *The Political Works of James I* (Cambridge, Mass., 1918). The alternative *Basilicon Doron* (adopted for the Craigie edn.) was used in James Montagu's preface to the 1616 *Workes* and also in the table of contents there; otherwise Greek letters are used throughout. For the texts cited here and for forms of reference see nn. 40, 81 below.

[14] See also Burns, 'George Buchanan and the Anti-Monarchomachs'.

them 'the best known commentary on a ruler's absolute power in
the sixteenth century, Jean Bodin's *De republica*'.[15] Bodin was no
doubt to be 'recognized as the greatest exponent of absolute monarchy'.[16] His disposition to assimilate royal and paternal power
undoubtedly nourished the patriarchalist element in the ideology
of royal absolutism,[17] yet his theory of sovereignty, though an
immensely useful, was not a sufficient support for kingship as
such against the monarchomach challenge. As Adam Blackwood
for one acknowledged, the *regia potestas* (which is evidently his
term for a Bodiniam sovereign power) required by any viable
system of government need not be lodged in the hands of a
monarch, let alone the kind of king Blackwood's *Pro regibus apologia* sought to defend.[18] Blackwood, as we have seen, argued in
juristic terms to prove that a true king had such *imperium merum
ac solutum* as no elective magistrate, not even the Roman *princeps*,
enjoyed or could claim. Such a king was, for one thing, *anointed*:
he had been consecrated by a rite Blackwood describes as 'a
symbol of divinity and, as it were, a sacrament'.[19] Secondly, royal
power was strictly and indefeasibly hereditary: the heir to the
crown becomes king immediately upon the death of his predecessor.[20] Blackwood also insists, however, that 'kings inherit, not
from [previous] kings, but from the realm [itself]'.[21] This, by implying that the realm subsists in some sense independently of the
king, may recall Winzet's concept of a *regnum* to which both king
and people are 'bound'; and it may appear, similarly, to limit that
full power over the laws which is the essence of *regia potestas*.
Blackwood, however, argues from the postulate that kings succeed to the realm rather than to their predecessors to the conclusion that, just as the king may abrogate or repeal any law he

[15] K. Pennington, *The Prince and the Law 1200–1600: Sovereignty and Rights in the
Western Legal Tradition* (Berkeley and Los Angeles, 1993), 276.
[16] D. Wootton (ed.), *Divine Right and Democracy: An Anthology of Political Writing
in Stuart England* (Harmondsworth, 1986), 35.
[17] See on this R. Tuck, *Philosophy and Government 1572–1651* (Cambridge, 1993),
26–7, 260–1.
[18] *Apologia* (1581), 197–8.
[19] *Apologia* in Blackwood's *Opera Omnia* (Paris, 1644), 9: from an opening chapter apparently added to the text sometime after the publication of the 2nd edn.
(Paris, 1588). In his 1575 *De conjunctione religionis et imperii* Blackwood had referred
to 'the hidden and almost divine power' of the oil used to anoint both kings and
priests in the period of the Old Testament (*Opera Omnia*, 232, 234).
[20] *Apologia* (1581), 71–3.   [21] Ibid. 113.

has himself made, so he is not bound by any agreement entered into by kings who have preceded him on the throne.[22] And to this we may add, finally, the point that Blackwood's theory of kingship is based upon a view of human society in which force is the inevitable origin and basis of authority.[23]

Before turning, as before, from Blackwood to Barclay, exemplifying as they do aspects of monarchist thinking in the period when James VI was to make his distinctive contribution, we may usefully look briefly at a writer with no Scottish connection or involvement. Pierre Grégoire (1540–1617), a slightly older contemporary of Barclay, was his colleague at Pont-à-Mousson from 1582 and his ally in the struggle against Jesuit influence in that recently founded university.[24] Unlike Barclay, he did not engage in the polemical struggle, preferring to expound his position in a more academic form. His *De republica* (1596) was a fundamentally Bodinian but eclectic 'detailed and exhaustive analysis of political forms and theories'.[25] Perhaps because of its eclecticism, it is a work susceptible of varying, if not contradictory, interpretations; but there can at least be no dispute as to Grégoire's essentially monarchist position. Following Bodin, he rejects the possibility of a mixed state; and he rejects too the Aristotelian distinction between royal power, with its willing subjects, and tyranny, imposed on subjects who are coerced. To have an authority dependent in any way upon the will of its subjects is, he argues, to preclude any possibility of a genuinely monarchical system.[26] Yet Grégoire does not deny that authority *originated* with the community: he appeals to the model of the Roman *lex regia*, but insists (in accordance with one major tendency in civil-law scholarship) that the people's transfer of power was total and irrevocable. On that basis it is, above all, hereditary monarchy that is defended; and a hereditary ruler can never be deposed, even if, by violating divine and natural law (for over 'the politic and civil

---

[22] Ibid. 114.   [23] Ibid. 61–3.

[24] See C. Collot, *L'École doctrinale de droit public à Pont-à-Mousson* (Paris, 1965). Grégoire's 'alliance' with Barclay did not extend (it may be worth noting) to ecclesiology; for he did not adopt the Gallican position in regard to papal authority.

[25] Salmon, in Burns and Goldie (eds.), *Cambridge History of Political Thought 1450–1700*, 234–5; and cf. D. R. Kelley, ibid. 88–9. For a helpful account of some of Grégoire's main ideas see Carlyle, *Mediaeval Political Theory*, vi. 441–5.

[26] *De republica libri sex et viginti* (Pont-à-Mousson, 1596; Frankfurt, 1609), VI. xviii. 15.

laws' he has complete command), he becomes a tyrant. He should of course rule in accordance with the laws of God and nature. Indeed it is his function to exhibit to his subjects 'the image and the power of God': it is God who has given him absolute power and whose vicar upon earth he is.[27] There are doubtless writers who press that kind of argument even further; but the image of the king as a quasi-divine and as a patriarchal figure is vividly presented in Grégoire's treatise.[28] This makes it all the more important to recognize at the same time that Grégoire, following Bodin's distinction between sovereignty and government, fully recognizes the function and the value of the institutions—magistracies, courts, councils, and perhaps especially the estates of the realm—through which a prudent king rules his people. All these institutions, however, subsist and operate at the discretion of the king, whose absolute power is always paramount.[29]

If Pierre Grégoire provided, in the mid-1590s, 'a detailed and exhaustive analysis' of what we might term the political science of monarchism, William Barclay was at work in the same period on what became, according to the same scholar, 'a kind of *summa* of the ideas of divine right, sovereignty, and Gallicanism developed by *politique* royalists during the later religious wars [in France]'.[30] Fellow jurists and disciples of Bodin though they were, however, the two Pont-à-Mousson professors wrote very different books. Barclay's *De regno et regali potestate* (Paris, 1600) began life, as we have seen, as a response to Buchanan's *De iure regni apud Scotos*; and though it may in the end have become indeed 'a kind of *summa*', it never lost its essentially polemical character. Having dealt with Buchanan in Books I and II, Barclay turned, in the next two Books, to the task of refuting 'Brutus'—the pseudonymous author of the *Vindiciae contra tyrannos*; and by the time he came to write Books V and VI he had to face what was, to him, the

[27] *De republica*, III. iv. 6; VI. xviii. 15; VII. v. 8; VI. ii. 9.

[28] The last passage cited in n. 27 is particularly striking: 'Neque in principibus tam personam singularem reveremur, quantum majestatem Dei et imaginem potestatemque consideremus et reveremus ex parte illius cujus delegati sunt, et vicarias in terra partes gerunt.' Salmon (*Cambridge History of Political Thought 1450–1700*, 234) suggests that Grégoire 'chose not to put as much stress on divine right as [Pierre de] Belloy' (in his *Apologie catholique* of 1585). For the patriarchalist element in Grégoire see, e.g. *De republica*, VI. xvii. 15; XIII. xii. 16.

[29] Ibid. v. i. 18; and cf. XXIV. iv. 6–8; XXIV. vi. 17.

[30] Salmon, *Cambridge History of Political Thought 1450–1700*, 235.

enormity of the Catholic Jean Boucher's having embraced the monarchomach heresy in his *De iusta Henrici Tertii abdicatione* of 1589. The polemics, harsh and prolix as they are, owe, to be sure, a great deal to Barclay's juristic learning; and he was also prepared to turn to others for the theological learning which could provide further support. Cuner Peeters and, especially, Ninian Winzet are summoned as witnesses in that connection.[31] In the end, however, the *De regno* is a work of controversy, not primarily of scholarship. That may be at least a partial explanation of the incoherence and inconsistency Locke was to point out and to exploit. On the other hand, there may be a deeper source: there were perhaps problematic issues in the theory of monarchy which were unlikely to be resolved in a book where theory was subordinated to the needs of ideological debate. The brief reference to Barclay's ambiguities in a previous chapter may now usefully be followed up by looking at his theory in more general terms.[32]

For Barclay, then, *utilitas*—speaking always in harmony with nature—is the basis of human society. The laws of nature must indeed be respected if the common good is to be furthered; but human circumstances vary widely and the task of adjusting human laws to the specific needs of a community calls both for legislative skill and for effective authority in the hands of a single ruler. That ruler is *legibus solutus*: free from the restraints, not of natural and divine law, but of the human laws that are made by his authority.[33] That he should take counsel in regard to this and other aspects of his government is both prudent and, as we might say, 'civilized'. In the words of the *Code* it is *humanum*; but it is not and cannot be obligatory. The councils, the assemblies, the estates, the whole institutional apparatus of counsel exists by the

[31] On Peeters, see J. H. Burns, 'Buchanan and the Anti-Monarchomachs', in N. Phillipson and Q. Skinner (eds.), *Political Discourse in Early Modern Britain*, 17 and n. 52.

[32] Cf. Burns, 'George Buchanan and the Anti-Monarchomachs', 152–8.

[33] *De regno*, 193–4, where Barclay cites a formidable list of earlier jurists from Guilielmus Durantis in the late 13th c. to Jason de Mayno and Felinus in the early 16th. Pennington (*The Prince and the Law*, 276) argues that Barclay's view 'is simply a statement of the Roman law principle . . . [that] the prince may transcend positive law through his absolute power' and that he takes a less extreme position than e.g. that of Albericus de Rosate (who is in Barclay's list of authorities) in the mid-14th c.

authority and at the discretion of the king, who retains the exclusive right to make law.[34]

It is indeed, as the title of his book makes clear, with kingship
that Barclay is concerned. Kings rule by divine right, their power
is ordained by God. That, however, does not preclude the possibility—perhaps even the necessity—of some kind of role for
'the people'. Even where direct divine intervention seems
most in evidence—in the appointment of kings over God's chosen
people—the community had its essential part to play. Saul
and David both achieved their regal position *populi suffragio*,
even though each had previously been anointed by Samuel. It
was God alone, however, who conferred power upon the kings
the community had instituted; and the same is true, according to
Barclay, of all kings. Moreover, this divinely ordained royal
power is superior to any power the community may have. In
particular, the people have no right to depose or take coercive
action against their king.[35] In regard to the hereditary monarchy
Barclay of course favours, the same principles apply. Succession
is precisely the kind of thing that calls for positive regulation by
human law, having regard to varying circumstances. Yet the king
who duly succeeds to the crown in accordance with such a law
receives his authority from God and is answerable to God alone
for his exercise of it.[36] The importance for Barclay of the patriarchal element in royalist thinking is perhaps debatable.[37] Again, we
have noted already the complications created by his having
'made vital concessions to resistance theory'; and it has been said
that he 'seems to be perplexed about the German Empire and
Poland'.[38] The fact remains that *De regno* came to be seen as,

---

[34] *De regno*, 194: 'Et Principem solum posse condere statuta, licet humanum sit,
quod consilio Procerum utatur, denique Principem posse tollere leges positivas,
quia illis non subiicitur, sed illae sibi.' Barclay is in fact quoting directly from
Durantis, *Speculum iuris*: I have been unable to verify the citation, but the implicit
Code reference is to 1, 14, 8. See also *De regno*, 41, 43, 44–7, 61, 98, 287–8 (where
Barclay cites Bodin), 336–7.

[35] Ibid. 112–13; 269–70.

[36] Ibid. 119–20. See also ibid. 66, 68, 195.

[37] Thus Salmon (*Cambridge History of Political Thought 1450–1700*, 235) refers to
Barclay's view that '[m]onarchy began with Adam, the first patriarch, and . . . was
the only form of government approved by God' (cf. *De regno*, 79–80). Tuck (*Philosophy and Government*, 28) finds, in Barclay as compared with Grégoire, less
'stress on the *familial* character of government'.

[38] Salmon, *Cambridge History of Political Thought*, 235; Carlyle, *Mediaeval Political
Theory*, vi. 450 (cf. *De regno*, 282–3).

essentially, the work of one of *'the great Vindicators of the Right of Kings'*;[39] and James VI, when he had become James I, was sufficiently impressed by Barclay's credentials (including his resolute Gallicanism) to seek, though without success, to attract him by preferment in England.

The English succession was of course very much in the king's mind as he wrote the two works which are the central subject of this chapter. This may prompt questions (which cannot, however, be discussed here) as to the extent to which the ground had been prepared in his new kingdom for the reception of his ideas. What is necessary for our purposes is to consider those ideas in two contexts: first, the general state of monarchist thinking sketched here in the last few pages; and secondly James's personal experience of the realities of kingship in Scotland.

The True Lawe of Free Monarchies has been called an 'academic treatise'; but it is difficult to accept that designation. James himself was surely nearer the mark in describing the work as a 'pamphlet'.[40] And even then, in an age when pamphleteering could be conducted on a massive scale, this would be notable for its brevity. Within its brief compass, again, a substantial part—perhaps one third—of the text is given over to scriptural exegesis. All James's direct references and almost all his quotations are biblical. This is not, of course, in any way unusual or surprising. 'Political theology', often largely scriptural in character, is characteristic of many works of the period that are much more elaborate and 'academic' than *The True Lawe*. In that sense James's approach to his theme was very much the same as was adopted by writers like

---

[39] Locke (ed. Laslett), *Two Treatises*, 190. In this passage (in the *First Treatise*), Locke groups Barclay with Blackwood and Sir John Hayward (*c.*1564–1627), arguing that they all *'admit with one consent the Natural Liberty and Equality of Mankind, for a Truth unquestionable'*.

[40] Wormald, *Court, Kirk, and Community*, 148. James uses the term 'pamphlet' twice in the 'ADVERTISEMENT to the Reader', though he does admittedly, towards the end of his 'discourse', refer to it as 'this treatise': *Minor Prose Works of King James VI and I*, ed. J. Craigie and A. Law (Scottish Text Society; Edinburgh, 1982; hereafter *MPW*), 58, 81. That edn., though inconveniently arranged, provides the best text, corresponding to the 1st edn. of 1598 rather than the later anglicized text included in James's *Workes* (London, 1616) and reproduced in C. H. McIlwain (ed.), *The Political Works of James I* (Cambridge, Mass., 1918; hereafter McIlwain edn.). *The True Lawe* appeared over the pseudonym 'C. φιλοπατρις'; and, while James's authorship must have been an open secret from an early stage, it was not publicly acknowledged until the work's inclusion in the 1616 collection.

Winzet and Barclay. The difficulty remains, however: the concise and compressed nature of the text and the absence of any non-scriptural apparatus make it hard to locate James's pamphlet in the wider context of late sixteenth-century monarchist writing. It has been suggested, albeit tentatively, that Blackwood's *Apologia* may have been the source of some of his arguments.[41] It is likely enough that James had read Blackwood, and his insistence that many monarchical regimes (including that which prevailed in Scotland) had originated in conquest is at least reminiscent of Blackwood's view that force was the basis of political power. On the other hand, James could have found that argument (if a specific source is needed) in Bodin's *Six livres de la République*, which we know to have been in his library by 1583.[42] So far as putative influence is concerned, it is noteworthy that there is, in *The True Lawe*, no such emphasis as we find in Blackwood's *Apologia* (and also in Winzet's *Velitatio*) on the significance of the anointing of kings. James mentions of course the facts that Samuel anointed Saul as king and that David, because of the sacred character this had conferred, refused to slay Saul when he had the opportunity to do so.[43] James, as noted above, had himself been anointed and was to be anointed again when he succeeded to the English throne. It may be significant, however, that he exercised the power to 'touch' for 'the king's evil' only with reluctance and some degree of evident scepticism.[44] Certainly he reveals no inclination to build his case for the 'divine' character of kingship on this particular doctrine.

To say this is not of course to deny that James is very much concerned, in *The True Lawe*, to uphold, precisely, the view that kingship is in some special sense an institution based on 'divine right'. That all 'the powers that be' were 'ordained by God' was, to be sure, common ground across virtually the entire spectrum of

[41] Carlyle, *Mediaeval Political Theory*, vi. 437.

[42] G. F. Warner (ed.), 'The Library of James VI, in the Hand of Peter Young, his Tutor, 1573–1583', *Miscellany of the Scottish History Society* (Edinburgh, 1893), p. xlii (the work is paginated throughout in lower-case Roman). James would not have had to read far in Bodin's prolix work before encountering the point in question: early in the sixth chapter of Book I, Bodin says, 'Reason and common sense alike point to the conclusion that the origin and foundation of commonwealths was in force and violence.'

[43] *MPW* 62, 67.

[44] See on this D. H. Willson, *King James VI and I* (London, 1956), 172–3.

political thinking in early-modern Europe.[45] This, however, makes it not less but all the more important to recognize the specificity of the divine right *of kings*. The point of James's 'sermon' in *The True Lawe*, with 1 Samuel 8: 9–20 as his text, may be missed if we do not bear in mind that God, in acceding to the request for 'a king to judge us like all the nations', was in effect appointing a replacement for himself in the government of his chosen people. True, the wielding of godlike authority by a human ruler carried with it the risk of all the burdens and exactions of which Samuel gave warning. Yet the authority *was* godlike: kingship was, in James's phrase 'the true patterne of Diuinitie': '*Monarchie* . . . as resembling the Diuinitie, approacheth nearest to perfection . . . Vnitie being the perfection of all things'.[46] Such a king should, to be sure, wield such authority 'as a louing Father'; but for this and for all his obligations he is 'countable to that great GOD, who placed him as his lieutenant' over his subjects.[47] The weight of scriptural exegesis in James's argument supports the hypothesis that one of his main concerns at this time was to refute the positions taken by Melville and his allies.[48] At the very outset of *The True Lawe* he emphasizes the necessity for a people to have 'knowledge of their God'. Next to that, however, nothing is more necessary than 'the right knowledge of their alleageance, according to the forme of gouernement established among them'.[49] This opens up another perspective in James's thinking.

The 'forme of gouernement established among' the first readers of *The True Lawe* was in effect the *ius regni apud Scotos*. This was the law from which, subject always of course to the overarching principles of divine and natural law, James's subjects were urged to derive their understanding of what he called in the subtitle of his pamphlet 'the reciprock and mutuall duetie betwixt a free King and his naturall subiects'. Now, while it may be the case that 'nineteen years seems a long time to wait before seeking to controvert another man's arguments, especially when that other's book had been written when its nominal addressee was only four years

---

[45] See, with particular reference to early 17th-c. England, C. S. R. Russell, 'Divine Right', in J. Morrill, P. Slack, and D. Woolf (eds.), *Public Duty and Private Conscience in Seventeenth-Century England: Essays Presented to G. E. Aylmer* (Oxford, 1993), 101–20.

[46] *MPW* 60, 59.   [47] Ibid. 61.   [48] See Craigie, ibid. 195–7.

[49] Ibid. 59.

old', there cannot be much real doubt that Buchanan's *De iure regni apud Scotos* was in James's mind as he wrote *The True Lawe*.[50] Intrinsic probability apart, there are echoes of the earlier text to be noted—the Ciceronian phrase about 'the speaking law and the dumb king', the invoking of the maxim *summum ius summa iniuria*, and other instances.[51] Much more weight, however, may and indeed must be accorded to critical points in the arguments deployed by James and by Buchanan. The most striking instance is surely James's reference, in his refutation of objections to his position, to 'the mutuall paction and adstipulation (as they call it) betweixt the king and his people'.[52] The phrase 'mutuall paction' echoes so precisely Buchanan's *mutua pactio* that it is difficult to believe that James did not have his tutor's text in his mind and perhaps indeed before him as he wrote.[53] It is now at all events time to consider more closely and systematically the case stated in *The True Lawe* in support of the king's position as 'a free and absolute *Monarche*'.[54]

The scriptural argument with which James opens his case has already been touched upon: the greater part of it is devoted to establishing the absolute duty of subjects to obey the commands of their king 'in all thinges, except directly against God, as the commands of Gods Minister'; and to denying to 'broyling spirites and rebellious mindes' any 'libertie . . . against any Christian Monarchie'.[55] This is preceded, however, by a briefer but important statement of the biblical grounds for the other side of the relationship—'[t]he princes duetie to his subjectes' which 'is so clearly set downe in many places of the Scriptures'. The king's obligations make familiar reading: he is '[t]o minister Iustice and Iudgement . . . [t]o advance the good, and punishe the evill . . . [t]o establish good lawes to his people, and procure obedience to the same . . . [t]o procure the peace of the people', acting throughout as 'the minister of God'. All this is linked to the oath sworn 'in the Coronation of our owne Kings, as well as of every Christian Monarche',

[50] The sceptical view is taken by Craigie, ibid. 194–5.

[51] Craigie, ibid. 194, lists the instances and observes that 'none is of any great significance'—perhaps a fair enough comment in view of the standard or even commonplace character of the points in question; but see below at n. 65.

[52] *MPW* 78.

[53] The *De iure regni* was of course in James's youthful library: Warner, 'Library of James VI', p. xlii.

[54] *MPW* 60.   [55] Ibid. 69, 67.

in honouring which priority is given to the upholding of religion, followed by the maintenance of 'all the lowable and good Laws made by their Predecessours'. The king is likewise 'to mainteyne the whole Countrie, and every state therein, in all their ancient priuiledges and liberties'.[56] If this account of the Scottish coronation oath is compared with that which had been sworn on James's behalf in 1567 by the earl of Morton, some interesting points emerge.[57] First, the king's explicit reference to maintaining the privileges and liberties of the various estates and the realm as a whole does not occur in the 1567 form. On the other hand, while the parliamentary text refers to 'the louabill Lawiis, and constitutiounis ressaifit in this Realme', James has 'the lowable and good Laws made by [the king's] Predecessouris'; and he goes on to suggest that the oath bound the king to the 'establishing of new' laws as well as to the preservation of the old.

The terms of the oath are important; for, in James's view, 'the oath in the Coronation is the cleerest ciuill and fundamentall law, whereby the Kinges office is properly defined'.[58] And it is to 'civil and fundamental law', together with the law of nature that his argument turns when its primarily biblical phase is completed. Natural law, in this view of it, issues above all in the king's becoming 'a naturall Father to all his Liegis', seeing to their 'nourishing, education, and vertuous gouernement'—that government involving, when required, 'a fatherly chastizement seasoned with pittie'. Even if 'pittie' should be lacking, there is no 'pretence of wickedness or rigour on [the king's] parte' that can 'be a iust excuse for his children to put hand into him'.[59] Similar consequences follow from the other analogy suggested by the natural order: 'the proper office of a King towardes his subiectes agrees very well with the office of the head towards the bodie'. The head is charged with 'discourse and direction', the members with 'the execution' of what the head has determined. That determination may, in extreme circumstances, necessitate the amputation of 'some rotten member . . . But what state the body can be in,

---

[56] Ibid. 60–1.

[57] Craigie (*MPW* 129–30, 131–2) reproduces from the parliamentary and Privy Council records the form of the oath prescribed in 1560 and both confirmed and actually administered in 1567. He does not refer to the interesting discussion by R. J. Lyall, 'The Medieval Scottish Coronation: Some Seventeenth-Century Evidence', *Innes Review*, 28 (1977), 3–21.

[58] *MPW* 62.   [59] Ibid. 62, 74–5.

if the head, for any infirmity that can fall to it, be cut off, I leaue it to the readers judgement.'[60]

Useful though these well-worn similitudes may have been for James's purposes, it is reasonable to suppose that they interested him less than the themes which, in developing his detailed argument, he set down ahead of them. These themes are derived from 'the fundamental and ciuil law, especially of this Countrie'; and the discussion begins with 'the first maner of establishing the lawes & forme of gouernement among vs'. Referring to 'the affirmation of those that pryde themselues to be the scourges of Tyrantes', James grants that 'in the time of the first age, diuers common-wealthes & societies of men chosed out one among them selues, who for his vertues & valour' was made ruler; but he insists that 'these examples are nothing pertinent to vs; because our kingdome, and diuers other Monarchies are not in that case, but had their beginning in a far contrary fashion'.[61] Fergus, the first king of Scots, became king by conquest: 'he and his successours, a long while after their being Kinges, made & established their lawes . . . as the occasion required.' The absolute priority of royal power is the peg on which James's argument hangs; 'The Kings . . . in *Scotland* were before any estates, or rankes of men within the same, before any Parliaments were holden, or lawes made.' They distributed land ('which at the first was whole theirs'), established estates, devised 'formes of gouernment'. In fine, 'the Kinges were the authors & makers of the lawes, and not the lawes of the Kings.'[62]

The argument here is not, for James, a mere matter of assertion and counter-assertion. In denying 'the false affirmation of such seditious writers, as would perswade vs, that the Lawes and state of our countrie were established before the admitting of a King', he is not content to proffer an alternative account of a remote past. His appeal is to the evidence of current practice and usage and to extant documents. Thus 'it is euident by the rolles of our Chancellerie (which contayne our eldest & fundamentall laws) that the King is *Dominus omnium bonorum*, and *Dominus directus totius Dominij*, the whole subjects being but his vassals, & from him holding all their lands as their ouer-lord'. In that feudal capacity the king acts 'without advise or authoritie of either

---

[60] *MPW* 74–5. [61] Ibid. 69–70. [62] Ibid. 70.

Parliament, or any other subaltern judiciall seat'. As for the parliamentary assembly itself, it 'is nothing else but the head courte of
the King, and his vassals', where 'the lawes are but craued by his
subjects, and onely made by him at their rogation, & with their
advise'. Moreover, the king can and does 'make daily statutes and
ordinances . . . without any advise of parliament or estates',
whereas 'it lies in the power of no Parliament to make any kinde
of law of statute, without his Scepter be put to it, for giuing it the
force of a law'.[63] The case is further supported by an appeal to
Scottish law regarding such matters as treasure 'found vnder the
earth', the reversion of land to the kind in default of 'any sorte of
heires', and the 'rehabling' of bastards—'which . . . only lyes in
the Kinges handes'. The king is indeed 'Maister ouer euery person
that inhabiteth the [land], hauing power over the life and death of
euery on[e] of them'. He should, to be sure, act as 'a speaking
lawe'; for although 'the King is aboue the law, as both the author
and giuer of strength thereto: yet a good King will not onely
delight to rule his subjects by the Law, but euen will conforme
himselfe in his own actions thervnto'. At the same time, 'least
[lest] *summum ius* be *summa iniuria*, he may interpret or mitigate
the same'; and this power extends to the suspension, 'vpon
causes onely knowne to him', of 'general lawes, made publikly in
Parliament'.[64]

Corresponding to the 'right & power a King hath ouer his land
& subjects' we have the 'allegeance & obedience his lieges owe
vnto him'. This, James says, 'is easie to be vnderstood', provided
we bear in mind that what is being expounded is the position of
'such free Monarches as our King is, & not of electiue Kings, and
much lesse of such sorte of gouernours, as the Dukes of Venice
are, whose Aristocratick and limited gouernment is nothing like
to free Monarchies: although the malice of some writers hath not
bene ashamed to misknow any difference to be betwixt them'.
Commonplace as the instance may be, it is difficult not to think
that James here had the 'malice' of George Buchanan immediately
in view.[65] At all events he proceeds to insist rigorously on the duty

[63] Ibid. 70–1.
[64] Ibid. 72. Craigie (*MPW* 135–7) conveniently transcribes passages from *Regiam
Maiestatem* and Bell's *Digest of the Laws of Scotland* (1861) on the relevant points of
law. On bastardy he also cites Erskine's 1838 *Institute of the Law of Scotland*.
[65] Cf. n. 51, above.

of obedience and non-resistance. Any other position, he says, must entail 'inuerting the order of al law & reason': only then can 'the commanded . . . be made to command their commander, the iudged to judge their Iudg, and they that are gouerned to gouerne their time about their lord & gouernnor'.[66]

This is followed in the text of *The True Lawe* by the arguments from natural law already considered here; and from these, his own case being complete, James turns to 'the solution of foure principall and most weightie doubtes, that the aduersaries may object'.[67] The first of these is the argument that 'good Citizens wilbe forced, for the natural zeale and dutie they owe to their owne natiue countrie, to put their hande to worke, for freeing their common-welth from' a king who is 'wicked and tyrannous'. To this James's answer is twofold. First, evil should never be done that good may result; and the evil here would consist in 'the people, or any parte of them (who all are but priuate men, the authoritie being alwaies with the Magistrate . . .)' taking upon themselves 'the vse of the sworde . . . against the publick Magistrate, whome to onely it belongeth'.[68] This is a passage of considerable interest. On the one hand, James is rejecting an argument much favoured by 'resistance theorists', in which the private-law right of self-defence was extended to the public domain by applying it to the situation of those oppressed by tyrannical rulers.[69] On the other hand, he explicitly denies that the community or any part of it can claim any corporate public status or authority. Implicitly this is to say that a people is to be regarded as a body politic only by virtue of its members' subjection to the authority of the ruler.

So much for the first aspect of James's response to the first of the 'doubtes' he is considering. Secondly, he adopts the classic position that resistance and rebellion must always be the greater of two evils. Those who advocate such action, 'in place of releeuiing the commonwealth out of distresse (which is their onely excuse and colour) . . . shall heape double distresse and desolation upon it'. No king, however 'vnrulie and tyrannous' can fail to keep society 'in better order then [than] it can be [by] his way-taking'; for 'no King being, nothing is vnlawfull to none . . . the

---

[66] *MPW* 73–4.   [67] Ibid. 75–6.   [68] Ibid. 76.
[69] See Skinner, *Foundations of Modern Political Thought*, ii. 125–6, 197–204, 217–24, 234–5.

commonwealth at that time resembling an vn-daunted yong horse, that hath casten his rider'. The relation between this and the first part of the argument is important: since the coherence of the community depends entirely upon the sovereign power, the removal of that power necessarily produces a situation in which, because 'nothing is lawfull' (there being no law), 'all things are lawfull to all men'.[70]

The second 'objection' to his position with which James deals is that, since the rule of a tyrant is a 'cursse, that hangs ouer the common-wealth', it must be an 'acceptable deed in the sight of GOD . . . to free the countrie of such a cursse, & vindicat to them their libertie, which is naturall to all creatures to craue'. To this his reply is again twofold. First, the 'cursse' is 'layde' on the people by God himself, and the only available remedy is prayer. Secondly, the people can have no right to 'reaue out of the Princes hand that superiority, which he & his Predecessors haue so long brooked [enjoyed]'—a superiority grounded, James now argues (perhaps in some degree at variance with the rest of his case), in the subjects' 'owne consent'. That consent is as irrevocable as the ruler's own grant of 'priviledges' to his subjects.[71] Here James seems to be using the *lex regia* model, interpreting it, of course, as implying an irreversible transfer of authority.

The third objection is closely linked to the second; for, James goes on to say, 'the vnhappie iniquitie of the time, which hath oft times giuen ouer good successe to their treasonable attempts', enables his adversaries to claim 'that God fauoured the iustnes of their quarrel'. This is met by the counter-argument that God, for his own purposes, often gives victory to 'them that haue the wrong side'—as he manifestly did on various occasions in the Old Testament history of his chosen people. Accordingly James agrees with 'all good writers, aswell Theologues, as other', that 'Duelles and singular combattes are disallowed: which are onely made vpon pretence that GOD will kythe [reveal] thereby the justice of the quarrell'; for 'it is oft times a very deceauable argument to judge of the cause by the event'.[72]

It is to the fourth and last objection 'grounded vpon the mutuall

---

[70] *MPW* 76–7.   [71] Ibid. 77.

[72] Ibid. 78. Craigie points out (ibid. 142) that James's early library included a Latin translation of Antonio Massa's *Contra l'use del duello* (1551) and cites (141–2) the Scottish act 'ANENT singular combattis' passed in 1600.

paction and adstipulation (as they call it) betwixt the king, and his people, at the time of his coronation' that James devotes most attention; and it is indeed, in theoretical terms, the most interesting. His concern is to 'deny any such contract to be made then, especially containing such a clause irritant'—the proviso, that is to say, whereby breach of the contract by either party frees the other from obligations under the agreement.[73] Yet the point is not entirely straightforward. After all, the subtitle of James's pamphlet refers to 'the reciprock and mutuall duetie betwixt a free King and his naturall subjects'. Quite early in the text he had referred to the 'mutuall, and reciprock bande' between 'the Lieges' and 'their King'—'bande', of course, being in Scottish usage a familiar and resonant term for contractual agreements.[74] Again, in his discussion of Old Testament history he had referred to the 'contract' entered into when God appointed kings in Israel.[75] Even in the immediate context of this 'objection' to his position, James cannot and does not deny 'that a King at his coronation, or at the entry to his kingdome, willingly promiseth to his people, to discharge honourably and truely the office giuen him by God ouer them'. The crucial question remains: 'presuming that thereafter he break his promise vnto them . . . who shuld be judg of the break[?]' Even if we grant the existence of a valid contract, James goes on,

I think no man, that hath but the smallest entrance in the ciuill law, will dout that of all law either ciuill, or municipal of any nation, a contract cannot be thoght broken by the one partie, & so the other likewise to bee fred therefro: except that first a lawfull triall and cognition be had by the ordinary Iudge of the breakers thereof . . . Now in this contract . . . betwixt the King and his people, God is doutles the only judg.

That judgement cannot be sought by way of what Locke was to call the 'appeal to Heaven': James has already ruled that out in dealing with the third objection. As for the notion that, in Locke's phrase, *'The People shall be Judge'*, this too is precluded. For James, the people can be no more than 'a headlesse multitude' incapable of any right 'to Iudge and punish him, whome by they should be judged & punished'.[76] Neither king nor people can, in equity, be a fit judge in such a case. For one party to allege a breach of contract

[73] *MPW* 78–9.   [74] Ibid. 62.   [75] Ibid. 66.   [76] Ibid. 78–9.

will merely elicit a similar charge by the other; and the result can only be a trial of strength, with 'the victors making the tyners [losers] the traitors'. It may be apposite to recall that it was about this time that Sir John Harington made the same point in a different way:

> Treason doth neuer prosper, what's the reason?
> For if it prosper, none dare call it Treason.[77]

With this James's argument is almost complete. He is careful, however, to add two further points. First, he insists on the permanence of 'the duty & allegeance, which the people sweareth to their prince'. The 'free monarchy' he is defending is strictly hereditary: 'he is their heritable ouer-lord, & so by byrth, not by any right in the coronation, commeth to his crowne. For at the very moment of the expiring of the king reigning, the nearest & lawfull heir entreth in his place.' And James takes the opportunity to condemn 'the superstitious rebellion of the Liguers' in France 'who, vpon pretence of heresie, by force of armes held so long out . . . their natiue and righteous King from possessing of his owne crowne and naturall kingdome'.[78] This aspect of the case he was concerned to argue obviously had special importance for James, since his claim to the succession in England—by the late 1590s his main preoccupation—rested entirely on hereditary right.

Only the peroration remains. James professes no exaggerated expectations: 'neither thinke I by the force & argument of this my discourse so to perswade the people, that none will herafter be raised vp, and rebel against wicked Princes . . . My only purpose & intention in this treatise is, to perswade . . . al . . . good Christian readers . . . to keepe their hearts & hands free from such monstrous and vnnaturall rebellions.' This does not mean, however, that the 'wickednesse' which provides the pretext for rebellion is to go unpunished. Kings are remitted 'to God (who is their only ordinary judge)' and thus to 'the sorest and sharpest Schoole-maister that can be deuised for them'. Nearing the end of *The True Lawe of Free Monarchies*, James foreshadows a theme that was to be central in the *Basilikon Doron*: 'the further a king is

---

[77] *Epigrams*, IV. 5, in *The Letters and Epigrams of Sir John Harington*, ed. N. E. McClure (Philadelphia, 1930), 225.
[78] *MPW* 80–1.

preferred by God aboue all other ranks and degrees of men, and the higher that his state is aboue theirs: the greater is his obligation to his maker.' And, behind the (doubtless somewhat flimsy) mask of his *nom de plume*, he 'hartely' expresses the wish for 'our kings behauiour so to be, & continue among vs, as our God on earth, & louing father'.[79]

James VI had married Anne of Denmark in 1590 and their eldest son, Henry, was born in 1594. *ΒΑΣΙΛΙΚΟΝ ΔΩΡΟΝ, or His Maiesties Instrvctions to his dearest sonne, Henry the Prince*, printed for the first time in 1599, was evidently written in the late summer or early autumn of the previous year, prompted by James's premonition that he might predecease Elizabeth and his consequent anxiety to prepare the prince for the succession in both Scotland and England.[80] In regard to the latter realm, it is true, he cautiously refrains from much comment apart from points in which he recommends English practice to his son as preferable to Scottish.[81] His 'instructions' are closely linked to his own experience of royal government in Scotland. Yet the view of kingship he presents is at the same time a general view, its principles applicable not in Scotland or England alone, but wherever 'the true law' prevails. The connection between the two works James wrote in 1597–8 is immediately apparent. The dedication of *Basilikon Doron* echoes the closing passage of *The True Lawe* by insisting that a king is to perceive himself as 'not excelling all [his] people so far in rank and honour, as in daylie care and hazardous painestaking, for the duetifull administration of that great office that God hath layde vpon [his] shoulders: laying so a just symmetrie and proportion, betwixt the height of [his] honourable place, and the heauie weight of [his] great charge'.[82] That charge is dealt with under two headings—in Book I, 'a kings Christian duetie towards God'; and in Book II, 'a kings duetie in his office'. The third book deals, in less deontological terms, with 'a kings behaviour in indifferent things'.

---

[79] *MPW* 81–2.　　　　[80] See on this Craigie edn., ii. 1–8.

[81] Ibid. i. 72/3; and cf. e.g. 74/5, 92/3. (Double page-numbers are given because the Craigie edn. prints both the 1599 and the 1603 printed texts below a transcript of the surviving MS, which is in James's hand. Textual quotations here are, unless otherwise specified, from the 1599 text, ignoring however the italic type in which it is printed throughout.)

[82] Ibid. i. 6/7–8/9.

Of these headings it is clearly the second that has most relevance in the present discussion. Yet the religious position James
adopts in Book I has its own importance; for a 'divine-right'
account of kingship presupposes a theological framework. For
James that framework is, as we have seen already in *The True
Lawe*, essentially scriptural. Even when, in the 1603 edition, the
text of *Basilikon Doron* is fully equipped with marginalia, all but
one of the references given in Book I are biblical, and the solitary
exception cites, not any patristic or other work of exegesis or
theology, but a line from Horace.[83] Moreover, James's attitude to
the scriptures is studiously Protestant: 'As to the Apocriphe
bookes, I omit them because I am no Papist . . . & indeed some of
them are as like the ditement of the spirite of God as an Egge is to
an Oyster.'[84] The religion he professed, and which his son
was expected to profess, 'was grounded vpon the plaine words
of the Scripture'.[85] The 'conseruer' of that religion was
'Conscience . . . the light of knowledge that God hath planted in
man', to be carefully guarded against both the 'Leaprosie' which
'is the mother of Atheisme' and 'Superstition', the source of 'Heresies'. The safeguard does not rest 'vpon the credit of your owne
conceits, neither yet of other mens humours, how great Doctors of
Divinity that euer they be: but . . . vpon the expresse Scripture'.
By careful and prayerful reading of the Bible 'two extreamities'
will be avoided: 'th'one, to beleeue (with the Papistes) The
Churches Authoritie, better nor your owne knowledge: th'other,
to leane (with the Anabaptists) to your own conceites & dreamed
revelations'.[86]

So far, so good. Yet the references to papists and anabaptists
have already indicated debatable lands in the territory of true
religion. The problematic aspect of the matter emerges even more
clearly when, near the end of Book I, James refers to the need 'to
discerne betwixt poyntes of saluation and indifferent thinges,

[83] It may be noted, for what it is worth, that theology is not particularly well
represented in James's youthful library, though contemporary Protestant divines
figure there in some number.

[84] Craigie edn., i. 34/5; but it is noteworthy that in the 1603 edn. the final words
are modified to read 'some of them are no wayes like the dytement of the Spirite
of God'.

[85] Ibid. i. 30/1. In the 1603 edn. the phrase 'al my Religion' is expanded to read
'all my Religion presently professed by me and my kingdome'.

[86] Ibid. i. 40/1–48/9.

betwixt substance and ceremonies'. Scrupulous care in regard to the former must be combined with flexibility 'as the time shall require' when dealing with 'all other things not conteyned in the scripture'. Here for the first time we encounter the problem of opposition to the king's will:

> when any of the spiritual office-bearers in the Church, speaketh vnto you anything that is wel warranded by the worde, reuerence and obey them as the Heraulds of the most high God: but if (passing that bounds) they would urge you to embrace anye of their fantasies in place of Gods word, or would colour their particulars with a pretended zeale, acknowledge them for vaine people passing the boundes of their calling; and (according to your office) grauely and with authoritie redact them in ordour againe.[87]

The parenthetic phrase 'according to your office' is critically important here; for when James turns in Book II to 'a kings duetie in his office', one of his major concerns will be with the ecclesiastical aspect of the subject. And indeed, as we shall see, that aspect was rarely far from his mind throughout the writing of *Basilikon Doron*.

A substantial part of Book II is organized by reference to the three estates—not primarily in their parliamentary aspect (though that is not overlooked and must be considered in due course), but as the constituent elements of the body politic. And pride of place must go, James acknowledges, to the church. Throughout Christian history 'all the Churches' have been afflicted by three 'naturall siknesses . . . Pride, Ambition, and Avarice'. These deservedly brought about 'the over-throwe of the Popish Church in this cuntry and diuers others'. In Scotland, however, this was achieved by 'a popular tumult & rebellion (as wel appeared by the destruction of our policie) . . . not proceeding from the Princes ordour (as it did in England)'. The result, in James's view, was that 'some of our fyerie ministers . . . begouth to fantasie to them selues a Democratik forme of gouernement', with the hope of becoming *Tribuni plebis* in 'that imagined Democracie . . . leading the people by the nose to beare the sway of all the rule'. They taught the people to believe that 'all Kings and Princes were naturally enemies to the liberty of the Church'. That liberty was to be secured only by 'Paritie in the Church'; but,

---

[87] Craigie edn., i. 48/9–50/1.

James argued, such an egalitarian view was simply 'the mother of confusion', being necessarily an 'enemie to Vnitie, which is the mother of ordour'.[88]

Nor was the danger confined to 'the Ecclesiasticall gouernement'; for the advocates of 'Paritie' and 'Democracie' in the church 'think (with time) to draw the politick and ciuill gouernment to the like'. On both grounds Henry is urged to '[t]ake heede . . . to these Puritanes, verie pestes in the Church and common-weill of Scotland; whom (by long experience) I haue found, no desertes can oblish, oathes nor promises binde, breathing nothing but sedition and calumnies . . . and making their own imaginations (without any warrant of the Worde) the square of their Conscience'.[89] The vehemence of this condemnation (broadened by implication in its scope when the words 'in Scotland' were deleted in the 1603 edition) was perhaps tempered somewhat in the prefatory address 'To the Reader' added to that version of the work. There James not only insists that his concern was solely with the 'morall faultes' of the 'Puritanes', but also seeks to narrow the connotation of the term. It belongs 'properly', he says, 'only to that vile sect among the Anabaptistes, called the Familie of loue', who believe 'all the rest of the worlde to be but abhomination in the sight of God'; and these he absolutely condemns, confident no doubt of general agreement. He acknowledges, however, that he has also 'give[n] this style to suche bransicke and headie preachers, their disciples and followers' as disclaim that kind of association and 'yet participates too muche with their humours, in maintayning the aboue mentioned errours'. In particular, James accuses them of 'aggreeing with the generall rule of all Anabaptistes, in the contempt of the ciuill Magistrate, and in leaning to their owne dreames and revelations'.[90]

To this, no doubt, even the extreme Presbyterians would have retorted that they fully respected the authority of the civil magistrate within his proper sphere, but that this did not include matters that were the concern of the church. This was indeed the crux. James went on to protest that his animadversions were not to be understood 'generally of all preachers, or others, that likes better

---

[88] Ibid. i. 72/3–76/7.   [89] Ibid. i. 78/9.

[90] Ibid. i. 15–16. (As in quotations from the 1599 edn., the italic type used throughout this prefatory part of the 1603 text has not been reproduced here.)

of the single forme of policie in our churche, then [than] of the manie ceremonies in the churche of England; that are perswaded, that their Bishops smels of a Papall supremacie, that the Surplice, the cornerd cap, and suche like, are the outward badges of Popishe errours'. Provided that, in matters he 'esteemed as indifferent', the law of the land was obeyed—provided above all that no 'rebellion or schisme' was provoked—a peaceable diversity of opinion was acceptable.[91] Yet James did not withdraw, in 1603, the advice he had given his son in 1599 to 'conteine your Church in their calling as *Custos utriusque tabulae*; for the ruling them wel is no small poynte of your office'. In particular, the future king must 'suffer them not to meddle with the policie or estate in the Pulpite'. Nor should he 'suffer . . . Conuentions nor meetings among Churchmen' except with his 'knowledge and permission'.[92] Again, James's attitude to questions of ecclesiastical polity was hardly as detached as the 1603 address to his readers might suggest. If we go back to his discussion of the church in his review of the three estates, we find him insisting that the notion of the 'Paritie' of ministers 'can not agree with a Monarchie'. In the 1603 edition this is elaborated: 'their conceited Paritie . . . and their other imaginarie groundes . . . can neither stand with the ordour of the Churche, nor the peace of a common-weale and well ruled Monarchie'. Accordingly, the prince is urged to 'aduance the godlie learned, and modest men of the ministrie . . . by their prefermente to Bishoprickes and Benefices'.[93] It is quite clear that James envisages an ecclesiastical role for the king quite different from that of behaving as 'God's silly vassal' in the kingdom of Christ. If he does not claim headship or governorship explicitly, it is plain that he has in mind some form of royal supremacy in the church. Not the least attractive aspect of the English succession must have been the fact that, once it was secured, such supremacy would be his in his new realm.

[91] Craigie edn., i. 16–17.

[92] Ibid. i. 144/5–146/7. While the substance of James's advice was allowed to stand in 1603, the language was noticeably softened. In the earlier text, James wrote, following the injunction to prohibit political preaching: 'But snibbe sickerlie [rebuke severely] the firste that minteth to [attempts] it: And (if hee like to appeale or declyne) when ye haue taken order with his heade, his brethren may (if they please) powle his haire and pare his nayles, as the King my Grande-father said of a Priest.' In 1603 this becomes simply, 'but punishe seuearlie the first that praesumeth to it'.

[93] Ibid. i. 78/9–80/1.

With a view to the promotion of learned and modest ministers to episcopal rank, James urges his son to annul 'that vile Act of Annexation', if he himself had not already done so.[94] In the event, three years after his succession in England, James did indeed have the 'vile Act' repealed. It has been said of the annulment that it 'was purely civil and financial in its effects and had no bearing on the ecclesiastical status of the bishops', while, to be sure, it 'stressed the importance of the episcopate as an essential part of the constitution of the kingdom'.[95] This was indeed a major consideration in James's mind. By following his advice, he pointed out, his son would 'reestablishe the olde institution of three Estates in Parliament'.[96] This brings us to the question of James's general view, in the *Basilikon Doron*, of the parliamentary assembly. We know already, from *The True Lawe*, that he regarded parliament as 'nothing else but the head courte of the King, and his vassals'.[97] It comes therefore as no surprise to find that, when addressing his son and heir, he says that 'a Parliament is the honorablest and highest judgement in the land (as being the King head Court)'. To this, however, he adds the proviso that parliament has this character 'if it be well vsed, which is by making of good lawes in it'. If, on the other hand, it is 'abused to mens particulars', it becomes

the injustest judgement-seate that may bee . . . irreuocable decreits against particulare parties being giuen therein under colour of generall laws, and oftimes the estates not knowing themselues whom thereby they hurt: And therefore hold no Parliamentes but for necessity of new lawes, which would be but seldome; for fewe laws and well put in execution, are best in a wel ruled common-weal.[98]

That last point is a recurrent theme in James's account of the business of government. Observing ruefully that 'in this country we haue alreadie mo good lawes then [than] are well execute', he abstains from advising his son about legislation—'I remit the making of [good laws] to your owne discretion, as yee shall finde the necessitie of new-rising corruptions to require them . . . and am onely to insist in your forme of gouernment anent their execution'.[99] As to this, James's advice is both general and specific.

[94] Ibid. i. 78/9. On the 1587 act see n. 8 above.
[95] Donaldson, *James V to James VII*, 205.   [96] Craigie edn., i. 80/1.
[97] *MPW* 71.   [98] Craigie edn., i. 58/9–60/1.   [99] Ibid. i. 58/9.

In general, he argues, a king newly come to the throne, as his son will come, 'not *precario*, nor by conqueste, but by right and due discente', should begin by being firm to the point of severity 'in giuing the lawe full execution against all breakers thereof but exception'. Once his authority has thus been securely established, he 'may thereafter al the dayes of [his] life mixe justice with mercie'. James claims that this advice is based on his own experience; 'for I confesse, where I thought (by being gracious at the beginning) to winne al mens hearts to a louing and willing obedience, I by the contrarie founde, the disorder of the cuntrie and the tinsall [loss] of my thankes to be all my rewarde'.[100]

The more specific aspects of James's counsel need not be followed in detail here. It is important, however, to consider in regard to the secular estates of the realm, as we have done in regard to the church, his diagnosis of the 'peccant humours' from which they are apt to suffer. A diagnostic procedure of this kind is, in James's view, essential for good government.[101]

First, as to the nobility, James describes them tartly as 'although second in rank [to the church], yet ouer-farre first in greatnes and power'; and it is 'a fectless arrogant conceite' of their power that leads them into oppression and disorder 'without respect to God, King, or common-weill'. They must be taught to obey the law 'as precisely as the meanest: feare not their orping [murmuring] nor taking the pet as long as ye rule well; for their pretended reformation of Princes taketh neuer effect, but where euill gouernment precedeth'.[102] That last point evokes resounding echoes of much that we have encountered earlier in this investigation, not least in the opening sketch of the reign of James III and in the propaganda of the Lords of the Congregation in 1559–60.

At the same time, a prudent king will cultivate the good will of the lesser nobility or gentry—'the honest men of your Barrones and Gentle-men'. Henry should encourage them to petition him directly, 'not making a bogle of you, in making the greate Lordes their intercessours (for intercession to Saints is Papistry)': in this way he would 'bring to a measure [the] monstrous backes' of the more powerful nobles.[103] This may be regarded as an attempt by James to mobilize the 'countervailing power' of a class in Scottish society which was certainly becoming more important and

---

[100] Craigie edn., i. 60/1–64/5.   [101] Ibid. i. 70/1–72/3.
[102] Ibid. i. 82/3–84/5.   [103] Ibid. i. 84/5.

influential in the second half of the sixteenth century.[104] On the
other hand, such power as the lairds or gentry wielded was at best
imperfectly embodied in effective institutions. Their significant
role in the new church was, to be sure, reflected in their participation in the General Assembly; but the act of 1597, providing
that one 'baron' should be appointed to the Assembly with three
ministers from each presbytery was 'not . . . invariably, if at all,
observed'. So far as parliamentary representation was concerned,
the 1567 provision that in future 'the barons of the shire were to
choose one or two of their number as commissioners' apparently
never took effect.[105] The 'Barrones and Gentle-men' were still, as
James acknowledged, merely 'an inferior part of the nobilitie and
of their estate'.[106]

Nor could there be, realistically, any question of effective royal
government in Scotland without the collaboration of the aristocracy. James insists that ways must be found to suppress their
'barbarous feides [feuds]': the laws—not least James's own 'lawis
made against Gunnes and trayterous Pistolettes'—must be 'put in
execution' without fear or favour, beginning with those nearest
and dearest to the king as 'an example to the reste'. At the same
time, it was important to avoid 'the other extreamitie', which
(James says) 'brake the King my grandfathers hearte': the 'errour'
of 'lightlying and contemning [the] Nobilitie . . . The worthines of
their antecessours craueth a reuerent regard to be had vnto them:
honour them therfore' (he urges his son) 'that are obedient to the
law among them, as Peeres and Fathers of your land'. As such, he
goes on, 'the principall poynts of seruice that ye craue of them, is,
in their persones to practise, and by their power to procure due
obedience to the lawe'.[107] There was indeed one form of aristocratic power which was 'the greatest hinder to the execution of
our law in this cuntry': namely, 'thir heritable Shirifdomes &
Regalities, which being in the hands of the great men wracketh
the whole country'. For this James saw 'no present remedie, but
by taking the sharper account of them in their offices' and refusing, when such offices fell vacant, to fill them again on heritable
terms. In the longer term, the hope must be that 'the lowable

---

[104] See on this Wormald, *Court, Kirk, and Community*, as index under 'lairds,
gentry'.
[105] Donaldson, *James V to James VII*, 278–9, 320.
[106] Craigie edn., i. 88/9.   [107] Ibid. i. 84/5–88/9.

custome of Englande' could be introduced in Scotland by a king reigning in both realms.[108] Despite efforts in this direction by Charles I, and apart from a few years during the Cromwellian interregnum, this was a hope not to be realized for a century and a half after James expressed it in *Basilikon Doron*.

This part of the book ends with James's far from flattering account of 'the third & last estate, which is our Burghes'. Merchants and craftsmen alike are condemned for sectional greed and malpractice. In both cases James advocates the advantages of bringing in foreign competitors: 'permit & allure forraine merchants, to trade here, so shall we haue best and best cheape ware ... [T]ake example by England, how it hath flurished both in wealth and pollicie, sen the strangers Craftes-men came in amonge them.'[109]

It is unnecessary here to examine James's 'political economy' more closely; but it is important to take note of his statement that 'one faulte in all the common people of this Lande subjecte as well Burgh as Lande ... is, to judge and speake rashelie of their Prince ... euer wearying of the present estate, and desirous of Nouelties'. Against this subversive tendency one remedy is, of course, 'the execution of the lawes that would be vsed against vnreuerent speakers'.[110] This was a theme James had already dealt with emphatically in his account of crimes the king is 'bounde in Conscience neuer to forgiue'. There he had added to 'Witch-crafte, wilfull-murther, Incest ... Sodomie, Poysoning, and false coyne' the unpardonable crime of 'vnreuerent writing or speaking of [the king's] Parents and Predecessours'. The biblical injunction to honour one's parents also required the 'lawful magistrat' not to allow 'both [his] Princes and [his] Parents to be dishonoured by any'. In the 1603 text James added the further point that such a prohibition was also in the king's interest as an example to be followed by his successors and thus a safeguard for his own posthumous reputation.[111] However, such direct legislative and executive action is not the only way of dealing with a problem James regarded as endemic. He also advocates what Jeremy Bentham would have called indirect means; and the point was one he elaborated when revising the *Basilikon Doron* for its second printing. He urged his son

---

[108] Craigie edn., i. 88/9.   [109] Ibid. i. 88/9–92/3.
[110] Ibid. i. 92/3. The 1603 text has 'execution of lawes that are to be vsed'.
[111] Ibid. i. 64/5–66/7.

so to rule, as may justly stop their mouthes, from all suche idle and vnreuerent speaches: and so to prop the weale of your people with prouident care for their good gouernment; that justly, *Momus* him self may haue no grounde to grudge at: and yet so to temper and mixe your seueritie with myldenesse, that as the vn-just railers may be restrayned with a reuerent awe; so the good and louing subjectes, may not onely liue in suretie and wealth, but be stirred vp and invited by your benigne courtesies, to open their mouthes in the just praise of your so well moderated regiment.[112]

James then went on to the point already made in the 1599 edition—the advisability of appointing days 'for delighting the people with publick spectacle of al honest games & exercise of armes, as also for conveening of neighbours for enterteyning friendship and hartlinesse, by honest feasting & merrines'. He remarks that 'this forme of alluring the people, hath bene vsed in all well gouerned Republickes'.[113]

Related to this is the importance James attaches to the king's being 'wel acquent with the nature and humoures of all [his] subjects . . . and . . . the estate of euery part of [his] dominions'. He should visit annually 'the principall parts of the cuntry . . . hearing your self their complaints'; and—looking to a situation in which more than one realm is involved—there should be 'ordinarie Councelles and justice-seates in euerie kingdome of their owne Cuntry-men', with 'the principall matters' always decided by the king in person when he comes there.[114]

It is indeed a profoundly personal and positive kingship that James envisages, reflecting no doubt the traditions of his Scottish realm as well as his own experience and predilections. The theme continues as he deals with such matters as the making of war and peace and, at greater length, with the king's court. To his courtiers, James points out, a king is 'both a Politicke & Oeconomick gouernour' and thus has 'a double care for the ruling-well of [his] owne seruantes'.[115] Again, the choice of those servants is a heavy responsibility, heaviest of all in respect of those who are to be appointed 'to the offices of the crowne and estate', where the choice affects the well-being of the people as a whole. They are to be chosen 'only for their worthinesse, and not

---

[112] Ibid. i. 92/3.   [113] Ibid. i. 93–94/5.   [114] Ibid. i. 94/5–96/7.
[115] Ibid. i. 106/7. Craigie (ibid. ii. 228) mistakenly suggests that 'Politick' here 'refers to the formulation of the State's policy', while 'Oeconomick' refers 'to the day-to-day administration of affairs'; but the entries in his glossary make the distinction correctly.

for pleasing of friends'; but at the same time they should be 'men of the Noblest bloud that can be had'. Courtiers in any case are, like all other subjects, to be paid 'with *praemium* or *poena* as they deserue, which is the verie ground-stone of good gouernement'.[116]

There is much detail here that need not concern the present investigation; and the same is true of James's careful advice to his son as to marriage and children. It may be sufficient to note the emphatic advice—'beware to Marie any but one of your owne Religion' and to 'suffer her neuer to meddle with the Politick gouernemente of the common-weale, but hold her at the Oeconomicke rule of the house, and yet all to bee subjecte to your direction'.[117] In regard to the royal offspring, James urges Henry not to divide his inheritance among his children but to maintain strict male primogeniture in the succession to all the realms of which he may die possessed.[118]

The account in *Basilikon Doron* of the cardinal virtues offers, predictably, little that is novel or striking, though the discussion of justice—'the greatest vertue that properly belongeth to a kings office'—prompts James yet again to some characteristic comments. As in *The True Lawe*, he invokes the maxim *Summum ius summa iniuria* to underline the point that even justice is to be pursued 'with such moderation as it turne not to Tyrannie . . . Lawes are ordeined as rules of vertuous and sociall liuing, and not to bee snares to trap your good subjects'. They are thus to be equitably 'interpreted according to the meaning, and not to the literall sense thereof, *Nam ratio est anima legis*'.[119]

To rule justly—to rule well in all respects—the king must know thoroughly his 'owne crafte'; but this entails his knowing all 'craftes', for his 'proper office' is to 'controll euerie one' of them. In particular he must 'be well seene in the Scriptures'; and next he is to 'studie well [his] owne Lawes'—which, however, should be 'as shorte and plaine as' possible; for legislative 'long-somnes serueth onely for the enriching of the Aduocates and Clerkes with the spoyle of the whole Countrie'. In this connection, Henry is urged, 'haunt whiles your Session, and spie carefully their

---

[116] Craigie edn. i. 106/7–120/1.

[117] Ibid. i. 128/9–130/1; 134/5. For the discussion of marriage at large see ibid. i. 120/1–134/5.

[118] Ibid. i. 134/5–136/7.   [119] Ibid. i. 140/1.

proceedings'; and again, 'Be an ordinary sitter in your secret Counsall: that judicatour is only ordeined for matters of estate, and repreassing of insolente oppressions', and the king should 'suffer no Aduocates to be heard there with their delatoures'. There is an essential role for 'the ordinary judicatoure', but it is the king's 'owne craft to take a sharpe counte of euery man in his office'.[120]

History as well as law is to be studied—but only 'in authentick histories', not 'such infamous inuectiues as BVCHANANES or KNOXES chronicles'. James fears that 'the Spirits of these archi-bellowces of rebellion, ar flitted into them that hoardeth their bookes, or mainteineth their opinions'. So much (it may be observed in passing) for any suggestion that James, by the late 1590s, could treat the views of Buchanan—or of Knox—as spent fires needing no further effort to extinguish them. Genuine history, on the other hand, would enable the king to 'learne experience by Theorick, applying the by-past things to the present estate'; and the lessons are to be learnt from 'the Chronicles of al nations', so that, among other things, the king will be equipped to deal knowledgeably with 'all Embassadoures and strangers'.[121]

The remainder of Book II of *Basilikon Doron* is devoted to James's advice regarding the virtues of magnanimity, humility, constancy, liberality, and wisdom. Salient points are his insistence that the just anger of a king is both part of magnanimity and compatible with 'true humilitie'; and that 'true Constancie' is not to be confused with 'that Stoick insensible stupiditie that proud inconstant LIPSIUS perswadeth in his Constantia'.[122] Liberality, again, is to be used 'in rewarding the good . . . but' (James added in the 1603 text) 'with . . . proportional discretion'. The king must avoid 'exactions vpon [his] subjects', behaving as a faithful trustee (*fidus depositarius*) with the people as beneficiaries. As for

---

[120] Ibid. i. 142/3–148/9. Craigie (ibid. ii. 246) points out that 'delatoures' here (1603, 'dilatours') 'is a now obsolete technical term in Scots law' meaning 'an objection . . . which, without touching the merits of the case, suspended further proceedings until it was disposed of'.

[121] Ibid. i. 148/9–150/1.

[122] Ibid. i. 152/3–156/7. In the 1603 text the reference to Lipsius is replaced by a more general reference to 'many in our dayes', who 'by their inconstant behauiour in their owne liues, belyes their profession'. Justus Lipsius, whose *De Constantia* was first published in 1584 (English trans., 1595), conformed at various times to Lutheranism, Calvinism, and Catholicism: he may have been a member of the 'Family of Love', so strenuously condemned by James.

wisdom, it is to be exercised 'principallie...in discerning... betwixt true and false reports' and in avoiding (as we might put it) paranoid suspicion, which 'is the Tirantes sicknes'.[123]

The religious doctrine of Book I and the political morality of Book II are backed, in the third Book, by advice on 'minor morals'—manners, diet, speech, dress, and so forth. Interesting though this is in many ways, it does not add substantially to our understanding of James's view of kingship. Yet the theme of 'a king's behaviour in indifferent things' does enable him to under-line and develop the argument 'That a King is as one set on a skaffold [1603, 'stage'], whose smallest gestures & actions al the people gazingly do behold' and that it is especially important for him to avoid incurring 'Contempt, the Mother of Rebellion and disorder'.[124] One detail of some significance is the distinction James urges between the king's 'forme of language in reasoning' and the style to be adopted in his 'pronouncing of sentences or declarator of [his] will in judgement': he should 'reason pleasntly & patiently, not like a King, but like a priuat man & a scholer'; but (he tells his son) 'in the points of your office, you should ripelie advise indeede before ye giue forth your sentence: but fra it bee giuen forth, the suffering of anie contradiction, diminisheth the majestie of your authority & maketh the processes endles; the like forme woulde also be observed by all your inferiour judges and Magistrates.'[125]

The *Basilikon Doron* ends, as it began, with a deliberate emphasis on 'the greatnesse of [a king's] charge' and the supreme import-ance of his endeavouring 'to excel in [his] owne craft'.[126] How far James VI had succeeded, how far James VI and I was to succeed, in that endeavour no doubt are and will remain debatable ques-tions. They are, in any case, questions beyond the scope of this enquiry. What can be said here is that the author of *The True Lawe* and of *Basilikon Doron* was no fool, wise or otherwise. His political writings as king of Scots provide a unique amalgam of late six-teenth-century royalist ideology with a shrewd appraisal of the problems of royal government in a particular kingdom. How James's thinking developed in the broader context—so heavily foreshadowed in *Basilikon Doron*—in which he reigned as 'king of Great Britain' is the question to be examined in the next chapter.

---

[123] Craigie edn., i. 156/7–158/9.   [124] Ibid. i. 162/3.
[125] Ibid. i. 182/3.   [126] Ibid. i. 206/7.

8

The Whole Isle and Beyond
James VI and I

THE period with which this chapter is concerned stands in an
ambiguous relationship to the rest of the discussion here. For
twenty-two years (almost to the day) James VI of Scotland ruled
in England as James I. To have said that he ruled as king of
England would have been both substantially and formally correct; but the king himself would have questioned its correctness,
and the ambiguity has at least one of its roots in that questioning.
James wished to be, and to be recognized as being, king of Great
Britain: that was how he had himself proclaimed, that was the
style published abroad by coinage, seals, and flag.[1] In a moment
we shall have to consider the implications, for our purposes, of
James's endeavours to give substance to that form and style.
When all was said and done, however, there were—and were to
be for another century and more—two crowns: the traditional
phrase 'Union of the Crowns' is, it has been rightly pointed out,
peculiarly inappropriate.[2] In Scotland, where our primary interest
lies, James still reigned as king of Scots; and although he ruled *in
absentia*—ruled, as he boasted, by his pen—he ruled through the
traditional institutions and methods of Scottish kingship. In his
experience of these he was (as he never tired of recalling) already
'an old king' by the time the English crown came to him in 1603.
He was, however, the last king of Scots who could lay claim to
such an understanding of monarchy in Scotland. As Sir Thomas
Craig, the most distinguished Scottish legal scholar of his day and
a vigorous advocate of union between the two realms, shrewdly
observed:

Henceforward, after the most noble prince, His Majesty's son, no Scottish
king will ever rule in Scotland; instead [our] kings will be born in

[1] See on these points B. R. Galloway, *The Union of England and Scotland 1603–
1608* (Edinburgh, 1986), 59–62, 82–4.
[2] Ibid. 1.

England, they will be Englishmen, they will live in England, and (in conformity with natural reason) they will favour their English attendants and courtiers . . . London will be the seat of the Court and the capital city where almost all our suits must be brought . . .

James himself, Craig argued, native Scot though he was, would have only limited freedom to avoid preferential treatment of his English courtiers: he too, the implication seems to be, would already be more of an English than a Scottish ruler.[3]

In the event, of course, neither 1603 nor 1625 marked the end of a distinctively Scottish monarchy. Yet the fact remains that the characteristic discourse of that monarchy acquired, in the seventeenth century, accents and emphases which inevitably differentiated it from what had gone before. And already, in the last two decades of James VI's reign, the theme of Scottish kingship changed its character as it became one note in the chord—and discord—of a developing British monarchy. With much of that development, even in James's reign, we cannot concern ourselves here. The historiographical debate in which traditional 'Whig' views of the political, constitutional, and religious history of Jacobean England are challenged by 'revisionist' interpretations, and these in their turn meet with post-revisionist or counter-revisionist rejoinders, is not part of our subject.[4] Here it will suffice to consider such issues as seem to have a particular bearing upon our enquiry into the conceptualization of Scottish kingship in the last century or so of its fully independent existence. Three topics of this kind will be considered in turn. The first, inevitably, is the question of union itself, which dominated the politics of the first half-dozen years after James's accession in England. The second, overlapping chronologically with the first, is an issue James had long faced—and still faced—in Scotland, but which he now confronted in a wider context: the issue, essentially, of 'church and state'. This was for a time translated into the European terms of the king's controversies with Bellarmine and

---

[3] Craig, *De Unione Regnorum Britanniae Tractatus*, ed. C. S. Terry (Scottish History Society; Edinburgh, 1909), 177–8; and cf. p. 440. (I have, however, made my own translation from the Latin text.) It is worth noting that even if Henry, Prince of Wales, had lived to succeed to the throne, much of his upbringing would have been in England. His brother Charles, though born in Scotland, was entirely English by education.

[4] This is not, of course, to deny that there is an important Scottish 'input' to that debate: see esp. J. Wormald, 'James VI and I: Two Kings or One?', *History*, NS 68 (1983), 187–209.

with Du Perron; but it remained a crucial issue in his relationship with the kirk, and this was again to be central during and after his visit to Scotland in 1617. A third theme, closely interwoven with both of these, but demanding separate consideration and forming a suitable conclusion to the chapter, is the further development, during these decades, of the ideology of divine-right monarchy as we have seen it in the writings of Blackwood, Barclay, and James himself.

The English succession had been a major concern of Scottish policy throughout James VI's life; it had indeed been a prime objective of diplomacy during his mother's brief personal reign. Such a policy might, to be sure, have been entirely dynastic in scope and intention: it need not, that is to say, have raised the issue of 'union' in anything like the terms with which James himself confronted both his English and his Scottish parliament in 1604. Yet the general conditions of sixteenth-century politics, and in particular the way in which Anglo-Scottish relations had developed during the period of the Reformation and Counter-Reformation, were such that a mere 'personal union' was unlikely to satisfy all aspirations. The concept—one could even say the vision—of a Britain united in the cause of Protestant reform and the security of 'true religion' was already inspiring the Marian exiles of the 1550s. They in turn looked back to ideas that had formed part of the propaganda campaign at the time of the 'Rough Wooing' in the late 1540s—in particular to the Protector Somerset's 1548 *Epistle to the Nobilitie of Scotland*.[5] True, such visions were clouded by the English claim, constantly renewed and as constantly rejected, to suzerainty over Scotland. Nevertheless John Knox for one can be seen as a powerfully prophetic advocate of a 'Davidic' kingdom which would bring together two peoples, already similar in character, language, and law, and now (above all) to be united in religion.[6]

[5] Printed, with other English pamphlets of the period, in the Early English Text Society's edn. of *The Complaynt of Scotland*: see Ch. 3 n. 65 above.

[6] The theme has been most fully explored by Williamson, *Scottish National Consciousness*: see esp. ch. 1 for the points made here. It may be going too far to say, as Williamson does (p. 11), that Knox's *First Blast of the Trumpet* is 'a treatise on behalf of Anglo-Scottish union'. In any case his views need to be read together with the interpretation offered by Dawson, 'The Two John Knoxes'. See also R. A. Mason, 'The Scottish Reformation and the Origins of Anglo-British Imperialism', in id. (ed.), *Scots and Britons: Scottish Political Thought and the Union of 1603* (Cambridge, 1994), 161–86.

The developing threats to Protestantism in the 1570s and 1580s could only enhance the attractions of such a vision. It offered the hope of security for English and Scottish Protestants against the Catholic League and the 'enterprise' which might have failed with the defeat of the Armada but which could at any time be renewed. It also offered the flattering prospect of 'British' leadership in a Protestant Europe embattled against Antichrist in the form of the papacy, the Society of Jesus, and their allies. It was at this point that James VI, then in his early twenties and still in the first flush of personal rule, made his entrance in this particular scene.

The scene, it must be borne in mind, was essentially an apocalyptic one. The language was above all the language of scriptural prophecy, denunciation, and exhortation. James was always attracted by discourse of this kind, and never more so perhaps than in the period after his mother's execution, during and following the crisis of the Armada. He wrote an elaborate paraphrase of *the* Apocalypse, the book of Revelation itself; and in 1588 he published *Ane Fruitfull Meditatioun* on Revelation 20: 7–10 (where we read of the final overthrow of Satan and the nations he has gathered together against 'the camp of the saints and the beloved city'). This was closely followed by, and must be read in conjunction with, James's 1589 *Meditatioun* on 1 Chronicles 15: 25–9 (dealing with the bringing to Jerusalem of the ark of the covenant).[7] A certain amount of reading between the lines is necessary if the 'political' implications of these apocalyptic writings are to be appreciated. To this end it is useful to consider not only James's own words but the prefaces 'To the Christiane Reader' contributed by Patrick Galloway, soon to be James's chaplain. In the second of these, for instance, Galloway explicitly looks beyond James's 'awin boundis' to what he calls the 'anefold conjunctioun in him with the haill reformed Christiane kirkes in the earth'. Those churches, James maintained, were threatened by the pope

---

[7] Both the *Fruitfull Meditatioun* and the *Meditatioun* were published in Edinburgh by Henry Charteris and reprinted in *The Workes of the Most High and Mighty Prince, James, By the Grace of God Kinge of Great Britaine France and Ireland* . . . (London, 1616; hereafter *Workes*), 73–90, 81–9. *A Paraphrase upon the Revelation of the Apostle S. John* was not published until its inclusion in *Workes*, 1–72. There, in Bishop James Montagu's Preface, it is said to have been written before the king was 20. Willson (*King James VI and I*, 81–2) treats it as an expansion of the *Fruitfull Meditatioun*, written at the same time: this does not seem very plausible.

as Antichrist, together with 'the Jesuites, his last and maist pernicious vermine', whom he had sent out 'to steir up the Princes of
the earth his slaues, to gather and league them selfis together for
his defence'.[8] Neither England nor its queen is mentioned explicitly (nor, for that matter, is Scotland); but the unity of 'the Ile'
of Britain against the enemy is assumed.

One may hesitate to accept unreservedly the description of
James, in this context, as 'the greatest Knoxian in all Scotland'.[9]
Yet it is hardly to be questioned that he had in mind a 'Davidic
kingdom', of which the Scotland he ruled could be at least the
germ and microcosm. In the *Meditatioun* of 1589 he makes an
explicit comparison and draws a striking conclusion. The 'elders
of Israel' who accompanied David when the ark was brought to
Jerusalem, he says, 'wer of twa sortes, magistratis in wallit
townes . . . and cheifes in trybis and fatheris of fameleis quho in
the countrie did lodge . . . Thir war not vnlyke to twa of the
estaitis of our kingdome, the Barrounis and the Burges.' With 'the
captains over thousands' and the Levites also participating,
therefore,

men of all estaitis wer present in this godlie wark. This is to be markit
weill of Princes, and of all thois of ony hie calling or degrie that mellis
[concern themselves] to do in Godis caus: Dauid dois nathing in matereis
apperteining to God without ye presence and speciall concurrence of
Goddis Ministeris appointit to be spirituall rewlleris in his Kirk . . . [A]ne
godlie King findis as his hart wishes godlie estaitis concurring with him.
Nixt ane godlie King of his godlie forsicht in choosing guid vnder
rewlaris reapes this profite and pleasure that as he gois befor, so his with
zealous hartis do follow.[10]

As for the 'godlie wark' this king and his zealous people were to
perform—or rather had begun, with God's help, to perform:

Is thair not now ane sinceir professioun of ye treuth amangest ws in this
Ile oppugnit by ye natiounis about, haiteris of ye holie word . . . ? [W]e as
Israell [are] ye defenderis of our natiue soil and patrie . . . Bot . . . hes
nocht our virtewe bene far mair notabill than that of Israell? . . . For as
God by blowing on ye toppes of ye trees . . . put ye Philistines to flicht,
hes he not ewen in ye lyke maner by brangling with his michtie wind

---

   [8] *Fruitfull Meditatioun*, 1588 edn., sig. B ii^v; *Workes*, 78.
   [9] Williamson, *Scottish National Consciousness*, 42.
   [10] *Meditatioun on . . . Chronicles*, 1589 edn., sigs. A ii^v–B i^r; *Workes*, 83–4.

thair timmer castellis scattered and shaken them a sunder to ye wrak of ane greit part and confusioun of the haill?[11]

Here 'this Ile' is implicitly treated as a 'patrie' common to Scots and English alike, as a single realm united above all by 'sinceir professioun of ye treuth'. And that, no doubt, is—as far as it goes—a sufficiently 'Knoxian' vision.

As always, it is important to take account of the immediate circumstances in which James was writing. Apocalyptic though his visions may at times have been, he rarely lost touch completely with the pragmatic necessities of politics. One of his goals at the period when the two 'meditations' were written was 'to reach a *rapprochement* with the presbyterians'. It was important to vindicate his commitment to 'true religion' both against the suspicions aroused by his attitude to the Catholic earls and against the aspersions cast upon him by Archbishop Bancroft in England.[12] Ten years later, when we next have substantial evidence for James's attitude to Anglo-Scottish union, circumstances were very different.

By the time *Basilikon Doron* was written and printed in 1598–9, James had already made significant advances in his campaign against Presbyterian extremism. At the same time, Elizabeth was ten years older, the question of her successor that much more urgent. On the other hand, James was addressing his son and heir at a time when he was prey to uncertainty as to whether he would himself live to inherit the English crown and whether, failing that, Henry would succeed in his stead. In either case the problems of ruling 'moe kingdomes nor this [of Scotland]' would have to be faced; and those problems would not be solved by apocalyptic enthusiasm.[13] James is careful to avoid assuming any right to criticize English institutions, though cautiously hopeful of acquiring in due course the experience he still lacked of how those institutions worked.[14] That some of them did in fact work better

[11] *Meditatioun*, 1589, sig. B ii[v]; *Workes*, 87–8.

[12] Donaldson, *James V to James VII*, 192.

[13] *Basilikon Doron*, Craigie edn., i. 198/9: 'my trust is, that God hath ordeined you for moe Kingdomes nor this . . .'. Cf. 96/7: 'I hope yee shal be King of moe cuntries then this . . .'.

[14] See ibid. i. 21: 'I will speake no thing of the state of England, as a mater wherein I neuer had experience.' This is in the 1603 preface 'To the Reader', where one of James's concerns was to dispel the suspicion that he harboured 'a vindictiue resolution against England' (pp. 14, 18). He had, however, already expressed in the main text (pp. 72/3) the same disclaimer: 'And as for England, I will not speake be-gesse of them, neuer hauing bene among them.'

than their Scottish counterparts, he was already sure. He advises
his son to deal with the problem of heritable jurisdictions by
striving to 'drawe' Scotland 'to the lowable custome of Englande,
which yee may the easelier doe being King of both, as I hope in
GOD yee shall'.[15] Yet, 'hauing learned both the theorick and
practick' of kingship, James advises a cautious approach in these
matters, recognizing, in particular, that the task in hand is that of
ruling distinct and separate realms: his son is urged 'once in the
three yeares to visie al your kingdomes, not lippening [trusting]
to Viceroys but hearing your self their complaints, and hauing
ordinarie Councelles and justice-seates in euerie kingdomev of
their owne Cuntry-men'.[16] In 'all indifferent thinges' the king's
aim must be 'to allure peece and peece the reste of [his]
Kingdomes to followe the fashiones of that kingdome' which he
finds 'most ciuill, easiest to be ruled, and moste obedient to the
lawes'. This is to be achieved without coercion—'brought on with
time & at leasure, speciallie by mixinge through allie and dailie
conuersatioun, the men of every kingdome with an other'. The
final goal is 'a naturall & inseparable vnitie of loue'; and this
'maye easelye bee done in this Ile of Brittane, being . . . al-ready
ioyned in unitie of Religion and language'.[17] The vision of ten
years before is still there; but it is to be realized (we might say in
later terminology) by 'piecemeal social engineering', not by seeking an apocalyptic utopia.

To say this is to foreshadow an endorsement of that more recent
view of James's 'union' policy at the outset of his reign in England
which rejects the charge of excessive haste and political naïvety.
To be sure, closer union between his two realms was perhaps his
principal goal at that time.[18] And his presentation of the case
lacked nothing in grandiloquent imagery. The apocalyptic note

[15] Ibid. i. 88/9. Later (p. 92/3), James advises his son to 'take example by
England' in regard to bringing in foreign craftsmen.

[16] Ibid. i. 96/7. For 'the theorick and practick' see James's 1603 preface,
ibid. i. 20.

[17] Ibid. i. 198/9–200/1. The phrase 'a naturall & inseparable vnitie of loue'
occurs in a significant expansion of the passage in the 1603 text, contrasting the
'hereditarie hatred' between Scots and English with its 'quenching . . . by the
meanes of this long & happie amitie, betweene the Queene my dearest sister &
me'.

[18] The reference above to James's 'two realms' implicitly ignores the fact that he
was also king of Ireland: cf. the subtitle of Maurice Lee, Jr.'s *Great Britain's Solomon:
King James VI and I in his Three Kingdoms* (Urbana, Ill., 1990). In fact, comparatively
little is said about Ireland either by Lee or by Willson (*King James VI and I*), and the
topic will not be touched on here.

was there in James's speech at the opening of his first English parliament on 19 March 1604: 'Hath not God first vnited these two Kingdomes both in Language, Religion, and similitude of maners? . . . And now in the end and fulnesse of time vnited, the right and title of both in my Person . . . whereby it is now become like a little World within it selfe . . . '. God's purposes in this were, for James, inseparably associated with the political theology of monarchy as well as of union:

What God hath conioyned then, let no man separate. I am the Husband, and all the whole Isle is my lawfull Wife; I am the Head, and it is my Body; I am the Shepherd, and it is my flocke: I hope therefore no man will be so vnreasonable as to think that I that am a Christian King vnder the Gospel, should be a polygamist and husband to two wiues; that I being the Head, should haue a diuided and monstrous Body; or that being the Shepheard of so faire a Flocke (whose fold hath no wall to hedge it but the foure Seas) should haue my Flocke parted in two.[19]

The Scottish estates assembled in the month of April, and James had already made clear north of the Border that his position was to be understood as that of a prince who had succeeded to a single 'imperiall kingdome' in which the two realms were 'now joyned togidder under ane head, as they haif bene of long tyme past in ane religioun, ane language, and ane commoun habitatioun of ane Ile'. Accordingly, his 'princelie care mon be to sie thame joyne and coalesce togidder in a sinceir and perfyte unioune, and' (James went on in a striking metaphor, followed by a firm political conclusion) 'as two twynes bred in ane bellie, love ane another as no moir twa but ane estate'.[20] The practical problem was, of course, to determine what kind of 'estate' it was to be, what 'perfyte unioune' implied in terms of actual institutions. The task of finding solutions was remitted to the joint commission set up in the autumn of 1604 to negotiate terms for a treaty of union.

Those terms, the debate to which they gave rise on both sides of the Border, and the eventual failure of the project have all been exhaustively analysed in recent scholarship and need not form part of the agenda here.[21] It is, however, important for our

---

[19] McIlwain edn., 271–2.
[20] *Register of the Privy Council of Scotland* (hereafter *RPC*), vi. 596 (12 Jan. 1604).
[21] A convenient summary of developments in 1604 is provided by B. R. Galloway and B. P. Levack (eds.) *The Jacobean Union: Six Tracts of 1604* (Scottish History Society; Edinburgh, 1985), pp. ix–xxvii. More generally, see Galloway,

purposes to take particular note of the way in which the issue was seen in Scotland in relation to the Scots' understanding of their monarchy. There was plainly an acute sense of a possible threat to what the king himself called, in June 1604, 'the liberteis and fredomes of that . . . ancient and honourable realme'.[22] These were safeguarded by 'fundamental laws', and the status and security of those laws became a major issue in the union debate. Scottish law might be a much less mature and sophisticated structure than that which prevailed in England; but both law and legal scholarship in Scotland were developing rapidly enough to constitute a major factor in relations between the two countries.[23] It is no mere coincidence that the most substantial contribution to the debate on union in the years from 1603 to 1607 should have been written by Scotland's leading jurist. Sir Thomas Craig of Riccarton's legal scholarship has, to be sure, a much wider significance.[24] What is most relevant here, however, is the fact that he brought his learning to bear on the question of union.

The *De Unione Regnorum Britanniae Tractatus* is, on the one hand, an elaborate defence of the terms of union negotiated by the 1604 commission, on which its author had been one of the Scottish representatives. On the other hand, it can be read (though the point is debatable) as advocating a much closer union than either the commissioners or the king himself envisaged. Craig, for instance, decisively rejects the opinion that the projected union is 'merely a kind of treaty'. The goal is rather to find means whereby 'two kingdoms, each possessed of sovereignty, may come together under the rule of one king so that the two become one'.[25]

Union of England and Scotland; B. P. Levack, *The Formation of the British State* (Oxford, 1987), esp. 31–58. For a longer perspective see J. Robertson, 'Empire and Union: Two Concepts of the Early Modern European Political Order', in id. (ed.), *A Union for Empire: Political Thought and the British Union of 1707* (Cambridge, forthcoming). See also J. Wormald, 'The Union of 1603', in Mason (ed.), *Scots and Britons*, 17–40.

[22] *RPC* vii. 458 (12 June 1604).

[23] See B. P. Levack, 'English Law, Scots Law and the Union, 1603–1707', in A. Harding (ed.), *Law-Making and Law-Makers in British History* (Royal Historical Society; London, 1980), 105–19; id., 'Law, Sovereignty and the Union', in Mason (ed.), *Scots and Britons*, 213–40.

[24] See esp. J. G. A. Pocock, *The Ancient Constitution and the Feudal Law: A Study of English Historical Thought in the Seventeenth Century* (Cambridge, 1957; 2nd edn., 1987), 79–90; also Cairns, Fergus, and MacQueen, 'Legal Humanism and the History of Scots Law', esp. 56–67.

[25] *De Unione*, 55, 56; and cf. pp. 281, 282. Terry's rendering in the second passage—'the fusion of two sovereign states into a single realm'—both loses some

Later, again using the verb *coalescere* to denote the process he has
in mind, Craig refers to it as capable of bringing the two peoples,
'in time [*aliquando*]' together 'into a single body, almost [*quasi*] a
single state'.[26] That is the conclusion of a chapter dealing expressly with the legal aspect of the problem: 'Whether harmony
between the laws of each kingdom is necessary for perfecting the
Union . . .'.[27] Craig also refers to the relationship between Scottish
and English law in his *Jus Feudale*; and it is important to take note
of the careful distinction he makes there between *jus* and *lex*. The
latter—the specific law of different societies—issues from 'the
magistrates or the ruler': it may be 'established by the consent of
the people or by immemorial custom'. This is quite distinct from
jus, which stems from nature and is therefore called *jus Naturale*,
jus Gentium, *jus Commune*. *Jus* is the natural, *lex* (which is , to be
sure, a species of *jus*) is the civil bond of human society. Now,
Craig argues, 'the Scots, as it happens, enjoy the same *jus* as the
English, and yet they do not have identical laws'.[28] In the *De
Unione*, where his primary concern is not so much with community of laws as with shared *mores*, he gives pride of place to the
virtual identity in religious belief between the two communities.
Law, to be sure, is still important; and Craig claims that 'now-
adays no peoples differ less than the English and the Scots in their
laws and ordinances [*in Legibus et institutis*]'. Above all, there was
close agreement on the fundamentals of *Jus*, and there need be no
insurmountable obstacle to a harmonizing of laws.[29]

That some such harmony was essential to virtually any kind of
union would have been generally accepted; but harmony did not
imply—indeed it precluded—identity. There would still be two

of the nuances in the Latin and suggests a more emphatic conclusion that Craig
intended.

[26] Ibid. 90; and cf. p. 328. Craig's juxtaposition of the terms *Corpus* and *Civitatem*
may appear to justify Terry's rendering as 'body politic'. It seems better, however,
to preserve Craig's disjunction of the two terms and, especially, his qualifying of
Civitatem by the adverb *quasi*, which is quite lost in Terry's version.

[27] Ibid. 68; and cf. p. 297, where 'whether the laws of the two countries should
be identical' surely goes too far beyond Craig's 'Legum utriusque Regni
consonantia'.

[28] Craig, *Jus Feudale*; ed. J. Baillie (Edinburgh, 1732), 49; cf. *The Jus Feudale of Sir
Thomas Craig of Riccarton*, ed. J. A. Clyde, 2 vols. (Edinburgh, 1934), i. 103.

[29] *De Unione*, 68, 74; and cf. pp. 297, 304. In translating the second passage Terry
uses 'rights' for both *morum* and (in the marginal heading) *juris*: it is not really
appropriate in either case.

legal systems. In this Craig and those who thought like him saw no bar to the kind of union they sought; but the event was to prove such expectations over-sanguine. Of course there were many reasons for the failure of James's plans to make 'Great Britain' more than a form of words. Yet legal difficulties played a substantial part in the breakdown. The problems posed in this connection by the deeply entrenched structure of English common law and by its professionally powerful practitioners are too familiar to need recapitulation here. What is necessary for our enquiry is a closer inspection of Scottish attitudes and anxieties, rooted as they were in the traditions of the Scottish monarchy as we have seen them develop since the later years of the fifteenth century.

It is best, none the less, to begin in England, and specifically with the king's speech to parliament on 31 March 1607. Several matters had by then come to a head—in particular the issue between 'gradual union' and 'perfect union'. The latter was now envisaged, on the English side, as 'an absolute unity involving the institutions of government as well as the laws'.[30] This was contrasted with the 'imperfect union' that would be produced by the terms agreed in the 'Instrument' produced by the 1604 commissioners. A particular difficulty was caused by the Scots' insistence that their 'Fundamentall Lawes' and the status of Scotland as 'a free Monarchie' must be safeguarded. James, in his speech, endeavoured to allay English anxieties on the first score by insisting that fundamental law meant, in the Scottish context, not—as in England—'the Common Law, for they haue none, but that which is called the IUS REGIS'. And that in turn meant 'onely those Lawes whereby confusion is auoyded, and their Kings descent mainteined, and the heritage of the succession and Monarchie'. As for 'free monarchy', this was a matter of avoiding a situation in which 'for want either of Magistrate, Law, or Order', the Scots might 'become like a naked Province, without Law or libertie vnder this Kingdome'.[31] James went on to elaborate the argument that the Scots had 'no Common Law'. Their law had three sources: part was 'drawn out of the Chauncerie of England'; part was 'Statute Lawes . . . Acts of Parliament'; and part was 'the Ciuill Law'. James dismissed, among other arguments, the

---

[30] Galloway, *Union of England and Scotland*, 112.
[31] McIlwain edn., 300–1.

suggestion that the king 'must passe all the Lawes agreed to by the Lords and Commons' in the Scottish parliament. In fact, it was only his consent, given by the touch of his sceptre, that made a statute effectively law.[32]

In the event, '[t]he English parliament of 1606–7 was an almost unmitigated disaster for James's plans of union for England and Scotland'.[33] In Scotland, those plans may seem superficially to have fared better, but in substance the result was equally negative. James might try to persuade the English parliament that English law and English influence must in the end predominate in a united realm. In Scotland, uneasy awareness that this would be so produced at best a reluctant acceptance of what the king sought. The estates met in August 1607 and duly passed 'An Act Anent the Unioun of Scotland and England' incorporating 'all the provisions in the Instrument'.[34] Much more revealing, however, is the letter addressed to James by the estates in the same month. There the questions of 'fundamentall lawis' and of 'free monarchie' are vigorously taken up. On the first point James in his speech on 31 March is said to have 'verie treulie interpreted oure meaning'. This, however, was somewhat disingenuous; for the letter goes on to classify as 'fundamental' not only the 'lawis whairby your Majestie . . . dois most happely injoy the crowne', but also those 'quhairby the frayme of this hole kingdome is established, togidder with suche speciall priviledgeis and prerogativeis quahirby all distinctioun of rankis and ordouris is manteynit amang us'. These are carefully distinguished from 'our particulair Actis or Statutis or other lawis or customes', which are 'alterable as the weale of the commounwelth and publict state sall require'.[35] This is plainly a much broader view of fundamental law than James's *Ius Regis*, albeit an entirely traditional one.

In regard to 'free monarchy' James and his Scottish parliament were in fuller agreement: 'we can never better interprete it', the letter says, 'then your Majestie has already done'. It had never, the estates now claimed, been their intention 'to except aganis anie confounding as it wer of these two befoir separatit kingdomes in one gloriose monarchie and impyre of the whole Yle'. Even in such an 'impyre', however, 'this your Majesteis antient and native

[32] McIlwain edn., 301–2.
[33] Galloway, *Union of England and Scotland*, 127.
[34] Ibid. 129.   [35] *RPC* vii. 535.

kingdome sould not be so disordourit and maid confusit by turneing of it . . . into a conquered and slavishe province to be governed by a Viceroye or Deputye'.[36] James himself, it is worth recalling, had said to the English parliament, 'I hope you meane not I should set Garrisons ouer [the Scots] . . . or gouerne them by Commissioners.' Some of his Scottish subjects may well have sensed the irony whereby this was followed immediately in James's speech by his boast that 'by a Clearke of the Councell I gouerne Scotland now, which others could not do by the sword'.[37] The sword as well as the pen was indeed to be needed in the governing of Scotland later in the century; but that government could never again be quite the 'free monarchy' it had been before 1603.

By the time the union project was running into the sand, the king had other matters on his mind which have a bearing upon our enquiry. The Gunpowder Treason of 1605 was followed by the imposition of the oath of allegiance which entailed denying the pope's right to depose James and swearing that 'I do from my heart abhor, detest and adjure, as impious and heretical, this damnable doctrine and position, that princes which be excommunicated or deposed by the pope may be deposed or murdered by their subjects or any other whatsoever'.[38] Catholics were expressly forbidden to take this oath by Paul V in September 1606, a prohibition renewed in August 1607 and defended by Cardinal Bellarmine in a letter addressed on 28 September 1607 to the Archpriest George Blackwell. These pronouncements evoked James's *Apologie for the Oath of Allegiance*, published in English, French, and Latin in 1607–8.[39] This was replaced by a revised edition in 1609 (English, French, Latin, and Dutch), to which the king added the *Monitory Preface*.[40] He was there responding to the

---

[36] Ibid.   [37] McIlwain edn., 301.

[38] 3 & 4 Jac. I, c. 4; and cf. 7 & 8 Jac. I, c. 6, where, in 1610, the obligation to take the oath was extended from recusants 'to all non-noble persons whatsoever, if eighteen and above' (McIlwain edn., pp. li–lii).

[39] *Triplici Nodo, Triplex Cuneus. Or An Apologie for the Oath of Allegiance*: McIlwain edn., 71–109. English translations of the papal documents and Bellarmine's letter are given (pp. 73–5, 80–1, 82–5).

[40] *A Premonition to All Most Mightie Monarches, Kings, Free Princes, and States of Christendome*: McIlwain edn., 110–68. The reference in the title to *States* may suggest that James had in mind the concurrent controversy between the papacy and Venice, following Paul V's imposition of an interdict on the city. Certainly a

attack on his *Apologie* by Bellarmine, who was also engaged in posthumous controversy with William Barclay over the nature and extent of papal authority.[41] Finally, when Cardinal du Perron, at the meeting of the French States General in 1615, defended the doctrine that subjects might be freed from their duty to obey heretical, unbelieving, or persecuting rulers, James again entered the debate with his *Déclaration ... pour le droit des Rois et indépendance de leurs couronnes.*[42]

This extensive controversy has, in its general aspects, been fully explored elsewhere.[43] Here it is necessary to examine it in the perspective of James's theory and practice of kingship in Scotland, having regard to the fact that he was himself aware of the important continuities between the English and European debate on the one hand and, on the other, the problems he had faced and still faced in regard to the claims of ecclesiastical authority in his native country. He had, as we know, denounced the Jesuits as 'pernicious vermine' in 1588. Twenty years later, embroiled directly with the Jesuit Bellarmine, he remarked acidly that '*Iesuits* are nothing but *Puritan-papists*'.[44] The argument which, from the pope's spiritual supremacy, derived an 'indirect power' whereby he could exercise control over those rulers who, as James understood the matter, owed responsibility directly to God and to God alone had an evident affinity with the Melvillian view of the king as a mere vassal in the kingdom of Christ, amenable to the discipline of Christ's body, the church. Andrew Melville himself had, as it happened, been firmly removed from the Scottish scene. Following the 'rebel' assembly of ministers in

presentation copy of the *Premonition* was sent to the Doge and Senate, though it is said to have been 'at once deposited in the most secret archives of the State where it has remained unmolested to the present day' (Willson, *King James VI and I*, 238).

[41] Barclay's *De potestate Papae* was published posthumously by his son John in 1609, Bellarmine's riposte in 1610. It is worth recalling that James had tried unsuccessfully to induce William Barclay to settle in England.

[42] McIlwain edn., 169–268. James's original French text (first published in 1615) is said to have been corrected by Pierre du Moulin (who may in fact have written a good deal of it himself). It was translated into English as *A Remonstrance for the Right of Kings, and the Independance of Their Crownes* and included in James's *Workes* (1616). It is commonly referred to by the running title used in that edn., *A Defence of the Right of Kings*.

[43] A brief but useful outline is provided by J. H. M. Salmon in Burns and Goldie (eds.), *Cambridge History of Political Thought 1450–1700*, 247–53. See also J. P. Sommerville, *Politics and Ideology in England 1603–1640* (London, 1986), 117–20. An older but much fuller account is in McIlwain edn., intro., pp. liii–lxxx.

[44] *Premonition*, in McIlwain edn., 126.

Aberdeen in July 1605, defiance had been met by imprisonment and banishment. Melville and seven of his colleagues 'were invited to London at the end of August 1606 for a consultation with the king'. His assertion of the right of free assembly brought him first to the Tower and then, in 1611, to the academic exile in which he spent the last eleven years of his life.[45] James meanwhile had both strengthened and consolidated his ecclesiastical policy in Scotland.

In this context the character and status of the office of bishops becomes critically important. Whether or not James believed in *jure divino* episcopacy—and the issue is a contentious one—there can be no doubt as to his conviction that bishops were essential to the good order of the church.[46] And as 'supreme governor' of the church—certainly in England, arguably in Scotland—that good order was a crucially important part of his responsibility to God. In Scotland, however, it was necessary—and James recognized the need—to proceed cautiously. A proposal to install 'constant moderators' of presbyteries had been rejected at the synodal level in February 1606 but approved by a far from independent 'assembly' ten months later; and it was only against strong resistance that the introduction of the same office for synods (which could be seen as corresponding more or less to episcopal dioceses) was accepted. Legislation by the estates in the same year, 1606, restored the parliamentary status and the revenues of the bishops who were to be constant moderators of synods. The upshot was that 'by 1609 something like diocesan episcopacy was again in operation'. Strictly spiritual functions were transferred from presbytery to bishop in 1610; and in the same year, on 21 October, episcopal consecration was received at Westminster by three Scottish bishops. Bearing in mind the anxieties that had been expressed during the union debate, it is important to note that this restoration of traditional episcopacy was achieved in such a way as to avoid any hint or trace of English ecclesiastical superiority over Scotland.[47]

---

[45] Donaldson, *James V to James VII*, 204–5.

[46] See e.g. *Premonition*, in McIlwain edn., 126: 'And as I euer maintained the state of Bishops, and the Ecclesiasticall Hierarchie for order sake; so was I euer an enemie to the confused Anarchie of the *Puritanes*.' On the *jure divino* question see Lee, *Great Britain's Solomon*, 167–71, and the references given there.

[47] Donaldson, *James V to James VII*, 205–6. See also Lee, *Great Britain's Solomon*, ch. 6, 'Supreme Governor', for a valuable general discussion of issues of ecclesiastical polity in James's reign.

Questions as to James's personal convictions in matters of religion may be essentially unanswerable. One historian, though by no means unfavourably disposed towards the king, claims that it 'is simply not true' that James was, for all his theological knowledge, personally 'pious'.[48] What cannot be doubted is the political importance he attached to theological positions and not least to ecclesiology. Episcopacy might be (as James certainly at one point professed to believe) 'an Apostolique institution, and so the ordinance of God'.[49] What mattered most, however, was the safeguard it afforded against positions, whether papist or presbyterian, which threatened the integrity of royal power and had, in James's lifetime, yielded, on both extremes, doctrines that justified resistance and even king-killing. It is, to be sure, the case that bishops as such would not serve the purpose. One reason, indeed, for James's uncertainty as to *jure divino* episcopacy was precisely that it might lay the foundation for a spiritual power potentially as independent and therefore as menacing as, in their several ways, both papistry and presbytery were. Bellarmine for one had defended not merely the papal monarchy but a concept of ecclesiastical autonomy and the supremacy of the spiritual power of which that monarchy was simply, in his view, the ultimate and essential expression.[50] If it is true that 'James's church . . . was Calvinist in doctrine and episcopal in polity',[51] it is also true that the Anglican polity he upheld (and hoped to parallel in Scotland) had a good deal in common with the Gallican Catholicism defended by such writers as William Barclay. Bishops were to rule the church, no doubt; but they were not to be the 'proude Papall Bishoppes' denounced in *Basilikon Doron*.[52] Papal they must not be, least of all in the sense advocated by Bellarmine, denying as he did 'that Bishops haue their Iurisdiction immediatly from God' and subordinating them to the authority of the pope.[53] And as for

[48] Lee, *Great Britain's Solomon*, 165–6.

[49] *Premonition*, in McIlwain edn., 126.

[50] See e.g. the references to Bellarmine in James's *Apologie*, in McIlwain edn., 109, citing 'De Clericis, cap. 28' (i.e. *Disputationes . . . de Controversiis Christianae Fidei*, I. xxviii) and translating (or paraphrasing): 'these very Church-men that are borne, and inhabite in Soveraigne princes countreys, are notwithstanding not their Subiects, and cannot bee iudged by them, although they [the churchmen] may iudge them [the princes].' Cf. the Latin text in Bellarmine, *Opera Omnia*, 8 vols. (Naples, 1872), ii. 201–5.

[51] Lee, *Great Britain's Solomon*, 167.   [52] Craigie edn., i. 80/1.

[53] *Premonition*, in McIlwain edn., 126.

pride there should at least be no room for the pride of rank which
had so often characterized bishops in the past. In Scotland, it has
been said, the episcopate James had succeeded in restoring was
essentially 'an office which he regarded as part of his administrative machine'; and such offices were to be filled by 'new men'—
men not 'of the same social standing as pre-reformation prelates
or connected with the oligarchy which had been dominant in the
past'.[54]

If, then, there may be uncertainties as to James's doctrinal position, there are none as to the principles and objectives of his
policy. To implement those principles, to achieve those objectives
was, of course, another matter. In Scotland, where our principal
interest lies, the restoration of effective episcopacy in 1610 may
have been the end of one phase, but it was also the start of
another, in the ecclesiastical conflict that had marked virtually the
whole of James's personal rule. A new crisis was to come with his
only visit to Scotland between 1603 and his death.

James may be said to have approached that crisis from an
unprecedentedly strong position. Already in 1606 he had been
acknowledged as governor of persons both temporal and spiritual in all cases throughout the realm. The bishops whose authority in the kirk was being restored held their authority, at least in
its jurisdictional aspect, from the crown.[55] On the other hand, the
General Assembly continued to meet until 1618 and never formally lost its position as the supreme authority in strictly ecclesiastical matters, on issues of faith and order. There were, of course,
as James had already shown (and was to show again), means
whereby assemblies could be induced to act as the king wished;
but it was still a body enjoying some measure of independence of
the royal will. Parliamentary action in 1617 to give the king,
advised by the bishops (but without the involvement of ministers), legislative power in the kirk could not be implemented.
There was in effect a combination of episcopacy and presbyterian-
ism: some historians would see this as 'a reversion to the system
which had operated in the 1560s and 1570s modified by the existence now of the presbytery . . . between the congregation and the
bishop's synod'.[56] So far, this 'Jacobean compromise' looked like

[54] Donaldson, *James V to James VII*, 221–2.
[55] *APS* iv. 282, 430; *RPC* viii. 604–5; and cf. Donaldson, *James V to James VII*, 206.
[56] Ibid. 207.

another success for James's skilful management as an absentee ruler.

The king, however, with a dozen years' experience of his English realm and its church, now sought to take matters further. Beginning in 1614 with a proclamation which enjoined the celebration of holy communion at Easter, he advanced rapidly towards more sweeping liturgical changes. These eventually crystallized, after James's Scottish visit in the summer of 1617, in the so-called Five Articles of Perth. Together with the restoration of the principal festivals of the traditional Christian year, there was provision for private baptism, private communion, the rite of episcopal confirmation, and—the most controversial article of all—the requirement that communion be received kneeling. Following the rejection of these articles by the Assembly at St Andrews (November 1617), James angrily convoked a more manageable Assembly at Perth on 25 August 1618, where the articles were approved. On 21 October they were ratified by the privy council; and parliamentary endorsement came in July 1621. As significant as the king's victory, however, is the degree of opposition against which it was achieved. Substantial minorities opposed the articles both in the Assembly and in parliament. James may, as he threatened in 1617, have let his opponents know 'what it is to draw the anger of a king upon them'; but there were some at least whose convictions were stronger than their fear of royal displeasure.[57] If 'the Princes ordour' had, as James understood the matter, sufficed for reformation in England and Denmark, he found it less than adequate to achieve his aims in the kirk at the end of his reign.[58]

It may be the case that, when James I contemplated the possibility of a fully independent *jure divino* episcopate, he asked himself, 'Was the spirit of Andrew Melville coming back to life, clad this time in a mitre?'[59] James VI, however, may have had even greater cause to ask himself whether Melville, who died in Sedan in 1622, had been, as it were, reincarnated in advance in such men as David Calderwood. Certainly the confrontation between

[57] Donaldson, *James V to James VII*, 207–10. In the assembly there were 41 adverse votes in a total of 127; in the estates, 51 in a total of 129. James's threatening words in 1617 are recorded in *Original Letters relating to the Ecclesiastical Affairs of Scotland . . . 1603–25*, 2 vols. (Bannatyne Club; Edinburgh, 18), ii. 524.

[58] For 'the Princes ordour' see *Basilikon Doron*, Craigie edn., i. 74/5.

[59] This splendid rhetorical question is posed by Lee, *Great Britain's Solomon*, 169.

Calderwood and the king in 1617 shows clearly how acute the problem of Christian obedience still was. For Calderwood obedience might, in the last resort, mean that one must 'rather suffer than practice' what was commanded contrary to the law of God. For James it was the obedience of the centurion's servants in the gospel; and in the polity of the church this meant that 'The bishops must rule the ministers, and the king rule both, in matters . . . not repugnant to the Word of God'.[60] As ever, the difficulty lay in determining whose interpretation of 'the word of God' should prevail. James certainly saw himself, in virtue of his royal office, as *custos utriusque tabulae*; and this may be interpreted as 'a right to impose his interpretation of Scriptures on the church'.[61] He was to exercise his authority 'by commanding obedience to be giuen to the word of God, by reforming the religion according to his prescribed will, by assisting the spirituall power with the temporall sword, by reforming of corruptions, by procuring obedience to the Church'—by acting, in fact, very much as the 'supreme Governour' envisaged in the oath prescribed in Scotland nearly half a century before the crisis over the Five Articles of Perth.[62] Such a royal supremacy was not, in principle, acceptable either to Catholics or to many Protestants; but in practice much would depend on the manner in which it was exercised. In Scotland, James (it can be claimed) 'knew where to stop, and even when to retreat'.[63] His son did not.

Through all the controversies of James VI and I's reign there runs the distinctive thread of a consistent doctrine—the doctrine of what the king himself had called 'free monarchy'. This involved divinely ordained hereditary kingship; and one of the essential attributes of such a king was his absolute power. That concept was certainly in some ways problematic and it was in time to become the centre of intense ideological debate. Yet in itself and at

[60] J. Spottiswoode, *The History of the Church of Scotland*, ed. M. Russell and M. Napier, 3 vols. (Spottiswoode Society; Edinburgh, 1847–51), iii. 241; D. Calderwood, *History of the Kirk of Scotland*, 8 vols. (Wodrow Society; Edinburgh, 1842–9), vii. 263; and cf. Lee, *Great Britain's Solomon*, 170.

[61] This is the interpretation suggested by Lee, ibid. 169. For kings as *custodes utriusque tabulae* see *Apologie*, in McIlwain edn., 108; and cf. *Basilikon Doron*, Craigie edn., i. 144/5. For a very elaborate statement of royal responsibilities in regard to the church, with copious scriptural references, see *Apologie*, in McIlwain edn., 107.

[62] Ibid. 108; and cf., for the 1571 oath, Ch. 5 at n. 12.

[63] Donaldson, *James V to James VII*, 211.

the period with which this enquiry is concerned the notion of absolute power was not controversial in quite the sense it has acquired in the conventional antithesis between 'absolutism' and 'constitutionalism'. By the early seventeenth century it had long been recognized, and recognized across a broad range of political thinking, that some kind of absolute power was a necessary element in the government of a well-ordered state or commonwealth.[64] The meaning of *potestas absoluta*, however, and its distinction from *potestas ordinata* or *ordinaria* must be understood not simply—indeed not primarily—in narrowly 'political' terms, but rather in the juristic and theological contexts in which such terminology had been developed.[65] Given the theological focus of so much of the polemics of James VI and I's reign, together with the king's own interest in theology, it is natural, and will not be misleading, to give that aspect of the subject initial emphasis. At the same time we need to bear in mind that it was as often as not in the field of law that the doctrines of what has been called 'Jacobean political theology' were brought to bear upon the concrete issues of government.[66]

By the second quarter of the thirteenth century theologians had formulated the concept and devised the terminology of God's absolute and his ordained power—the latter manifested in what God has in fact chosen to do, the former referring to the infinite number of things he could and might have done. From such writers as Alexander of Hales (d. 1245) this language passed rapidly into juristic thinking—notably in the work of one of the outstanding canon lawyers of the time, Hostiensis (d. 1271). Applied in particular to the papacy, it meant that the pope, as God's vicegerent, could dispense with the ordinary positive law of the church and even with divine law itself: 'he can', Hostiensis declared, 'dispense in all things provided that he does not violate

[64] See Burns, *Lordship, Kingship, and Empire*, as index under 'absolutism, absolute monarchy' and '*potestas absoluta*'.

[65] See F. Oakley, *Omnipotence, Covenant, and Order* (Ithaca, NY, 1984), ch. 4, 'Divine Sovereignty, Papal Miracle, Royal, Grace'; Pennington, *The Prince and the Law*, as index under '*Potestas absoluta et ordinata*', esp. 54–75, 106–18; W. Courtenay, *Causation and Volition: A History of the Distinction of Absolute and Ordained Power* (Bergamo, 1990).

[66] See F. Oakley, 'Jacobean Political Theology: The Absolute and Ordinary Powers of the King', *Journal of the History of Ideas*, 29 (1968), 323–46; id., 'The "Hidden" and "Revealed" Wills of James I: More Political Theology', in J. R. Strayer and D. E. Queller (eds.), *Post Scripta* [*Studia Gratiana*, 15 (1972)], 363–75.

the faith and provided that his dispensation does not lead to a mortal sin.'[67] There was of course to be prolonged and intricate discussion throughout the three centuries and more between Hostiensis and the period with which we are concerned as to whether the concept of *potestas absoluta* could indeed be pushed so far. And there would be a broad consensus that this power did not in fact exempt the ruler—whether pope or prince—from the dictates of divine and natural law; and, moreover, that he should in general respect the ordinary law and govern in accordance with it, using his *potestas ordinata* only.

Much—perhaps most—of this flowed without interruption from the work of medieval theologians and jurists into the early-modern theory of sovereignty and absolute monarchy.[68] If we now return to the reign of James VI and I, we shall find ample evidence for this. Thus, in Edward Forset's 1606 *Comparative Discourse of the Bodies Naturall and Politique*, the distinction between God's working '*naturally*, by the mediate causes' and his performing 'his owne pleasure by *extraordinarie* meanes, drawne out of his absolute power' is presented as a 'likenesse' of the king's 'Sovereigntie'. And at the end of the reign, writing in 1625, Sir John Davies says that the king 'doth imitate the Divine Majesty' when 'by the positive law [he] was pleased to limit and stint his absolute power, and to tye himself to the ordinary rules of the law'.[69]

James himself seems not to have used the precise terminology of absolute and ordinary power; but the essential distinction was certainly part of his thinking.[70] Thus in his speech to the English

[67] Quoted by Pennington, *The Prince and the Law*, 61 and n. 87.

[68] This is the essential theme of Pennington's 'Epilogue: The Sixteenth Century and Beyond', ibid. 269–90.

[69] The passages from Forset and Davies are quoted by Oakley, *Omnipotence, Covenant, and Order*, 109. Davies is a particularly interesting 'witness' in this connection, since he is primarily remembered, in the history of ideas, as a representative of 'the common-law mind': see e.g. Pocock, *The Ancient Constitution and the Feudal Law: A Study of English Historical Thought in the Seventeenth Century: A Reissue with a Retrospect* (Cambridge, 1987), 32–5, 59–63, 263–5; also the extract from Davies's *Primer Report* in Wootton (ed.), *Divine Right and Democracy*, 131–43.

[70] The passage cited by Oakley (*Omnipotence, Covenant, and Order*, 105 and n. 32, where the page-reference should be 602) to support the suggestion that James 'came even closer' than in the 1610 speech to using the absolute/ordinary terminology is not wholly convincing. James does indeed speak of his 'doble prerogative', distinguishing that which, pertaining to his 'absolute authoritie royall', 'his supreame and imperiall power and soveraigntie ... ought not to bee

parliament on 21 March 1610 he insisted that 'we are to distinguish betweene the state of Kings in their first originall, and betweene the state of setled Kings and Monarches, that doe at this time gouerne in ciuill Kingdomes'. And he went on to invoke the parallel distinction between 'the olde Testament', where God 'spake by Oracles, and wrought by Miracles', and the situation after the redemptive work of Christ, when 'it pleased [God] to setle a *Church* . . . Hee euer after gouerning his people and Church within the limits of his reueiled will'. In a similar way, kings (whether their power had been achieved by conquest or by consent) ruled originally on the basis that

their wills . . . serued for Law; Yet how soone Kingdomes began to be setled in ciuilitie and policie, then did Kings set downe their mindes by Lawes, which are properly made by the King onely; but at the rogation of the people, the Kings grant being obteined thereunto. And so the King became to be *Lex loquens*, after a sort, binding himselfe by a double oath to the obseruation of the fundamentall Lawes of his kingdome: *Tacitly*, as by being a King, and so bound to protect aswell the people, as the Lawes of his Kingdome; And *Expresely*, bu his oath at his Coronation . . .[71]

Earlier in the speech, in a well-known passage, James had, on the one hand, given a magniloquent account of the godlike power of kings:

they make and vnmake their subiects: they haue power of raising, and casting downe: of life, and of death: Iudges ouer all their subiects, and in all causes, and yet accomptable to none but God onely. They haue power to exalt low things, and abase high things, and make of their subiects like men at the Chesse; A pawne to take a Bishop or a Knight, and to cry vp, or downe any of their subiects, as they do their money.

On the other hand, he distinguished between 'a Kings power in *Abstracto*' and his power 'in a setled state of a Kingdome which was gouerned by his owne fundamentall Lawes and Orders'.[72]

There is a certain intriguing ambiguity in that last phrase. The possessive 'his' should probably be taken as equivalent to 'its' in

disputed . . . in vulgar argument', and that which 'was ordinary, and had relacion to his private interest'. The latter, however, is hardly what was meant by a ruler's *potestas ordinata*. James used similar language in his 1616 Star Chamber speech, distinguishing his 'priuate Prerogatiue' from 'the absolute Prerogatiue of the Crowne, that is no Subiect for the tongue of a Lawyer, nor lawfull to be disputed' (McIlwain edn., 333).

[71] Ibid. 309.   [72] Ibid. 308.

modern English: the 'fundamentall Lawes and Orders' are thus, as James says further on, 'the fundamentall Lawes of [the ruler's] kingdome'. Yet 'his' could also be read as attributing the laws to the king; and certainly James wished to assert that law is 'properly made by the King onely', however much it may arise from the people's 'rogation'. What he calls 'the generall power of a King in Diuinity' may be modified in 'the settled and established State of this'—or any other—'Kingdome'.[73] In the end, however, it remains the case that 'Kings are not onely Gods Lieutenants vpon earth, and sit vpon Gods throne, but euen by God himselfe they are called Gods'; and that is why 'The State of MONARCHIE is the supremest thing vpon earth'.[74]

There is, of course, a great deal more in the 1610 speech, much of it of considerable importance. That importance, however, lies largely beyond the range, or on the margins, of the present enquiry. In regard to political ideas, with particular reference to the conception of kingship brought by James VI into the realm of James I, what the speech provides is at once a condensation and, in certain respects, an elaboration of the doctrine expounded in *The True Lawe*.[75] The elaboration (modest in scope, but still interesting) is in James's 'political theology'—a development perhaps carried further in the Star Chamber speech of 1616.[76] It would not be easy, however, to identify any notable change or development in his understanding of what he calls 'the grounds of Policie and Philosophie' on which his theory of kingship stood.[77] He referred in the 1616 speech to his having acquired 'that knowledge, that an Acte of Parliament can doe greater wonders' than would have been involved in his frustrated scheme for the union of the realms: we may surely assume that such knowledge was already his by 1610 and that he could then too have cited the authority of 'that old wise man the Treasourer *Burghley* [who] was

[73] Ibid.   [74] Ibid. 307.

[75] For discussion of both *The True Lawe* and *Basilikon Doron* in the 'Anglo-Scottish' context, see J. Wormald, 'James VI and I, *Basilikon Doron* and *The Trew Law of Free Monarchies*: The Scottish Context and the English Translation', in L. L. Peck (ed.), *The Mental World of the Jacobean Court* (Cambridge, 1991), 36–54, 278–83 (notes).

[76] See e.g. McIlwain edn., 333: 'It is Atheisme and blasphemie to dispute what God can doe: good Christians content themselues with his will reuealed in his word. [S]o it is presumption and high contempt in a Subiect, to dispute what a King can doe . . . but rest in that which is the Kings reuealed will in his Law.'

[77] Ibid. 307.

wont to say, Hee knew not what an Acte of Parliament could not doe in *England*'.[78] Whatever James may have learned of 'parliamentary sovereignty' in his southern kingdom, however, does not seem to have altered the view he had formed before 1603 as to where supreme power lay in a 'free monarchy'.

In reviewing what had become of James's earlier ideas by the time he reached the middle and later years of his reign in England, we must of course consider *Basilikon Doron* as well as *The True Lawe*. In that connection a somewhat neglected text may be helpful. James's 1620 *Meditation vpon the 27, 28, 29 Verses of the XXVII chapter of St Matthew, or A paterne for a Kings inauguration* was not included in the Harvard edition of his *Political Works*; and it has been dismissed as a 'strange effort, a product of premature senility'.[79] Yet it deserves some attention. Written expressly for Prince Charles, who had taken his dead brother's place as heir apparent, it is essentially a brief recapitulation of the doctrine of *Basilikon Doron*.[80] Its structure—somewhat loose, to be sure—is provided by the ceremonies and symbolic objects used at a royal inauguration, James's text being the account of the mocking 'coronation' of Jesus by Pilate's soldiers. It is neither necessary nor appropriate to follow in detail his exposition of the theme, but there are some interesting restatements of essential elements in his concept of kingship, and perhaps some emphases or turns of phrase that are worth noting.

To begin with a point near the end of James's *Meditation*, it is no surprise to find him still insisting that 'laws without execution are without life'.[81] Again, at an early stage in the text, we find the king's persistent, almost obsessive, hostility to 'our foolish superstitious *Puritanes*'; and it may be permissible to guess that recent

[78] McIlwain edn., 329.

[79] Published separately in 1620, the *Paterne* (as it may best be referred to) was added (with continuous pagination and an additional colophon) to the 1620 reprint of *Workes*. The dismissive comment is by D. H. Willson, 'James I and his Literary Assistants', *Huntington Library Quarterly*, 8 (1944–5), 55; cf. id., *King James VI and I*, 302–3, where the verses of James's text are said to be 'wrenched from their context'.

[80] In his dedication to Charles, dated 29 Dec. 1619, James remarks that in *Basilikon Doron* he had been concerned to give Henry 'aduice anent the gouernment of Scotland in particular'. That kind of specific advice has no place in the *Paterne*; but, in his 'Aduertisement to the Reader' James states his intention, in a later work, 'to set downe at large . . . the whole principall points belonging to the office of a King'. That intention was not to be fulfilled.

[81] *Paterne*, 125; *Workes* (1620), 621.

developments in Scotland are reflected in a particular emphasis on their refusal

> to kneele at the receiuing of the blessed *Sacrament*. For, if euer at any time *Christ* is to be worshipped, it is in time of prayer; and no time can be so fit for prayer and meditation, as is the time of our receauing the *Sacrament*, & if any place can be more fit than other for worshipping of *God* and his *Christ* in, it is the *Church*, where is the ordinarie assembly and meeting of his Saints.[82]

With this we find a predictable insistence on the king's ecclesiastical authority. Kings, 'as GODS Deputie iudges vpon earth, sit on thrones, clad with long robes, not as laiks and simply *togati*, as inferior secular Iudges are, but as *mixtae personae*'. This does not mean 'that they ought to vsurpe any point of the Priestly office . . . but it is the Kings office to ouersee and compell the Churche to do her office, to purge all abuses in her, and by his sword, as *vindex vtriusque tabulae*, to procure her due reuerence and obedience of all his temporall subiects'.[83]

The sword is carefully differentiated from 'the scepter, which represents the authority of a King toward all his subiects, as well good as bad'; whereas 'the sword . . . is only ordeyned for the punishment of the euill'. The context for this is James's argument that 'wise Kings will be loth to put their prerogatiue vpon the tenterhooks'—that is, to stretch it to the limit—'except a great necessity shall require it'.[84] This is one of the lessons Charles must learn if he is to come into his kingdom, not 'like a raw Spanish *Bisogno*, but rather like an old souldier of a trayned band'—if, 'in the science of gouernement', he intends, as he should, 'to presse to bee an arts-master'.[85]

That a king's 'entres' upon his inheritance should be accompanied by 'the loue & acknowledgment of his people' (symbolized by 'the diademe or crowne') and that 'it is a great signe of

[82] *Paterne*, 12–13; *Workes* (1620), 608.

[83] *Paterne*, 35–7; *Workes* (1620), 611. James refers, after the words *mixtae personae*, to his *Basilikon Doron*: the Latin phrase does not occur there, but cf. Craigie edn., i. 172/3, where, after arguing that a king has both a civil and a military role, being both *togatus* and *paludatus*. James adds a comparison: 'as your office is likewise mixed betuixte the Ecclesiasticall and ciuil estate: for a king is not *mere laicus*, as both the Papistes and Anabaptists would haue him, to the which errour also our puritanes incline ouer-far.'

[84] *Paterne*, 60–1; *Workes* (1620), 614.

[85] *Paterne*, sig. [A 11]ʳ, 123; *Workes* (1620) 606, 621.

the blessing of *God* when he enters on it with the willing applause of his subiects' are for James unquestionably true propositions. Yet 'a Monarchie or hereditary Kingship cannot iustly be denied to the lawfull successor, what euer the affection of the people bee'.[86] The assertion of strict hereditary right, which had been the essential basis of James's acquisition of the English crown, is as firm as ever. At the same time, James now comments on the basis of royal authority in relation to the society over which it is exercised in ways that merit some notice here. Of course, 'all succeeding Kings receaue their crownes from God onely, yet the people at their inauguration giue a publike acknowledgment of their willing subiection to his power & authority, submitting themselues to the power of God, who is the onely giuer of it'. And James is prepared to go further: 'Neither will I denie that many Kings of the nations [i.e. the Gentiles] had their diademes or crownes giuen them by the people, who translated or transferred by that act all their power vnto their Kings, but it followeth not that God therefore did not set those Kings vpon their thrones.' In contrasting such cases with that of God's chosen people, among whom '*God* visibly ruled', James reverts to the distinction between 'revealed ' and 'secret' wills. God was at work in both situations; but 'what *God* did directly by his word and oracle among his own people in the election of Kings, he did it only by his secret writing in the harts of other nations'.[87] On either basis, however, 'Kings are anoynted of *God*, sitting in his seate and therefore called *Gods*'. Yet the king 'must remember . . . that hee is ordeyned for his people, and not his people for him. For he is a great watchman and shepheard . . . : and his eye must neuer slumber nor sleepe for the care of his flocke.'[88]

It cannot reasonably be claimed that James's *Paterne for a Kings inauguration* is other than a minor work by an author who had written more substantially on its themes. Yet it is certainly more than an indication of 'premature senility'. It is, rather, a significant epilogue to James's thinking about kingship and, as far as it goes,

[86] *Paterne*, 40, 118–19; *Workes* (1620), 612, 620–1.
[87] *Paterne*, 41–2, 44–7; *Workes* (1620), 612. James had also used the distinction between God's revealed and his 'secret' will in the *Meditation on the Lords Prayer* which, like the *Paterne*, was added to the 1620 printing of his *Workes* (580).
[88] *Paterne*, 71–2; *Workes* (1620), 614.

an epitome of some of his most essential doctrine. If it suggests that the views of James I, king of Great Britain, in his last years, were not fundamentally different from those of James VI, king of Scots, in his prime, this in turn may point to the conclusion that its author had 'learnt nothing and forgotten nothing'. Yet James's reputation as a ruler and his standing as a political thinker are both a good deal higher as we near the quatercentenary of his accession in England than they have been for most of the intervening centuries. Nor is it as obvious as it once seemed to be that the doctrine of divine-right kingship he espoused was an alien import into a society, whether English or 'British', radically hostile to such ideas. As we return to the Scottish context and approach the conclusion of the enquiry, one question for consideration is whether James's 'free monarchy' represented continuity with, or divergence from, the political traditions which had prevailed in his native country.

Conclusion

THE investigation pursued in this book began with an adolescent king of Scots for whom 'fre impyre' was being claimed in 1469. It ends with an elderly king of Great Britain resolutely upholding 'his supreame and imperiall power and soveraigntie'. That sovereignty was, for James I, to be exercised over what James VI's Scottish estates called 'one gloriose monarchie and impyre of the whole Yle'. Yet it is as well to bear in mind that, as late as 1705, almost on the eve of the Union which was to extinguish the realm of Scotland as a separate entity, the 'imperial and independent' status of the Scottish crown was still being vehemently asserted.[1] Again, if we look back at the writers whose ideas have been the main focus of interest here, we find at the outset a theologian whose 'A.B.C. of Cristianite' ends resoundingly in what is, substantially if unoriginally, a 'mirror of princes'.[2] At the other end of the story we have a king minded to be a theologian who, if his contemplation of the mirror was notably narcissistic, was doubtless sincere in believing that the 'paterne' he offered was one his successors should follow. Between the Scotland of James III and John Ireland and the Scotland of James VI we have, of course, moved from a predominantly scholastic to an essentially humanist culture. And over much the same period the Catholic Scotland of the fifteenth century became the Protestant Scotland which was to be such a decisive factor in the formative early-modern history of Britain.[3] Yet it is remarkable how often, in the political literature of Scotland from James III to James VI one experiences a sense of *déjà vu* (or *déjà lu*). These resemblances or echoes (at times resounding in unexpected places) merit some further consideration. If they prove to be largely

---

[1] See James Anderson, *An Historical Essay, Shewing that the Crown and Kingdom of Scotland, is Imperial and Independent*, ed. W. Ferguson, in *Stair Society Miscellany*, iii (Edinburgh, 1992), 1–130.

[2] For 'the A.B.C. of Cristianite' as the subtitle or alternative title of Ireland's *Meroure of Wyssdome*, see *Meroure*, i. 14; ii. 151.

[3] At the same time, it is worth recalling that scholastic theology was still important for the leading Scottish Protestant writer of the first half of the 17th c., Samuel Rutherford.

commonplaces, we should remember that such commonplaces are not the least important evidence we have as to the 'mental world' in which a society lived. The essence of a truism, after all, is that it embodies what people in general believed (rightly or wrongly) to be true.

Thus James VI and I, in his final exposition of the 'paterne' a king should imitate, says he 'must remember . . . that hee is ordeyned for his people, and not his people for him'. This might well have been said, more or less verbatim, by James's tutor and bugbear Buchanan, or indeed by John Mair. The fundamental Aristotelian distinction between rulers who use their power for the benefit of their subjects or fellow citizens and those who abuse it for selfish or sectional interests is, as it were, the ground-bass—or at least an essential note in the ground-bass—of political thinking throughout this period. That dissonant variations could be built upon that common foundation is abundantly clear; and it may well seem that the differences were the natural result of divergent interpretations of the word 'ordeyned' in James's formulation. Even here, however, matters are by no means straightforward. No Christian writer—and we are dealing throughout with a professedly Christian culture—could question the Pauline doctrine that—to use, appropriately, the words of the 'King James Bible'—'the powers that be are ordained of God'. God, it was true, had given his chosen people kings 'in his anger'.[4] And he might punish the sins of a nation by sending a tyrant to oppress them. Yet the general tendency of the biblical evidence was to endorse and reinforce the classical view: the ruler exercised his authority as 'the minister of God . . . for good . . . he beareth not the sword in vain: for he is . . . a revenger to execute wrath upon him that doeth evil', to be obeyed 'for conscience sake' by all who 'do that which is good'.[5] On the other hand, both classical and biblical sources also told another story—not necessarily contradicting the Pauline concept of divine ordination, yet capable of yielding problematic conclusions when combined with it. The Roman lawyers maintained that imperial authority (and it was *imperium*, 'fre impyre', that kings were to claim in the sixteenth century) was derived, originally, from a grant by the *populus Romanus*. And

---

[4] Hosea 13: 11: 'I gave thee [Israel] a king in mine anger'; and cf. the account of the establishment of kingship in 1 Samuel 8–10.

[5] Romans 13: 3–5.

even in the case of the most directly and evidently 'divine' of all 'divine-right' monarchies, the kingdom of Israel, God's appointment and the prophet's anointing were combined with some kind of 'popular' authorization. Thus Saul was acclaimed by the people as well as having been anointed by Samuel.[6] David, anointed long before by the prophet, was anointed again by 'all the elders of Israel'; and moreover this anointing was preceded by a covenant (or 'league') between the king and the representatives of the people.[7]

The critical importance of this 'contractual' model for kingship scarcely needs to be emphasized. What does call for particular notice is the point that the notion of covenant or pact in this connection was not found only in theories where it was used to justify resistance to the ruler. James VI, as we saw, both took care to reject that kind of contractual resistance theory and yet accepted the validity of the notion of a pact which imposed 'reciprock' obligations upon both parties. Neither Ninian Winzet nor (following his lead in this respect) William Barclay could exclude the possibility of justifiable resistance when a ruler failed obstinately in his office, however much they might be concerned to safeguard 'the Lord's anointed' against the laying on of seditious and sacrilegious hands. George Buchanan's 'mutual pact' between king and people might be rejected by his critics; John Knox's 'mutuall contract' might appear to Mary Stewart to be merely another way of expressing the belief that her subjects must obey Knox rather than their queen. Yet the notion of mutuality was too pervasive and fundamental, it seemed (one might almost say) too natural to be expelled by anything less than the sharpest and stoutest of dialectical pitchforks. Perhaps, among the writers we have considered here, it is only Adam Blackwood who achieves the expulsion; and it is certainly a striking fact that he goes out of his

---

[6] 1 Samuel 10: 24.

[7] 2 Samuel 5: 1–3: 'league' is the Authorized Version translation, 'covenant' replacing it in the Revised Standard Version. It is worth noting that David had already been anointed 'king over the house of Judah' by 'the men of Judah' (ibid. 2: 4). The double ceremony reflects the fact (not lost on those concerned with Anglo-Scottish union in the early 17th c.) that this was a case where two distinct groups of tribes were, somewhat uneasily, united. James himself, twice anointed as he had been, does not seem to have been greatly interested in the possible parallel.

way to reject the Roman *lex regia* as a model applicable to the kingdom of the Scots.

For those who did accept that model, or (more generally) the model of a mutual or reciprocal relationship between ruler and subjects, the pact or covenant involved, almost necessarily, a reference to 'fundamental law'. Terminology varies; and there was, needless to say, sharp dissension as to the precise and substantive content of that law. Yet once again the persistence and pervasiveness of the notion is beyond question. John Mair, for instance, may make little or no explicit use of 'contractual' ideas as such; but he is committed to the belief that political (as distinct from paternal) authority is grounded in the consent of its subjects and instrumental to their well-being. And it is essential to that well-being that the ruler be bound by certain *leges regni*: these 'laws of the realm' define the basis of his authority and prescribe the limits which differentiate his *dominium* over the realm as a 'public person' from the private rights enjoyed by his subjects over their property. These are, for Mair, defining characteristics of 'a free people' (*liber populus*) such as he clearly believed the Scots to be. Freedom here has, in addition to its implicit rejection of proprietorial monarchy, a constitutional—even a constituent—aspect. A *libera communitas* has authority to 'impose binding laws' upon the ruler; but it also has the ultimate power 'to change the polity', to replace one form of government by another. And such 'constitutionalism' seems to be remote indeed from the 'absolutism' we associate with the rebuttal of 'resistance theory' later in the century.

Certainly there would be a hint of indulging in a mere play on words if one were to suggest any simple filiation between Mair's 'free people' and James VI's 'free monarchy'. The latter evidently has to do with *liberum imperium*, with a power that is 'freed from the laws' (*legibus solutus*). From this it would be tempting to conclude that the two 'freedoms' were incompatible: to argue either that no 'free people' could live with 'free monarchy'—with a ruler enjoying *liberum imperium*, or that the subjects of 'free monarchy' could not themselves be 'free'. Yet these were not in fact the conclusions drawn, in general, by political thinkers in the period with which we are concerned. This was because, for one thing, 'freedom from the laws' did not, plainly, imply freedom from *all* law. The laws of God and of nature, the precepts of religion and morality, bound the king no less than his subjects. Given, indeed, the weight of his responsibilities, and perhaps especially his duty (so strongly inculcated by both Buchanan and his royal pupil) to provide a moral exemplar for his subjects to imitate, there was a sense in which the king was even more restricted than ordinary people were by those primary rules of conduct. And if we bring in, as we must, that third category of law from which kings were not 'freed'—Mair's *leges regni*, Winzet's *leges politicae*—we have norms that, by their very nature and purpose, bind the ruler rather than those over whom he rules.

This may be regarded as the sense in which, *par excellence*, we should understand the notion of 'fundamental law'. And we have seen how difficult, even virtually impossible, it was to interpret that notion in a way that was compatible with what we might perhaps call 'mere absolutism'. James I tried to persuade his English parliament that, in Scotland, the term meant no more than *ius regis*, concerned solely with 'the heritage of the succession and Monarchie'. Even in that context, however, he found it impossible to leave aside the closely associated concern of his Scottish subjects to avoid being left 'without Law or Libertie vnder this Kingdome'.[8] And we have seen how the Scottish estates, for their part, were anxiously concerned to insist that the 'fundamentall lawis' of Scotland established 'the frayme of this hole kingdome' and the 'speciall priviledgeis and prerogativeis' of its constituent 'rankis and ordouris'. Nor was the free monarchy of Scotland to be reduced to 'a conquered and slavishe province'. We may well recall how, nearly half a century earlier, the Lords of the Congregation had claimed to be upholding the *pristina libertas* of their country against a similar threat from a different direction. James himself had referred in 1604 to 'the liberteis and fredome of that . . . ancient and honourable realme'; and already in *The True Lawe* itself, for all his studied insistence upon the priority of kings over laws, James had acknowledged the ruler's obligation 'to mainteyne the whole Countrie, and euery state therein, in al their ancient priuiledges and liberties'. Later in that text, indeed, he explicitly invokes, more than once, the concept of fundamental law, insisting of course that 'the fundamental laws & practize of this country' uphold the 'free monarchy' he is expounding.[9] In

---

[8] McIlwain edn., 300–1.   [9] *RPC* vii. 458; *MPW* 61.

Basilikon Doron, an intriguing manuscript emendation may suggest both a degree of uneasiness with such language, combined none the less with a recognition of the importance of 'the auncient and fundamentall pollicie of our Kingdome'.[10]

As it happens, the passage just referred to provides a cue for the next stage in this concluding review. By the 'fundamentall pollicie' of the realm, James says, 'the whole subiectes of our country . . . are deuided into three estates'; and it is the role of the estates in the late-medieval and early-modern understanding of the kingdom that now needs consideration. There are two aspects to be kept in mind, which may perhaps be called the parliamentary function of the estates and, underlying that, their broader socio-political significance.

In regard to the parliamentary assembly of the estates, something was said in the Introduction to indicate how it operated as an essential part of the machinery of royal governance; and the point has recurred at various stages in later chapters—notably in connection with the problems of ecclesiastical policy, but also in the discussion of 'resistance'. In terms of 'theory', it is clear that John Mair for his part saw the estates in their parliamentary guise as an essential part of the *politia regalis et optima* exemplified in his native country. Willing though he was to ascribe legislative authority to a well-counselled king in terms even James VI might have been happy to endorse, Mair insisted that the estates had exclusive and final authority over such matters as the regulation of the succession to the crown, the safeguarding of the public domain, and the levying of taxes. There might indeed be emergencies when the leading men of the realm, the *proceres*, must act outside the framework of parliamentary procedure. Parliament, however, was the normal means by which the community acted; and it was no mere sprinkler-system activated by the flames, or even by the 'clear and present' smoke of tyranny and misrule. It was a mechanism essential for the operation of legitimate monarchical government.

That the community of the realm might indeed have to resist an oppressive ruler when the measures taken to prevent such

---

[10] See Craigie edn., i. 72/3. In the MS, the phrase originally read, 'the auncient & fundamentall lawis of oure cuntrey': 'lawis' was later corrected to 'policie' and 'cuntrey' to 'kingdome', and, with variations in spelling, this corrected text was used in both the printed editions.

oppression had failed to do so was of course part of Mair's theory. He was, however, exceedingly circumspect in identifying cases in which resistance of this kind had actually, and justifiably, occurred. In regard to the kingdom of the Scots, indeed, it is hard to find, in Mair's account, any such instance apart from the (admittedly crucial) case of John Balliol's replacement by Robert Bruce. In the more urgent circumstances of the third quarter of the sixteenth century, something more than a theory allowing for the possibility of resistance was required by those who opposed the established authorities. What was needed was a positive doctrine advocating as well as authorizing a rebellion which might well entail the deposition of the ruler and might even include an apologia for tyrannicide. Yet, except perhaps for that last point, the resistance urged or defended by a Knox or a Buchanan is essentially institutionalized resistance. Such doctrines, as Knox said in 1564, 'speik of the peopill assembled togidder in one bodie of ane Commounewelth'; and the estates as a parliamentary assembly form, with the nobility, the essential means of giving the 'Commounewelth' a voice with which to speak and power with which to act. The estates, for Knox, are 'bridels, to represse the rage and insolencie of your Kinges'.[11] Mair would not—could not, consistently—have disagreed with that metaphor; yet it belongs to a form of political discourse strikingly different from his.

With Buchanan, again, there is a different rhetorical tone and colour. There is also, however, a difference in substance so far as parliament is concerned. It is not simply that, having learned from Hector Boece of the vicissitudes of the Scots under their mythical early kings, he can cite alleged instances in which the estates acted for the community by disposing of tyrants. Nor is it merely that he can point, almost within living memory, to the fate of James III as another example of parliamentary action against an oppressive king. All this and more can be alleged in support of interpreting Buchanan as the ideologue of an 'ancient constitution' still operating in his own day to the downfall of Mary Stewart. There is also, however, a point of great importance in regard to the legislative process which merits closer scrutiny here.

---

[11] Laing edn., ii. 442; Dickinson edn., ii. 129 (for the 1564 passage). The 'bridels' phrase is from Knox's *Appellation* (Laing edn., iv. 504), where it is specifically addressed to the nobility; but cf. e.g. ibid. 494–5 for the 'Nobils and Estates' as jointly charged with such responsibilities.

Mair had of course ascribed legislative powers to the estates; but he had not granted them a monopolistic sovereignty in that respect. James VI was to acknowledge the legislative role of parliament and indeed to insist that 'Parliaments are onlie ordeined for making of Laws'. In parliament as 'the Kings head Court', however, 'lawes are but craued by his subjects, and onely made by him at their rogation, & with their advise'. Yet James still found it necessary to reassure his English parliament that *his* legislative will did ultimately prevail in the Scottish estates; that he had a decisive 'negatiue voice' there; and that only the touch of his sceptre could convert bills into acts.[12]

Buchanan's view of the legislative process is very different. Laws, to be properly made, should be made by the people, whose shield against oppression they constitute: the ruler should have power neither to make law nor to interpret it. Lawmaking by Buchanan's *populus*, however, is to be understood by reference to 'our custom' in Scotland. This means that bills are considered first by *selecti ex omnibus ordinibus*—by the Lords of the Articles, in fact, with the final decision taken by the estates in plain parliament, embodying for this purpose the entire *populus*. Buchanan would have had no difficulty in endorsing what James VI and I sought to convey to the English parliament when he said that 'the forme of Parliament [in Scotland] is nothing inclined to popularitie'. James, however, would have found it impossible to recognize a legislative procedure in which the estates made law without reference to the king or the touch of his sceptre. And it need hardly be said that the king's view, here as elsewhere, comes a good deal closer to political reality than his tutor's theoretical model. In Scotland as in England, *mutatis mutandis*, 'the king in parliament' legislated. Without entering into complex questions raised in later English controversy as to whether the crown was itself an 'estate' of the realm, we may accept the fact that in Scotland, in this regard, common ground is shared by Mair, by David Lindsay, by Buchanan's anti-monarchomach critics, and by James VI. For all of them the king is the head of the body politic, necessarily involved in articulating the rules by which it is to live. Buchanan's ruler—*Rex Stoicus* though he may be—does not enjoy that organic position: he both can and should be excluded from the legislative process.

[12] Craigie edn., i. 58/9; *MPW* 71; McIlwain edn., 302.

Realism rather than the exhibiting of 'ideal types' is very much in evidence when we turn from the estates in parliament to the estates considered as the constituent parts of the body politic. When political thought meets and mingles with social analysis, we encounter a chorus of criticism. Targets (to employ another metaphor) differ and ammunition varies; but Wedderburn's *Complaynt of Scotland* could serve as a title for much that we find in Henryson and Ireland, in Mair and Boece, in Lindsay of course, but also in Knox and, perhaps above all, in James VI (whose 'view from the throne' in *Basilikon Doron* is arguably the shrewdest of all). There is no need here to recapitulate the sometimes threadbare themes—aristocratic faction, clerical rapacity, and immorality, the sectional selfishness of the burgesses. It will, however, be useful to take a retrospective view of one of these variously culpable estates of the realm. The position of the church was so often at the heart of politics during the century and more examined here that no concluding review could be adequate without some final reflections on that theme.

A starting-point for such reflections may be found in David Lindsay's great mid-century *Satyre*. There, it will be recalled, the church, having endured savage and sustained attack throughout the play, is in effect eliminated at the end. Its representatives leave in dudgeon or dejection; and while their places are in a sense taken by worthier pastors of the Christian flock, these are hardly seen as occupying the position of the irremediably corrupt ecclesiastical estate. Now there certainly was a view at this time and later according to which the church need not and indeed should not constitute an estate in that sense at all. Yet it was hard to square that view with the need, in an early-modern society, to have priests, pastors, or ministers fulfilling the tasks required of them without granting them (or insisting that they accept) a place in what we may broadly call the political system. 'No bishop, no king' might be, for some, an unacceptable way of expressing the point: 'no church, no state', if anachronistic in its terminology, may none the less express a principle few at that period would have rejected.

The difficulty lay, of course, and had lain for centuries, in finding an acceptable equilibrium between the spiritual and temporal powers which were both regarded as essential to a well-ordered society. The issue—or at least the terms in which the issue was presented—no doubt changed with the Protestant rejection of what purported to be the universal spiritual sovereignty of the papacy. Yet the conciliarism and Gallicanism to be found in a writer like John Mair suffice to remind us that papal supremacy was far from being accepted, in a still Catholic Latin Christendom, at the face-value claimed for it by the popes and papalists of the later Middle Ages. And nearly a century after Mair wrote, we can see from the affinity and potential alliance between a Gallican Catholic like William Barclay and the 'Anglicanizing' James VI and I how vigorously such issues had survived the schism between Catholicism and Protestantism. James indeed, the adversary of both Andrew Melville and Robert Bellarmine, had unique experience of the problem and uniquely epitomizes the monarchist response to it.

The author of *The True Lawe* and *Basilikon Doron*, of the *Apologie* and the *Remonstrance for the Right of Kings*, acted, as a ruler, with a good deal of politic circumspection, building in both his Scottish and his English realm a position of considerable strength. That position was to crumble gradually but with increasing rapidity during the reign of his son. This is not the place to enter into vexed questions as to 'what went wrong' with the Stewart monarchy under Charles I. What is both evident and relevant here, however, is that the monarchism which in some sense triumphed in James's reign still faced a challenge and a threat. The catastrophic end of Charles's reign shows how grave a threat it was.

The challenge was certainly based in part upon a view of the nature of the church that was incompatible with the claims of royal supremacy. What was increasingly seen as an intolerable 'Erastianism' continued for generations to alienate various and varying groups from any kind of 'establishment' of the church in Scotland. Even in the last decade of the eighteenth century, some of the comments by parish ministers on dissenting congregations reflect the depth of that alienation.[13] A hundred and fifty years earlier such factors certainly contributed to the making of civil strife.

---

[13] For example, James Rutherford, minister of Hounam in Roxburghshire, writing in 1799, refers to a neighbouring 'meeting-house of the wildest kind of Seceders, the Antiburghers, who are zealous in disseminating their principles, not supposed very favourable to morals and true piety': *The Statistical Account of Scotland*, ed. D. J. Withrington and I. R. Grant, iii, *The Eastern Borders* (Wakefield, 1979), 278.

Yet if religion (in regard both to ecclesiastical polity and to other points) was one source of conflict, there were certainly others that had to do with civil (if hardly with secular) authority. Some of these have already been touched on in these concluding pages, but more remains to be said. 'Divine right and democracy' may or may not be an appropriate (as it is certainly a convenient) piece of shorthand for one aspect of this early-modern debate.[14] James VI certainly saw himself as contending against an 'imagined Democracie' which, taking root among the 'Puritanes' in the kirk, would undermine the civil order too.[15] Yet none of those who (like Mair, Knox, and Buchanan) upheld, in one way or another, the authority of 'the people' against that of the prince would have pleaded guilty to what they as much as James would have regarded as an accusation. There is, to be sure, no doubt that the social order in James VI's Scotland was changing, and with that change would come, in time, a shift in the distribution of political power. Whatever else they may have been, however, these changes can hardly be interpreted as a process of democratization. The post-Union phase of James VI's reign can be seen as marking the beginning of a transition of which the eventual result, by the mid-eighteenth century, would be that 'direct magnate power gave way to influence and patronage'.[16] Again, the character of James VI's 'pen-government' after 1603 (already foreshadowed in his administration before the Union) suggests that royal government was undergoing a change which, if we cannot safely call it professionalization, did mean an increasing divergence from the traditional pattern of rule by an alliance of crown and nobility.[17] And it is as well to bear in mind the point that what we tend to think of as the characteristic 'absolute monarchy' of early-modern Europe had perhaps as much to do with greater administrative sophistication as with 'political theology'. Inchoate movement in such directions had, however, had little if

[14] See D. Wootton, *Divine Right and Democracy*, Preface (pp. 9–19) and Intro. (pp. 21–86).

[15] In the MS of *Basilikon Doron* (Craigie edn., i. 74), James wrote that 'sum of oure fyrie ministers . . . begouth [began] to fantasie to thame selfis a democratik forme of gouernment'. Craigie (ibid. ii. 215) noted that this use of the adjective 'democratic' antedates by several years what was (and is still, in the 2nd edn.) the earliest instance cited in the *Oxford English Dictionary*.

[16] R. Mitchison, *Lordship to Patronage: Scotland 1603–1745* (London, 1983), 162.

[17] See on this Mitchison, *Lordship to Patronage*, ch. 1; Donaldson, *James V to James VII*, 215–37.

any effect on political thinking in Scotland by the end of the period with which we are concerned. Final consideration here must be directed neither to the issue of monarchy versus democracy, nor to questions about 'absolutism', 'constitutionalism', 'bureaucracy', or patronage, but rather to the relationship, over the period we have surveyed, between kingdom and commonwealth.

The matter is one that is properly seen as a relationship rather than an 'issue'; for there was no intrinsic or necessary opposition between *regnum* and *respublica*. If conflict or contradiction arose—as it certainly could and did—this was conceived as being the result of misconception or malpractice on one side or the other. If the king betrayed his public responsibilities in the furtherance of selfish interests, he did indeed set himself (but not the kingship of which he was for the time being the unworthy embodiment) at variance with the commonwealth; and corporate action might be needed to restore the right relationship. If the estates of the realm in which the *respublica* was articulated should stubbornly 'go backward', as in Lindsay's *Satyre*, this was of course a situation calling for the remedy of sharp correction; and it was, above all, for the king to administer the cure. Yet again, however, this did not mean that the commonwealth in its essential nature had, or could have, alienated itself from the kingdom. Three pieces of evidence may be recalled to illustrate the point here. We have seen Ninian Winzet, in 1582, insisting that *rex* and *populus* are alike 'bound to the realm itself' by a tie imposing grave and weighty responsibilities on each side. In 1564, we heard John Craig declaring that every kingdom was, or should be, a commonwealth, and no doubt that 'or should be' was pregnant with future political possibilities. Both Craig and Winzet might, however, have responded warmly to the crowning image in David Lindsay's *Satyre of the Thrie Estaitis*, when John the Commonweal, gorgeously robed, is 'set . . . doun amang them in the Parliament'.

No one concerned with the study of political ideas will be in any danger of confusing image with actuality, however much we may (and should) insist that image and idea helped to shape actuality as it developed in 'the real world of politics'. We began with Shakespeare; but it may be salutary to end with Eliot—

Between the idea
And the reality
Between the motion
And the act
Falls the Shadow

For Thine is the Kingdom

Bibliography

PRIMARY SOURCES

AITKEN, J. M. (ed.), *The Trial of George Buchanan before the Lisbon Inquisition including the Text of Buchanan's Defences with a Translation and Commentary* (Edinburgh, 1939).

ANDERSON, JAMES, *An Historical Essay, Shewing that the Crown and Kingdom of Scotland, is Imperial and Independent*, ed. W. Ferguson, in *Stair Society Miscellany*, iii (Edinburgh, 1992), 1–130.

AQUINAS, ST THOMAS, *Summa Theologiae*, ed. T. Gilby *et al.* (61 vols.; London, 1964–80).

BARCLAY, WILLIAM, *De regno et regali potestate adversus Buchananum, Brutum, Boucherium, & reliquos monarchomachos, libri sex* (Paris, 1600).

——*De potestate Papae an et quatenus in reges et principes seculares jus et imperium habeat* (Pont-à-Mousson, 1609).

BELLARMINE, ROBERT, *Disputationes . . . de Controversiis Christianae Fidei*, 3 vols. (1586; Ingolstadt, 1590).

——*Opera Omnia*, 8 vols. (Naples, 1872).

BELLENDEN, JOHN, *The Chronicles of Scotland*, ed. R. W. Chambers, E. C. Batho, and H. W. Husbands, 2 vols. (Edinburgh, 1938–41).

——*The Hystory and Croniklis of Scotlande* (Edinburgh, n.d. [1540?]; facsimile edn., The English Experience; Amsterdam, 1977).

——*The History and Chronicles of Scotland*, 2 vols. [vols. i and ii in *The Works of John Bellenden*, 3 vols. (Edinburgh, 1821–2)].

BLACKWOOD, ADAM, *Opera Omnia* (Paris, 1644).

——*De coniunctione religionis et imperii libri duo* (Paris, 1575).

——*Adversus Georgii Buchanani dialogum, De iure regni apud Scotos, pro regibus apologia* (Poitiers, 1581; 2nd edn., Paris, 1588).

BOECE, HECTOR, *Murthlacensium et Aberdonensium Episcoporum Vitae* (Edinburgh, 1825; ed. J. Moir, Aberdeen, 1894).

——*Scotorum Historiae* (Paris, 1527; 2nd edn., with continuation by Giovanni Ferreri, Paris, 1574).

BUCHANAN, GEORGE, *Opera Omnia*, 2 vols. (Leyden, 1725).

——*De iure regni apud Scotos . . . dialogus* (Edinburgh 1579; facsimile edn., The English Experience, Amsterdam, 1969).

——*The Powers of the Crown in Scotland*, ed. C. F. Arrowood (Austin, Tex., 1949).

——*The Art and Science of Government among the Scots*, ed. D. H. MacNeill (Glasgow, 1964).

——*Rerum Scoticarum Historia* (Edinburgh, 1582).

——*The Tyrannous Reign of Mary Stewart: George Buchanan's Account*, ed. W. A. Gatherer (Edinburgh, 1958).

CALDERWOOD, DAVID, *History of the Kirk of Scotland*, 8 vols. (Edinburgh, 1842–9).

CALVIN, JEAN, *Opera*, xv [*Corpus Reformatorum* (Brunswick, 1863–1900), vol. xliii].

CAMERON, A. I. (ed.), *The Scottish Correspondence of Mary of Lorraine* (Edinburgh, 1927).

CAMERON, J. K. (ed.), *The First Book of Discipline: With an Introduction and Commentary* (Edinburgh, 1972).

CRAIG, Sir THOMAS, *De Unione Regnorum Britanniae Tractatus*, ed. C. S. Terry (Edinburgh, 1909).

——*Jus Feudale*, ed. J. Baillie (Edinburgh, 1732).

——*The Jus Feudale of Sir Thomas Craig*, ed. J. A. Clyde, 2 vols. (Edinburgh, 1934).

CRANSTOUN, J. (ed.), *Satirical Poems of the Time of the Reformation*, 2 vols. (Edinburgh, 1891).

FORTESCUE, Sir JOHN, *De Laudibus Legum Anglie*, ed. S. B. Chrimes (Cambridge, 1942).

GALLOWAY, B. R., and LEVACK, B. P. (eds.), *The Jacobean Union: Six Tracts of 1604* (Edinburgh, 1985).

GERSON, JEAN, *Opera Omnia*, ed. L. E. Du Pin, 5 vols. (Antwerp, 1706).

——*Œuvres complètes*, ed. P. Glorieux, 10 vols. (Paris, 1960–73).

GRÉGOIRE, PIERRE, *De republica libri sex et viginti* (Pont-à-Mousson, 1596; Frankfurt, 1609).

GREGORY OF RIMINI, *In primum librum Sententiarum* (Paris, 1482).

——*Lectura in Primum et Secundum Sententiarum*, ed. D. Trapp and V. Marcolino, 6 vols. (Berlin, 1979–82).

HENDERSON, G. D. (ed.), *Scots Confession, 1560 (Confessio Scoticana) and Negative Confession, 1581 (Confessio Negativa)* (Edinburgh, 1937).

HENRYSON, ROBERT, *The Poems and Fables of Robert Henryson*, ed. H. Harvey Wood (Edinburgh, 1933).

HESSE, T. (ed.), *The Confession of Faith professit and belevit be the Protestantis within the Raelme of Scotland*, in W. Niesel (ed.), *Bekenntnisschriften und Kirchenordnung der nach Gottes Wort reformierten Kirche* (Munich, 1938), 15–117.

IRELAND, JOHN, 'Quaestiones in librum III Sententiarum'; 'Quaestiones in librum IV Sententiarum' (Aberdeen University Library, MS 264).

——*The Meroure of Wyssdome composed for the use of James IV, King of Scots A,D, 1490 by Johannes de Irlandia Professor of Theology in the University of Paris*, 3 vols. (Edinburgh: vol. i, ed. C. Macpherson, 1926; vol. ii, ed. F. Quinn, 1965; vol. iii, ed. C. McDonald, 1990).

——*Of Penance and Confession*, in W. A. Craigie (ed.), *The Asloan*

Manuscript, 2 vols. (Edinburgh, 1923–5), i. 1–80.

JAMES VI and I, King, *The Workes of the Most High and Mightie Prince IAMES . . . King of Great Britain* (London, 1616; 2nd edn. 1620).

——*Ane fruitfull Meditatioun contening ane plane and facil exposition of ye 7, 8, 9, and 10 verses of the 20 chap. of the Reuelatioun in forme of ane sermone* (Edinburgh, 1588).

——*Ane meditatioun upon the xxv., xxvi., xxvii., xxviii., and xxix. verses of the xv. chap. of the first buke of the Chronicles of the Kingis* (Edinburgh, 1589).

——*A Meditation vpon the 27, 28, 29 Verses of the XXVII chapter of St Matthew, or A paterne for a Kings inauguration* (London, 1620).

——*The Political Works of James I*, ed. C. H. McIlwain (Cambridge, Mass., 1918).

——*The Basilicon Doron of King James VI*, ed. J. Craigie, 2 vols. (Edinburgh, 1944–50).

——*Minor Prose Works of King James VI and I*, ed. J. Craigie and A. Law (Edinburgh, 1982).

KIRK, J. (ed.), *The Second Book of Discipline: with an Introduction and Commentary* (Edinburgh, 1980).

KNOX, JOHN, *The Works of John Knox*, ed. D. Laing, 6 vols. (Edinburgh, 1846–64).

——*John Knox's History of the Reformation*, ed. W. C. Dickinson, 2 vols. (Edinburgh, 1949).

——*The Political Writings of John Knox*, ed. M. A. Breslow (Washington, 1985).

——*John Knox: On Rebellion*, ed. R. A. Mason (Cambridge, 1994).

LASKI, H. J. (ed.), *A Defence of Liberty against Tyrants [Vindiciae contra Tyrannos]* (London, 1924).

LAUDER, WILLIAM, *Ane Compendious and Breue Tractate concernyng ye Office and Dewtie of Kyngis, Spirituall Pastoris, and Temporall Iugis* (1556), ed. F. Hall (London, 1864; rev. edn., 1869).

——*The Minor Poems of William Lauder*, ed. F. J. Furnivall (London, 1870).

LESLEY, JOHN, *The History of Scotland from the Death of King James I in the Year MCCCCXXXVI to the Year M.D.LXI* (Edinburgh, 1830).

——*De origine, moribus, et rebus gestis Scotorum* (1578; Rome, 1675).

LINDSAY, Sir DAVID, *The Works of Sir David Lindsay of the Mount 1490–1555*, ed. D. Hamer, 4 vols. (Edinburgh, 1931–6).

LOCKE, JOHN, *Two Treatises of Government*, ed. P. Laslett (Cambridge, 1988).

MAIR, JOHN, *Quartus Sententiarum* (Paris, 1509).

——*In primum Setentiarum* (Paris, 1510).

——*In secundum Setentiarum* (Paris, 1510).

——*Quartus Sententiarum* (Paris, 1512).

——*In quartum Sententiarum* (Paris, 1516).

——*Super tertium Sententiarum* (Paris, 1517).

——*In Mattheum ad literam expositio* (Paris, 1518).

——*Historia Majoris Britanniae tam Anglie quam Scotie* (Paris, 1521).

——*In quatuor Euangelia* (Paris, 1529).

——*Ethica Aristotelis . . . Cum Jo. Majoris commentariis* (Paris, 1530).

——*Historia Majoris Britanniae*, ed. R. Freebairn (Edinburgh, 1740).

——*A History of Greater Britain as well England as Scotland*, ed. A. Constable (Edinburgh, 1892).

MELVILLE, JAMES, *The Autobiography and Diary of Mr James Melvill*, ed. R. Pitcairn (Edinburgh, 1842).

Original Letters relating to the Ecclesiastical Affairs of Scotland . . ., 2 vols. (Edinburgh, 1851).

ROBINSON, H. (ed.), *Original Letters Relative to the English Reformation*, 2 vols. (Cambridge, 1846–7).

SEYSSEL, CLAUDE DE, *La Monarchie de France et deux autres fragments*, ed. J. Poujol (Paris, 1961).

SPOTTISWOODE, JOHN, *The History of the Church of Scotland*, ed. M. Russell and M. Napier, 3 vols. (Edinburgh, 1847–51).

Statistical Account of Scotland, ed. D. J. Withrington and I. R. Grant, iii, *The Eastern Borders* (Wakefield, 1979).

STEWART, WILLIAM, *The Buik of the Croniclis of Scotland: or a Metrical Version of the History of Hector Boece*, ed. W. B. Turnbull, 3 vols. (London, 1858).

TEULET, A. (ed.), *Papiers d'état relatifs a l'histoire de l'Ecosse*, 3 vols. (Paris, 1852–60).

The Thre Prestis of Peblis how thai tald thar talis, ed. T. D. Robb (Edinburgh, 1920).

WEDDERBURN, ROBERT, *The Complaynt of Scotland*, ed. J. Leyden (Edinburgh, 1801).

——*The Complaynt of Scotland*, ed. J. A. H. Murray (London, 1872–3; repr. 1891).

——*The Complaynt of Scotland (c.1550) by Mr Robert Wedderburn*, ed. A. M. Stewart (Edinburgh, 1979).

WINZET, NINIAN, *Flagellum Sectariorum . . . Accessit Velitatio in Georgium Buchananum circa Dialogum quen scripsit de iure regni apud Scotos* (Ingolstadt, 1582).

——*Certain Tractates together with the Book of Four Score Three Questions and a Translation of Vincentius Lirinensis . . .*, ed. J. K. Hewison, 2 vols. (Edinburgh, 1888–90).

WOOTTON, D. (ed.), *Divine Right and Democracy: An Anthology of Political Writing in Stuart England* (Harmondsworth, 1986).

SECONDARY SOURCES

ANDERSON, W. J., 'Rome and Scotland, 1513–1565', in D. McRoberts (ed.), Essays on the Scottish Reformation (Glasgow, 1962), 463–83.

BARTH, K., The Knowledge of God and the Service of God According to the Teaching of the Reformation: Recalling the Scots Confession of 1560 (London, 1938).

BLACK, J. B., 'Boece's Scotorum Historiae', in W. D. Simpson (ed.), Quatercentenary of the Death of Hector Boece (Aberdeen, 1937), 30–53.

BROADIE, A., The Circle of John Mair: Logic and Logicians in Pre-Reformation Scotland (Oxford, 1985).

——The Tradition of Scottish Philosophy: A New Perspective on the Enlightenment (Edinburgh, 1990).

BURNS, C., 'Papal Gifts to Scottish Monarchs: The Golden Rose and Blessed Sword', Innes Review, 20 (1969), 150–94.

BURNS, J. H., Lordship, Kingship, and Empire: The Idea of Monarchy 1400–1525 (Oxford, 1992).

——'The Scotland of John Major', Innes Review, 2 (1951), 65–76.

——'The Political Ideas of George Buchanan', Scottish Historical Review, 30 (1951), 60–8.

——'New Light on John Major', Innes Review, 5 (1954), 83–100.

——'The Political Ideas of the Scottish Reformation', Aberdeen University Review, 36 (1956), 251–68.

——'John Knox and Revolution 1558', History Today, 8 (1958), 565–73.

——'The Political Background of the Reformation', in D. McRoberts (ed.), Essays on the Scottish Reformation (Glasgow, 1962), 1–38.

——'Politia reglis et optima: The Political Ideas of John Mair', History of Political Thought, 2 (1981), 31–61.

——'St German, Gerson, Aquinas, and Ulpian', History of Political Thought, 4 (1983), 443–9.

——'The Idea of Absolutism', in J. Miller (ed.), Absolutism in Seventeenth-Century Europe (London, 1990), 21–42.

——'John Ireland: Theology and Public Affairs in the Late Fifteenth Century', Innes Review, 41 (1990), 151–79.

——'Conciliarism, Papalism, and Power, 1511–1518', in D. Wood (ed.), The Church and Sovereignty (Oxford, 1991), 409–28.

——'George Buchanan and the Anti-Monarchomachs', in R. A. Mason (ed.), Scots and Britons (Cambridge, 1994), 138–57; also in N. Phillipson and Q. Skinner (eds.), Political Discourse in Early Modern Britain (Cambridge, 1993), 3–33.

——and GOLDIE, M. (eds.), The Cambridge History of Political Thought 1450–1700 (Cambridge, 1991).

BURROWS, M. S., Jean Gerson and De Consolatione Theologiae (1418): The Consolation of a Biblical and Reforming Theology for a Disordered

Age (Tübingen, 1991).

CAIRNS, J. W., FERGUS, T. D., and MACQUEEN, H. L., 'Legal Humanism and the History of Scots Law: John Skene and Thomas Craig', in J. MacQueen (ed.), *Humanism in Renaissance Scotland* (Edinburgh, 1990), 48–74.

CAMERON, J. K., 'The Conciliarism of John Mair: A Note on *A Disputation on the Authority of a Council*', in D. Wood (ed.), *The Church and Sovereignty c.590–1918: Essays in Honour of Michael Wilks* (Oxford, 1991), 429–35.

CARLYLE, Sir R. W., and A. J., *A History of Mediaeval Political Theory in the West*, 6 vols. (Edinburgh, 1903–36).

COLLOT, C., *L'École doctrinale de droit public à Pont-à-Mousson* (Paris, 1965).

COURTENAY, W., *Causation and Volition: A History of the Distinction of Absolute and Ordained Power* (Bergamo, 1990).

COWAN, I. B., *The Scottish Reformation: Church and Society in Sixteenth-Century Scotland* (London, 1982).

CRAIGIE, J., 'Lyndsay, Sir David (1486–1555)', in *Chambers's Encyclopaedia* (London, 1955), viii. 744–5.

DAWSON, J. E. A., 'The Two John Knoxes: England, Scotland and the 1558 Tracts', *Journal of Ecclesiastical History*, 42 (1991), 555–76.

DE LA BROSSE, O., *Le Pape et le Concile: La Comparaison de leurs pouvoirs à la veille de la Réforme* (Paris, 1965).

DONALDSON, G., *Scotland: James V to James VII* (The Edinburgh History of Scotland; Edinburgh, 1971).

—— 'Knox the Man', in D. Shaw (ed.), *John Knox: A Quatercentenary Reappraisal* (Edinburgh, 1975), 18–32.

DREXLER, M., 'Fluid Prejudice: Scottish Origin Myths in the Later Middle Ages', in J. Rosenthal and C. Richmond (eds.), *People, Politics and Community in the Later Middle Ages* (Gloucester, 1987), 60–77.

DUNCAN, A. A. M., *Scotland: The Making of the Kingdom* (The Edinburgh History of Scotland; Edinburgh, 1975).

DURKAN, J., 'John Major: After 400 years', *Innes Review*, 1 (1950), 131–9.

—— 'The School of John Major: Bibliography', *Innes Review*, 1 (1950), 140–57.

—— 'Early Humanism and King's College', *Aberdeen University Review*, 48 (1979–80), 259–79.

—— 'The Cultural Background in Sixteenth-Century Scotland' in D. McRoberts (ed.), *Essays on the Scottish Reformation* (Glasgow, 1962), 274–331.

DWYER, J., MASON, R. A., and MURDOCH, A. (eds.), *New Perspectives on the Politics and Culture of Early Modern Scotland* (Edinburgh, 1982).

ÉLIE, H., *Le Traité 'De l'infini' de Jean Mair* (Paris, 1938).

ELTON, G. R., 'Introduction: The Age of the Reformation', in id. (ed.), *The New Cambridge Modern History*, ii, *The Reformation 1520–1559*

302   *Bibliography*

(Cambridge, 1958), 1–22.

FARTHING, J. L., *Thomas Aquinas and Gabriel Biel: Interpretations of St Thomas Aquinas in German Nominalism on the Eve of the Reformation* (Durham, NC, 1988).

GALLOWAY, B., *The Union of England and Scotland 1603–1608* (Edinburgh, 1986).

GANOCZY, A., 'Jean Major, exégète gallicain', *Recherches de science religieuse*, 56 (1968), 457–95.

George Buchanan: Glasgow Quatercentenary Studies (Glasgow, 1907).

GREAVES, R. L., *Theology and Revolution in the Scottish Reformation: Studies in the Thought of John Knox* (Grand Rapids, Mich., 1980).

HARDING, A. (ed.), *Law-Making and Law-Makers in British History* (London, 1980).

HARPER, R., 'Modernizing Scotland's Laws Should be Priority', *Scotsman*, 6 May 1992.

HAZLETT, W. I. P., 'The Scots Confession 1560: Context, Complexion and Critique', *Archiv für Reformationsgeschichte*, 78 (1987), 287–320.

——' "Jihad" against Female Infidels and Satan: Knox's *First Blast of the Trumpet*', in W. van H. Spijker (ed.), *Calvin: Erbe und Auftrag* (Kampen, 1991), 279–90.

HUME BROWN, P., *George Buchanan Humanist and Reformer: A Biography* (Edinburgh, 1890).

INNES, T., *A Critical Essay on the Ancient Inhabitants of the Northern Parts of Britain or Scotland* (1729; Edinburgh, 1885).

KENDRICK, T., *British Antiquity* (1950; New York, 1970).

KRETZMANN, N., KENNY, A., and PINBORG, J. (eds.), *The Cambridge History of Later Medieval Philosophy from the Rediscovery of Aristotle to the Disintegration of Scholasticism 1100–1600* (Cambridge, 1982).

KYLE, R., 'John Knox and the Purification of Religion: The Intellectual Aspects of his Crusade against Idolatry', *Archiv für Reformationsgeschichte*, 77 (1986), 265–80.

LEE, M., Jr., *Great Britain's Solomon: King James VI and I in his Three Kingdoms* (Urbana, Ill., 1980).

LEVACK, B. P., *The Formation of the British State* (Oxford, 1987).

——'English Law, Scots Law and the Union, 1603–1707', in A. Harding (ed.), *Law-Making and Law-Makers in British History* (London, 1980), 105–19.

LINDER, R. D., *The Political Ideas of Pierre Viret* (Travaux d'Humanisme et Renaissance, lxiv; Geneva, 1964).

LORIMER, P., *John Knox and the Church of England* (London, 1875).

LYALL, R. J., 'The Medieval Scottish Coronation: Some Seventeenth-Century Evidence', *Innes Review*, 28 (1977), 3–21.

LYNCH, M. (ed.), *Mary Stewart: Queen in Three Kingdoms* (Glasgow, 1987).

MCDONALD, C., 'John Ireland's *Meroure of Wyssdome* and Chaucer's *Tale of Melibee'*, *Studies in Scottish Literature*, 21 (1987), 23–34.

MACDOUGALL, N., *James III: A Political Study* (Edinburgh, 1982).

—— *James IV* (Edinburgh, 1989).

—— ' "It is I, the Earle of Mar": In Search of Thomas Cochrane', in id. and R. A. Mason (eds.), *People and Power in Scotland* (Edinburgh, 1992), 28–49.

—— (ed.), *Church, Politics and Society: Scotland 1408–1929* (Edinburgh, 1983).

—— and MASON, R. A. (eds.), *People and Power in Scotland: Essays in Honour of T. C. Smout* (Edinburgh, 1992).

MCEWAN, H., ' "A Theolog Solempne": Thomas de Rossy, Bishop of Galloway', *Innes Review*, 8 (1957), 21–9.

MCFARLANE, I. D., *Buchanan* (London, 1981).

MACFARLANE, L. J., *William Elphinstone and the Kingdom of Scotland 1431–1514: The Struggle for Order* (Aberdeen, 1985).

—— 'The Primacy of the Scottish Church, 1472–1521', *Innes Review*, 20 (1969), 111–29.

MACKAY, A., 'Ritual and Propaganda in Fifteenth-Century Castile', *Past and Present*, 107 (May 1985), 3–43.

MCKECHNIE, W. S., '*De Jure Regni apud Scotos*', in *George Buchanan: Glasgow Quatercentenary Studies* (Glasgow, 1907), 211–96.

MACQUEEN, J., *Robert Henryson: A Study of the Major Narrative Poems* (Oxford, 1972).

—— 'Aspects of Humanism in Sixteenth- and Seventeenth-Century Literature', in id. (ed.), *Humanism in Renaissance Scotland* (Edinburgh, 1990), 10–31.

—— (ed.), *Humanism in Renaissance Scotland* (Edinburgh, 1990).

MCROBERTS, D. (ed.), *Essays on the Scottish Reformation* (Glasgow, 1962).

MAHONEY, M., 'The Scottish Hierarchy, 1513–1565', in D. McRoberts (ed.), *Essays on the Scottish Reformation* (Glasgow, 1962), 150–94.

MAPSTONE, S., 'The Advice to Princes Tradition in Scottish Literature, 1450–1500' (Oxford University D. Phil. thesis, 1986).

—— 'A Mirror for a Divine Prince: John Ireland and the Four Daughters of God', in J. D. McClure and M. Spiller (eds.), *Bryght Lanternis: Essays on the Language and Literature of Medieval and Renaissance Scotland* (Aberdeen, 1989), 308–23.

MASON, R. A., '*Rex Stoicus*: George Buchanan, James VI and the Scottish Polity', in J. Dwyer *et al.* (eds.), *New Perspectives on the Politics and Culture of Early Modern Scotland* (Edinburgh, 1982), 9–33.

—— 'Covenant and Commonweal: The Language of Politics in Reformation Scotland', in N. Macdougall (ed.), *Church, Politics and Society* (Edinburgh, 1983), 97–126.

—— 'Kingship, Tyranny and the Right to Resist in Fifteenth Century Scotland', *Scottish Historical Review*, 66 (1987), 125–51.

MASON, R. A., 'Scotching the Brut: Politics, History and National Myth in 16th-Century Britain', in id. (ed.), *Scotland and England* (Edinburgh, 1987), 60–84.

—— 'Kingship, Nobility and Anglo-Scottish Union: John Mair's *History of Greater Britain* (1521)', *Innes Review*, 41 (1990), 182–222.

—— 'Chivalry and Citizenship: Aspects of National Identity in Renaissance Scotland', in N. Macdougall and id. (eds.), *People and Power in Scotland* (Edinburgh, 1992), 50–73.

—— 'The Scottish Reformation and the Origins of Anglo-British Imperialism', in id. (ed.), *Scots and Britons* (Cambridge, 1994), 161–86.

—— (ed.), *Scotland and England 1286–1815* (Edinburgh, 1987).

—— (ed.), *Scots and Britons: Scottish Political Thought and the Union of 1603* (Cambridge, 1994).

MINER, B., 'The Popular Theology of John Ireland', *Innes Review*, 13 (1962), 130–46.

—— 'John Ireland and the Immaculate Conception', *Innes Review*, 17 (1966), 24–39.

MITCHISON, R., *Lordship to Patronage: Scotland 1603–1745* (The New History of Scotland; London, 1983).

NICHOLSON, R., *Scotland: The Later Middle Ages* (The Edinburgh History of Scotland; Edinburgh, 1974).

OAKESHOTT, M., *Rationalism in Politics and Other Essays* (1962; London, 1974).

OAKLEY, F., *Omnipotence, Covenant, and Order: An Excursion in the History of Ideas from Abelard to Leibniz* (Ithaca, NY, 1984).

—— 'On the Road from Constance to 1688: The Political Thought of John Major and George Buchanan', *Journal of British Studies*, 2 (1962), 1–32.

—— 'Jacobean Political Theology: The Absolute and Ordinary Powers of the King', *Journal of the History of Ideas*, 29 (1968), 323–46.

—— 'The "Hidden"and "Revealed" Wills of James I: More Political Theology', in J. B. Strayer and D. E. Queller (eds.), *Post Scripta* [*Studia Gratiana*, 15 (1977)], 363–75.

OBERMAN, H. A., *The Harvest of Medieval Theology: Gabriel Biel and Late Medieval Nominalism* (1963; 3rd edn., Durham, NC, 1983).

PECK, L. L. (ed.), *The Mental World of the Jacobean Court* (Cambridge, 1991).

PENNINGTON, K., *The Prince and the Law, 1200–1600: Sovereignty and Rights in the Western Legal Tradition* (Berkeley and Los Angeles, 1993).

PHILLIPSON, N., and SKINNER, Q. (eds.), *Political Discourse in Early Modern Britain* (Cambridge, 1993).

POCOCK, J. G. A., *The Ancient Constitution and the Feudal Law: A Study of English Historical Thought in the Seventeenth Century: A Reissue with a Retrospect* (Cambridge, 1957; 2nd edn. 1987).

RIDLEY, J., *John Knox* (Oxford, 1968).

ROBERTSON, J., 'Empire and Union: Two Concepts of the Early Modern European Political Order', in id. (ed.), *A Union for Empire* (Cambridge, forthcoming).

——(ed.), *A Union for Empire: Political Thought and the British Union of 1707* (Cambridge, forthcoming).

ROBERTSON, W., *The History of Scotland during the Reigns of Queen Mary, and of King James VI*, 2 vols. (1759; Edinburgh, 1791).

ROSENTHAL, J., and RICHMOND, C. (eds.), *People, Politics and Community in the Later Middle Ages* (Gloucester, 1987).

RUEGER, Z., 'Gerson's Concept of Equity and Christopher St German', *History of Political Thought*, 3 (1982), 1–30.

RUSSELL, C. S. R., 'Divine Right', in J. Morrill *et al.* (eds.), *Public Duty and Private Conscience in Seventeenth-Century England: Essays Presented to G. E. Aylmer* (Oxford, 1993), 101–20.

SALMON, J. H. M., 'An Alternative Theory of Popular Resistance: Buchanan, Rousseau and Locke', in *Diritto e Potere nella Storia Europea: Atti del quarto Congresso Internazionale della Società Italiana della Storia del Diritto, in onore di Bruno Paradisi* (Florence, 1982), 824–49.

SCHMITT, C. B., SKINNER, Q., and KESSLER, E. (eds.), *The Cambridge History of Renaissance Philosophy* (Cambridge, 1988).

SEELEY, Sir J., 'The Eighty-eights', *Good Words*, 29 (1888), 373–80.

SHAW, D. (ed.), *John Knox: A Quatercentenary Reappraisal* (Edinburgh, 1975).

SIMPSON, W. D. (ed.), *Quatercentenary of the Death of Hector Boece, First Principal of the University of Aberdeen* (Aberdeen, 1937).

SKINNER, Q., *The Foundations of Modern Political Thought*, 2 vols. (Cambridge, 1978).

——'The Origins of the Calvinist Theory of Revolution', in B. Malament (ed.), *After the Reformation: Essays in Honour of J. H. Hexter* (Manchester, 1980), 309–30.

SMYTH, A. P., *Warlords and Holy Men: Scotland AD 80–1000* (The New History of Scotland; London, 1984).

SOMMERVILLE, J. P., *Politics and Ideology in England 1603–1640* (London, 1986).

STEWART, I. H., *The Scottish Coinage* (2nd edn., London, 1967).

TAYLOR, M., 'The Conflicting Doctrines of the Scottish Reformation', in D. McRoberts (ed.), *Essays on the Scottish Reformation* (Glasgow, 1962), 245–73.

THOMSON, J. A. F., 'Innocent VIII and the Scottish Church', *Innes Review*, 19 (1968), 23–31.

TORRANCE, T. F., '1469–1969. La Philosophie et la théologie de Jean Mair ou Major de Haddington (1469–1550)', *Archives de philosophie*, 32 (1969), 531–47; 33 (1970), 261–93.

TREVOR-ROPER, H. R., *George Buchanan and the Ancient Scottish*

Constitution [*English Historical Review*, Supplement 3], 1966.

TUCK, R., *Natural Rights Theories: Their Origin and Development* (Cambridge, 1979).

——*Philosophy and Government 1572–1651* (Cambridge, 1993).

WARNER, G. F., 'The Library of James VI, in the Hand of Peter Young, his Tutor, 1573–1583', in *Miscellany of the Scottish History Society* (Edinburgh, 1893), pp. ix–lxxv.

WATT, D. E. R., *Fasti Ecclesiae Scoticanae Medii Aevi ad annum 1638: Second Draft* (St Andrews, 1969).

WILLIAMSON, A. H., *Scottish National Consciousness in the Age of James VI: The Apocalypse, the Union and the Shaping of Scotland's Public Culture* (Edinburgh, 1979).

WILLSON, D. H., *King James VI and I* (London, 1956).

——'James I and his Literary Assistants', *Huntington Library Quarterly*, 8 (1944–5), 35–57.

WOOD, D. (ed.), *The Church and Sovereignty c.590–1918: Essays in Honour of Michael Wilks* [Studies in Church History: Subsidia 9] (Oxford, 1991).

WORMALD, J., *Court, Kirk, and Community: Scotland 1470–1625* (The New History of Scotland; London, 1981).

——'James VI and I: Two Kings or One?', *History*, NS 68 (1983), 187–209.

——'James VI and I, Basilikon Doron and *The Trew Law of Free Monarchies*: The Scottish Context and the English Translation', in L. L. Peck (ed.), *The Mental World of the Jacobean Court* (Cambridge, 1991), 36–54, 278–83.

Index

DATE DUE

DEMCO 38-297